The Marginal Revolution in Economics

The Marginal Revolution in Economics

in Economics

Interpretation and Evaluation

Papers presented at a conference
held at the Villa Serbelloni, Bellagio,
Italy, August 22–28, 1971

Edited by
R. D. Collison Black
A. W. Coats
Craufurd D. W. Goodwin

1973
Duke University Press
Durham, North Carolina

© 1972, 1973, Duke University Press

L.C.C. card no. 72-91850

I.S.B.N. 0-8223-0278-0

PRINTED IN THE UNITED STATES OF AMERICA
BY THE SEEMAN PRINTERY, INC.

Contents

Preface

Tʜᴇ remarkable continuity of the main "orthodox" tradition of economic analysis, from Adam Smith to John Maynard Keynes and beyond, has often been cited as evidence for the view that economics is a science—indeed, that it is the most scientific of all the social sciences. During the past decade, however, it has been widely held that the history of science is marked by periodic discontinuities, "crises," or "revolutions," and it is therefore appropriate to reconsider the question whether the "marginal revolution" in economics can be fitted into this category. As is well known, during the early years of the 1870's a handful of brilliant innovators in several different countries published a series of pathbreaking ideas which, taken collectively, exerted a significant influence on the course of economic science in the ensuing century. But was this episode really an exception to the apparent continuity in the development of economics? Were the pioneer marginalists sufficiently united in purpose and comparable in performance to justify us in grouping them together? When their works are compared with the writings of their predecessors and successors, do their contributions seem sufficiently novel and significant to warrant the dramatic designation usually accorded them? In short, was there in fact a marginal revolution? And if so, is it worth commemorating?

This symposium was organized in the hope of casting light on these and related questions. The essays published herein examine the marginal revolution in a variety of perspectives: in terms of the predecessors, the revolutionaries themselves, the diffusion of ideas by their disciples and descendants, and their aggregate impact. The selection of topics and the range of coverage are necessarily incomplete, partly owing to unforeseeable circumstances and unavoidable logistical obstacles, but partly because there is already a substantial literature in the field, e.g., that dealing with the second generation of marginalists.

The articles in this volume are based on papers that were prepared for and discussed at a series of meetings held at the Villa Serbelloni,

Bellagio, Italy, from August 22 to 28, 1971, and the participants wish to record their warm appreciation of the direct support and generous hospitality provided by the Rockefeller Foundation and its staff. During the five days of vigorous, continuous, and stimulating discussion, many significant differences of opinion and interpretation emerged, with respect to both the specific topics under review and a number of wider questions of method and purpose in the history of economics. Some of these matters are examined in the opening and closing essays by Messrs. Blaug and Coats. Others recur repeatedly throughout the volume. While some papers were modified in response to the proceedings at Bellagio, neither the authors nor the editors have deliberately sought agreement on controversial matters. Indeed, in some instances disagreements have been emphasized for the reader's benefit.

In conclusion, it should be noted that the symposiasts left Bellagio with the heady feeling—no doubt influenced by the beauty and exhilarating qualities of the environment—that the history of economics is a field of rich intellectual promise. There are so many unanswered questions, untried methods of approach, and untapped research opportunities. Hence this collection should be regarded as a provisional agenda for future work, not as a final word on the marginal revolution.

R.D.C.B.

A.W.C.

C.D.W.G.

The Marginal Revolution in Economics

Was There a Marginal Revolution?

Mark Blaug

I

THE TERM "marginal revolution" is usually taken to refer to the nearly simultaneous but completely independent discovery in the early 1870's by Jevons, Menger, and Walras of the principal of diminishing marginal utility as the fundamental building block of a new kind of static microeconomics. It constitutes, so the argument goes, one of the best examples of multiple discoveries in the history of economic thought, which simply cries out for some sort of historical explanation: it is too much to believe that three men working at nearly the same time in such vastly different intellectual climates as those of Manchester, Vienna, and Lausanne could have hit by accident on the same idea; it must be due to some common cause, which it is the job of the intellectual historian to identify. The only trouble is that none of the standard explanations are convincing.[1] The levels of economic development of England, Austria, and France were so different in the 1860's that all crypto-Marxist explanations in terms of changes in the structure of production, or in the relationship between social classes, tend to strain our credulity. Likewise, the utilitarian-empiricist tradition of British philosophy, the neo-Kantian philosophical climate of Austria, and the Cartesian philosophical climate of France simply had no elements in common that could have provoked a utility revolution in economics. In matters of economic policy, there was in fact continuity with classical thinking, and when Jevons and Walras wrote on policy questions, as they did, there was little or no connection between practical recommendations and their views on value theory. As for an alleged "need" to defend the capitalist system, there was hardly

MARK BLAUG *is Professor of Economics of Education at the Institute of Education of the University of London.*

1. I canvassed the various explanations in my *Economic Theory in Retrospect*, 2d ed. (Homewood, Ill., 1968), pp. 303–8. The present note is an attempt to rethink the issue raised in those pages.

anything more suitable than the old wages-population mechanism of classical economics or the writings of Bastiat, which owed nothing to marginal utility. Lastly, there was no real sense of intellectual crisis in the 1860's either in England or on the Continent which might have encouraged a search for alternative economic models; besides, historicism was such an alternative model which continued to gain new adherents after 1860, not only in Germany but also in England. In short, the simultaneous discovery of marginal utility may call for an explanation, but none of the available explanations is satisfactory.

Perhaps the difficulty is that the idea of a "marginal revolution" is the sort of "rational reconstruction" of the history of economic thought, like the concept of "mercantilism" or that of "classical economics" as defined by Keynes, that is bound to generate spurious historical puzzles. This is a large part of the problem, I think, but it is not the whole of it. The debate over the marginal revolution so-called has in fact confused two quite different things: the explanation of the origins of the revolution (if revolution it was) and the explanation of its eventual triumph. Some carelessness in the use of the concept of "explanation" in intellectual history has further clouded the debate.

II

A useful way to begin is to ask ourselves whether the discovery of marginal utility by Jevons, Menger, and Walras was in fact a "multiple," in Robert Merton's sense of the term.[2] After an intensive investigation of hundreds of multiple discoveries in the history of science, Merton concluded that "all scientific discoveries are in principle multiples, including those that on the surface appear to be singletons" (p. 477). Lest this should appear to be "a self-sealing hypothesis, immune to investigation," Merton conceded that it was only true of certain kinds of science at certain stages of their development: "A great variety of evidence . . . testifies then to the hypothesis that, once science has become institutionalized, and significant numbers of men are at work on scientific investigation, the same discoveries will be made independently more than once and that singletons

2. R. K. Merton, "Singletons and Multiples in Scientific Discovery: A Chapter in the Sociology of Science," *Proceedings of the American Philosophical Society* 105, no. 5 (1961).

can be conceived of as forestalled multiples'' (p. 482). Although two-thirds of his 264 intensively investigated multiples involved an interval of ten years or less, Merton refused to confine the concept of multiples to nearly simultaneous discoveries: ''Even discoveries far removed from one another in calendrical time may be instructively construed as 'simultaneous' or nearly so in social and cultural time, depending upon the accumulated state of knowledge in the several cultures and the structures of the several societies in which they appear'' (p. 486). Enough has now been said to indicate that the concept of ''multiples'' is difficult to interpret, particularly in fields less professionalized than the natural sciences. The gist of the argument, however, seems to be that ''mature science'' is characterized by cumulative, continuous progress such as to make the next leap forward, if not absolutely inevitable, at least highly predictable.[3]

We may now ask: Was the state of economic science in the 1860's such as to make the eventual emergence of the marginal utility principle a perfectly predictable phenomenon, in which case it is hardly surprising that Jevons, Menger, and Walras discovered it at just about the same time? The answer to that question must surely be No.

First of all, it is highly doubtful that we can speak of one economic science in the 1860's as if it were a heritage shared between economists all over the world, studying the same treatises, reading the same journals and employing a common set of tools in the analysis of a similar range of problems. A glance at Hutchison's terse accounts of the state of economic thought around 1870 in England, Germany, Austria, France, and the United States will show that there were at least two, if not three or four, ''models'' of economic science extant at that time.[4] Although Jevons struggled against the tyranny of Mill's influence, German economists had long since rejected ''Smith-

---

3. Merton guards himself against misinterpretation by denying that his thesis implies that ''all discoveries are inevitable in the sense that, come what may, they will be made, at the time and the place, if not by the individual(s) who in fact made them'' (p. 485). For a similar qualification, see his ''Resistance to the Systematic Study of Multiple Discoveries in Science,'' *European Journal of Sociology* 4, no. 2 (1963): 246.

4. T. W. Hutchison, *A Review of Economic Doctrines, 1870-1929* (Oxford, 1953), chaps. 1, 8, 12, and 16; see also the writers cited by Jevons, Menger, and Walras in their treatises, with hardly a name in common. R. S. Howey, *The Rise of the Marginal Utility School, 1870-1889* (Lawrence, Kans., 1960), chaps. 1-5.

ianismus'' and all Ricardian varieties thereof, while French economists
for their part never exhibited much interest either in the analytical
features of English classical political economy or in the rallying cries
of the German historical school. The insularity of British economics
and the lack of communication between economists in different countries right up to the 1890's[5] is perfectly exemplified by the fact that
Jevons, a leading economic bibliophile, died in 1882 without realizing
that a man called Menger had written a book on economics which
would one day be likened to his own *Theory of Political Economy*.
Secondly, the notion that economic science as such was inexorably
moving towards the discovery of marginal utility somewhere around
the middle of the century is simply a rationalization after the fact.
Surely, the much more likely next step in English classical economics in the 1860's was either the generalization of the marginal
concept in Ricardian rent theory to all factors of production, that is,
the breakthrough to a marginal productivity theory of factor pricing,
or perhaps the further refinement of Ricardian value theory into something like linear input-output analysis? But as we know, the former
came only belatedly in the 1890's among the generation that succeeded our marginal utility trio, and the latter has only emerged in
the twentieth century.

What of the counterargument, however, that marginal utility was
not discovered but only rediscovered in the 1870's? Lloyd and Longfield had developed the distinction between total and marginal utility
in 1834, followed soon after by Senior (I ignore Bernoulli in the
eighteenth century as an ''outlier''). If Jevons, Menger, and Walras
do not constitute a ''multiple,'' perhaps Lloyd, Longfield, and Senior
deserve the title. But Lloyd, Longfield, and Senior made little substantive use of marginal utility and thus only illustrate Whitehead's
adage that everything new has been said before by someone who did
not discover it. The same objection does not apply to Dupuit (1844),
Gossen (1854), and Jennings (1855), all of whom not only rediscovered marginal utility but employed it to analyze consumer behavior
(and Gossen did so with all the confidence and revolutionary ardor of
Jevons and Walras). Nevertheless, the same argument that applied to
Jevons, Menger, and Walras applies now to Dupuit, Gossen, and

5. See T. W. Hutchison, ''The Marginal Revolution and the Decline and
Fall of English Classical Political Economy,'' below in this volume.

Jennings: they struck on the law of diminishing marginal utility at about the same time, but in response to totally different intellectual pressures and without the benefit of an inherited corpus of similar economic ideas.

We have now collected three trios, nine names in all, of economists who between 1834 and 1874 seized on the idea of marginal utility, four of whom saw it indeed as the stock from which a new economics could be evolved. If we deny that this constitutes a Mertonian "multiple," are we not splitting hairs?

It is clear how we might escape the dilemma. Recall Merton's own words: "Even discoveries far removed from one another in calendrical time may be instructively construed as 'simultaneous' . . . depending upon the accumulated state of knowledge in the several cultures and the structures of the several societies in which they appear." Thus, from the fact that marginal utility was independently discovered over and over again in different countries between 1834 and 1874, we might argue that there must have been a core of economic ideas which was held in common by economists all over the world, whose inner logic would eventually dictate the exploration of consumer's demand with the tools of utility theory. In other words, we can infer the state of the science from the existence of a multiple, instead of the other way around. But that is to deprive the theory of multiples of its most attractive feature, namely, the idea that the development of a science is to some extent predictable. So long as we take Merton's argument seriously as providing something more than an inductive generalization with many exceptions, we must deny that even nine names necessarily make a "multiple." The point is very simple: if communication between scientists were perfect, all multiples would be forestalled and we would only observe singletons; at the other end of the spectrum, if there were no communication whatsoever between scientists, multiples would have no more significance than the fact that lightning does occasionally strike twice in the same place; thus, multiples are only interesting phenomena if there is a high but nevertheless imperfect degree of communication between the practitioners of a discipline.

It is true that classical economics had no theory of demand and that its theory of price determination would sooner or later strike someone as peculiarly asymmetrical. But as the example of Cournot shows, it would have been perfectly possible to repair this deficiency without introducing utility considerations. It is also true that marginal utility was "in the air" throughout the nineteenth century and kept turning up afresh every ten years or so: Lloyd and Longfield, 1834; Dupuit, 1844; Gossen, 1854; Jennings, 1855; Jevons, 1862 (the date at which he first publicly proclaimed his theory); Menger, 1871; and Walras, 1874. But that is a far cry from saying that marginal utility economics was, in some sense, inevitable. We might as well say that the emergence of macroeconomics in the 1930's was inevitable because certain Swedish economists were thinking along the same lines in the 1920's as Robertson and Keynes. *Post hoc ergo propter hoc* is a perennial temptation in intellectual history.

III

Howey's *Rise of the Marginal Utility School, 1870–1889* has taught us that the "marginal revolution," like the Industrial Revolution, went unrecognized by those who lived through it. The now standard version, which dates the revolution near 1871 and links together the names of Jevons, Menger, and Walras as having written essentially about the same thing, was first announced in the late 1880's and (despite Marshall's endorsement in 1890) did not become a regular feature of histories of economic thought until well past the turn of the century.[6] The long-delayed acceptance of the marginal utility theory of value, which went hand in hand with the delayed acceptance of a rational account of its history, is perhaps the best indication we can have that it was indeed an anomaly which did not emanate logically from classical economics. This suggests, in other words, that the last quarter of the nineteenth century was one of those revolutionary phases in the history of economics when, in the language of Thomas Kuhn, economists adopted a new "paradigm" to guide their work.

Unfortunately, there appears to be no agreement as to just what the new paradigm was that Jevons, Menger, and Walras put forward. Was it a new emphasis on demand rather than supply, on consumer utility rather than on production costs?[7] Was it something as am-

6. Howey, chaps. 26 and 27.
7. See A. W. Coats, "The Economic and Social Context of the Marginal Revolution of the 1870's," below in this volume.

bitious as a subjective theory of value, which was to supplant the
objective labor-cost theories of the past?[8] Was it rather the extension
of the principle of maximization from business firms to households,
making the consumer and not the entrepreneur the epitome of rational
action?[9] Was it perhaps the equimarginal principle, enshrined in the
proportionality of marginal ultilities to prices as the condition of
consumer equilibrium?[10] Was it instead, as Schumpeter liked to say,
the explicit or implicit discovery of general equilibrium analysis?[11]
Or lastly, was it simply the first conscious recognition of constrained
maximization as the archetype of all economic reasoning? Whichever
version we adopt, it is difficult to sustain the thesis that Jevons,
Menger, and Walras were really preoccupied with the same paradigm.

Menger is in any case the odd man out: he was not self-consciously
aware, as Jevons and Walras were, of being a revolutionary; he eschewed mathematical formulations and hence the pure logic of ex-
tremum problems; he only formulated "Gossen's third law" in words
and certainly did not emphasize it; he certainly rejected cost theories
of value, but on the other hand he was deeply suspicious of all determinate theory of pricing and he underlined discontinuities, un-
certainties, and bargaining around the market price.[12] In other
words, there is a great deal more to be said for coupling Jevons
and Walras with Gossen than with Menger, and the only reason for
the standard version is that Menger's name was continually invoked
by his disciples Wieser and Böhm-Bawerk, both of whom were determined to persuade the profession that Austrian economics was a
differentiated product. Similarly, it takes hindsight to see much in
common between Jevons—a precisely formulated theory of barter
exchange, an explicit mathematical statement of "Gossen's third
law," a theory of the short-run supply schedule of labor, and some
grandiose but unfulfilled promises of a new kind of utility economics
—and Walras, who really did derive demand curves from utility

8. See R. L. Meek, "Marginalism and Marxism," below in this volume.
9. Ibid. It is worth noting that Adam Smith's theory of occupational choice
certainly treats individual workers as maximizers. There was nothing new in the
idea of extending the sphere of rational action to households, but the notion
of extending it to consumer behavior was new.
10. Blaug, *Economic Theory in Retrospect*, pp. 301–2.
11. A. Schumpeter, *History of Economic Analysis* (New York, 1954), p. 918.
12. For a somewhat extreme statement of this argument, see E. Streissler,
"To What Extent Was the Austrian School Marginalist?" below in this volume.

schedules, struggled likewise to derive supply curves from marginal productivity considerations, worked out a theory of market pricing, and wove all the elements together within a general equilibrium framework.

The whole question is made more difficult by the ironic fate which history visited on the founders. In the end, what proved important about marginal utility was "the adjective rather than the noun."[13] Utility theory was gradually deprived of all its bite, to end up as merely "revealed preferences"; cost theories of value were shown not to be wrong, but only valid as a special case; and general equilibrium virtually disappeared, only to be revived in the 1930's by Hicks and Samuelson as "everybody's economics." Could anyone have foreseen in 1871 the tortuous path by which marginal utility economics led via Paretian welfare economics to cost-benefit analysis and dynamic programing? Not for nothing do we speak of a "marginal revolution" and not a "marginal utility revolution," but marginalism as a paradigm of economic reasoning is a twentieth-century invention; there is as much marginalism in Ricardo as in Jevons or Walras, but it is applied to different things.

IV

The term "paradigm" as a self-authenticated viewpoint no doubt raises as many questions as it answers,[14] but if we equate it loosely with Schumpeter's Vision—"a preanalytic cognitive act that supplies the raw material for the analytic effort"—we may describe the last quarter of the nineteenth century as a period when economists did

13. Hutchison, *Review of Economic Doctrines*, p. 16.
14. Masterman has counted twenty-one different definitions of "paradigm" in Kuhn's *Structure of Scientific Revolutions*, ranging from "a universally recognized scientific achievement" to a "general metaphysical viewpoint." M. Masterman, "The Nature of a Paradigm," in *Criticism and the Growth of Knowledge*, ed. I. Lakatos and A. Musgrave (London, 1970), pp. 61–65. Without precisely defining his sense of the term, Coats has argued that economics "has been dominated throughout its history by a single paradigm—the theory of economic equilibrium via the market mechanism." A. W. Coats, "Is There a 'Structure of Scientific Revolutions in Economics'?" *Kyklos* 22 (1969): 292. Similarly, Bronfenbrenner first defines a paradigm as a "mode or framework of thought and language" and then gives instances of paradigms, such as the demand-and-supply cross, the equation of exchange, and Hicksian IS-LM curves, which are much more specific than a mode or a framework. M. Bronfenbrenner, "The 'Structure of Revolutions' in Economic Thought," *History of Political Economy* 3 (Spring 1971): 150.

develop a new view of their research agenda. A brief way of describing this new Vision is to say that pricing and resource allocation with fixed supplies of the factors of production became *the* economic problem, setting aside all questions about changes in the quantity and quality of productive resources through time. Whether we want to describe this shift as a ''revolutionary phase,'' given the fact that it took at least twenty to thirty years and in some sense is still going on, is a matter of words. Jevons, Menger, and Walras are not the founders of this new way of looking at economic problems, but they are important landmarks in the early stages of the shift of emphasis. That they published nearly simultaneously is a pure coincidence, because their reflections on the problem are actually separated by more than a decade. Only biographical data can tell us why Jevons and Walras (and Gossen) each insisted on the novelty of his ideas, whereas Menger (and Lloyd and Longfield and Jenkin) did not.[15] Therefore, to try to explain the origin of the marginal utility revolution in the 1870's is doomed to failure: it was not a marginal *utility* revolution; it was not an abrupt change, but only a gradual transformation in which the old ideas were never definitively rejected; and it did not happen in the 1870's.

V

The fact that Jevons, Menger, and Walras all published their works within the span of three years, while a coincidence, was not an insignificant coincidence; it encouraged the acceptance of marginal utility economics, or at any rate greatly increased the probability of its early acceptance. Nevertheless, the new economics still failed to make much headway for at least a generation, despite the fact that all three founders were academic economists with established reputations, who argued their case persuasively and subsequently spared no efforts to push their ideas. The historical problem, therefore, is to explain, not the point in time at which the marginal concept

15. For some convincing biographical evidence, see R. D. Collison Black, ''W. S. Jevons and the Foundation of Modern Economics,'' and W. Jaffé, ''Léon Walras's Role in the 'Marginal Revolution' of the 1870's,'' below in this volume. As N. B. de Marchi argues, Mill and Cairnes were actually in possession of all the pieces required to make the breakthrough to marginal utility economics, but could not do so because of their Ricardian blinkers. ''Mill and Cairnes and the Emergence of Marginalism in England,'' below in this volume.

was applied to utility, but rather the delayed victory of marginal utility economics.

This is not a difficult problem provided we do not insist that historians "retrodict" in essentially the same way that scientists predict; in other words, that historical explanations can be regarded as valid only if they take the form of counterfactual hypotheses based on some general "covering law." What historians do is to make past events intelligible—they illuminate rather than explain—and in the nature of the case, therefore, there can be no hard and fast rules on whether A caused B or was merely associated with B.[16] It is, therefore, fruitless to argue whether the diffusion of marginal utility economics, as distinct from its genesis, was largely the result of endogenous or of exogenous influences. It is precisely in this period that economics began to emerge as a professional discipline with its own network of associations and journals, the dilettante amateur of the past giving way for the first time to the specialist earning his livelihood under the title of "economist." A professionalized science necessarily develops its own momentum, the impact of external events being confined to the shell and not reaching the core of the subject.[17] But in 1870, or 1880, or even 1890, core and shell were still deeply intertwined. To argue, therefore, as Stigler does, that the retarded adoption of utility theory in economics can *only* be explained by "the rise of new values as the discipline became increasingly academic"[18] is merely to throw back the problem one stage further: Why did economics become professionalized in the last quarter of the nineteenth century and why should a professionalized science of economics find the truth of utility theory so self-evident that resistance to it becomes impossible?

It seems clear that no monocausal explanation can do justice to the long uphill struggle of the marginal revolution. One is struck in reading the treatises of the 1870's and 1880's by the bewildering

16. I am making tacit reference to a great debate that was started in the 1940's with an article by C. G. Hempel. See P. Gardiner, ed., *Theories of History* (Glencoe, Ill., 1959); and S. Hook, ed., *Philosophy and History: A Symposium* (New York, 1963).

17. For this useful distinction, see J. J. Spengler, "Exogenous and Endogenous Influences in the Formation of Post-1870 Economic Thought: A Sociology of Knowledge Approach," in *Events, Ideology, and Economic Theory*, ed. R. V. Eagly (Detroit, 1968).

18. G. J. Stigler, "The Adoption of the Marginal Utility Theory," below in this volume.

variety of attitudes adopted towards the principal tenets of classical economics, such as the labor theory of value, the quantity theory of money, the Ricardian theory of differential rent, et cetera. Jevons, Menger, and Walras each in his own way emphasized the method-ological advantages of abstracting from historical and institutional con-siderations in the interest of obtaining perfectly general results from the minimum number of assumptions. But such considerations had little appeal to most contemporary economists, who still cared more about relevance than about rigor. As far as applied problems were concerned, marginal utility was, as we have said above, largely irrelevant, and the methodological problem that troubled most econ-omists in the critical decade of the 1880's was the issue of induction versus deduction, the conflict between fact gathering and model build-ing. Wherever there was a historicist bias—a pervasive bias in Ger-many and a widespread one in England—marginal utility economics was dismissed, together with English classical political economy, as excessively abstract and permeated with implausible assumptions about human behavior. The fact that Jevons and Walras chose to express themselves in mathematical terms was undoubtedly responsible for further resistance to their ideas; the notion of reducing social phenomena to mathematical equations was still new and profoundly disturbing to nineteenth-century readers. It was the rise of Marxism and Fabianism in the 1880's and 1890's that finally made subjective value theory socially and politically relevant; as the new economics began to furnish effective intellectual ammunition against Marx and Henry George, the view that value theory really did not matter became more difficult to sustain. Furthermore, the addition of mar-ginal productivity to marginal utility in the 1890's related the new economics to the problem of distribution, making it virtually im-possible to deny a logical conflict between the ideas of Jevons, Menger, and Walras and those of Smith, Ricardo, and Mill. In 1891 Marshall provided a reconciliation between marginal utility economics and classical economics which made the new ideas palatable by showing that they could be fitted together into a wider context. But even at this late stage, the Marshallian integration was not immediately accepted on the Continent, and the three interlocking "revolutions" that had characterized the last two decades of the nineteenth century

—the marginal utility revolution in England and America, the subjectivist revolution in Austria, and the general equilibrium revolution in Switzerland and Italy—continued well into the twentieth century.

VI

It may be convenient to seize on 1871 as marking the date from which all this started. But that date has no more special claim on our attention as historians of economic thought than any other. Classical political economy did not begin in 1776, and the birth of marginal utility economics—marginalism, modern economics, by whatever name we choose to characterize it—similarly, cannot be pinned down to any particular date. To sum up: (i) the "marginal revolution" was a process, not an event; (ii) there was no "multiple" discovery of marginal utility, but only the temporal coincidence of three or more singletons; and (iii) the success of the marginal revolution is intimately associated with the professionalization of economics in the last quarter of the nineteenth century, and it is this which constitutes the problem that must be, and to some extent has been, explained by historians of economic thought.

Jevons,
Menger,
& Walras

The Origins of Marginalism

Richard S. Howey

I

JOHN A. HOBSON coined the word "marginalism" in his *Work and Wealth* (1914) when he needed an expression to cover the acceptance by economists of both marginal utility and marginal productivity.[1] The first coinage occurred when he wrote of "the wide acceptance which 'marginalism' has won in academic circles." The acceptance, of course, had been of the idea, not of the word. By context, Hobson gave the word a disparaging tinge, since he found the concept faulty and its policy conclusions unwelcome. He repeated the word "marginalism" seven times in his *Work and Wealth*. In 1909 Hobson had referred to economists who used marginal analysis as "marginalists."[2]

The word "marginalism" was infrequently used in the twenty-five years after Hobson's innovation. None of the reviewers of Hobson's *Work and Wealth* identified the word "marginalism" as a neologism. Almost alone, Hobson helped to keep the word in circulation by inserting a chapter, "Marginalism in Neo-Classical Economics," in his *Free Thought in the Social Sciences* (1926). Two years later, the thorough index of the fourth edition of the *Handwörterbuch der Staatswissenschaften* contained only one reference, a reference to Hobson, under the subject heading of "Marginalismus." The words "marginalism" and "marginalist" seldom appeared in the *Encyclopaedia of the Social Sciences* (1930–35).[3]

The widespread employment of marginal cost, marginal revenue, marginal rate of substitution, and marginal propensity to consume in economic analysis during the 1930's provoked Richard A. Lester to complain in 1946 that the "minutiae of marginalism" were con-

RICHARD S. HOWEY *is Professor of Economics at the University of Kansas, Lawrence.*

1. Pp. 174–75, and 331.
2. John A. Hobson, *The Industrial System* (New York, 1909), p. 114.
3. 1:166, 175, 176; and 10:609.

suming one-half to one-third of the leading American textbooks.[4] This complaint by Lester marks the reintroduction of the word "marginalism" into economics, once again as a disparaging term. The next year, Lester gave further prominence to the word "marginalism" by inserting it in the title of an article.[5] Fritz Machlup, who prepared the longest reply to the antimarginalists, assented to the acceptance of the word by adopting it in the first part of his reply.[6]

The marginalism controversy that Lester had begun in 1946 died out by 1961. It left the word "marginalism," however, flavored by the discussions of that controversy. For example, the meaning of "marginalism" is restricted to considerations of the helpfulness of marginal cost or marginal productivity in economic analysis in the subject index of the American Economic Association's *Index to Economic Articles* (formerly *Index of Economic Journals*), which listed no articles under "marginalism" from 1925 to 1945, listed largely articles on the Lester controversy from 1946 to 1961, and listed nothing under "marginalism" from 1962 to 1966. At least two authors have characterized "marginalism" as the essence of non-Marxist economics.[7]

The newness of the word "marginalism" is evident from the dictionaries. The word first entered a general dictionary in English in 1966 when *Webster's Third* defined "marginalism" as "economic analysis that stresses use of marginal qualities in the determination of equilibrium." Portuguese dictionaries are the only ones in another language that define "marginalism" in terms of more than one of its "qualities."

4. Richard A. Lester, "Shortcoming of Marginal Analysis for Wage-Employment Problems," *American Economic Review* 36 (1946): 63.

5. Richard A. Lester, "Marginalism, Minimum Wages, and Labor Markets," *American Economic Review* 37 (1947): 135–48.

6. Fritz Machlup, "Marginal Analysis and Empirical Research," *American Economic Review* 36 (1946): 518–54.

7. The following are the longer histories of marginal utility: George J. Stigler, "The Development of Utility Theory," *Journal of Political Economy* 58 (1950); R. S. Howey, *The Rise of the Marginal Utility School, 1870-1889* (Lawrence, Kans., 1960); and Emil Kauder, *The History of Marginal Utility Theory* (Princeton, 1965). A great sourcebook of the history of marginal utility is William Jaffé, *Correspondence of Léon Walras and Related Papers* (Amsterdam, 1965), in three large, packed volumes. Fuller information on many of the subjects treated below can be located in these works by consulting their subject headings and indexes.

A recognizable and continuous history of marginalism began with the advent of the "quality" now called "marginal utility." There already are several studies[8] of the beginnings of marginal utility, and hence of this aspect of the origins of marginalism. According to the conventional accounts, marginal utility, in a form later acceptable to economists, was first successfully and independently created during the twelve years from 1862 to 1874 by Willam Stanley Jevons, Carl Menger, and Léon Walras. It is generally agreed that the most fruitful of these years was 1871, the year when both Jevons and Menger published their books on the subject.

Marginal productivity, the second "quality" which Hobson's term "marginalism" covered, also had many antecedents. It was not fully discovered and identified, however, until after 1890 and hence did not receive systematic consideration until after marginal utility had been accepted by a number of potentially influential economists.

This acceptance was crucial. This first marginal "quality" was not quickly welcomed as a part of economic theory. Acceptance required a conscious effort by Jevons, Menger, and Walras to win supporters, an effort that met with considerable indifference and some opposition. Perhaps the time was ripe for eventual success. After 1870 the universities, the only locale where marginalism has ever flourished, not only grew rapidly but also accepted economics as a subject for study.

II

William Stanley Jevons (1835–1882) was the *only* writer to publish accounts of a general marginal utility theory in the 1860's. Jevons, twenty-four years old and a student at University College, having just returned to London following five years of work in Australia, wrote in his diary on February 19, 1860, that he had arrived at "a true comprehension of *Value*."[9] Later that year he wrote to his brother: "One of the most important axioms is, that as the quantity of any commodity . . . which a man has to consume, increases, so the utility or benefit derived from the last portion used decreases in degree." "I have no idea," he added, "of letting these things lie by

8. Leo Köppel, *Grenznutzentheorie und Marxismus* (Leipzig, 1930); Hermann Lehmann, *Grenznutzentheorie* (East Berlin, 1968).

9. J. A. LaNauze, "The Conception of Jevons' Utility Theory," *Economica*, n. s. 20 (1953): 357.

till somebody else has the advantage of them, and shall therefore try to publish them next spring."[10]

Jevons' first public statement, however, was delayed until October 7, 1862, when he was barely twenty-seven. On that date, in Cambridge, the Secretary read, to Section F of the British Association for the Advancement of Science, Jevons' "Notice of a General Mathematical Theory of Political Economy." No one besides the Secretary is known to have heard the paper read. The next year an abstract was printed in the *Report of the Thirty-Second Meeting of the British Association for the Advancement of Science* (1863). No one is known to have mentioned this printed abstract in the next ten years.

Obviously, whatever circumstance started Jevons toward marginalism had to have influenced him before, or during, the first months of his twenty-fourth year. Earlier he had felt the impulse to accomplish. "I have an idea," he wrote to his sister when he was twenty-two, "which I do not object to mention to you, that my insight into the foundations and nature of the knowledge of man is deeper than that of most men or writers. In fact, I think it is my mission to apply myself to such subjects, and it is my intention to do so."[11] In the same letter he told of his discovery that political economy was "a sort of vague mathematics which calculates the causes and effects of man's industry." He took seriously his inclination to make use of mathematics, for he wrote, while still in Australia, looking forward to returning to England and having in mind his mission and the nature of political economy, "I wish especially to become a good mathematician, without which nothing, I am convinced, can be thoroughly done."[12]

Jevons had also acquired an equally essential inclination to connect utility with economic analysis. It is likely that his interest in utility came partly from Jeremy Bentham's writings, with which he could have become familiar while attending University College after returning to England. Bentham's influence on Jevons appeared first in the published abstract of Jevons' paper where, though he did not refer to Bentham, he used Bentham's phraseology, for example,

10. Harriet A. Jevons, ed., *Letters and Journal of W. Stanley Jevons* (London, 1886), pp. 151-52.
11. Ibid., p. 101.
12. Ibid., p. 119.

Bentham's phrase "springs of action." His mother had provided an earlier source of his inclination toward utility when she read to him, at the age of nine, Richard Whately's *Easy Lessons on Money Matters for Young People* (1833). Jevons himself said, when he was older, that he had learned his "first ideas of political economy" from this book.[13] Whately, according to his biographer, regarded his *Easy Lessons* "as of more real importance than his larger works."[14] Jevons' recollection of the purport of Whately's dictum, "It is not . . . labour that makes things valuable, but their being valuable that makes them worth labouring for,"[15] or of Whately's vivid illustration of his statement, may have survived the intervening fifteen years and helped guide Jevons in the first months of 1860.

Of his own abilities Jevons wrote, "Give me a few facts or materials, and I can work them up into a smoothly-arranged and finished fabric of theory, or can turn them out in a shape which is something new."[16] Jevons had recognized a few of his "facts or materials" before he arrived in London. He soon found more. Besides studying philosophy, he enrolled in Augustus De Morgan's class in calculus, and in the class in political economy given by Jacob Waley, a star pupil himself of De Morgan's mathematics. In Waley's class he found the opportunity to consider the details of John Stuart Mill's *Principles of Political Economy* and, of course, from De Morgan he secured welcome instruction in the differential calculus. Early in 1860, Jevons worked all of his "facts or materials" into a "finished fabric of theory" that he realized was "something new."

III

Unlike Jevons, Carl Menger (1840–1921) left no correspondence or diaries that could disclose the sources of the new ideas contained in the *Grundsätze der Volkswirtschaftslehre* (1871), his first, and last, published contribution to marginalism. Although nothing is known that would directly invalidate the surmise that the *Grundsätze* resulted from ideas generated much earlier, a statement in the

13. W. Stanley Jevons, *Political Economy* (New York, 1878), p. 5.
14. E. Jane Whately, *Life and Correspondence of Richard Whately, D.D.* (London, 1866), 1:377.
15 .[Richard Whately], *Easy Lessons on Money Matters for the Use of Young People* (London, 1833), p. 33.
16. Harriet A. Jevons, *Letters and Journal of W. Stanley Jevons*, p. 96.

Grundsätze made it seem likely that the book was largely developed shortly before 1869 when Menger needed a *Habilitationsschrift* to qualify for a lectureship at the University of Vienna. In the statement in question Menger said that the field treated was "in no small degree . . . the product of recent development in German political economy."[17] This "recent development" was a discussion on value among German scholars that continued into 1869,[18] and to which Menger apparently intended to add the last word.

The German scholars gave Menger a subject for his *Habilitationsschrift* when they confronted him with the rudiments of an unsatisfactory non-labor theory of value. To improve this theory Menger added the key idea of marginalism, expressing it by saying that value equaled "the importance of the least important of the satisfactions assured by the whole available quantity and achieved with any equal portion."[19] No similar idea can be found in the writings of any German scholar that Menger had read earlier. In a way, the key idea is a mathematical one, and both Jevons and Walras acknowledged the relation between the calculus and their formulations of marginal utility. Menger, on the other hand, never publicly associated his version with the calculus. For this reason, as well as for the reason that his expressed views on methodology appeared hostile to the use of mathematics in economics, it has been presumed that mathematics played no part in the development of Menger's ideas on economics before 1871. J. A. Schumpeter attempted to explain the mathematics of Menger by saying that "the Austrian utility theorists, by operating the concept of marginal utility, actually discovered the calculus."[20]

However, there is evidence that Menger's formulation of marginal utility may not have been the simple rediscovery of the calculus that Schumpeter implied. It would not be, if, as seems to be the case, Menger was familiar with the calculus before 1869. The likelihood of his familiarity is established by a letter he wrote to Sigismund Feilbogen, who published a translation of it in 1911 in the *Journal des Economistes*.[21] "La philosophie et la mathématique," Menger

17. Carl Menger, *Principles of Economics* (Glencoe, Ill., 1950), p. 49.
18. Ibid., p. 306.
19. Ibid., p. 139.
20. Joseph A. Schumpeter, *History of Economic Analysis* (New York, 1954), p. 18.
21. *Journal des Economistes*, 6e série, 31 (1911): 56–57.

wrote, "ont compté de tout temps parmi mes études préférées."
Menger's first letter to Walras contained additional evidence of his
familiarity with mathematics. Walras first learned of Menger in a
letter of June 22, 1883, from Aulnis de Bourouill who had just (twelve
years after its publication) discovered Menger's *Grundsätze* and who
described it as "un livre de *théorie pure* avec des idées de mathématiques (comparaison de quantités distinctes) et arrivant par là
à la doctrine sur le taux d'échange."[22] Walras hastened to open correspondence with Menger. Menger's reply contained a discussion of
mathematical economics which it seems unlikely that he would have
written had he not had an interest in and knowledge of mathematics.[23]
In the reply Menger listed ten mathematical works on political economy which he had in his library and offered to lend to Walras. A
library of this kind and size would hardly be owned at this time,
even by a bibliophile such as Menger, if he had only faint connections
with mathematics. Further, one of the ten books was by Cournot. In
his letter to Feilbogen, Menger had said that the writings of Cournot
"devaient exercer sur mon esprit une influence particulière."

It is lamentable, especially in connection with a consideration of
Carl Menger's mathematics, that nothing is known of the relations
between him and his slightly younger brother, Anton. Anton Menger
began pursuing mathematics as a hobby in 1867, and between 1891
and 1894 published a number of memoirs on the reform of the calculus
under the assumed name of Dr. Julius Bergbohm. Carl Menger may
have felt, between 1867 and 1871, the influence of his brother's strong
interest.

IV

The first political economist to have direct cognizance of the
marginal analysis of Léon Walras (1834–1910) was Joseph Garnier,
editor of the well-established *Journal des Economistes*. Walras, then
thirty-eight years old, had in 1873 sent Garnier sixty pages of proof
from his forthcoming *Eléments d'économie politique pure*,[24] asking
him, as editor, to consider them for publication.

Two months later, in a second attempt to draw attention to his
book, which was still being printed, Walras read a summary paper,

22. Jaffé, *Correspondence of Léon Walras*, 1:766.
23. Ibid., 1:768–69.
24. Ibid., 1:318–19.

"Principe d'une théorie mathématique de l'échange" before the Académie des Sciences morales et politiques. Of this first appearance in public of his major ideas he wrote to a friend: "J'ai fait dans ma science une importante découverte. C'est celle que j'ai communiquée à l'institut aux vacances. La communication entière a été froidement reçue."[25]

After some hesitation, the Académie published Walras's paper in its *Séances et travaux* for January 1874, the first appearance in print of his contribution to marginalism. Walras realized that few would ever see his paper if it did not appear elsewhere. Accordingly, he repeated his request to Garnier to publish part of his manuscript in the *Journal des Economistes*. After a delay Garnier refused on the ground that "cela ne serait pas apprécié par les 0,99 de notre public."[26] Garnier, who often befriended Walras, tempered his refusal with the promise of other assistance, "en votre qualité de fils de A. Walras, de professeur d'économie politique, d'abonné, d'homme d'esprit, quoiqu'un peu rageur."[27] Walras accepted at once, gratefully.[28] Garnier, as part of his promised assistance, reprinted Walras's paper from the *Séances et travaux* in the April 1874 issue of the *Journal des Economistes*. From this reprinting Jevons first noticed the similarity of Walras's views to his own.

Walras had sought, from mid-1873 on, to enlist the support of A. A. Cournot, to whom he felt a debt, inviting him to the lecture Walras gave before the Académie, discussing with him their differences of viewpoint, asking for intervention with the publisher Hachette, and requesting his help in writing an article on mathematical political economy.[29] Cournot, who died in 1877, was willing and interested, but he could help little, not only because he was busy with his own publications and family matters but also because he had lost the effective use of his eyes shortly after he had published his *Recherches sur les principes mathématiques de la théorie des richesses* (1838), with the consequence that he had given up all mathematics for the preceding thirty years.[30]

25. Ibid., 1:354.
26. Ibid., 1:350.
27. Ibid.
28. Ibid., 1:351–52.
29. Ibid., 1:326, 330–32, 366–67, 375, 421–22.
30. Ibid., 1:331–32.

Walras's interest in political economy, according to his own account, had been first aroused in 1848 by overhearing his father, Auguste Walras, reading from one of his own manuscripts on political economy. "J'ai appris ainsi, à quatorze ans," Léon Walras reminisced, "que la terre et son service avaient une valeur intrinsèque provenant de leur utilité combinée avec la limitation de leur quantité."[31] This suggestion of a reasonable connection between value and utility may have helped lead Walras to marginalism. It was, however, almost ten later that Léon Walras first began to think of himself as a political economist. The turn came in the summer of 1858 when, after being forgiven by his father for having wasted four years and 7,000 francs in an unsuccessful attempt to become a mining engineer, Léon Walras began his professional career by promising to carry on his father's unfinished work in political economy.[32] Twenty-five years later, in writing to his mother of his own intellectual history, he said, "C'est un peu comme un tableau à l'huile dont mon père m'aurait fourni l'esquisse au crayon."[33]

What did "l'esquisse au crayon" contain? It contained an emphasis on utility and its relation to scarcity, resulting in the concept of *rareté*, which took the form of a ratio and was far from marginalism. It also contained Auguste Walras's unexplained encouragement of the use of mathematics in political economy. The sketch left much either to be filled in or corrected.

Léon Walras struggled vainly from 1858 through 1870 to earn a living and to obtain a foothold in political economy. In those twelve years in Paris, he failed to add the vital connection between mathematics and utility to the sketch, although he tried twice, first in 1860 and again in 1869–70.[34]

Walras's career might have continued in this way had he not received an unexpected appointment as a professor at Lausanne. This appointment brought him release from old obligations and offered new opportunities. Undoubtedly it altered the course of the marginal revolution. He arrived in Lausanne on December 11, 1870,

31. Léon Walras, "Un initiateur en économie politique: A. A. Walras," *Revue du Mois* 6 (1908): 181.
32. Jaffé, *Correspondence of Léon Walras*, 1:2.
33. Ibid., 1:761.
34. Ibid., 1:216–21.

in part because of his parents' payment of 3,000 francs, or more, to hire a substitute for his army service. In these fresh surroundings he renewed at once his effort to combine political economy with mathematics. "Le dimanche matin," he wrote to his wife shortly after he had arrived in Lausanne, "je suis allé voir un autre de mes collègues M. Gay, professeur de mathématiques à l'Académie, avec lequel j'ai travaillé quelques problèmes d'économie politique."[35]

When did Walras first capture the elusive, essential idea of marginal utility? William Jaffé, who has read *all* the correspondence and related papers, published and unpublished, said that there was "not the slightest inkling of a theory of maximization of utility either in L.W.'s pre-Lausanne papers or in the various outlines and prospectives of his work up to October 19, 1872."[36] The "inkling" on that date was Walras's remark in a letter to a colleague that he was going over his forthcoming publication with Antoine Paul Piccard, professor of mechanics at Lausanne, "en vue de la correction des formules algébriques."[37] Earlier, Piccard had given an expository note to Walras which, Jaffé said, "played more than a casual role in bringing mathematical light to L.W."[38] If Piccard brought the "mathematical light" to Walras, then Walras's *Eléments* came close to being published with no marginal utility in it, since Walras already had a manuscript and had begun to seek a publisher. Over a month earlier, in a letter to the publisher Guillaumin, he had said that his work on pure economics "est aujourd'hui presque entièrement terminé," and that it was in a form "tout-à-fait nouvelle," meaning that he had used the mathematical method.[39]

V

The preceding sections are intended to show that marginalism was developed between 1862 and 1873 by newcomers to political economy. The newcomers, Jevons, Menger, and Walras, having the outlook of young men, felt free from allegiance to prevailing and encumbering views on political economy. Each also had a marked sense of mission. Through different circumstances each had come to magnify the part

35. Ibid., 1:264.
36. Ibid., 1:309.
37. Ibid., 1:307.
38. Ibid., 1:308.
39. Ibid., 1:298.

that wants or utility play in an understanding of economics. Marginal utility emerged when these three men, from different countries, coupled their ideas of wants or utility with a basic concept of the differential calculus.

The further history of the development of marginalism, from 1873 through most of the 1880's, was the history of a search for acceptance and support of marginal utility. Marginalism, as a recognized part of economics, did not originate until supporters were found and acceptance achieved. Jevons, Menger, and especially Walras were the principal figures in this struggle for recognition. The fact that they were newcomers deprived them for a long time of allies.

Jevons and Walras soon discovered each other, but it was almost ten years later when Walras and Menger first corresponded. It was quickly pointed out to them that there had been predecessors. The main predecessor was Hermann Heinrich Gossen, whose discovery Jevons announced by letter to Walras in 1878.[40] Walras and Jevons agreed without delay that Gossen had preceded them. They did not agree on the other predecessors. Johann Heinrich von Thünen was called to Walras's attention by George Friedrich Knapp in 1874,[41] and to Jevons' attention by Robert Adamson in 1876.[42] Walras found little to interest him in Thünen, saying finally in a letter to Jevons, ''je doute malgré tout qu'il y ait grand'chose à y prendre.''[43] Jevons never commented on Walras's evaluation; but he only mentioned Thünen's name in the 1879 edition of his *Theory*, where he gave almost seven pages to Gossen.[44] Charles Letort advanced the name of Jules Dupuit in his review of Walras's *Eléments* in 1874.[45] As in the case of Thünen, but for different reasons, Walras did not accept Dupuit as a predecessor. Walras gave Jevons in 1874 a judgment on ''le mémoire de M. Dupuit'' saying that ''Dupuit y a effectivement abordé le problème de l'expression mathématique de l'utilité; mais il ne l'a nullement résolu.''[46] Jevons later wrote to Walras, ''It is impossible not to allow that Dupuit had a very profound comprehension of the sub-

40. Ibid., 1:581.
41. Ibid., 1:401.
42. Ibid., 1:508.
43. Ibid., 1:532.
44. Pp. xxxv–xlii, xliv.
45. Jaffé, *Correspondence of Léon Walras*, 1:458.
46. Ibid., 1:456.

ject and anticipated us as regards the fundamental ideas of utility."[47] Walras replied at once that he was not of Jevons' "avis sur le mérite des Mémoires de M. Dupuit."[48]

Carl Menger seemingly won followers with little exertion. The amount of his exertion, however, may be underestimated, since more is known about his results than his activities. Apparently he first captured the allegiance of his two principal supporters, Eugen Böhm-Bawerk and Friedrich von Wieser, on the merits of his *Grundsätze* alone. The start of the Austrian School, however, was delayed, for Wieser published nothing on marginalism until 1884, and Böhm-Bawerk did not start until 1886. No details of Menger's part in these publications are known.

Jevons realized that he had to seek out means to spread his views. Accordingly, he published, in 1866, a longer version of his original paper in a place more certain to be noticed, the *Journal of the Royal Statistical Society*. Later he prepared and was able to have published by Macmillan a book-length elaboration, his *Theory of Political Economy* (1871). In 1875 Jevons wrote to Walras, whom he had come to regard as an ally, "I have no doubt whatever about the ultimate success of our efforts, but it will take some fighting."[49] In the second edition of his *Theory* (1879), Jevons provided marginalism with its first history and its first bibliography, both of which gave status to the subject and furthered understanding. But Jevons was busy with other things, lacked a taste for pushing, and, unfortunately, died in 1882. He never learned that Menger had similar views.

Walras was the most energetic of the three in systematically and continually seeking recognition and support. A good part of the three large volumes of William Jaffé's superbly arranged *Correspondence of Léon Walras and Related Papers* recounts the ups and downs of Walras's unremitting efforts from 1873 to 1909 to ensure acceptance of the new economics.

Walras thought that he knew what had to be done. He had a plan for scientific revolution that went beyond the announcement of the revolutionary discovery. "Ce n'est pas tout que de faire des découvertes," Walras wrote to his mother in 1883, "il faut savoir se

47. Ibid., 1:533.
48. Ibid., 1:535.
49. Ibid., 1:474–75.

faire une position qui vous permettra de les faire connaître.''[50] He had sufficient revolutionary fervor to spend his own capital to help finance the marginal revolution. Walras estimated, in 1901, that he had spent, from his inherited capital, 50,000 francs (equal to ten times his highest annual salary) to spread his doctrines.[51]

From the beginning, Walras fancied that French political economists would ignore his work. Walras's fancy spurred on the internationalization of the struggle to introduce marginal utility into political economy. This internationalization was one factor contributing to the eventual success of the struggle, and hence to the origin of marginalism.

The plan for internationalization first appeared when Walras told Joseph Garnier in 1873 that if the French persisted in dismissing him as "un rêveur," he would appeal "au jugement public de l'étranger.''[52] He actually began systematically to seek foreign supporters on March 12, 1874, at which time he addressed similar letters to "un ami en Angleterre et un en Allemagne," both fellow members in the cooperative movement, and to a professor at Geneva who was familiar with Italy.[53] In these three letters he asked for a select list of professors and editors to whom he could send an offprint of his article in the *Journal des Economistes* with the hope of subsequently entering "en relation avec celles qui seraient disposeés à approfondir mes idées pour les discuter.''[54] Walras apologized in one of these letters for appearing "quelque peu altéré de publicité," saying that since his work was "très scientifique et peu populaire," he had to look far to find even a small group of readers.[55] He explained further that readers were especially necessary to him, since his publisher would print the second part of his forthcoming volume only after the first part was certain to sell enough copies to pay for itself, an agreement which delayed the printing of the second part of Walras's *Eléments* until 1877.[56] He estimated that his *Eléments* would have a chance to succeed if thirty persons in France, England, Germany, and Italy

50. Ibid., 1:761.
51. Ibid., 3:187.
52. Ibid., 1:344.
53. Ibid., 1:359–61.
54. Ibid., 1:360.
55. Ibid.
56. Ibid., 1:361.

could be found "en état de le lire, de le juger et de le faire avaler au public."[57]

Walras's first three letters turned up two Italian, seven German, and sixteen English prospects; but only one Italian and two English correspondents responded to Walras's overtures. The Italian was Alberto Errera, who opened Italy to marginalism. Jevons was the first Englishman to reply, saying that he had already read Walras's article in the *Journal des Economistes*. "It is satisfactory to me to find that my theory of exchange," he wrote on May 12, 1874, "which, when published in England, was either neglected or criticized, is practically confirmed by your researches."[58] This union of purpose between Walras and Jevons strengthened the forces creating marginalism. Of the coincidence of their discoveries Walras wrote to another correspondent that he hoped that "la singularité de cette rencontre piquera votre curiosité et vous amènera à vouloir prendre une connaissance approfondie de l'ouvrage de M. Jevons et du mien."[59] The other Englishman to answer was Professor T. E. Cliffe Leslie, who pointed out that Jevons had a similar theory with which neither he nor John Stuart Mill agreed.[60]

Walras repeated that same procedure for entering into correspondence with interested economists when the first part of his *Eléments* (1874) appeared, sending copies "à presque tous les professeurs d'économie politique de l'Europe."[61] On this occasion, Jevons provided Walras with the names of six economists who might respond;[62] only one, G. H. Darwin, became a correspondent. Walras mailed the second part of the *Eléments* (1877) with no more effect. In fact, his campaign for readers must have resulted in far fewer than he had anticipated; after all his effort, by 1881 he could count only three "élèves dignes de ce nom": Aulnis de Bourouill, von Winterfeld, and del Pezzo.[63]

After 1881, prospects brightened. In almost every year between 1881 and 1890, additional writers recognized and supported the idea

57. Ibid.
58. Ibid., 1:393.
59. Ibid., 1:420.
60. Ibid., 1: 395.
61. Ibid., 1:424.
62. Ibid., 1:427.
63. Ibid., 1:681.

of marginal utility. In 1882, Herbert Somerton Foxwell, who became Walras's principal English consultant following Jevons' death, sent Walras a list of twelve English prospects.[64] From the list Walras was able to open a correspondence with Alfred Marshall and F. Y. Edgeworth which, in some ways, was encouraging. In 1883, Aulnis de Bourouill brought Menger and Walras together, with the consequence that the marginal revolution now added another national dimension. In his first letter to Walras, Menger said that he had been aware of Walras's writings for some time, but it is not clear that he had appreciated the extent of the similarity of his viewpoint with that of Walras.[65] Perhaps the appreciation was absent because Menger did not think the similarity present. On the other hand, Walras emphasized their similarity when he wrote to Menger, "Nous nous sommes évidemment posé le même problème, Monsieur; et nous avons évidemment entrepris de le résoudre par la même méthode."[66]

The year after Menger was introduced to Walras, Friedrich von Wieser published his *Über den Ursprung und die Hauptgesetze des wirtschaftlichen Werthes* (1884). It was a book based on Menger's views, the first indication that there would be an Austrian School, and the book in which the word *Grenznutzen* was first used. It had a narrow circulation. Walras did not know it in 1886[67] and did not obtain a copy until 1887.[68] Charles Gide's proposal to Walras in 1885 to found a new French journal "ouverte aux idées critiques" indicated some warming of the French coolness that Walras had felt so long.[69] In 1886, Eugen Böhm-Bawerk's "Grundzüge der Theorie des wirtschaftlichen Güterwerts" appeared in the *Jahrbücher für Nationalökonomie und Statistik*, a primary forum for German professional opinion on economics. Walras wrote Böhm-Bawerk at once of "un premier et rapide examen m'en ayant fait connaître toute l'importance."[70] In this same year Walras wrote the second history of marginalism, which he put in the preface to his *Théorie de la monnaie* (1886). Late in 1887, Walras found a Russian mathematical economist,

64. Ibid., 1:738–39.
65. Ibid., 1:768–69.
66. Ibid., 1:771.
67. Ibid., 2:152.
68. Ibid., 2:187.
69. Ibid., 2:42.
70. Ibid., 2:152.

Ladislaus von Bortkiewicz, who became a valued correspondent and a reliable defender.[71]

Walras had first heard from Philip Henry Wicksteed in 1884 when Wicksteed wrote, "I am now reading your 'Eléments' with extreme interest."[72] Four years went by before Walras heard from him again. Foxwell, who continued to advise Walras on English economists, recommended Wicksteed in 1886 as "a very able man, an enthusiastic follower of Jevons" and in 1888 as an "admirable writer" who "is bringing out an Introduction to Mr. Jevons' Theory of P.E."[73] Wicksteed sent Walras a copy of his *Alphabet of Economic Science* (1888), and Walras responded that he had read the volume with "un vif plaisir."[74] The next year, "un vif plaisir" was also the exact phrase with which he described his feelings after examining the copy of *Principii di economia pura* (1889) which Maffeo Pantaleoni had sent him.[75] The hold that marginalism had in Austria in 1889 was shown by the appearance in that year of three other books using marginal analysis: Rudolph Auspitz's and Richard Lieben's *Untersuchungen über die Theorie des Preises*, Eugen Böhm-Bawerk's *Kapital und Kapitalzins, Zweite Abteilung, Positive Theorie des Kapitales*, and Friedrich von Wieser's *Natürliche Werth*.

VI

In the years 1862 to 1887, diverse names were given to the new way in which utility was being treated. Jevons coined the expressions "final degree of utility," "final utility," and "terminal utility" in the search for a satisfactory term. Menger used "importance of the least important of the satisfactions" to denote the same idea. Walras tried three forms, "intensive utility," "*rareté*," and "the intensity of the last want satisfied" to cover an identical concept. By 1887 it seemed likely that "final utility" might win out as the standard term, at least in English. Even the term *Grenznutzen* which Friedrich Wieser had introduced in his *Ursprung* (1884) was translated as "final utility."

Late in 1888 a word appeared that in time replaced "final utility"

71. Ibid., 2:229–37.
72. Ibid., 2:12.
73. Ibid., 2:160–61, 259.
74. Ibid., 2:307.
75. Ibid., 2:331.

in English and that will probably also replace all terms previously used in other languages. It was the word "marginal," first introduced by Philip H. Wicksteed in his *Alphabet*, where it occurred on an average of twice on each page, a massive occurrence for a first use. Adoption followed slowly. For example, the word "marginal" is not found in Edgeworth's review of the *Alphabet* in 1889.[76] Nor is it found in Edgeworth's Presidential Address before Section F of the British Association later that year, even though he referred to Wicksteed's *Alphabet* and mentioned "final utility" and "final disutility" many times.[77]

It has been easy to surmise that Wicksteed adopted the word from Wieser. Wieser had first translated "final utility" into *Grenznutzen* in 1884, hardly a literal translation. There is no evidence, however, in the *Alphabet* or elsewhere, that Wicksteed had been influenced in his introduction of the word "marginal" either by Wieser's *Ursprung* or by any of the infrequent uses by other writers of the word *Grenznutzen*. It may be added that "marginal utility" is a non-literal translation. It is an unlikely one as well, particularly since the expression "final utility" had been used increasingly for seventeen years as an equivalent. The *Annals of the American Academy of Political and Social Science* for 1890, contained two translations of articles by Böhm-Bawerk in which the word *Grenznutzen* was rendered, as would be expected, on every occasion into "final utility."[78] The word *Grenze* was also found in Menger's *Grundsätze*, but it should be, and was in the English edition, translated as "limit" and not as "margin."

Edgeworth, in his article "Margin (in economics)" for Palgrave's *Dictionary of Political Economy* (1896), said that Wicksteed "first used the phrase 'marginal' instead of 'final utility.' " Another reliable reporter, James Bonar, said in 1889 that " 'marginal utility' is a happy phrase used by P. H. Wicksteed."[79] Neither Edgeworth nor Bonar suggested any connection wih Wieser. Strangely, Wicksteed never mentioned "marginal utility" in the article "Final Degree of

76. *The Academy* 35 (1889): 71.
77. *Report of the Fifty-Ninth Meeting of the British Association for the Advancement of Science* (London, 1890).
78. 1:244–71, 361–84.
79. *Quarterly Journal of Economics* 3 (1889): 344.

Utility'' that he wrote for Palgrave's *Dictionary*. A statement at the end of Wicksteed's article said, ''Jevons's 'Final Degree of Utility' is the *Grenznutzen* of the Austrian School.''

The second book to include the word ''marginal'' was Alfred Marshall's *Principles of Economics* (1890). Marshall used the word less frequently than Wicksteed, averaging one use to every fifteen pages. It might be thought that Marshall learned the word ''marginal'' from Wicksteed. Yet no one has said that such was the case. In the first edition of the *Principles* Marshall gave a personal explanation of the origin of the term. ''The term 'marginal' increment I borrowed from von Thunen,'' he wrote, ''and it is now commonly used by German economists. When Jevons' *Theory* appeared, I adopted his word 'final,' but I have been gradually convinced 'marginal' is the better.''[80] Marshall's explanation was inexact in some ways. Thünen did not use the term '' 'marginal' increment''; neither, for that matter, did Marshall outside the passage just cited. Thünen used the noun *Grenze* only once, and then in the sense of the ''limit'' beyond which the employer would hire no laborers.[81]

Marshall felt that his explanation was amiss and consequently changed the footnote in the second edition to read thus:

> The term ''marginal'' increment is in harmony with von Thünen's methods of thought and was suggested to me by him, though he does not actually use it. It has been for some time commonly used by Austrian economists on the initiative of Prof. Wieser, and it has been adopted by Mr. Wicksteed. When Jevons' Theory appeared, I adopted his word ''final''; but I have been gradually convinced that ''marginal'' is the better. [In the first edition this footnote implied wrongly that the phrase, as well as the idea of, ''marginal increment'' could be traced to von Thünen.][82]

This was scarcely an improvement. What did he mean by ''adopted''? Marshall also introduced twice in the index of the second edition the sentence ''Wieser first used the term Marginal Utility.'' Later editions dropped this misleading sentence.

80. Alfred Marshall, *Principles of Economics* (London, 1890), p. x.
81. Johann Heinrich von Thünen, *Der isolirte Staat*, Zweiter Theil, Erste Abtheilung (Rostock, 1850), p. 178.
82. Marshall, *Principles*, 2d ed., p. xiv.

The new word "marginal" did appear, perhaps for the first time, as the English translation of the German word *Grenze* when Böhm-Bawerk's *Positive Theorie des Kapitales* (1889) was turned into English by William Smart in 1891. It was also so rendered by Christian A. Malloch's translation of Wieser's *Natürliche Werth* (1889) in 1893. But Smart, and his student Malloch, must have learned the word "marginal" from Marshall's *Principles* rather than from their German-English dictionaries.

The word "marginal" was applied by Wicksteed to ten different nouns and by Marshall to thirteen different nouns. The only noun modified by "marginal" that Wicksteed and Marshall had in common was "utility." The other nouns of Wicksteed were desire, desiredness, effect, effectiveness, usefulness, value, value-in-use, want, and worth. The other nouns of Marshall were capital, cost of production, demand price, disutility of labor, dose, efficiency of a factor of production, effort, expenses, increment, produce, return, supply price, and utility of money.

It is probable that the word "marginal" was introduced, not as a translation of *Grenze*, but as a handier substitute for "final." "Marginal" was more flexible, since it permitted, among other things, the use of such phrases as "at the margin" or "on the margin." Both Wicksteed and Marshall made use of this advantage. Wicksteed employed the noun "margin" twenty-four times, Marshall half that many. This was appealing because it brought marginal analysis in line with a type of analysis, long met with in English political economy, which consisted in centering attention on the circumstances at the "margin of cultivation." "Margin" was thought to be widely used, in this sense, when Wicksteed and Marshall wrote. "The expression 'margin of cultivation' has become," Simon N. Patten said in 1889, "through long usage, a classical expression for one of the most fundamental ideas of economics."[83]

The expression "margin of cultivation" had been introduced by Thomas Chalmers in his *On Political Economy in Connection with the Moral State and Moral Prospects of Society* (1832). Following the example of "Sir Edward West and Mr. Malthus," he began his discussion with a consideration of "the extreme limit of cultivation."[84]

83. *Quarterly Journal of Economics* 3 (1889): 356.
84. P. 2.

Chalmers repeated this expression once and then switched, without explanation, to "the extreme margin of cultivation," an alternative expression which he only used twice.[85] He also used the expression "last and farthest margin."[86] After those three uses of the word "margin" he reverted to his original term "limit," using it frequently, often writing "extreme limit," "certain limit," "natural limit," "least possible limit," or "existing limit." A German translation of "the limit" is *die Grenze.*

Chalmers alone probably could not have introduced the word "margin" into the vocabulary of political economy. The introduction became effective when it received, in addition, the approval of John Stuart Mill. In his *Principles of Political Economy* (1848), Mill included Dr. Chalmers among "authors of the highest name and of great merit," a position not usually given to him.[87] Mill said that Chalmers had the merit of expressing his opinions "in a language of his own, which often uncovers aspects of the truth that the received phraseologies only tend to hide."[88] "It is well said by Dr. Chalmers," Mill wrote, "that many of the most important lessons in political economy are to be learned at the extreme margin of cultivation."[89] Mill mentioned the "margin" a number of other times, attributing the word to Chalmers. The translation of the word "margin" into German is interesting. Adolph Soetbeer turned "at the extreme margin" into "auf dem äussersten Rande" in his German translation (1852) of Mill's *Principles,*[90] and he translated Mill's expression "extreme limit" as "die äusserste Grenze."[91] Thus the word "margin" (and hence the word "marginalism") links, as it properly should, the work of Jevons, Menger, and Walras with that of West, Malthus, and Mill. In this sense, marginalism appears as the confluence of two streams of analysis.

VII

The incorporation of marginal analysis in the general treatises of economics marked the final or acceptance stage in the origin of

85. Pp. 21 and 45.
86. P. 32.
87. 1:82–83.
88. 1:94.
89. 2:234.
90. 2:149.
91. 2:206.

marginalism. For the sake of conciseness, only American textbooks are considered here.

Richard T. Ely's *Outlines of Economics* (1893), the American textbook most widely selected by professors of economics during the next forty years for use in their classes, had been prepared as a revision of his *Introduction to Political Economy* (1889), which had hardly contained a trace of marginalism. The *Outlines* included a little more marginalism. It introduced Jevons, Menger, and Walras in a short history of economics and commented on the Austrian School, then becoming known in the United States. In its index it listed "Marginal Utility," but in the text, only a sketch of the idea of marginal utility was found, and no mention of the word itself.

The first edition of Ely's *Outlines* served from 1893 to 1907. In these fifteen years marginal analysis entered the competing textbooks of A. T. Hadley (1896), C. J. Bullock (1897), H. J. Davenport (1897), E. T. Devine (1898), F. W. Blackmar (1900), F. A. Fetter (1904), H. R. Seager (1904), and E. R. A. Seligman (1905). For the most part the textbooks discussed only marginal utility, although marginal productivity was also a topic in those of Hadley and Seligman.

The appearance of Ely's revised *Outlines* (1908) reflected a change in marginalism. After its editors had added marginal productivity as part of the explanation of the return to labor and capital, no other textbook excluded it. Ely's *Outlines* went through four later editions, 1916, 1923, 1930, and 1937, keeping approximately the same content of marginalism.

Other leading American textbooks of the period from 1908 to 1936, all of which gave essentially the same coverage as did Ely's textbook, were those of Alvin Johnson (1909), F. W. Taussig (1911), Irving Fisher (1911), F. M. Taylor (1911), J. R. Turner (1919), Henry Clay (1919), T. N. Carver (1919), O. F. Boucke (1925), Lionel Edie (1926), L. A. Rufener (1927), F. B. Garver and A. H. Hansen (1928), P. F. Gemmill (1930), F. R. Fairchild (1930), Broadus Mitchell (1932), and F. S. Deibler (1936). This was a twenty-eight-year plateau. Both marginal utility and marginal productivity had been accepted. There was no other use of marginal analysis in these textbooks.

In the 1930's new uses for the marginal concept were introduced in the journals and the specialized literature. Marginal utility lost favor, and the marginal rate of substitution took its place, partly as an immediate result of J. R. Hicks and R. G. D. Allen's "A Reconsideration of the Theory of Value" (1934).[92] Marginal cost and marginal revenue, twin guides to maximization that had for long appeared in isolated instances, came in for extended use in Edward Chamberlin's *The Theory of Monopolistic Competition* (1933) and in Joan Robinson's *Economics of Imperfect Competition* (1933). John Maynard Keynes began the unusual use of marginal terms as constants in *The General Theory of Employment, Interest and Money* (1936).

These changes reached the textbooks between 1937 and 1947. Two texts, one by A. L. Meyers, the second by A. M. McIsaac and J. G. Smith, both published in 1937, first showed plainly the acceptance of the ideas of Edward Chamberlin and Joan Robinson. Lorie Tarshis' textbook in 1947 gave the Keynesian marginal terms a prominent place.

A textbook which represented the new character of American textbooks after 1947 was P. A. Samuelson's *Economics* (1948), a book which came to dominate the growing market. It was still flourishing at the time of its revision in 1970. This revision covers essentially the same marginalistic subjects as the first edition, but devotes more than twice as much space to them. The amount and character of marginalism in other current textbooks is much the same as in Samuelson's textbooks.

Marginalism in American textbooks has had three acceptance plateaus: the first, 1893–1907; the second, 1908–1936; an interval of change, 1937–1947; and the third, 1948–   ?

92. *Economica*, n. s. 1 (1934) : 52–76, 195–219.

The Economic and Social Context of the Marginal Revolution of the 1870's

A. W. Coats

I

THIS essay is focused on a particular aspect of a general philosophical problem, i.e., the problem of explanation in history.* The fundamental question at issue is this: From what standpoint, in what terms, and to what extent, can the historian of economics "explain" the marginal revolution? As the title indicates, I do not believe it can be adequately explained solely in terms of the immanent development of the logic of economic theory. But, on the other hand, none of the familiar environmentalist theories has proved convincing, for as George Stigler has justly complained, exponents of this approach have usually failed "to offer hypotheses on the portions of the social environment which do or do not influence economic theorizing. Of course the environment has some influence, but until we can specify when and where we only have a *deus ex machina*."[1]

The problem of explanation in science and history has been the subject of considerable scholarly controversy in recent decades.[2] With-

A. W. COATS *heads the Department of Economic and Social History at the University of Nottingham.*

* This article is based on a paper designed to provide a background for the conference discussions. It therefore poses questions rather than offering solutions and is reproduced substantially as originally presented. Further comments on many of the issues raised can be found in "Retrospect and Prospect" at the end of the volume.

1. Review of Robert V. Eagly, *Events, Ideology and Economic Theory* (Detroit, 1968) in the *Journal of Economic History* 29 (June 1969): 337. In an earlier paper, "The Influence of Events and Policies on Economic Theory," reprinted in his *Essays on the History of Economics* (Chicago, 1965), pp. 16-30, Stigler attempted to identify those parts of the environment which exerted an influence both on economic theory and on other branches of economics. For a brief résumé of his argument and comments on two environmentalist theories see the Appendix at the end of the present article.

2. See, for example, Patrick Gardiner, ed., *Theories of History* (Glencoe, Ill., 1959); Robert Brown, *Explanation in Social Science* (London, 1963); William H. Dray, ed., *Philosophical Analysis and History* (New York, 1966); and Leonard

out entering into the details of the debate it may be said that the prerequisite of any explanation is a clear definition of the explanandum. A survey of the historiography of economic thought reveals innumerable competing, overlapping, and conflicting interpretations of the nature and significance of the marginal revolution of the 1870's. It may therefore clear the ground for subsequent discussion if I express my support for the conventional view that despite the existence of numerous earlier versions of the marginal concept, the combined achievements of Jevons, Menger, and Walras in the early 1870's did constitute a significant intellectual breakthrough in the development of economic analysis and may be regarded as revolutionary in their implications, if not in their novelty or in the speed of diffusion.[3] The changes included not only a major shift in the focus of economic theory —towards an emphasis on subjective factors, on demand and consumption rather than supply, production, and distribution; they also laid the basis for a comprehensive systematization of the subject matter of economics, including the elaboration and eventual completion of competitive price theory, the integration of value, production, and distribution theories, the refinement of economic logic, and the extension of mathematical modes of analysis. As Mark Blaug has observed, "The theory of utility supplied most of the excitement of discovery in the seventies and eighties, but it was the introduction of marginal analysis as such that marked the true dividing line between classical theory and modern economics. The significance of marginal utility theory was that it provided the archetype of the general problem of allocating given means with maximum effect."[4]

In considering how to account for this breakthrough in economic

I. Krimerman, ed., *The Nature and Scope of Social Science* (New York, 1969), for selections from a large and growing literature. Against this background one may well question the meaning of George Stigler's protest at "the peculiar belief that intellectual history is exempt from the requirements of respectability of proof, which are imposed on all scientific work." Review of Eagly, pp. 336–37. The concept of "respectability of proof" is sociological or psychological, rather than logical, and is dependent on the currently recognized methodological rules or decisions. For further discussion of this matter see n. 27 below.

3. For a recent contrary opinion see George J. Stigler, "Does Economics Have a Useful Past?" *History of Political Economy* (Fall 1969): 225: ". . . the marginal utility revolution of the 1870's replaced the individual economic agent as a sociological or historical datum by the utility-maximizing individual. The essential elements of the classical theory were affected in no respect."

4. Mark Blaug, *Economic Theory in Retrospect*, 2d ed. (Homewood, Ill., 1968), p. 299. Sentence order reversed.

analysis the first problem is the choice of perspective. This is largely a subjective matter, but to my mind a satisfactory explanation must encompass the common characteristics of the ideas and experiences of the three cofounders of modern marginalism and must also place their work in its wider intellectual and socioeconomic setting. According to Blaug, previous explanations have fallen into four broad categories, regarding the marginal revolution respectively as (i) an autonomous intellectual development within the discipline of economics, (ii) the product of philosophical currents, (iii) the result of definite institutional changes in the economy, and (iv) a counterblast to socialism, particularly to Marxism.[5] These four categories are not mutually exclusive, and recent research in the history, philosophy, and sociopsychology of science points the way to a further type of explanation which incorporates logic, methodology, personality, and environmental factors in fruitful new combinations. To say this is not, of course, to suggest that a "complete" explanation is available, or is ever likely to be; nor does it mean that the new approach is entirely novel. Nevertheless, as it is a source of fruitful hypotheses, it merits some consideration in a volume devoted to the history of marginalism in economics.

II

The sociology of science (or the science of science) is a subdivision of the sociology of knowledge, which is a field of research rather than a specific theory. The sociology of knowledge may be defined as "the branch of sociology which studies the relations between thought and society . . . [it] attempts to relate the ideas it studies to the socio-historical settings in which they are produced and received";[6] and as this approach has sometimes been associated

5. Ibid., pp. 304–8. As the significance of the marginal revolution was recognized only after an appreciable time lag, an attempt to account for this breakthrough should, strictly speaking, include the first two decades or so of the diffusion process. However, as that phase has been admirably treated in Richard S. Howey, *The Rise of the Marginal Utility School* (Lawrence, Kans., 1960), I shall concentrate on the conditions of production rather than the reception of the new ideas.

6. Lewis Coser, "The Sociology of Knowledge," in *International Encyclopedia of the Social Sciences* (New York, 1968), 8:428; also Robert Merton, *Social Theory and Social Structure*, 2d ed. (New York, 1957), chap. 12; W. Stark, *The Sociology of Knowledge* (London, 1958). As Merton has noted, "each type of imputed

with rigid deterministic theories of the influence of events upon ideas, it should immediately be noted that there are in fact numerous competing theories of the relationship between thought and society, some loose, idealistic, and sweeping (macrosociological), others more precise and empirically grounded (microsociological). The current orthodoxy among students of the history and sociology of science supports the contention that endogenous (or internal) influences largely explain the growth of scientific knowledge. Indeed one authority, after commenting on the ''virtual disappearance'' since World War II ''of attempts to explain the content and theories of science on the basis of social conditions,'' adds:

> Historical studies of the development of scientific thought, and sociological investigation of the way scientists work, have unquestionably shown that the problems investigated by scientists are overwhelmingly determined by conditions internal to the scientific community, such as the ''state of the art'' and the resources for and organization of scientific work. This is not to say that general philosophical ideas and social concerns may not influence science at all, but that the growth of scientific knowledge cannot be *systematically* explained as resulting from such external conditions.[7]

However, before directly applying this generalization to the marginal revolution in economics, two significant qualifications must be noted. Most work in the sociology of science is concerned with the natural sciences rather than the social sciences, which are, on the whole, much less self-contained bodies of knowledge; and even with the natural sciences there has been considerable disagreement as to where the boundary line should be drawn between ''internal'' and ''external'' conditions. Secondly, statements derived from twentieth-century conditions are not necessarily applicable to earlier periods, when the ''scientific community,'' if it existed at all, was much smaller and less tightly organized.

One further preliminary observation is in order. While it is true

---

relation between knowledge and society presupposes an entire theory of sociological method and social causation'' (p. 476).

7. Joseph Ben-David, ''Introduction'' to the Sociology of Science issue of the *International Social Science Journal* 22 (1970): 19–20. Italics supplied.

that current research in the history and philosophy of science favors explanations of scientific change in terms of "conditions internal to the scientific community," there has nevertheless been a significant shift in the prevailing interpretation of those conditions. While turning away from such broad exogenous influences as the state of the economy, the social structure, ideology, and class bias, scholars have tended to emphasize the variety and complexity of factors at work within the scientific community. It is no longer fashionable to accept the logical empiricists' clear-cut distinction be. tween the sociology of scientific knowledge and the philosophy of science, a distinction sometimes expressed as a dichotomy between the "context of discovery" and the "context of justification." Instead, attention is increasingly focused on actual scientific practice rather than correct scientific method, the latter representing an ideal seldom attained in practice. Likewise, it is increasingly recognized that "theoretical and philosophical factors are presupposed in every aspect of scientific inquiry . . . in the meanings of observational and theoretical terms, in the characterization of the problems tackled by a science, and in what is to count as solutions to those problems."[8] It remains to be seen how far this new species of microsociological analysis can contribute to a reappraisal of the marginal revolution of the 1870's.

III

Sociological analysis of the marginal revolution can begin at any one of a number of points, for example, the concept of multiple discoveries in science.[9] As the subjective originality of the three co-

8. R. G. A. Dolby, "Sociology of Knowledge in Natural Science," *Science Studies* 1 (Jan. 1971): 9. This article contains a useful survey of recent research. Robert K. Merton accepted the logical empiricists' distinction as embodied in the works of R. Carnap, H. Reichenbach, C. G. Hempel, E. Nagel, and K. R. Popper, whereas the newer approach can be found in the writings of N. Hanson, P. K. Feyerabend, S. Toulmin, and T. S. Kuhn, among others. There is a penetrating critique of the contrasting views of Merton and Kuhn in M. D. King, "Reason, Tradition and the Progressiveness of Science," *History and Theory* 10 (1971): 3–32. I have drawn heavily on this article, and on my discussions with the author.

9. The concept of multiple discoveries is, of course, especially associated with the work of Robert Merton. Cf. his "Singletons and Multiples in Scientific Discovery: A Chapter in the Sociology of Science," *Proceedings of the American Philosophical Society* 105 (Oct. 1961): 470–86; and "Resistance to the Systematic Study of Multiple Discoveries in Science," *Archives Européenes de Sociologie* 4 (1963): 237–82. For some comments on the relevance of this notion to economics

founders is not in question, the approximate similarity and contemporaneity of their achievements link the creativity of the individual innovator to the mainstream of scientific knowledge, thereby strengthening the impression that the growth of knowledge has an organic life of its own. This aspect illustrates the problem of perspective mentioned earlier: when we view the process of scientific development as it were from a distance, the common characteristics seem relatively more important; whereas on closer inspection, the idiosyncratic features of the individual innovators assume greater significance; and there can be no single uniquely correct perspective. Of course the extent to which an apparent multiple is in fact a genuine one is a matter for detailed historical investigation; but the very existence of multiples in the history of economics[10] helps to distinguish the field as a scientific discipline from less systematic areas of intellectual endeavor, the assumption being that in economics, as contrasted with the creative arts, if one scientist does not "discover" something there is a reasonable expectation that somebody else will.[11]

see Stigler, "Does Economics Have a Useful Past?," pp. 225–27. While acknowledging the importance of multiples, Stigler emphasizes the difficulties in assessing the significance of discoveries widely spaced in time.

10. Alfred Marshall's views on multiples are especially interesting considering his emphasis on the continuity of economic ideas and the fact that he may have been an independent, but inadequately recognized, codiscoverer of the marginal utility idea. "The substance of economic thought cannot well be to any great extent the work of one man. It is the product of the age. Perhaps an exception should be made for Ricardo: but everything of importance that was said in the five generations 1740–65, 1765–90, 1815–40, 1840–65, 1865–90, seems to me to have been thought out concurrently more or less by many people." To L. L. Price, 19 Aug. 1892, in *Memorials of Alfred Marshall*, ed. A. C. Pigou (London, 1925), pp. 378–79.

11. "There is only one world to discover, and as each morsel of perception is achieved the discoverer must be honored or forgotten. The ivory tower of the artist can be a one-man cell; that of the scientist must contain many apartments so that he may be housed among his peers." Derek J. de Solla Price, *Little Science, Big Science* (New York, 1963), p. 69. More recently, however, it has been suggested that science and art are less different than formerly supposed. Cf. the contributions by J. S. Ackerman, E. M. Hafner, G. Kubler, and T. S. Kuhn, to *Comparative Studies in Society and History* 2 (1969): 371–412. In a well-known survey, "Marginal Utility Economics," in the *Encyclopedia of the Social Sciences* (New York, 1931), 5:357–63, Frank H. Knight argued that owing to the "wreck" of the classical system by the late 1860's "a new start became inevitable." However, he did not maintain that marginal utility was the only possible foundation of a new system, merely a very likely one: "The utility theory should be seen as the culmination, historically and logically, of the rationalistic and individualistic intellectual movement of which the competitive economic system itself is one aspect and modern science and technology are others. To its admirers it comes near

In this sense the extent and speed of recognition of a multiple tell us something about the level of intellectual coherence and organization of the research area in which it occurs. As any given science becomes more institutionalized, and as increasing numbers of specialists are at work on the same or closely related problems, any given discovery is increasingly likely to be made independently more than once. Swift recognition of a multiple is, of course, a function of the efficiency of communication among specialists in the field;[12] and in the case under consideration the contacts between Jevons and Walras reveal the existence of an embryonic international network of scientific economists in the 1870's.[13]

The occurrence of a multiple naturally invites the historian of ideas to investigate the intellectual context from which it emerged.[14] He should, for example, consider whether the discovery was unexpected by contemporaries or sprang from an acknowledged intellectual "crisis"—and in the latter case he should examine the nature of that crisis and the extent to which the discovery represented a genuine solution of the intellectual difficulties recognized at the time.

---

to being the fulfilment of the eighteenth-century craving for a principle which would do for human conduct and society what Newton's mechanics had done for the solar system."

12. With perfect communication there would be no separate independent discoveries; the original innovator's achievement would be instantly recognized everywhere and subsequent rediscoveries would be forestalled. As Merton has put it, "There, but for the grace of swift diffusion, goes a multiple." "Singletons and Multiples," p. 478. For a preliminary discussion of the diffusion process see, for example, Joseph J. Spengler, "Notes on the International Transmission of Economic Ideas," *History of Political Economy* 2 (Spring 1970): 133–51. Spengler distinguishes between the source, the media of transmission, the content transmitted, and the receiver. For a relevant case study see T. W. Hutchison, "Insularity and Cosmopolitanism in Economic Ideas, 1870–1914," *American Economic Association Papers and Proceedings*, May 1955, pp. 1-16. The rate of acceptance of a new idea may be a function of the rate at which new, and presumably young and receptive, persons enter the field.

13. See, for example, the correspondence in William Jaffé's magnificent edition, *Correspondence of Léon Walras and Related Papers* (Amsterdam, 1965), vol. 1, 1857–1883. An investigation of the growth and scientific importance of this international network of economists in the nineteenth century would be a fruitful topic of research. Such a project might, indeed, begin with a detailed examination of the sources cited in the early works and correspondence of Jevons, Menger, and Walras.

14. Neil de Marchi's examination of the British background to Jevons' *Theory of Political Economy* (see his article below in this volume, "Mill and Cairnes and the Emergence of Marginalism in England") provides an admirable illustration of this point. I have profited greatly from reading and discussing his work.

Unlike natural scientists, economists are rarely confronted with crises resulting from an accumulation of experimental results which conflict with existing theories;[15] indeed, their theories have rarely been subjected to rigorous empirical testing, and it is consequently more difficult for the historian to determine the precise reasons why one economic theory displaced another. Two or more rival theories often coexist,[16] and it rarely happens that one is superior to its competitors in all respects—e.g., generality, manageability, and congruence with reality.[17] A shift of allegiance from one theory to another may result from a change of intellectual fashions, the emergence of a new and ambitious school of writers, or a shift in the range of problems thought to be important.[18] There seems no reason to believe

15. For a penetrating discussion of intellectual crises of this kind see Thomas S. Kuhn, *The Structure of Scientific Revolutions*, rev. ed. (Chicago, 1970), chaps. 7–9. Kuhn's critics have not merely objected to his notion of paradigm change on the grounds that the paradigm concept is vague and misleading; they have also questioned the validity of his fundamental distinction between ''normal'' and ''revolutionary'' phases in the history of science. For example, while Karl Popper considers that Kuhn has exaggerated the distinction, he nevertheless regards it as of ''great importance.'' Stephen Toulmin, on the other hand, believes that the notion of revolution is useful as a descriptive label, but useless as an explanatory concept. Imre Lakatos, a disciple of Popper, adopts an intermediate position which assimilates many of Kuhn's ideas. See the discussion of these problems in Imre Lakatos and Alan Musgrave, eds., *Criticism and the Growth of Knowledge* (Cambridge, 1970), esp. pp. 41, 52, 93ff.

16. One of Kuhn's more vigorous and effective critics, Imre Lakatos, maintains that competition between rival theories is endemic and healthy in the natural sciences, especially in periods of rapid advance. ''Instant rationality,'' he argues, is impossible in practice: one theory does not supplant another overnight, nor is the full significance of a new theory quickly appreciated. Even in the natural sciences anomalies do not (as Kuhn claims) accumulate until they become intolerable, and so-called ''crucial experiments'' do not immediately establish the superiority of one theory over its rivals, for there is usually a substantial time lag before the significance of such experiments is recognized. Like other philosophers of science (e.g., Karl Popper, M. Polanyi, and Morris Cohen), Lakatos recognizes the ''principle of tenacity''—the legitimate desire to retain a theory of proven value despite the accumulation of anomalies and counterexamples. Cf. Lakatos' long essay, ''Falsification and the Methodology of Scientific Research Programmes,'' in Lakatos and Musgrave, pp. 91–195. A penetrating review of this essay by David Bloor appears in *Science Studies* 1 (Jan. 1971): 101–15.

17. These characteristics of successful theories are discussed by George J. Stigler in his classic article, ''The Development of Utility Theory,'' reprinted in his *Essays*, pp. 148–55. Other characteristics could be suggested, for example, simplicity, elegance, fruitfulness, ''heuristic power.'' Cf. Lakatos and Musgrave, pp. 132ff.

18. This list of possible causes is by no means exhaustive. For a valuable account of the wide range of factors involved see Joseph J. Spengler, ''Exogenous and Endogenous Influences in the Formation of Post-1870 Economic Thought: A

that the marginal revolution of the 1870's was the product of an acute sense of intellectual crisis; on the contrary, as Schumpeter observed, many of the cofounders' "fellow scientists felt no attachment to the old doctrines."[19]

This state of affairs can be explained in a variety of ways. On a purely intellectual level emphasis may be laid on the manifest theoretical and empirical shortcomings of the received doctrines—though this calls for an explanation of the revival of interest after a phase of intellectual stagnation.[20] On the other hand, the absence of a sense of crisis may also be due to the loose social structure of the scientific community of economists, especially the small number of scientific practitioners and the low level of "social acoustics" in the field.

While we recognize the interdependence of logical, psychological, and sociological elements in the marginal revolution, it is nevertheless essential to attempt a precise estimate of the scientific nature and importance of the changes involved. How far, for instance, did the subjective-value theorists accept the classical economists' "scientific vision"?[21] Which theoretical and empirical propositions of classical

Sociology of Knowledge Approach," in *Events, Ideology and Economic Theory, the Determinants of Progress in the Development of Economic Analysis*, ed. Robert V. Eagly (Detroit, 1968), pp. 159–87. On fashions cf. R. D. Collison Black, *Economic Fashions* (Belfast, 1963). For an interpretation of the history of science in terms of shifts in what does not need to be explained, see Stephen Toulmin, *Foresight and Understanding: An Inquiry Into the Aims of Science* (London, 1961), chaps. 3 and 4.

19. Cf. his essay on Eugen Böhm-Bawerk in *The Development of Economic Thought: Great Economists in Perspective*, ed. Henry W. Spiegel (New York, 1952), p. 570. This assertion needs careful documentation.

20. Joseph J. Spengler has advanced the notion of a "conceptual freeze" which may be broken by the emergence of "intractable policy problems, flaws in consensual explanations, new empirical findings, and technological and methodological developments (for example, computers, input-output) which consensual explanations cannot effectively incorporate." See his "Economics: Its History, Themes, Approaches," *Journal of Economic Issues* 2 (March 1968): 21.

21. In the nineteenth century an economist's attitude to the value problem was often regarded as providing a clue to his entire outlook. For example F. von Wieser, *Natural Value*, ed. W. Smart (1893), p. xxx: "As a man's judgment about value, so, in the last resort, must be his judgment about economics. . . . Every great system of political economy up till now has formulated its own peculiar view on value as the ultimate foundation in theory of its applications to practical life, and no new effort at reform can have laid an adequate foundation for these applications if it cannot support them on a new and more perfect theory of value"; J. S. Mill, *Principles of Political Economy* (Toronto, 1965), 2:456: "Almost every speculation respecting the economical interests of a society . . . implies some theory of Value: the smallest error on that subject infects

economics were (i) accepted *in toto*, (ii) modified, and if so, how
drastically, (iii) rejected, by the marginalists? To put the matter
differently: while agreeing that the marginal revolution represented a
breakthrough in theory and technique, rather than the applications
of theory, we may still enquire whether it constituted a breakthrough
in methodology, in the content and focus of theory, in the conceptual
language employed (e.g., the use of mathematics), and in the extent
to which theory became congruent with reality, amenable to verification, or relevant to policy. An attempt to answer these (somewhat
rigidly taxonomic) questions would enable us to judge how far the
classicists and marginalists were employing "incommensurable" conceptual frameworks, and how far the revolution involved genuine
scientific disagreement rather than the rhetorical exaggeration so
often associated with assertions of scientific novelty.[22] Of course, no
final answers to these questions can be given, not merely because there
is no uniquely correct historical perspective but also because the
historian's judgment is itself influenced by his philosophical and
methodological preconceptions.[23]

As already noted, the occurrence of multiple discoveries highlights
the relationship between the general growth of scientific knowledge
and the contributions of individual scientific innovators, and it is
appropriate to consider each of these aspects in turn. The innovator's
role is commonly regarded as analogous to that of a biological mutation
in the evolutionary process of nature,[24] and from this standpoint
science appears as a special type of adaptive social system—what
Ernest Nagel has termed "a social mechanism for sifting warranted

with corresponding error all our other conclusions; and anything vague or misty
in our conception of it, creates confusion and uncertainty in everything else."
These statements serve as a reminder that value theory occupied a central place
in late-nineteenth-century economics.

22. The "technique of persuasion" is discussed in George J. Stigler, "The Nature and Role of Originality in Scientific Progress"; cf. his *Essays*, pp. 4ff.

23. For a provocative treatment of this problem see Imre Lakatos, "History
of Science and Its Rational Reconstructions," in PSA 1970, in memory of
Rudolf Carnap *Boston Studies in the Philosophy of Science*, vol. 8, ed. Roger
C. Buck and Robert S. Cohen, pp. 91–136; also the accompanying "Notes on
Lakatos" by Thomas S. Kuhn, ibid. pp. 137–46.

24. Cf. Kuhn, *Structure of Scientific Revolutions*, pp. 170–73; Karl Popper,
The Logic of Scientific Discovery (London, 1959), p. 108; also his *Conjectures
and Refutations* (London, 1963), p. 52.

beliefs.''[25] This mechanism connects the subjective activity of the individual scientific researcher to the collective quest for objective knowledge, and this relationship has become familiar to historians of economics largely through T. S. Kuhn's analysis of the behavior of scientific groups in so-called ''normal'' and ''revolutionary'' periods of scientific advance. It has been well said that Kuhn's scientist is ''a man engaged in the interpretation, elaboration, modification, and even on occasions overthrow of a professional tradition of practice, rather than an automaton whose activities are finally monitored by a fixed inexorable logic'';[26] and although Kuhn has been criticized for overemphasizing psychological and sociological aspects, and minimizing the importance of rational elements in scientific practice (a contention he has strenuously denied),[27] his approach is compatible with a kind of ''epistemological agnosticism'' according to which some of the more vexing, theoretical difficulties in the philosophy of science can be allowed to recede into the background.

The sociology of science is a fruitful source of hypotheses about the immediate social context of the marginal revolution. For example,

Who were the people taking part in scientific activity? What were their numbers, education, social position, means of livelihood, personal motives and opportunities, means of communication, institutions? What critical audience was there to be convinced by, use, transmit, develop, revise or reject their conclusions? What social pressures were there within the sci-

25. Ernest Nagel, *The Structure of Science: Problems in the Logic of Scientific Explanation* (New York, 1961), p. 489.
26. King, ''Reason, Tradition,'' p. 25.
27. Lakatos, for example, attacks Kuhn's emphasis on the importance of the collective judgment of the scientific community as ''mob psychology,'' but stresses the crucial role of methodological decisions, such as the decisions which determine whether a particular proposition should be viewed as a fact or a theory in the context of a given ''research programme''; what part of a scientific program is to be regarded as the ''irrefutable'' hard core; and what constitute acceptable criteria of falsification of a scientific theory. He concedes that his approach tends to blur the dividing line between science and metaphysics, a line that was carefully drawn by positivist philosophers, and rejects what he calls naive or dogmatic falsificationism. While insisting that ''experience'' is the impartial arbiter of scientific controversy, he readily admits the difficulty of knowing what experience proves or disproves. Lakatos, ''Falsification,'' and the comments by Popper, Feyerabend, and Kuhn, in Lakatos and Musgrave. See also Bloor's review article referred to in n. 16 above; and the Lakatos-Kuhn exchange cited in n. 23 above.

entific community itself to affect the consensus of opinion in favour of the old or the new ?[28]

Obviously if a "scientific community"[29] of economists can be said to have existed in the early 1870's, it was much smaller, less tightly organized, and less immune to external influences than the twentieth-century body of natural scientists, with which so much recent work in the sociology of science has been concerned. Nevertheless, the degree of social organization required need not be elaborate; indeed, the mere recognition of a "problem area" within a scientific discipline may be a sufficient condition, since this problem area can be regarded as the prototype of a more formal and stable organization designed to produce and foster innovation. The essential need is for a "social circle" or scientific group—a "critical mass" comprising "an audience of sufficient size and competence to provide an adequate feedback" in the form of professional recognition.[30] Once this exists, the establishment of common scientific values, standards, and goals, with the concomitant attributes of "conviviality" and "commitment" so vividly portrayed by Michael Polanyi,[31] cannot be far behind.

These remarks may help to point the way towards a more systematic comparative study of the sociointellectual context of the marginal revolution, an undertaking which can only be hinted at here. Such a study would seek to identify the principal differences between the personal histories, scientific backgrounds, and intellectual beliefs and objectives of the three cofounders. On a broad level it would show

28. Cf. A. C. Crombie, ed., *Scientific Change* (London, 1963), p. 10. These remarks draw attention to the processes of professionalization and academicization which were repeatedly referred to in the conference discussions. Cf. ''Retrospect and Prospect,'' Sec. III, below in this volume.

29. The term ''scientific community'' was introduced by Michael Polanyi to describe the way scientists enforced strict discipline amidst a great deal of individual freedom through training, refereeing of publications, and purely informal sanctions of approval and disapproval. He also showed how this informal system was related to the intrinsic characteristics of research. Cf. Joseph Ben-David, ''Introduction,'' p. 12.

30. Cf. Norman Storer, ''The Internationality of Science and the Nationality of Scientists,'' *International Social Science Journal* 22 (Feb. 1970): 92; also his book *The Social System of Science* (New York, 1966); and Warren O. Hagstrom, *The Scientific Community* (New York, 1965). The development of a ''social circle'' of marginalists after 1871 has been traced by Richard S. Howey, *Rise of the Marginal Utility School*. In the present context, however, it is more pertinent to ask, To what audience did Jevons, Menger, and Walras address themelves?

31. See especially his *Personal Knowledge* (Chicago, 1958), chaps. 7, 10.

that when they published their major works they were all comparatively young[32] members of the moderately well-to-do social class which had access to higher education in nineteenth-century Europe, and they were all brought up in the mainstream of European ideas which laid the foundations for the growth of modern science.[33] However, there were, at the same time, significant differences in their backgrounds and knowledge, for example, in the extent to which a professional tradition of economic thought existed in their respective countries during the 1860's and the extent to which each cofounder could be regarded (or could regard himself) as a deviant from his inherited intellectual beliefs. While the academic community was doubtless more open and flexible in Jevons' England than on the European continent, Jevons faced a more powerful and firmly entrenched corpus of economic ideas than either Menger or Walras, both of whom suffered from lack of congenial and stimulating scientific colleagues until after they had produced their major works. From this point it would be appropriate to examine how far their academic backgrounds and connections shaped their approach to economics, for it has often been noted that from the 1870's most of the significant advances in economics were made by academics. If this is in fact the case, we should surely examine the changing university environment in which this occurred and endeavor to assess its precise influence on the development of economic ideas.

A comparative study of the type indicated would need to consider the psychological dimensions of the marginal revolution, in addition to the social situation within the scientific community, for these two levels of discourse necessarily interact. To recall the evolutionary analogy mentioned above, if the scientific innovator resembles a biological mutant, then in psychological terms "learning, perception and other increases in knowledge at the individual level, and increases in the accuracy and scope of scientific knowledge, are

32. The major creative achievements of Jevons, Menger, and Walras compare favorably with other performances in economics and political science analyzed in Harvey C. Lehman, *Age and Achievement* (Princeton, 1953), esp. pp. 137–38, 296–97, 302–3. Such achievements tended to occur later in the nineteenth century than nowadays because innovators usually derived less aid from their teachers and were more dependent on the development of their own intellectual tools. Moreover, the pecuniary rewards and prestige value of innovativeness are probably higher now.

33. Cf. the comment by F. H. Knight cited in n. 11 above.

part processes of the more general case of increases in the adaptive fit of organism to environment."[34] How far any given scientist will strive to advance knowledge in his special field will, of course, depend on a subtle combination of circumstances, some intrinsic to the individual, others reflecting the pressures and opportunities presented by his particular sociocultural environment.

In the past the process of scientific discovery has too often been regarded as a mystery, the product of some inherently unanalyzable characterological traits summed up in the expression "creative genius." More recently, however, efforts have been made to study this phenomenon as a social process, and although it is impossible to explain the specific content of mental phenomena in terms of physical facts,[35] it is nevertheless possible to shed light on the more general influences bearing on multiple discoveries. Thus numerous efforts have been made to specify the characterological traits to be found in the representative innovator—such qualities as insight and motivation, personal attributes such as erudition, xenophilia (love of the unexpected), visualization (e.g., insight into logical, spatial, or mechanical relationships), alertness, and consistency of purpose.[36] Research in this area is still in its infancy; for instance, there is much to be learnt about the elements in motivation, such as the role of curiosity, aggressiveness, self-esteem, vanity, power;[37] and there is obviously no

34. Donald T. Campbell, "Objectivity and the Social Locus of Scientific Knowledge," Presidential Address to the Division of Social and Personality Psychology of the American Psychological Association, 1969, to appear in R. S. Cohen and M. W. Wartofsky, eds., Boston Studies in the Philosophy of Science. For an extended discussion of the links between psychology and the philosophy of science, with special reference to the problem of scientific discovery, see also Campbell's "Evolutionary Epistemology," to appear in The Philosophy of Karl R. Popper, ed. P. A. Schilpp, Library of Living Philosophers (La Salle, Ill., forthcoming). Campbell emphasizes the "blind-variation-and-selective-retention process" in scientific enquiry: "What is characteristic of science is that the selective system which weeds out among the variety of conjectures involves deliberate contact with the environment through experiment and quantified prediction, designed so that outcomes quite independent of the preferences of the investigator are possible."

35. This is forcefully argued in F. A. von Hayek, The Sensory Order (London, 1952), pp. 192–93.

36. Cf. "Great Men and Scientific Progress," in History, Psychology and Science: Selected Papers by Edwin G. Boring, eds. Robert I. Watson and Donald T. Campbell (New York, 1963), pp. 29–49. See also Bernice T. Eiduson, Scientists: Their Psychological World (New York, 1962).

37. Watson and Campbell, Editor's Foreword, p. vii.

unique scientific "type," for there are many different functions to be performed by members of the scientific community.[38]

Historians of economics differ markedly in the importance they attach to the role of biographical factors in the development of their subject. For example, while George Stigler is inclined to think that "biography distorts rather than illuminates the understanding of scientific work,"[39] William Jaffé has argued that

> a great original discovery or a great innovation, be it in economics or in any realm of scientific or artistic endeavor, is not a composite product, but the product of the imagination of some one individual whose identity marks the achievement indelibly in a thousand and one subtle ways, giving it, to be sure, a bias. . . . We miss some essential trait of an argument, or of a theory, or even of a piece of description in economics, if we ignore the distinctive individuality of its author. One does not need to be an out-and-out Marxist to concede that the particular social status of the economist must exert an influence directly or indirectly on his ideas and interests; nor need one be an out-and-out Freudian to acknowledge the impact of childhood experience and education on his fundamental attitudes.[40]

This is surely a claim that needs to be tested by historians of economics —for example, as part of our proposed comparative study of the

38. As George Stigler noted in a pioneering essay, much valuable scientific work—the testing of hypotheses, the accumulation of knowledge, the refinement or elaboration of economic theory—requires little or no originality; and there may even be an excess of originality which impedes the essential process of "scientific fermentation"; cf. "Originality in Scientific Progress," pp. 12–14. The less original phases of scientific activity are reminiscent of Kuhn's conception of "normal" scientific puzzle-solving. As is well known, Jevons was an "ideas" man, a man of immense intellectual fertility in a variety of fields, who was eager to flick his ideas at the world rather than to work them out fully and painstakingly. In the conference discussions it became clear that Walras often chose to concentrate his attention on relatively limited problems which could be fully solved, whereas Menger's *Grundsätze* was far more open-ended and consequently provided many hints and incompletely worked-out ideas which his disciples could refine and elaborate.

39. Cf. his review of *The Evolution of Modern Economic Theory* by Lord Robbins, in *Economica* 37 (Nov. 1970): 426.

40. William Jaffé, "Biography and Economic Analysis," *Western Economic Journal* 3 (Summer 1965): 227. See also Spengler, "Economics: Its History," pp. 26–28.

marginal revolution.[41] All three cofounders exhibited in striking
fashion the psychological attributes commonly found among scientific
innovators, while Jevons and Walras in particular were highly self-
conscious about their scientific contributions.[42]

The interdependence between the subjective approach of the individual scientist and the collective judgment of the scientific community has been most perceptively depicted by Michael Polanyi.
"Discoveries are made," he observes,

> by pursuing unsuspected possibilities suggested by existing
> knowledge. And this is how science retains its identity through
> a sequence of successive revolutions. . . . Only plausible ideas
> are taken up, discussed and tested by scientists. Such a decision
> may later be proved right, but at the time that it is made, the
> assignment of plausibility is based on a broad exercise of in-
> tuition guided by many subtle indications, and *thus it is al-
> together undemonstrable. It is tacit.*

But while different scientists proceed on the basis of different methods,
questions, and objectives,

> it is not rare for two or more scientists to make the same dis-
> covery independently—because different scientists can actualize
> only the same available potentialities; and they can indeed be
> relied on to exploit such chances.[43]

IV

These remarks take us back to our starting point—the relationship
between individual scientific discovery and the corpus of knowledge
from which it emerged. Can it be said that Jevons, Menger, and
Walras actualized "the same available potentialities" in economic
theory? And if so, does this reveal significant parallels between scientific progress in nineteenth-century economics and the paradigm

41. This point was vigorously debated at the conference. Cf. below in this
volume, "Retrospect and Prospect," Sec. IV.
42. Thus Jevons discussed the "Character of the Experimentalist" in his
book *The Principles of Science: A Treatise on Logic and Scientific Method*
(London, 1874), chap. 26.
43. "The Growth of Science in Society," *Minerva* 5 (1966–67): 539, 536,
542, reprinted as chap. 5 in his volume of essays, *Knowing and Being* (London,
1969). Italics are in the original.

of natural science? Or, by suggesting that the marginal revolution was a break comparable to a biological mutation, have we implied that the new departure was by no means an inevitable product of the organic growth of scientific knowledge? How far can the marginal revolution be regarded as a typical example of the "learning process" in scientific work, and how far do explanations of this type depend on the assumption that economics, like natural science, is a comparatively closed intellectual system?

It is at least conceivable that a study of the marginal revolution in economics will shed light on the general process of intellectual innovation in economics and, indeed, in other branches of the social sciences. It may also even shed new light on the age-old question of the similarities and differences between the natural and social sciences, especially with respect to their developmental patterns.[44]

APPENDIX

Any attempt to explain the marginal revolution (or, indeed, any other historical occurrence) as a product of environmental influences must be specific if it is not to be merely tautological, for in its broadest sense the term "environment" embraces all the possible antecedent causes of the phenomenon to be explained. Many hypotheses about the interrelationships between events and ideas have been advanced, but most have been partial and selective and seldom has any serious effort been made to explicate the underlying logical structure.

The difficulties involved in the environmentalist's approach are exemplified by Werner Stark's interpretation of the marginal revolution as an instance of what Schumpeter termed a "classical situation." To Stark, this state of affairs was no mere intellectual phenomenon but a "life situation," for the 1870's was a time when

44. In the first (1962) edition of *The Structure of Scientific Revolutions*, Kuhn began by emphasizing the differences between the natural and the social sciences, and he has since described the latter as "proto-sciences—in which practice does generate testable conclusions but which nevertheless resemble philosophy and the arts rather than the established sciences in their developmental patterns." Cf. Lakatos and Musgrave, p. 244; also the "Postscript—1969" to the 2d edition (1970) of Kuhn's *Structure*, esp. pp. 207–10, and his "Comment" in *Comparative Studies in Society and History* 11 (1969): 403–12.

"capitalism was so to speak most fully and clearly itself, in which social and economic reality approached, comparatively speaking, most closely to a state of integration in a determinate equilibrium." There was, he admitted, no *social* equilibrium in the early 1870's; indeed, the existence of a sociopolitical gulf between capitalist and proletarian helps to explain the theoretical economist's "retreat" to an abstract concept of economic equilibrium: "In Walras' day competition was as perfect as it is possible in the nature of things, . . . the economies of the leading countries came as near then to the realization of a free, automatically functioning market as never before and never since. Chapter and verse for this assertion can be found in any textbook of economic history," and this bold claim was backed by references to free trade, the general existence of free competition, and the absence of obstacles to international payments or controls over the labor market and the wage contract.[45]

The foregoing example may be too extreme to be taken seriously; yet its very excesses serve to highlight the difficulties inherent in the environmentalist approach. Stark's account is couched in such vague and general terms that it is virtually impossible to decide what empirical evidence, if any, could be cited to confirm or refute his claims. Notwithstanding his confident assertion about economic history textbooks, there is ample evidence incompatible with his contention that society approximated a state of "perfect competition" when "the utility theory of values arose."[46] Indeed, if "perfect competition" is a purely mental construct, should we seek an empirical counterpart? And if the answer is in the affirmative, where should we look, and when? Are we to infer from Stark's account that competition was more nearly perfect in Jevons' England, Menger's Austria, and Walras's Switzerland (or France) than elsewhere? And if not, why were

45. W. Stark, "The Classical Situation in Political Economy," *Kyklos* 12 (1959): 59, 62–63. Cf. Joseph A. Schumpeter, *History of Economic Analysis* (Oxford, 1954), pp. 51, 87, 143, 380.

46. Cf. W. Stark, *The History of Economics in Its Relation to Social Development* (London, 1944), p. 56. There is, of course, room for dispute as to when "the utility theory of values *arose*." Although Stark considered it a remarkable coincidence that the first edition of Walras's *Éléments* appeared in the years which show "a maximum approach to a free economy in practice" ("The Classical Situation," p. 62) it is noteworthy that another, more subtle environmentalist has emphasized that Walras's theory was entirely in conflict with contemporary economic conditions. Cf. Leo Rogin, *The Meaning and Validity of Economic Theory* (New York, 1956), p. 438.

marginal utility theories absent from other countries? Would any serious economic historian suggest that economic and social conditions were essentially similar in England, Austria, and Switzerland (or France) when it is well known that the first of these three was by far the most advanced industrially?[47] How should we account for the fact that earlier versions of marginal utility theory were enunciated in several widely differing historical settings? If we accept Stark's contention that ideas appear in historical perspective not merely as "conditioned by reality" but also "determined by it—provided that we do not forget that the formation of ideas has never been subject to absolute necessity in its time,"[48] we must presumably seek causal connections, not merely correlations, between events and ideas. But what particular connections should we expect to find between an individual thinker and his socioeconomic environment? Is there any reason to expect the same parallels in the cases of all the codiscoverers of an important theoretical concept or system? Should we seek clues in the individual's life history, in that of his family or social group, or in the broader background of his national culture? Again, what time lags should we expect to discover between the (slowly or rapidly) changing socioeconomic environment and the intellectual products to which it gives rise?

A more subtle example of the environmentalist approach is Nikolai Bukharin's contention that the Austrian School's version of marginal utility economics reflected the individualistic outlook that represented a fundamental trait of the bourgeoisie, while the emphasis on the psychology of the consumer was characteristic of the *rentier* class. Bukharin's Marxist standpoint embraced methodological, historical, sociological, and logical elements, for he was anxious to disassociate himself from the antitheoretical biases of the German historical school. As a Marxist he advocated recognition of "the priority of society over the individual," the essentially "temporary nature of any social structure," and the "dominant part played by production" in economic life, whereas the Austrian School was characterized by "extreme individualism in methodology, by an unhistorical point of view, and by its taking consumption as a point of departure." While

47. The operative term here, of course, is "essentially"; i.e., in what crucial respect was there similarity of "conditions"?

48. Stark, *History of Economics*, p. 7.

acknowledging the need for abstraction in economic science, Bukharin nevertheless argued that psychology was the basis of logic, and the psychology of the *rentier* was present-minded, whereas the proletarian viewpoint was dynamic and forward-looking—presumably up to the classless utopia. The consuming *rentier* stood apart from the processes of production and trade; he was concerned only with luxury consumption such as "riding mounts, with expensive rugs, fragrant cigars, the wine of Tokay." Thus the historical conditions favorable to the growth of subjective value theories included "the rapid evolution of capitalism, the shifting of social groupings and the increase in the number of the class of rentiers, all these produced in the last decades of the nineteenth century all the necessary sociopsychological presuppositions for bringing these delicate plants to efflorescence."[49]

Like Stark's account, Bukharin's explanation was couched in general terms; but he was at least aware of the crucial distinction between the genesis, the formulation, and the diffusion of marginal utility theory. After noting the works of some earlier and later forerunners he commented that "only at the beginning of the decade 1870-80 did the theory of marginal utility find a sufficient prop in the 'social public opinion' of the ruling scientific circles and rapidly become *communis doctorum opinio*." It is not entirely clear whether the triumvirate—Jevons, Menger, and Walras—were thought to be fully aware of their historical mission, though it is clear that subsequent authors used their theories "in order to justify the modern order of society." However, Bukharin avoided some of the more specific environmentalist difficulties by emphasizing that the Austrian School was not distinctively *Austrian* at all, adding that it had "actually become the scientific implement of the international bourgeoisie of *rentiers* regardless of their domicile."[50]

Reverting to the basic issue stated in the second sentence of this essay, we must again ask what kind of "explanation" is required. Is it necessary to embrace all the dimensions of Bukharin's approach —methodological, historical, sociological, and logical—or would any two or three dimensions suffice? According to Mark Blaug, "it is not

49. *The Economic Theory of the Leisure Class* (London, 1927), pp. 36, 26, 34. The book was substantially written in 1914, and a Russian edition appeared in 1919 or 1920.
    50. Ibid., p. 34. For further discussion of the role of environmental influences see "Retrospect and Prospect," Sec. IV, below in this volume.

far-fetched to see a connection between changes in the economic structure of society around the middle of the century and the theoretical
innovations of the subjective value trio'';[51] but precisely what kind
of connection must be sought? The most constructive discussion of
this problem is George Stigler's article on "The Influence of Events
and Policies on Economic Theory,"[52] in which he endeavored to specify
the points at which the environment impinged on economic theory.
While recognizing the multiplicity of possible connections, he contended that the majority of events, whether of major or minor importance, have been routine with respect to economic theory in the
period since economics became "a discipline pursued by professional
scholars" (p. 19). Indeed, he regarded this comparative immunity
from external influences as a mark of the maturity of the discipline.
Prior to 1870, however (and the date is obviously significant with
respect to the marginal revolution), economists were oriented toward
contemporary problems and institutions, and economics was "dominated by controversies over policy" (ibid.). For a problem to affect
the main corpus of economic theory it must be pervasive, persistent,
and of "vast importance" in relation to the conditions of all economies at all times. Otherwise theory (though not other parts of economics) would be unaffected, since "the dominant influence upon
the working range of economic theorists is the set of internal values
and pressures of the discipline" (p. 22). Facts do, of course, influence the economic theorist's work; indeed the "pedestrian, even
vulgar" fact "of diminishing marginal utility of objects" influenced
Jevons, Menger, and Walras (pp. 22–23); but facts are increasingly
being provided through the professional expertise of the empirical
research economist. Public policy, on the other hand, is a separable
part of the environment and is not closely geared to events. Once
again, only "general and persistent policy questions are likely to
call forth permanent advances in theory" (p. 25), and the classical

51. Blaug, p. 306. For comments on this subject see also S. G. Checkland,
"Economic Opinion in England as Jevons Found It," *Manchester School* 19
(May 1951): 151–52; and his *The Rise of Industrial Society in England* (Lon-
don, 1964), pp. 428–29. For an explanation in ideological terms see Daniel R.
Fusfeld, "Neo-Classical Economics and the Ideology of Capitalism," *Papers of
the Michigan Academy of Science, Arts and Letters* 43 (1958): 191–202.

52. Reprinted in his *Essays in the History of Economics*, pp. 16–30. Subsequent
page references are included in the text in parentheses.

problems of tariffs, monetary standards, monopoly, control of business fluctuations, the role of government and unions in labor markets, the incidence of taxes, and the treatment of the indigent fall into this category. ''The development of related disciplines'' is also part of the environment within which economic theory evolves, and this is felt mainly through the progress of such technical subjects as mathematics and statistics and through the development of other substantive fields (e.g., Darwinian theory and positivism) on the economist's ''scientific vision.''

Hence, on the whole, Stigler emphasized ''the immense degree of autonomy that any successful science must apparently possess'' (p. 29). However, if this argument is accepted, the question remains: How far was economics intellectually autonomous in the period immediately prior to the marginal revolution?

Marginalism and the Boundaries of Economic Science

Donald Winch

I

THOSE who speak of a marginal revolution necessarily commit themselves to the view that the introduction of marginalism marks a decisive change in the direction, and possibly even the nature, of economics as an organized body of knowledge. One important interpretation of marginalism, for example, maintains that it was responsible for the first clear conception of what is quintessentially "economic" in the economic behavior of individuals and in the description of economic systems taken as a whole. We speak of the marginal revolution as having altered the agenda and methods of economics, of new problems being made central while old ones were either revamped, subsumed, or set aside. In short, we speak of a transition from classical political economy to neoclassical economics.

As successive generations of interpreters have applied themselves to the problem of establishing what this transition entailed, the contrast between the old and the new has acquired a number of dimensions. To those concerned mainly with the history of economic analysis, independent of political, philosophical, and ideological issues, the significance of the marginal revolution lies in the scientific advance which it made possible. Partial and erroneous theories of value and distribution were replaced by others which were more rigorous and general. For such historians as Knight, Schumpeter, and Stigler, the introduction of the marginal principle, first as applied to consumer evaluations of economic goods and subsequently developed to cover a wider range of economic quantities, marks a kind of coming of age, when "economic theory was transformed from an art, in many

DONALD WINCH *is Dean of the School of Social Sciences at the University of Sussex, Brighton.*

respects literary, to a science of growing rigour.''[1] Associated with an advance on the analytical front were certain methodological gains. Economists, it is claimed, acquired a stricter sense of what was logically, rather than politically or morally, relevant to explanations of economic reality. The categories of economic analysis were made more distinct from those sanctioned by philosophical, political, and ethical debate. Prescientific vestiges and survivals were purged; economists became more self-conscious about maintaining the distinction between improvements in their analytical tools and more effective solutions to social problems. In this way, therefore, marginalism both reflected and contributed to the process of professionalization and internationalization of economics as an organized discipline which took place after 1870.

At the other end of the spectrum there is the amorphous group of interpreters, chiefly historicist, institutionalist, and Marxist in complexion, who look upon the transition from classical political economy to neoclassical economics as one of retreat and evasion. For such writers marginalism ''set the seal upon that process of abstraction from the socio-economic relations between men in production which began after Ricardo's death.''[2] It should be regarded, therefore, not as a scientific advance, but as an ideological reflex designed to ward off criticism of the way in which production and distribution are organized under capitalism and as a device for sustaining the myth that competitive capitalism constitutes a rational and socially beneficial economic system. Instead of being concerned with the social relations between men and men in historically determined class systems, under the banner of marginalism economics retreated further towards becoming a discipline concerned only with fetishistic relations between abstract individual atoms and things.

Insofar as these two implacably opposed schools of thought base themselves on similar observations as to *what* actually occurred as a result of the advent of marginalism as opposed to *why* it happened, they have more in common with each other than might at first appear to be the case. In recent years, however, an intermediate position has been formulated which alters the picture by drawing attention to

1. See George J. Stigler, *Production and Distribution Theories* (New York, 1941), p. 1.
2. Ronald L. Meek, *Economics and Ideology* (London, 1967), p. 208.

substantive differences in the aims of the classical and neoclassical approaches to the economic problem. This intermediate position is generally associated with a more sympathetic interpretation of the classical concern with the problems of capital accumulation, population increase, and economic growth. For if scientific advance is no longer viewed exclusively in terms of solutions to the problem of relative prices, a different set of contrasts comes to the fore. Thus we speak of a shift of emphasis from classical growth theory to neoclassical concern with the economics of allocation and efficiency; of a shift from macrodynamics to microstatics.[3] The intermediate interpretation speaks more of differences than of advance or retreat and remains neutral as between the two polar views on this question.

In spite of the apparent boldness of the title of this essay I shall not attempt to survey the whole field of controversy outlined above. I shall mainly be concerned with the contrast—or supposed contrast —between the classical and neoclassical views of the proper boundaries of economic science as it emerges from the methodological pronouncements of the three rediscoverers of the marginal principle. As is frequently the case with methodology, the firm conclusions are chiefly negative ones. But I hope to shed some light on the larger issues of interpretation by disentangling what I regard as essential qualities of the contrast from unwarranted accretions. One more prefatory remark may be in order. I am aware of the vagueness attached to the term "boundary" in my title, but in view of the close connection between questions of method, scope, and substance in any intellectual revolution, I do not wish to be overcommitted in advance.

II

When dealing with the marginal revolution there is less need than usual to make the ritual apology for introducing dry methodological issues. The event can be seen partly as an "internal" process of renewal, whereby certain questions which had always been of interest to economists were subjected to new and more rigorous treatment, and partly as a response to "external" pressures in the form of widespread contemporary criticism of the accepted methods and scope of economic science. In addition to the more well-known similarities in

3. One of the earliest works in this vein was H. Myint, *Theories of Welfare Economics* (London, 1948).

the work of the three rediscoverers of the marginal principle there is the fact that they exhibited a common desire to proclaim the methodological significance of what they had achieved. And while they did not arrive at exactly the same conclusions on this matter, it is worth noting that they upheld similar positions on many of the important issues where the discipline was under fire. They were in agreement on the question of the true province of economic theory in its pure form, and, to a lesser extent, on the question of the relationship between pure theory, empirical evidence, and policy conclusions.

As far as pure theory is concerned, the essential idea on which they concurred was in recognizing scarcity of given means in relation to alternative ends as *the* economic problem. According to Jevons, economic science was a rational, logical, deductive, and ultimately mathematical pursuit. Its scope was narrowly confined to ''the mechanics of self-interest and utility''; but since it dealt with universal laws of human wants it also possessed great generality.[4] Once the autonomy of economic science was thus established, it was possible to propose a viable division of labor between the various branches of social and economic inquiry. Subdivision became Jevons' favorite remedy for the methodological dissension of his day. ''We must distinguish the empirical element from the abstract theory, from the applied theory, and from the more detailed art of finance and administration. Thus will arise various sciences, such as commercial statistics, the mathematical theory of economics, systematic and descriptive economics, economic sociology and fiscal science.''[5] One of the remarkable features of Jevons' career is the fact that he contributed to several of these different branches of inquiry, though at the possible cost of not completing a well-rounded treatise on economics.

Walras confined pure economics to ''the theory of the determination of prices under a hypothetical regime of perfectly free competition,'' adding that pure economics was synonymous with the theory of social wealth because ''the sum total of all things, material

4. As Professor Hutchison has pointed out in his *Review of Economic Doctrines, 1870–1929* (London, 1953), pp. 35–36, Jevons arrived at this conception of economics at a very early stage in his studies. The relevant passage in his Journal for 1858 reads: ''Economy, scientifically speaking, is a very contracted science; it is in fact a sort of mathematics which calculates the causes and effects of man's industry, and shows how it may best be applied.''

5. W. S. Jevons, *Theory of Political Economy*, 2d ed. (London, 1879), p. xvii.

or immaterial, on which a price can be set because they are scarce
(i.e., both *useful* and *limited in quantity*) constitutes social wealth."[6]
Like Jevons, though on different lines, Walras also went on to mark
out clear dividing lines between *l'économie politique pure, l'économie
politique appliquée,* and *l'économie sociale,* each having its own characteristic aims and virtues. Pure science was distinguished by "the
complete indifference to consequences, good or bad, with which it
carries on the pursuit of pure truth."[7] On this foundation of pure
science an applied economics could be built which would comprise the
study of the technical and economic conditions most favorable to the
production of social wealth. Applied economics, regarded as an art or
applied science concerned with ways of increasing material well-
being, had as its distinguishing criterion usefulness rather than truth.
Social economics involved the study of property, taxation, and the
distribution of social wealth. Its questions were ethical rather than
industrial in character: they depended entirely on human decisions
and were to be judged not in terms of truth or usefulness but in
terms of justice and morals.

Menger's life-long struggle to achieve *Lebensraum* for a theoretical
science of economics against the claims of the German historical school
needs no emphasis. No less than Walras or Jevons, though possibly
with greater thoroughness, Menger defined the limits of theoretical
economics by reference to the conditions under which individuals exchange economic goods. Only by seeking the causal connections between
the simplest phenomena of exchange was it possible to establish the
fundamental laws underlying the more complex phenomena of human
economic activity. As a result of the *Methodenstreit,* Menger's methodological position was elaborated at great length. Here it is only
necessary to mention the basic distinctions which he made between
various branches of the science of social phenomena. The most important was that between sciences which deal with "individual (concrete) phenomena and their individual (concrete) relationships in
time and space," and sciences which deal with "types (empirical
forms) and their typical relationships (laws in the broadest sense

6. L. Walras, *Elements of Pure Economics,* trans. W. Jaffé (London, 1954), p.
40.
    7. Ibid., pp. 69–70.

of the word).''[8] History and statistics belonged to the former category, while theoretical economics, with its concern for what is truly "general" in the nature and connections between economic phenomena, belonged to the latter category. Political economy was made up of a combination of theoretical economics with a third type of science—the practical or technological sciences of national economy, which were concerned with the "principles of suitable action" in the field of policy and finance. Given the dominance of the historical school, the failure to maintain a rigid separation between historical, theoretical, and practical knowledge provided the chief reason, in Menger's view, for the neglect of economic theory in Germany.

Although these schemata exhibit a common awareness of the desirability of establishing the autonomy of pure science in terms of the scarcity view of the economic problem, they are the result of different philosophical traditions which on other questions produced divergent answers. The main divergence can be seen in the respective positions adopted by Jevons and Menger on the relationship of pure theory to empirical evidence. Not only was Menger dubious about the use of mathematics in economic theory—a topic on which Jevons and Walras were enthusiasts—but his fundamental dichotomy between theoretical and historical-cum-statistical sciences allowed no bridge to be built between them. There was no question of the a priori deductions of pure theory being verified by a posteriori inductive methods. Indeed, Menger maintained that "testing the exact theory of economy by the full empirical method is simply a methodological absurdity, a failure to recognize the basis and presuppositions of exact research"; it was as absurd as "testing the principles of geometry by measuring real objects."[9]

More in conformity with his training in the natural sciences, Jevons took the opposite view on this matter, using "exact" in a different sense to characterize not merely a science in which theoretical relationships were expressed in mathematics, but one in which the terms referred to measurable quantities. It was possible for economics to exist as a mathematical science of human enjoyment prior to the measurement of feelings; he also spoke of economic theory as "almost

8. Carl Menger, *Untersuchungen über die Methode der Socialwissenschaften* (Leipzig, 1883); English version: *Problems of Economics and Sociology*, trans. F. J. Nock (Urbana, Ill., 1963).
9. Ibid., pp. 60–70.

certain truth" proceeding from intuitively established axioms à la Euclid. But Jevons' scheme of science allowed for cross fertilization, and he expressed great optimism concerning the possibility of transforming economics from a mathematical into an exact science. Measurement of feelings was already conceivable in principle: like gravity it could be measured by its effects on motion or human action. His main hopes in this field rested on the existence of large quantities of statistical evidence which only needed to be properly interpreted by means of "correct theory." He took especial comfort from the fact that "questions which appear, and perhaps are, quite indeterminate as regards individuals, may be capable of exact investigation in regard to great masses and wide averages."[10]

The methodological differences between Menger on the one side and Walras and Jevons on the other have been examined by Emil Kauder in his *History of Marginal Utility Theory*.[11] Kauder maintains that Menger made a more fundamental disjunction between ethics and science: not only was pure science to be pursued as an end in itself, but the possibilities of conflict between hedonism and morals were not as extensively explored as they were by Walras and Jevons. More important than this, however, is Menger's adoption of the principles of philosophical realism, whereby the mind is held to be capable of grasping the essential qualities of objects. According to this view, theory does not proceed by isolating ideal types and by forming mental constructions; it aims at direct understanding of the reasons for the existence of objects and proceeds by constructing exact types and typical relationships between them which are valid for all times and places. Within such a scheme, genetic causality replaces the ideal of mutual interdependence. This helps to explain Menger's attitude towards mathematics as well as his antipathy to the idea that empirical evidence was in any way relevant to theoretical understanding. He could never have accepted, for example, Jevons' belief in the value of evidence of a statistical or aggregative kind; the only way of understanding social wholes was by means of methodological individualism, whereby spontaneous or unconscious social order is treated as the result of individual actions.

This difference of opinion may have been important to the way

10. Jevons, *Theory*, p. 17.
11. (Princeton, 1965), chap. 8.

in which the English, Austrian, and Walrasian versions of neo-classicism subsequently developed, but it should not be allowed to obscure the basic similarity in the positions adopted by our three authors in the face of attacks on the scope and methods of economic science by the historically minded. Menger's stance as a forthright opponent of the claims of the historical school was matched in essence, if not bitterness, by both Jevons and Walras. Thus, while Jevons held that "there must arise a science of the development of economic forms and relations," he was prepared to hand over to others the study of social and institutional change in order to free pure economic science from such entanglements.[12] He was certainly not in favor of the view advanced by one of his English historical critics, T. E. Cliffe Leslie, that "wide historical investigation must precede the construction of the true theory," and that no theory of consumption could be put forward "without a study of the history and the entire structure of society, and the laws which they disclose."[13] Indeed, in his *Principles of Science* Jevons was highly sceptical about the claims made for this kind of inquiry, maintaining apropos of Buckle and Comte, that "a science of history in the true sense of the term is an absurd notion."[14] Nevertheless, like many others of his generation in England, it would appear that Jevons put his faith in the eventual emergence of some kind of evolutionary sociology along the lines being mapped out by Spencer.

Walras too remained unimpressed by the claims of the historical school as presented to him in 1874 by two Italian adherents to the position adopted by German *Kathedersozialisten*, Vito Cusumano and Alberto Errera.[15] While accepting many of their criticisms of the Manchester School and its French adherents, and while acknowleging the artificial character of property and the industrial system, Walras reminded them that just as it was necessary to have a knowledge of the natural properties of matter in order to construct good machines, so "pour bien organiser la societé économique il faut connâitre les

12. Jevons, *Theory*, p. xvi.

13. T. E. Cliffe Leslie, *Essays in Political and Moral Philosophy*, 2d ed. (London, 1888), pp. 71, 72.

14. W. S. Jevons, *Principles of Science* (London, 1873), p. 761.

15. The correspondence can be found in W. Jaffé, *Correspondence of Léon Walras*, vol. 1, Letters 309–11, 317, 318, 323, 326, and 415. See also Walras's review of Errera in the *Journal des Economistes*, 3d ser. 36, no. 107 (Nov. 1874): 329–34.

tendances naturelles de la richesse sociale.'' Moving over to the attack, he doubted whether statistics and history alone would repair the defects in classical theories. Facts were one thing, laws of their nature, causes, and consequences another: mere empiricism led to unsubstantiated dogma. ''Il serait temps de finir d'accorder le piano et de commencer à nous jouer un peu de musique.'' The importance attached by Walras to a rigid distinction between the universalism of pure science and the particularities of applied science can also be seen in the proposals he put forward in 1879 for the reform of French educational institutions, where one of the objects in view was to avoid the German experience of confusion between theory and practice, science and politics.[16]

III

Do the similarities in the methodological positions adopted by Jevons, Walras, and Menger enable us to locate essential points of contrast between the classical and neoclassical views of the economic problem? How far do they help to substantiate some of the contrasts mentioned at the outset? Do they, for example, confirm the view that marginalism was associated with a clearer, more ''professional'' recognition of the distinction between ''science'' and ''art,'' and between positive and normative propositions?

The answer to these questions seems to be a negative one. In one form or another the desire to uphold the theoretical/practical and the positive/normative distinctions can be found in a variety of classical authors, and notably in the work of Senior, Whately, J. S. Mill, and Cairnes.[17] A similar impulse lies behind Ricardo's well-known complaints against Malthus that he failed to realize that political economy was ''a strict science like mathematics,''[18] and that he was prone to make premature appeals to ''experience.''[19] That marginalism was in no way necessary for belief in the autonomy of economic science can also be demonstrated by reference to J. S. Mill's elaborate defense of the a priori deductive method in his ''Essay on the Definition

16. L. Walras, ''De la culture et de l'enseignement des sciences morales et politiques,'' *Bibliothèque Universelle et Revue Suisse*, July and Aug. 1879.
17. On this see J. A. Schumpeter, *History of Economic Analysis* (London, 1954), pp. 535–41.
18. *Works and Correspondence*, ed. P. Sraffa, 8:331.
19. Ibid., 6:295.

and Method of Political Economy'' in Book VI of his *Logic*, and in his tract *Auguste Comte and Positivism*. In spite of his earlier sympathies Mill resisted the attempt by the Saint-Simonians and Comte to subsume political economy under history or sociology. There was still a need for a positive science which dealt with man ''as a being who desires to possess wealth, and who is capable of judging the comparative efficacy of means for obtaining that end,'' even though the process of abstracting one element from among the many motives attributable to men in society meant that conclusions with regard to actual conduct would need to be supplemented by other branches of knowledge.

It is doubtful if any of the rediscoverers of the marginal principle went much further than Mill. Even Jevons, who hardly ever missed an opportunity to score off Mill, did not express dissent on these matters.[20] Indeed, as T. W. Hutchison has recently reminded us, the revival of ''utility-arianism'' which accompanied the marginal utility theory in England enabled economists to maintain an air of neutrality with respect to the objects of consumer evaluation while advancing the claim that practical questions of economic policy and social justice, though formally separate from pure economic science, could also be treated scientifically. It frequently led to a more ambitious view of the role of the economist in policy matters—more ambitious than, say, the stricter views of Senior and Cairnes would have allowed.[21] The careful marking-out of the boundaries between pure and applied economics, therefore, does not correspond with the division between classical and neoclassical economics.

But perhaps one should ask a slightly different question: How far was marginalism associated with a narrowing of the aims of economic theory? Or, to introduce a more tendentious range of comparisons, how far was the marginalist view of the economic problem responsible, in itself, for reducing the importance and attention previously paid by economists to historical, institutional, and sociological variables?

In one important sense, of course, marginalism was responsible for

20. Jevons does not deal with the methodology of the social sciences in the second edition of his *Principles of Science* (London, 1877); his criticisms of Mill's *Logic* in the *Contemporary Review*, vol. 31 (Dec. 1877, Jan. 1878) and vol. 32 (April 1878), do not bear directly on these issues.

21. T. W. Hutchison, *Positive Economics and Policy Objectives* (London, 1964), pp. 40–41.

extending the boundaries of economics. The chief merit of the re-constructed science was that it demonstrated both the unity and the universality of the laws of choice in economic situations. By defining *the* economic problem as one of allocating scarce means between al-ternative uses, and by explicitly including both material and im-material goods and services, moral and immoral, the proponents of marginalism stressed the universal application of the laws of human choice. The marginal approach made it possible to explain the determination of all prices, including the prices of factors of pro-duction, as special cases of a single general principle. It was this aspect of the revolution that led Schumpeter to speak of the "rush for generality" which was implicit in the logic of marginalism, and led him to conclude that "the historical importance of the utility and marginal utility theory of Jevons, Menger, and Walras rests mainly upon the fact that it served as the ladder by which these economists climbed up to the conception of general economic equilibrium."[22] The search for and achievement of generality in this sense was not a marked characteristic of classical writers; Schumpeter's condemna-tion of the "Ricardian vice" is to a large extent the obverse of his admiration for Walrasian general equilibrium.

Schumpeter's enthusiasm carried him beyond theoretical generality and led him to speak of the "transcendental" qualities of marginalism. The early marginal utility theorists made it possible for us to recog-nize that at the common core of all economic problems was a prob-lem of constrained maxima or minima. And once having recognized this, we may, in Schumpeter's words, "transcend economics and rise to the conception of a system of undefined 'things' that are simply subject to certain restrictions and then try to develop a perfectly gen-eral mathematical logic of systems."[23] Still following this line of thought, and after mentioning Barone's application of the mathemat-ical apparatus to the collectivist state, Schumpeter speaks of lifting "the logical core of the economic process above the ground of the institutional garb in which it is given to observation."

It is here that one comes closest to the two polar interpretations of marginalism mentioned at the beginning of this essay. There is a great

22. Schumpeter, *Ten Great Economists* (New York, 1951), p. 126; and his *History of Economic Analysis*, p. 918.

23. Schumpeter, *Ten Great Economists*, pp. 123–24.

deal to be said for the view that marginalism enabled neoclassical economists to go further towards excluding historical and institutional categories from pure economics, so that even if the idea of drawing a clear boundary between pure and applied science was shared with the classical economists, there remain differences as to where the boundaries of pure science itself should be drawn.

IV

The best-known exclusion was a theory of population. It would be difficult to imagine classical political economy, with its concern for the problems of growth and macrodistribution, without some version of the population doctrine. Yet while Jevons fully accepted the "truth and vast importance" of this doctrine, he judged that "it forms no part of the direct problem of Economics," which he defined as follows: "Given, a certain population, with various needs and powers of production, in possession of certain lands and other sources of material: required, the mode of employing labour which will maximize the utility of the produce."[24]

Classical political economy in its abstract form largely treated technology as exogenous, but the supplies of factors of production remained within the boundaries of science, as did a variety of institutional factors. Here is J. S. Mill on the subject:

> Political Economy considers mankind as occupied solely in acquiring and consuming wealth; and aims at showing what is the course of action into which mankind, living in a state of society, would be impelled, if that motive, except in the degree in which it is checked by [the aversion to labour, and desire of the present enjoyment of costly indulgences], were absolute rulers of all their actions. Under the influence of this desire, it shows mankind accumulating wealth, and employing that wealth in the production of other wealth; sanctioning by mutual agreement the institution of property; establishing laws to prevent individuals from encroaching upon the property of others by force and fraud; adopting various contrivances for increasing the productiveness of their labour; settling the division of the produce by agreement, under the influence of competition . . . ;

24. Jevons, *Theory*, p. 289.

and employing certain expedients (as money, credit, etc.) to facilitate the distribution.[25]

There is little doubt that a decisive simplification was achieved as a result of making the problems of scarcity and exchange central to pure theory. According to Walras's tripartite division of the subject matter of economics, for example, neither the production nor the distribution of social wealth fell within the scope of "natural science." Respectively, they dealt with relations between men and things and men and men, and were concerned, therefore, with "human" and not "natural" phenomena. In other words, they dealt with matters that were entirely subject to human will and social contrivance. Pure science was reserved for value in exchange, which "once established, partakes of the character of a natural phenomenon, natural in its origins, natural in its manifestations and natural in essence." *Rareté* was comparable with velocity in mechanics; value in exchange was a measurable magnitude, and therefore a fit subject for mathematical treatment. For "if the pure theory of economics or the theory of exchange and value in exchange . . . is a physico-mathematical science like mechanics or hydrodynamics, then economists should not be afraid to use the methods and language of mathematics."[26]

The narrowing of pure economics to concentrate on value in exchange made it possible to be more ruthless in separating economic adjustment mechanisms from their social and historical integument, thereby strengthening claims to cross-cultural and intertemporal validity. The contrast here with classical political economy exists, but again is not as straightforward as might at first appear. J. S. Mill, as we know, was sensitive to the criticisms of political economy advanced by Comte and Saint-Simonian writers to the effect that it took for granted "the immutability of arrangements of society, many of which are in their nature fluctuating or progressive."[27] His *Prin-*

25. J. S. Mill, "On the Definition of Political Economy; and on the Method of Investigation Proper to It," in his *Essays on Some Unsettled Questions* (London, 1844), p. 138. It is perhaps worth noting, however, that Mill, for all the emphasis which he placed on the population doctrine, regarded it as an interpolation—"the strictness of purely scientific arrangement being thereby somewhat departed from for the sake of practical utility." Ibid., p. 140. He might not have objected too strongly to Jevons' excision.

26. Walras, *Elements*, pp. 69–71.

27. J S. Mill, *Essays on Economics and Society*, in *Collected Works* (Toronto, 1967), 4:225.

ciples was designed to reconcile, where possible, the implicit universalism of a deductive science with historical and social relativism. Hence the chapters on custom and competition, on socialism and alternative property systems. Hence also the use of Comte's distinction between statics and dynamics, and the division which he made between laws of production which "partake of the character of physical truth" and laws of the distribution of wealth which are "a matter of human institution solely."[28]

The apparent agreement between Mill and Walras on the question of distribution does not survive closer examination. It is frequently overlooked that Mill went on to say that the consequences of any given set of rules or institutions for distributing the social product "are as little arbitrary, and have as much the character of physical laws, as the laws of production"—a statement which Walras could not have accepted. The difference is also terminological and arises out of divergent interpretations of what a theory of distribution should attempt to explain. One of the main charges made against the classical writers by their marginalist successors, of course, was that they failed to put forward an integrated theory of distribution, where this was seen as involving the derivation of the prices of higher-order goods and services from the value of their joint products. In other words, they failed to recognize that a single rather than tripartite theory of distribution could only be arrived at via an adequate theory of exchange value and production.

The intermediate form of interpretation mentioned above counters this charge by stressing the differences between the quasi-dynamic classical interest in macro or class distribution, and the static, micro-oriented, neoclassical theory of distribution, with its emphasis on limited substitutability between factors of production within the constituent productive units of an economy.[29] And to mitigate the harshness of the judgment that the classical writers perceived only fitfully the vital connection between exchange value and distribution, attention can be drawn to the fact that the labor theory of value was also intended as a welfare indicator or yardstick to be used in mea-

28. J. S. Mill, *Principles of Political Economy*, ed. Ashley, pp. 199–200.
29. The fact that these productive units or firms were given only shadowy existence (if that) by the early marginalists adds support to Schumpeter's "transcendental" interpretation.

suring intertemporal changes in national income and exchange value—
a problem which did not present itself in the same form to neoclassical
economists. When this line of approach is adopted, the substantive
differences become clear while the issue of whether or not the classical
or neoclassical writers can be said to have put forward *the* theory
of distribution becomes one of mere definition. Nevertheless, it is
possible to conclude that a narrowing of the boundaries of theoretical
economics was achieved as a result of the marginal revolution because distribution in the neoclassical sense was treated as simply an
extension of the theory of final goods prices, while the classical interpretation of the distribution problem, with its implied connections with institutional forms and rules, was left outside the sphere
of what could be known by pure science.

The conclusion must be qualified immediately by remembering
that the early rediscoverers of marginalism, and Jevons in particular,
were not always able to break away from the classical view of distribution, and that outside the sphere of pure economic science there
were other continuities which justify the use of the term *neo*classical.
In England, for example, interest in the measurement of poverty and
the class distribution of income and wealth was a marked feature of
social, economic, and statistical inquiry in the last quarter of the
nineteenth century; so that even if marginalism implied that such
questions lay outside the boundaries of pure economics, and no
widely accepted theory existed to deal with macrodistribution, the
problems of distributive justice occupied a major place on the agenda
of applied science.

The early marginalists also shared many of the tacit institutional
assumptions accepted by their classical forebears. There is a great
deal of truth in Schumpeter's statement that they "had no explanatory scheme of economic change other than the one they had
inherited from Adam Smith," and that "the formative influence of
environments, group attitudes, group valuations, and so on, were not
taken into account in any other way than they had been by J. S.
Mill.''[30] In this respect both classical and neoclassical economists were
targets for those sociological critics who charged that many of the
conclusions of economics were vitiated by the assumption of given
tastes and by the failure to explore the connection between market

30. Schumpeter, *History*, pp. 889, 892.

choices and what Marshall, in a later effort to make the connection, lumped together under the term "activities."[31]

Nevertheless, the continuities should not be exaggerated. Mill went further than any of his immediate neoclassical successors were willing to go in meeting the historical and sociological critics of political economy. On the one hand Mill claimed that the methods of investigation appropriate to political economy were universally applicable: "as he who has solved a certain number of algebraic equations, can without difficulty solve others, so he who knows the political economy of England, or even Yorkshire, knows that of all nations actual or possible."[32] On the other hand he subsequently conceded that "only through the principle of competition has political economy any pretension to the character of a science."[33] Edgeworth drew attention to this inconsistency when he pointed out that it was not really possible for Mill to retain belief in the a priori deductive method once "he began to doubt the universality of the principle of self-interest, which he once regarded as the foundation of economic reasoning."[34]

The conciliatory stance adopted by Mill provided an opportunity to undermine claims to universality. This became obvious later when Bagehot, seeking to preserve a sphere of relevance for the old political economy, went further in this direction by restricting the science to "a single kind of society—a society of grown-up competitive commerce, such as we have in England."[35] Bagehot's answer furnished only temporary and uncertain grounding for an autonomous science of political economy, though it perhaps implied that the sphere of competence would widen as other nations "grew up." Potentially, at least, Mill's answer was equally damaging to the universal claims of the science: he had suggested that in the society of the future, cooperation would replace competition and that a comfortable form of "stationariness" could abolish the need for economic striving.

Some evolutionist critics of political economy exploited the openings provided by these concessions. They were not content to accept

31. This question is exhaustively treated by Talcott Parsons in *The Structure of Social Action* (London, 1937), chap. 4.
32. J. S. Mill, *Essays on Economics and Society*, p. 226.
33. J. S. Mill, *Principles of Political Economy*, ed. Ashley, p. 242.
34. See R. H. I. Palgrave, ed., *Dictionary of Political Economy* (London, 1893–99), 2:757.
35. Walter Bagehot, *Economic Studies* (London, 1886), pp. 16–20.

a division of labor whereby the economists simply relinquished claims to deal with social and institutional change. Mill and Bagehot had acknowledged that political economy did not apply to custom-bound societies; but was it any more applicable to complex industrial societies? Single-cause explanations deduced from dubious psychological premises failed to take account of the ways in which economic behavior presupposed and was modified by an increasingly complex institutional order.[36]

In view of the widespread enthusiasm for evolutionary and interdisciplinary modes of explanation during the second half of the nineteenth century, the concern of the early marginalists to establish the autonomy of a pure deductive science within narrowed boundaries is all the more remarkable. Against this background the use of mathematics together with the more thoroughgoing individualism entailed by an economics which placed the rational maximizer at the center of things can only be seen as a decisive movement against the prevailing intellectual tide, in the face of which Mill, and later Marshall, made significant concessions. But perhaps it is better to describe the movement as *un recul pour mieux sauter*, particularly important when a new structure of economic theory was being built. Responsibility for certain outlying and inconvenient territories could be denied or handed over with an appearance of good grace to other disciplines. Border disputes continued, but the new arrangements proved more comfortable to professional scruples, while not ruling out extensive forays into neighboring fields, as instanced by Jevons' statistical and policy writings, and Walras's interest in social reform along liberal-socialist lines.

It was this kind of accommodation which enabled Foxwell in his survey of English economics in 1887 to praise mathematical marginalism in the following terms:

> It has introduced continuity and precision for the first time into economic reasoning; it has shown how hopelessly the old theory fell below the ordinary scientific standard; it has overhauled the whole system of definitions and assumptions; it has been full of suggestions, both as to unobserved truths and as

36. See, e.g., T. E. Cliffe Leslie, *Essays in Political and Moral Philosophy*; and L. Stephen, ''The Sphere of Political Economy,'' in his *Social Rights and Duties* (London, 1896).

to the exact limits and best expression of those already observed; it has given organic unity to the science; and, most valuable service of all, it has made it henceforth practically impossible for the educated economist to mistake the limits of theory and practice. . . .[37]

This was also the basis for Marshall's claim that "the retiring disposition of general principles and general propositions has been accompanied not by a diminution but by an increase of their real authority,"[38] and for his distinction between "a body of concrete truth" and "an engine for the discovery of truth."

V

Even after taking into account qualifications and continuities, therefore, it remains true that the advent of marginalism led to a pervasive shift of emphasis within economics, and that this shift was associated with a narrowing of the boundaries of the science which could be interpreted—and was interpreted by many of those most directly concerned—as entailing closer attention to what was knowable by means of deductive theory and thus more defensible from a "professional" point of view. This unexciting conclusion leaves open the question which has been much discussed in recent years by philosophers and historians of science as to whether the transition from classical to neoclassical economics is best seen as part of a gradual process of falsification and scientific advance à la Popper, or conforms more to the Kuhnian notion of revolutionary discontinuity.[39] Nor does it imply any simple resolution of the conflict between say the Schumpeterian and Marxian views of the marginal revolution. It will be obvious perhaps that I adhere to the intermediate position described above and find neither of the polar points of view entirely compelling; they both seem to contain a large element of unsubstantiated rhetoric and wishful or teleological thinking. Schumpeter's account of marginalism as a purely technical innovation and his idea that "in analysing economic phenomena, categories other than those suggested by

37. H. Foxwell, "The Economic Movement in England," *Quarterly Journal of Economics* 2 (1887): 88.

38. Marshall, "The Old Generation of Economists and the New," in *Memorials of Alfred Marshall* ed. A. C. Pigou (London, 1925), p. 297.

39. For an extended version of the Popper-Kuhn debate see I. Lakatos and A. Musgrave, eds., *Criticism and the Growth of Knowledge* (Cambridge, 1970).

the class structure of society have proved more useful, as well as more satisfactory, logically'' may be correct, but need to be supported by more than the odd assertion about ''the inevitable consequence of analytic advance.''[40] Similarly with some of the Marxian interpretations, the view that special virtue attaches to the Ricardo-Marx categories of analysis cannot be established simply by internal reference or by an implicit appeal to criteria which lie beyond economics or any other attempt to construct an empirically verifiable science of society.

For the historian of economic thought one of the ironies about some current revivals of interest in classical-Marxian modes of analysis is that they frequently require us to admire holistic features of the classical economists' approach which contemporary critics condemned them, as well as their marginalist successors, for neglecting. The shift from classical to neoclassical entailed an accentuation—not the invention—of economic individualism. Yet another irony surrounds the process whereby what are essentially neoclassical optimizing techniques have been accommodated in recent years within the Marxian canon, a development which Schumpeter would have welcomed as proof of his thesis about marginalism and the ''institutional garb.'' For this purpose it is the Austrian view of marginalism as praxiology, or the principles of rational action, that is accepted. According to this view economics is not an empirical science, but a body of necessary truths. The irony arises from the fact that the Austrian School provided the most implacable opponents of Marxism and was the only branch of neoclassicism to deny the economic rationality of socialism. Any guilt I would normally feel in skating round these larger problems is mitigated by the fact that they are dealt with more extensively and authoritatively by Professor Ronald Meek in his contribution to this volume, ''Marginalism and Marxism,'' below.

40. Schumpeter, *History*, p. 551.

Mill and Cairnes and the Emergence of Marginalism in England

N. B. de Marchi

I

I⊤ IS well known that marginalist concepts appeared in economic literature before 1871. As far as England is concerned, the notion of diminishing marginal utility, for example, was spelt out in the 1830's and again in the 1850's. And Jevons hit upon and outlined his special view of political economy a full decade before the *Theory of Political Economy* was published.

For the most part, successive expositions of the utility theory were ignored by economists practicing in the dominant Ricardian tradition. This is not quite true of the leading adherents of that tradition, John Stuart Mill and J. E. Cairnes, who openly opposed it in certain respects. We have come to accept their opposition as entirely natural. But it is not self-evident that they should have opposed it. Indeed, Schumpeter has argued that Mill was influenced by Say and by Senior more than he was aware, or was prepared to admit, so that his system offered "all the elements of the complete model that Marshall was to build."[1] Certainly Mill was early and (probably) independently in possession of isolated elements of marginalist theory—for instance, the notion of calculating, economic man and the principle of marginal cost pricing—which we tend rather to associate with Senior and W. F. Lloyd.[2] Further, Mill was, in terms of his schooling, at least as well

NEIL B. DE MARCHI *is Assistant Professor of Economics at Duke University.*

1. J. A. Schumpeter, *History of Economic Analysis* (New York, 1954), pp. 529–30, 569–70.

2. Compare [Mill] "The Nature, Origin, and Progress of Rent" (1828) in *Collected Works of John Stuart Mill* (Toronto, continuing), 4:163–80, esp. pp. 166–67, and "On the Definition of Political Economy; and on the Method of Investigation Proper to It" (1836), ibid., pp. 309–39, at p. 323, and also "War Expenditure" (1824), ibid., pp. 3–22, at pp. 16–18, with B. J. Gordon, "W. F. Lloyd: A Neglected Contribution," *Oxford Economic Papers*, n.s. 18 (1966): 64–70, at pp. 69–70, and Schumpeter, pp. 575–76.

fitted as Jevons to develop an "hedonic calculus."[3] Then, too, Mill and Cairnes were well versed in the writings of the so-called French school, with whom, according to Jevons, the truth (about distribution) really lay.[4] Cairnes was even an intimate of Leonard Courtney, who broadly adhered to this "school" and was one of the two men in England—after Fleeming Jenkin and George Darwin—who Jevons thought might appreciate Walras's work.[5]

Why, then, did Mill and Cairnes fail to develop their theoretical structure in the same direction as Jevons? To provide an answer to that question is the task of this essay.[6]

II

It is convenient to begin by listing the principal theoretical advances embodied in Jevons' political economy.

There is, firstly, the distinction between total and "final" utility, and the enunciation of the law that to a buyer the utility of a commodity diminishes as successive increments of it are acquired and consumed.[7]

Secondly, there is the explicit assumption of maximizing behavior, and the statement of what it implies—for consumers, that purchasing

3. Cf. R. D. C. Black, Introduction to the Pelican Classics (1970) ed. of W. S. Jevons, *The Theory of Political Economy* (1871), p. 30.

4. The expression "French school" was used both by Jevons and by Mill and Cairnes. Jevons meant by it the tradition of regarding commodities and factor services as subject to the same laws of value-in-exchange, and it is employed above in that sense. For a list of writers included by Jevons in this tradition, see Preface to the 2d ed. of his *Theory of Political Economy* (1879), p. xlix.

5. See Black, Introduction, pp. 32-33. Leonard Courtney was professor of political economy at University College, London, 1872-75. He published little on economic theory, but his adherence to the "French school" is sufficiently shown by two anonymous pieces: "Economistes Modernes," *London Review* 5 (12 July 1862): 35-37 and 5 (2 Aug. 1862): 106-8; and "Mr. Thornton on Labour," *Times*, 16 Oct. 1869, p. 4.

6. The enquiry is not as open-ended as this way of putting the question implies. We start with the knowledge that Mill and Cairnes shared roughly the same set of economic notions as Say, Senior, Longfield, Jennings, and Jevons. (In particular, they were familiar with the concept of the margin and the general notion of satiety.) What is at issue for the most part, then, is not why Mill and Cairnes failed to discover notions which these, and other of their contemporaries, hit upon, but what kept them from extending, applying, or combining common notions in precisely the same way as their contemporaries? To be specific, why, possessing the notion of the margin, did they not arrive at a clear distinction between total and marginal utility? And why, being familiar with satiety, did they not enunciate the principle of diminishing (marginal) utility?

7. Jevons, *Theory*, 2d ed., pp. 49-57.

should be so spread that the ratios of utilities derived from the last units consumed of each desired commodity are equal to the ratios of their prices.[8]

Thirdly, there is the insight that value in exchange is the pivot of the economic process, the laws of value applying equally to commodities and to agents of production, since factors or agents are rewarded out of the value of the product for which they are jointly responsible. In the case of both agents and commodities there is ''a general balance of producing power and of demand as measured by the final degree of utility.''[9]

Of course, Jevons' *Theory of Political Economy* contained other novelties—notably his discussion of capital and interest—but the three outlined are the ones most relevant to our purpose.

In what sense and in what measure were our two representatives of Ricardian thought aware of these ideas? And, insofar as they were known and understood, what stood in the way of their being developed within the Ricardian tradition?

III

We take up these questions firstly in relation to the distinction between total and marginal utility, and the law of diminishing marginal utility.

Marshall was inclined to see in Ricardo's differentiation of ''value'' from ''riches'' a hint that he had been ''feeling his way towards the distinction between marginal and total utility.'' Marshall continued:

> For by Riches he means total utility, and he seems to be always on the point of stating that value corresponds to the increment of riches which results from that part of the commodity which it is only just worth the while of purchasers to buy; and that when the supply runs short . . . there is a rise in that marginal increment of riches which is measured by value, at the same time that there is a diminution in the aggregate riches, the total utility, derived from the commodity.

All that Ricardo lacked, Marshall suggested, was the language in

8. Ibid., pp. 63–66, 198–201, 205–9.
9. Ibid., Preface, pp. xlix-lii, and pp. 204, 295–96.

which to express this neatly—"the terse language of the differential calculus."[10]

Marshall's assessment was overgenerous. If this was indeed the direction of Ricardo's thought, and the calculus the one tool lacking, it would be reasonable to expect his able follower John Stuart Mill to have arrived at a clear statement of the distinction. For Mill knew that price usually varies inversely as the quantity offered for sale. Also, he made more explicit than Ricardo the idea that the price prevailing in a market at a given time indicates that buyers consider it just worthwhile to purchase the last unit offered at that price.[11] Further, he had the advantage over Ricardo of having read Senior's —admittedly brief—exposition of the principle of diminishing marginal utility.[12] Finally, while he was, on his own admission, less thoroughly grounded in the calculus than in algebra and geometry, nevertheless, his mathematical education was sufficient to enable him to perceive possible applications of the distinction between a differential increment and a sum.[13] Yet Mill, in discussing the gain from

10. Marshall, *Principles of Economics*, 9th (variorum) ed., ed. C. W. Guillebaud, 2 vols. (London, 1961), 1:814.

11. On these points see Mill's essay, "Of the Laws of Interchange Between Nations; and the Distribution of the Gains of Commerce Among the Countries of the Commercial World," in *Collected Works*, 4:232–61, at pp. 237–38; his review article, "De Quincey's Logic of Political Economy" (1845), ibid., pp. 393–404, at pp. 399–401; and his *Principles of Political Economy, with Some of Their Applications to Social Philosophy* (1848), *Collected Works*, 3:465–68.

12. Mill's notes on Senior's *An Outline of the Science of Political Economy* (1836) are to be found reprinted in *Economica*, n.s. 12 (1945): 134–39.

13. For Mill's admission see J. Stillinger, ed., *The Early Draft of John Stuart Mill's Autobiography* (Urbana, Ill., 1961), p. 42. It was made concerning his education from age 8 to age 12. For the list of his mathematical reading during that period, which included some works on fluxions, see Francis E. Mineka, ed., *The Earlier Letters of John Stuart Mill, 1812–1848*, vols. 12 and 13 of *Collected Works*, at 12:7–8. Mill's mathematical training was, however, extended during a visit to France in 1820, when he worked partly under the supervision of M. P. Lenthéric, professor of higher mathematics in the Faculté des Sciences, Montpellier. By the end of this visit Mill had worked through Lacroix's *Traité du calcul différentiel et du calcul intégral* (1814), Lagrange's *Théorie des fonctions analytiques* (1813) and Laplace's *Exposition du système du monde* (1813)— performing "over and over" all the problems in Lacroix's work. For further details see Anna Jean Mill, ed., *John Mill's Boyhood Visit to France* (Toronto, 1960), pp. 29, 82, 86, 88, 90. (The dates of the French works listed above are those of the editions in Mill's library at Somerville College, Oxford.) Mill's library contains these and other works by the same authors, and William Whewell's *Doctrine of Limits* (1838). We know too that Mill was familiar with De Morgan's *Differential and Integral Calculus* (1842): see Mill's essay, "Berkeley's Life and Writings," *Fortnightly Review* n.s. 10 (Nov. 1871): 505–24, at pp. 521–22. Over-

trade, wrote as if the total gain were measured by the terms of trade—an apparent conflation of marginal with total utility for which he was sharply criticized by Jevons.[14] More basically, Mill showed no inclination to set down laws of consumer behavior, let alone laws of enjoyment resolvable into quantities of pleasure and pain.

One important factor in Mill's hesitancy is readily explained. He knew that different individuals experience a particular pleasure with different intensity. This difference might be attributed to a difference in circumstances; but even if the circumstances are common, he said, they may produce different effects because the characters of the persons involved differ. Indeed, the causes determining human character are "so numerous and diversified . . . that in the aggregate they are never in any two cases exactly similar." Hence, even in given circumstances, "no assertion, which is both precise and universally true, can be made respecting the manner in which human beings will think, feel, or act."[15]

Mill's methodological caution, it should be stressed, was reserved for attempts to specify *precise* and *universal* laws of behavior: laws which might be regarded as rules or precepts, applicable without thought for the possible peculiarities of each case.[16] However, this

all, Mill's mathematical education probably was not inferior to that available to Cambridge undergraduates in the early 1820's; on this see W. W. Rouse Ball, *A History of the Study of Mathematics at Cambridge* (Cambridge, 1889), chap. 7. Clearly, however, an adeqaute training in one discipline is not a guarantee that its techniques will be seen as applicable to the problems of another. Conversely, this perception may be present when the technical skill to exploit it is lacking. Malthus in 1829 confessed to "never having been very familiar with the present algebraic notation," yet saw that "there are many of the results in political economy which have some resemblance to the problems de maximis et minimis." Malthus to William Whewell, 26 May 1829, Whewell Papers, Trinity College, Cambridge.

14. Mill, *Principles, Collected Works,* 3:615; Jevons, *Theory,* 2d ed., pp. 154–56.

15. Mill, *A System of Logic, Ratiocinative and Inductive,* 2 vols. (London, 1843), 2:494, 506–7. In the latter passage Mill suggested that differences of "mental susceptibility" may be "original and ultimate facts," or "consequences of . . . previous mental history," or related to differences in the constitution or physiology of different individuals.

16. Cf. Mill's opposition to certain political economists (among whom he classed Robert Lowe) for their apparent readiness to identify political economy with "a set of catch-words, which they mistake for principles—free-trade, freedom of contract, competition, demand and supply, the wages fund, individual interest, desire of wealth, &c.—which supersede analysis, and are applicable to every variety of cases without the trouble of thought." "Professor Leslie on the Land Question" (1870), in *Collected Works,* 4:671–95, at p. 671.

still left it plenty of scope. For just as Mill was sensitive to the fact that the desire of different individuals for the same commodity might vary in strength, so too he recognized that there is no uniform relation between price and the quantities demanded of different commodities. Thus,

> some things are usually affected in a greater ratio than that of ... [a given] excess or deficiency, others usually in a less: because, in ordinary cases of demand, the desire, being for the thing itself, may be stronger or weaker: and the amount of what people are willing to expend on it, being in any case a limited quantity, may be affected in very unequal degrees by difficulty or facility of attainment.[17]

Money alone, of all commodities, he said, is desired as "the universal means of purchase"; and its value tends to vary in inverse proportion as its amount. Again, though Mill asserted, in his discussion of international exchange, that the terms of trade adjust to the "inclinations and circumstances of the consumers on both sides," he left the precise result unspecified. For, "as the inclinations and circumstances of consumers cannot be reduced to any rule, so neither can the proportions in which the . . . [traded] commodities will be interchanged."[18]

In the light of this it is not surprising that Mill in 1871 reacted negatively to Jevons' attempt to express the laws of consumer behavior in mathematical form. It mattered little whether it was a demand schedule or a schedule of variations in utility that was translated into symbols. In either case, Mill might have said, an important principle governing the use of scientific language was being violated. For Mill regarded algebraic relations as universal technical rules, applicable, without regard to the meaning of the signs or the peculiar circumstances of each case, *only* where the investigation comprised ascertaining a relation between mere numbers. In his view the laws of consumer behavior were preeminently not of this sort; and in investigating such subjects, he said, "the things on which we reason should be conceived by us in the concrete, and 'clothed in cir-

17. *Principles, Collected Works,* 3:512; cf. p. 467.
18. "Of the Laws of Interchange Between Nations," in *Collected Works,* 4:239–40. The passage was repeated in the *Principles, Collected Works,* 3:598–99.

cumstances.' ''[19] Jevons, Mill suggested, had ''a mania for encumbering questions . . . with a notation implying the existence of greater precision in the data than the questions admit of.''[20]

Mill's followers Cairnes and Cliffe Leslie held similar views, and they displayed much the same reaction to Jevons' *Theory of Political Economy.*[21]

The belief that mechanical reasoning should not be applied to consumer behavior no doubt blinded all three to the clarity which Jevons' mathematics imparted to the notion of the margin. Nonetheless, mathematics was not essential to the concept of marginal utility nor to the principle of diminishing (marginal) utility. Supplementary reasons must therefore be sought to explain why Mill and his followers failed to arrive at these ideas. Four will be suggested here.

Firstly, Mill inherited from Ricardo a bias against giving consumption a place equal to that held by production and distribution in the schema of economic science. ''Political economists,'' Mill averred, ''have never treated consumption on its own account, but always for the purpose of the enquiry in what manner different kinds of consumption affect the production and distribution of wealth.''[22] In part this was a defensive pose, adopted lest any concession appear to be made to those who believed in the possibility of a general glut.[23] And in part it reflected the Ricardian concentration on long-run, competitive value, as distinct from short-run or market

19. *System of Logic*, 2:292–98.

20. Mill to Cairnes, 5 Dec. 1871, Mill-Taylor Collection, vol. LV, British Library of Political and Economic Science.

21. In a letter of 23 Oct. 1871 to Mill, Cairnes wrote, apropos of Jevons' book: ''I own I have no faith in the development of economic doctrines by mathematics. What you have said on the subject of nomenclature in the second vol. of your Logic seems to me decisive upon this point.'' Mill-Taylor Collection, vol. LVIA. See also Cairnes's review of the work: ''New Theories in Political Economy,'' *Fortnightly Review*, n.s. 11 (Jan. 1872): 71–76, at p. 76. Leslie's views are given in his review of the 2d ed. of Jevons' *Theory. The Academy*, 26 July 1879, pp. 59–60.

22. ''On the Definition of Political Economy,'' in *Collected Works*, 4:318 n.; cf. his views on the place of the theory of value, *Principles, Collected Works*, 3:455.

23. Although the main battles on this point had been fought before 1830, Mill maintained his opposition to the ''chimerical supposition'' (as he referred to it) in the *Principles*. See *Collected Works*, 2:66–68 and 3:570–76. Cairnes, as late as 1874, evidently felt it necessary to reiterate the grounds of that opposition. See Cairnes, *Some Leading Principles of Political Economy, Newly Expounded* (London, 1874), pp. 17-34.

value. Given sufficient time, the Ricardians believed, the value of
a commodity whose supply can be increased will conform to the cost
or supply price of the particular amount of it demanded. Conversely,
they urged, a great demand, unattended by "some principle of limitation in the supply," is not sufficient to induce a high price.[24]

For Mill, then, there was to be no approach to marginal utility
theory via the investigation in its own right of consumption and the
laws of enjoyment. This position was reinforced by a technical objection to the idea that demand might be measured subjectively, according to the intensity of desire (or anticipated satisfaction). This notion had appeared in Senior's *Outline of the Science of Political
Economy*. If a shortage of wheat occurs, Senior had said, the consumers of oats and barley will not thereby have any greater power
of purchasing these substitute commodities, nor will the quantity of
them which is purchased increase, supply being given. There is, however, a sense in which the demand for them may be said to increase,
namely, that they are now *desired* in greater degree than before.[25]
Mill, commenting on this suggestion, rejoined that there would be
more purchasers at the previous market price, and in this sense an
increase in demand. Furthermore, this sense was to be preferred;
since if one is to speak of a law of demand and supply, these two
things must be expressed in comparable terms:

> Now as ordinary usage makes it almost impossible to use the
> word *supply* in any sense but that of *quantity of the commodity*,
> viz., the quantity actually in the market or ready to be brought
> into it, *demand* must I think be used also in the sense of quan-
> tity of the commodity, and in that sense it can only be taken
> to mean, the quantity for which at the market price, pur-
> chasers can be found.[26]

Mill repeated this argument in his *Principles of Political Economy*
(1848).[27]

It is possible, thirdly, that Mill's methodological convictions exerted

24. Mill, *Principles, Collected Works*, 3:475–76; "Nature, Origin, and Progress
of Rent," *Collected Works*, 4:164.
25. Senior, *Outline of the Science of Political Economy* (reprint ed.,
1938), p. 15.
26. "Notes on N. W. Senior's *Political Economy*, by John Stuart Mill,"
Economica, n.s. 12 (1945): 134.
27. *Collected Works*, 3:465.

a critical influence. Recall for a moment his view that no precise and universal laws of human feeling or action are to be found. At the same time Mill did allow that this standpoint was unnecessarily strict for many practical purposes. Frequently it is found, he said, that a few general causes, and qualities common to large bodies of men (though not to all mankind), will yield propositions which are "almost always true." Mill called these approximate generalizations, or observation statements, "empirical laws." However, they could not be regarded as truly scientific laws until they were resolved into the basic causes of the phenomena they described.[28] Now the law of diminishing marginal utility was of this purely empirical variety.[29] On Mill's view, then, to use this law to explain the shape of the demand curve would amount to setting one unexplained uniformity to explain another.[30] Outside the context of maximizing behavior, such a substitution must have appeared peculiarly sterile.

If the "empirical" law of diminishing marginal utility was itself to be explained, the explanation would have had to run in terms of the laws of psychology. The psychology adopted by Mill was the so-called associationist psychology. One of its laws stated that "greater intensity in either or both of . . . [two] impressions, is equivalent, in rendering them excitable by one another, to a greater frequency of conjunction."[31] This was not meant to imply that a more intense pleasurable sensation is reducible to a greater number of confrontations of the senses with a desired object. Such a supposition would be contrary to the commonsense implications of satiety. What was in view was the efficiency of the stimulus-response mechanism. It was not unreasonable to suppose that excitation would be more effective if a

28. *System of Logic*, 2:494-96.

29. Senior and Richard Jennings represented the law as a matter of common experience. Senior, pp. 11-12; Jennings, *Natural Elements of Political Economy* (London, 1855), pp. 98-99. Jevons actually called it an empirical law. *Theory*, 2d ed., p. 159.

30. Jevons himself regarded the law of diminishing marginal utility as an exploratory device. He doubted whether "any exact explanation" of the laws of utility could be given, and likened them to "the empirical formulae used in many of the physical sciences—mere aggregates of mathematical symbols intended to replace a tabular statement." *Theory*, 2d ed., p. 159.

31. Mill, *System of Logic*, 2:501. Cf. James Mill, *Analysis of the Phenomena of the Human Mind* (1829), a new edition, with notes illustrative and critical by Alexander Bain, Andrew Findlater, and George Grote, edited with additional notes by John Stuart Mill, 2 vols. (London, 1869), 1:82-90.

particular stimulus-response association was more frequently renewed. Nonetheless, the strict adherent of this psychology might be excused for failing to arrive at a clear conception of marginal satisfaction. Not only was attention directed more to the conjunction of sensations than to the senations themselves, but, although "degrees of pleasurable sensation" were sometimes spoken about, there was no clear separation made between the sensation itself and the degree of pleasure which might go together with it. As late as 1869 John Mill could write, in a cautious note to his father's *Analysis of the Phenomena of the Human Mind,* that

> it is open to question whether the pleasure or pain, especially
> the pleasure, is not something added to the sensation, and
> capable of being detached from it. . . . It is often observable that
> a sensation is much less pleasurable at one time than at another,
> though to our consciousness it appears exactly the same sensa
> tion in all except the pleasure. This is emphatically the fact in
> cases of satiety, or of loss of taste for a sensation by loss of
> novelty.[32]

Mill concluded that it is in principle possible to abstract the pleasure or pain attending a sensation from the sensation itself and to consider the pleasure or pain alone. However, he made no attempt to exploit this possibility or to show what implications it might hold for the study of human enjoyment.

Associationism did not constitute an absolute barrier to the clear conception of marginal satisfaction. Richard Jennings proceeded on the basis of the associationist psychology, yet he enunciated with remarkable clarity the principle that the "degrees of satisfaction" derived from consuming a commodity diminish with each installment of it offered to the senses.[33] It is significant, however, that Jennings had long been dissatisfied with the Ricardian theory of value and was deliberately casting about for an hypothesis which could equally well explain—as the cost of production theory could not—such diverse phenomena as why light, air, and water generally command no price;

32. In James Mill, 2:185.
33. Jennings, pp. 96–99. A useful statement of Jennings' views is given by Ross M. Robertson, "Jevons and his Precursors," *Econometrica* 19 (1951): 229–49, at pp. 234-37.

why silks vary less in price with a given change in quantity than do potatoes; and why a copy of the *Times* which costs fourpence in the morning falls to tuppence when the evening news is out.[34] Mill, by contrast, felt no such inducement to investigate the laws of enjoyment.

Lack of interest in the laws of enjoyment led to blunted perception. Thus Cairnes, who was the only one of Mill's disciples to comment on Jennings' work, dismissed it with the comment that no new light had been thrown on production, division of labor, and exchange by Jennings' attempt to exhibit the psychological and physiological bases of these phenomena of wealth.[35]

To summarize: Mill had specific reasons for not wanting to admit into economic science the study of human wants and the laws of enjoyment. These reasons had to do with his belief that the forces of supply were of prime importance. Consistently with this, he insisted that in speaking of demand and supply a measure of demand must be adopted conformable with that—namely, quantity—in terms of which supply is commonly understood. He therefore deemed unsatisfactory a subjective measure of demand. Further, it is probable that Mill would not have accepted the law of diminishing marginal utility as a genuine explanation of the shape of the demand curve. But in any case, his adherence to associationist psychology made it unlikely that he would enunciate even this "empirical law" for himself.

An assessment of the relative importance of these several reasons will be held over till after the examination of the position of Mill and Cairnes with respect to the other new elements in Jevons' *Theory of Political Economy*.

IV

The central figure in Jevons' calculus of pleasure and pain was the utility-maximizing individual. Mill based his own political economy on the not dissimilar assumption that man is "determined, by the

34. Jennings, pp. 84, 97, 210–11; idem, *Social Delusions Concerning Wealth and Want* (London, 1856), pp. 70–71.

35. Cairnes, *The Character and Logical Method of Political Economy* (1857), 2d ed. (London, 1875), Appendix B. Cairnes also protested against Jennings' suggestion that "such relations as those of Quantity and Value . . . may be exhibited in the formulae and analyzed by the different methods of Algebra and of Fluxions." Jennings, pp. 259–60; Cairnes, *Character and Logical Method*, 2d ed., pp. 110–12 n.

necessity of his nature, to prefer a greater portion of wealth to a smaller," save only that he is averse to labor and also prefers the present enjoyment of the fruits of his efforts. Mill added that man is "capable of judging of the comparative efficacy of means" to the attainment of wealth. In other words, he assumed man to be motivated by "the desire of obtaining the greatest quantity of wealth with the least labour and self-denial."[36] We have seen that Mill's acquaintance with the idea of satiety did not impel him in the direction of the law of diminishing marginal utility. Nor did his readiness to deduce economic laws from the premise that man desires wealth and is calculating in its pursuit lead him to enunciate the theorem that if a maximum of satisfaction is to be derived from any good (including labor or money) capable of satisfying different wants, it must be allocated to these different uses in such a way as to equalize its marginal utilities in all of them.[37] Nonetheless, Mill's thinking approached most closely to Jevons's at this point.

The closeness of their views is obscured by Mill's concern with minimizing real cost or sacrifice, rather than with maximizing utility. But, as the following examples show, he had firmly grasped the essence of the optimizing procedure—the ordering of alternative possible uses of resources in terms of their respective effects on some maximand (say, output) or minimand (such as cost). Thus, Mill opposed the Corn Laws because, he said, under their influence "a portion of the labour and capital of the country is diverted out of a more into a less advantageous employment: a quantity of labour is employed in growing corn, which would otherwise have produced, not only cloth, or hardware, sufficient to purchase the same quantity of corn in the foreign market, but much more."[38] Similarly, Mill judged the Saint-Simonian system of cooperation superior to that proposed by Robert Owen, because he thought it likely to be more efficient. According to the former scheme each man was to be employed "according to his capacity," and his reward "proportioned as far as possible to his services." Owen, however, advocated that individuals "be freely permitted to receive from the general store of the community whatever

36. "On the Definition of Political Economy," in *Collected Works*, 4:321–22, 323.
37. Cf. Schumpeter, pp. 910–11.
38. [Mill] "The Corn Laws" (1825), in *Collected Works*, 4:47–70, at pp. 51–52. Cf. the discussion of discriminating duties in *Principles, Collected Works*, 3:847–48.

they may require," irrespective of the value of their particular contribution. This policy, Mill believed, would weaken the incentives to work; as a result, the "powers of production" would not be called into full activity.[39] Both these examples deal with society's allocation of its resources. Right social policy was indeed Mill's chief concern.[40] But the process of individual maximizing behavior did not wholly escape his attention. In an exchange of letters with Cairnes, Mill outlined a case where a consumer is unable to afford as much as he would like of each of two commodities, and he is therefore forced to "share his demand" between them. His "apportionment of self-denial," Mill suggested, is likely to vary with the relative prices of the commodities, and in such a way—so Mill's phrasing implies—as to reduce the total of forgone satisfaction to a minimum.[41]

This last example directs us to the elements separating Mill from Jevons. What was lacking in Mill's treatment was a statement as to just how far consumption should proceed in each direction for the optimum result to obtain.[42] He was prevented from spelling this out by his not having the notion of marginal utility (in this instance, disutility), or the principle—essential to a maximum or minimum solution—that marginal utility diminishes as successive units of each

39. Owen, *Report to the County of New Lanark* (1820), in G. D. H. Cole, ed., *Robert Owen: A New View of Society and Other Writings*, Everyman Library (London, 1963), pp. 245–98, at p. 289; also Mill's "Closing Speech on the Cooperative System" a speech delivered at the Cooperative Society Debates of 1825, reprinted as "Further Reply to the Debate on Population," *Archiv für Sozialwissenschaft und Sozialpolitik* 62 (1929): 225–39, at p. 232; and his anonymous article, "St. Simonism in London," *Examiner*, 2 Feb. 1834, p. 68.

40. In one sense, Mill's concentration on social policy may be said to have made it unnecessary for him to develop a detailed theory of individual maximizing behavior. Choices, if acted upon, will issue in observable behavior. Assuming, then, that social conflicts, if they appear, are resolvable according to some set of higher criteria, nothing more need be postulated about private maximization than that each individual, being informed about alternatives, knows what he wants and pursues it. On the other hand, even if a theory of individual utility-maximization is developed, it may be deemed inapplicable to the social sphere because of the difficulty of making comparisons of satisfactions between persons. This, we know, was a problem of which Mill was very much aware: see, for example, Hugh S. R. Elliot, ed., *The Letters of John Stuart Mill*, 2 vols. (London, 1910), 2:116.

41. Mill to Cairnes, 5 Jan. 1865, printed in Appendix H of Mill's *Principles, Collected Works*, 3:1089. The other portions of the exchange are also contained in this Appendix.

42. In the other two examples given, complete adoption of one of the alternative courses of action meant that the analogue of this problem on the side of production did not arise.

commodity are consumed (marginal dissatisfaction increases as less of each commodity is available for consumption).

Some possible reasons why Mill did not possess these notions have been examined in the preceding section. The same reasons suffice to account for his inability to transform the postulate of man as a calculating seeker after wealth into the precise rules of behavior which Jevons derived from the maximization principle. It needs only to be added that, from the present viewpoint, Mill's prohibition against the use of mathematics may have been as critical to the final result as was his unwillingness to enquire directly into the laws of enjoyment. The obvious tool for elaborating the assumption of maximizing behavior was the differential calculus. Had Mill applied it, he might have been led to the distinction between total and marginal utility in the process of interpreting his mathematical results.

V

We turn next to Jevons' insight that the laws of value apply equally to commodity prices and to the rewards of the agents of production. In a long preface to the second edition of his *Theory of Political Economy* he wrote: "we must regard labour, land, knowledge and capital as conjoint conditions of the whole produce," and the share of each in that produce as "entirely subject to the principles of value and the laws of supply and demand."[43] This was said by way of showing in which general direction "a true doctrine of wages" must be sought. Jevons did not claim to have worked out the details of the theory of distribution hinted at in these passages, but he saw clearly that it would run counter to several characteristic features of the Ricardian theory of distribution. For example, the ideas that agents jointly determine final output and that each must bargain for "the best share of the produce which the conditions of the market allow him to claim successfully" upset the doctrine that rent forms no part of value and is determined quite independently of "normal" wages and profits.

In outlining his own approach to distribution Jevons indicated that he thought he was only restating a view which had been held by a series of French writers, from Condillac, through Say, to Bastiat and Courcelle-Seneuil. Mill and Cairnes knew the works of most of these

43. Jevons, *Theory*, 2d ed., Preface, pp. l-li.

writers, but they esteemed them much less highly than did Jevons. From their criticisms—especially those of Cairnes—we may hope to learn something of why they preferred their own views on the relation between value and distribution.

These criticisms were wholly methodological. Mill placed great stress on the importance in science of attending carefully to nomenclature and classification: that is, to the names of kinds of things and the arrangement of those kinds into larger classes. He commented on the latter process: "The ends of scientific classification are best answered, when the objects are formed into groups respecting which a greater number of general propositions can be made, and those propositions more important, than could be made respecting any other groups into which the same things could be distributed."[44] Cairnes accepted Mill's views and from this standpoint offered an assessment of Courcelle-Seneuil and Bastiat.

Of Courcelle-Seneuil's *Traité théorique et pratique d'économie politique* (1858) Cairnes wrote:

> The chief fault I find with it is—what I think is characteristic of the French school—a tendency to vicious generalization . . . which, instead of elucidating, darkens the problems. Thus he regards abstinence as a form of labour, rent as a form of interest. Capital is made to cover land as well as wealth in general. . . . It is of course only by dint of straining language that he can make his facts fit into this framework; and thus a sort of haze is thrown over the whole exposition. . . .[45]

A similar comment might have been made about Bastiat's writings.[46] Indeed, in an essay published late in 1870, and which had Mill's approval, Cairnes argued that Bastiat's central results were founded upon "the shifting uses of an ambiguous term."[47]

44. Mill, *System of Logic*, 2:302.
45. Cairnes to Mill, 13 Jan. 1870, Mill-Taylor Collection, vol. LVIA. Mill had previously written to Cairnes saying that, in his view, French political economists shared largely in the defects of French philosophic writers in general, these being "decidedly inferior in closeness and precision of thought to the best English." Mill to Cairnes, 16 Nov. 1869, Mill-Taylor Collection, vol. LV.
46. Compare the points singled out in the passage quoted with pp. 178, 179, 182, 277 of Bastiat's *Economic Harmonies*, trans. W. Hayden Boyers, ed. George B. de Huszar (Princeton, 1964).
47. "Bastiat," in Cairnes, *Essays in Political Economy, Theoretical and Applied* (London, 1873), pp. 312–44, at p. 337.

The term was "service." "Value," Bastiat had written, "is the relation of two services exchanged." He applied this doctrine to all useful objects and acts, including property in land, as well as labor and capital. The ambiguity of which Cairnes complained lay in the fact that "service" might stand, and was intended by Bastiat to stand, for such disparate elements in value as the degree of usefulness, scarcity, and effort embodied in a commodity or act, plus the subjective judgment of the consumer and the pains which he is spared by the fact that others supply the commodity or act which he desires.[48] Cairnes insisted that no single term could embrace these varied and distinct conditions and still retain explanatory power. He compared Bastiat's theory unfavorably with Ricardo's on these grounds. Thus,

> Ricardo, seeking to ascertain the laws to which exchange-value in its various manifestations conforms, analyzes the various conditions under which the phenomenon is found to present itself, classifies them according to their essential distinctions, marking these distinctions by distinct names [monopoly values, (competitive) "market" and "natural" values, domestic and international values], and is thus enabled to show in what way and under what circumstances each class contributes to the ultimate result—the phenomenon of value.

Cairnes continued:

> To tell me . . . that value represents "service" and varies with "service" is to tell me nothing, unless I am told further the elements of "service" which are operative in the given case. This is what Ricardo's theory in effect does: this is what Bastiat's theory fails to do.[49]

48. Bastiat, *Economic Harmonies*, pp. 105–6, 143–45.
49. "Bastiat," in Cairnes, *Essays*, pp. 338, 340. In an anonymous review of Cairnes's *Essays in Political Economy* Jevons dissented from the author's estimate of Bastiat. "On the whole, we think that Mr. Cairnes might have discovered more merit in Bastiat. . . . He remarks that the most recent and important works on political economy, those, for instance, of M. Courcelle-Seneuil, make little reference to Bastiat, so that he has no following; but we are much mistaken if the general disposition of the subject by Seneuil, followed since by Professor Hearn, of Melbourne, in his "Plutology," is not derived from Bastiat. While Mr. Mill has most erroneously denied that consumption of wealth is a branch of political economy, Bastiat logically commenced with human wants and

Elsewhere, Cairnes made precisely the same criticism of Jevons' use of the term "utility."[50] And when Leonard Courtney, in a review of Thornton's *On Labour*, sought to comprehend the cost-of-production theory of value under an extended form of the law of demand and supply, Cairnes evidently felt that an important distinction was thereby obscured, and he wrote to state his emphatic dissent.[51]

Not surprisingly, then, when Cairnes faced the specific suggestion that the phenomena of wages, profits, and rent might be elucidated by the same theory as explains the value of commodities, he expressed a serious doubt whether a comprehensive formula could be found to do the job. Certainly, he agreed, *relative* rewards can be ascertained by applying the laws of value. But the problems of commodity prices, on the one hand, and of the *positive* returns to agents, on the other, were in his view "essentially discrepant." Cairnes objected in particular to the idea that the two problems can be reduced to one by considering each as amenable to the law of demand and supply. Confining himself to the question of wages, he urged that commercial motives, whereby the supply of commodities is adjusted to the demand, do not apply to the supply of labor. To adapt a single formula to these distinct cases would, he said, issue in solutions either true merely by verbal shifts, or false to the real facts.[52] Similarly, Cairnes implied that an attempt to treat land and its reward on the same basis as "the ordinary products of industry" would violate the fundamental truth that products directly or indirectly using land as an input—but *only* they—are subject to the limiting principle of diminishing returns.[53]

---

made the consequent demand and consumption of commodities the natural basis of the science of human wealth. It is probable that when the true logical order of treatment of the doctrines of the science comes to be carefully reconsidered, the order adopted by Mr. Mill will be rejected, and that of Bastiat more nearly followed." *Manchester Guardian*, 10 April 1873, p. 6.

50. Cairnes, *Some Leading Principles*, pp. 11–16.

51. Cairnes to Courtney, 1 Sep. 1869, Courtney Collection, vol. I, British Library of Political and Economic Science. Courtney had written: "the normal or natural as much as the temporary or market value of any commodity depends upon an equilibrium of supply and demand; for, though it is strictly measured by the cost of production under the most unfavorable circumstances under which production is sustained, that range of circumstances is attained only when the quantities produced and brought to market (supply) is equal to the quantities withdrawn from market and consumed (demand)." *Times*, 16 Oct. 1869, p. 4.

52. Cairnes, *Some Leading Principles*, pp. 173–79.

53. "Bastiat," in Cairnes, *Essays*, pp. 327–28, 343. For Mill's views on the

In both these instances Cairnes drew attention to disparities in the conditions governing the *supply* of commodities and agents as his reason for ruling the law of demand and supply inapplicable to the problem of the average rate of wages and to the determination of rent. Certainly he was right to attend carefully to the forces of supply. But he failed in not asking seriously whether a basis for applying the laws of value to factor rewards might be found on the side of demand. To account for this failure it will be helpful to recall Mill's criteria for a good classification. They were two: that it bring out the most numerous, and the most "important," features peculiar to the kinds of things under scrutiny. Mill admitted that what is "important" may vary with the object in view; "and the same objects, therefore, may admit with propriety of several different classifications."[54] Now Cairnes was interested primarily in the average remuneration enjoyed by the whole class of workers or capitalists, and the causes influencing the average well-being of all classes taken together, in questions such as, Why is the return to capital and labor higher in one country than in another? and, Why is it progressing faster in one than another?[55] His interest in these questions, plus his Ricardianism, made him jealous for a classification which brought out, for example, the distinctiveness of the motives governing the supply of labor, and of the forces governing the rate of return in agriculture and related industries. Had Cairnes given more attention to the question of the relative rewards of different laborers and capitalists amongst themselves, and had he been less set against supply-and-demand analysis, he might have come to see, as Marshall did, that the demand for factor services is a derived demand, that for short periods at least price governs cost, and that the rewards of specific types of labor and capital may embody an element of quasi-rent. As it was, he quite failed to appreciate that with the aid of the new principle that values are governed by marginal utility, the value of the product due to an agent of production, and its value to a consumer, may "with propriety" be classified anew, and begin to be investigated, as aspects of a single problem.

---

significance of the principle of diminishing returns see *Principles, Collected Works,* 2:173.

54. Mill, *System of Logic,* 2:305.

55. Cairnes, *Some Leading Principles,* p. 174.

On this interpretation, then, it was Cairnes's choice of problems, together with the ordering of causal factors from which solutions to his chosen questions flowed, that separated him from Jevons and the French tradition of treating value and distribution by the same general laws.

VI

A number of partial explanations have now been offered as to why Mill and Cairnes failed to take the steps necessary to reach the Jevonian position. These steps were of three kinds:

1. The fashioning of new tools: for example, *marginal* utility, and the law of diminishing marginal utility;
2. A redirection of interests and a rewriting of procedural rules, so that the new tools seemed relevant and appropriate (examples of this are the switch in emphasis from the supply side to wants and demand, and the decision to employ mathematics);
3. The envisaging of a unified economic science, organized around the notion of utility maximization.

The relative significance of the reasons outlined above varies according to which step is being considered.[56]

We have not been much occupied with discovery, since the concept of marginal utility and the law of diminishing (marginal) utility were accessible, and actually known, to Mill (in the work of Senior) and to Cairnes (in the writings of Jennings and—almost certainly—of Longfield). The only factor among those mentioned which bears on discovery is the associationist psychology; this made it unlikely that Mill would forge the link between satiety and the idea of diminishing marginal utility.

What of the factors inhibiting Mill and Cairnes from appropriating this idea? Here two things are pertinent. On the one hand there are Mill's methodological convictions, from which we can infer that he would have said that nothing more is explained by speaking of diminishing satisfaction than by saying that a lowering of price

56. The separation of the steps is not complete, nor the ordering fixed. Thus the concept of marginal utility was formed before the new vision, yet without the latter this concept would not have been seen to be of such wide applicability.

is usually necessary if potential buyers are to be induced to consume more of a particular commodity. And, on the other hand, there
is the fact that both Mill and Cairnes were interested mainly in questions which could be answered without paying any special attention
to the laws of enjoyment. There is no way of knowing which of these
factors weighed more heavily in their thinking. Mill's rejection of
a subjective measure of demand, however, follows naturally from,
and therefore probably was secondary to, his interest in the supply
side of things.

So far as the vision of a unified economic science is concerned, here
too methodological factors and the orientation of their interests both
played a part in circumscribing the view taken by Mill and Cairnes,
though in this case methodological factors were secondary. No doubt
their methodological belief that mathematical reasoning ought not to
be applied to wants and enjoyment prevented them from grasping
the significance of Jevons' mechanics of utility maximization. But
what really stopped them from treating value and distribution as
aspects of a single problem was their insistence that land is different
and that labor is not simply a commodity. And this insistence, in turn,
stemmed from a concern with typically Ricardian problems—the price
of food, and the average standard of comfort of the laboring class (in
the determination of which laborers were supposed to be capable of
exercising choice)—and a commitment to Ricardian solutions to those
problems.

Overall, it is probable that Mill and Cairnes were more constrained
by their initial selection of questions to be tackled and by their special
view of what constituted adequate answers than by their methodological beliefs. For Jevons was acutely conscious of the methodological
pitfalls in what he was doing, and he expressed much the same doubts
about them as Mill and Cairnes.[57] Yet he was not deterred from ex-
ploring, as potentially illuminating, lines of thought which simply
failed to spark any interest in them.[58]

57. See, Jevons, *Theory*, chap. 1.
58. This essay was prepared while the author was supported by a Nuffield
Foundation Dominion Travelling Fellowship. Thanks are due to the Foundation and
to Professor A. W. Coats for his helpful comments on an earlier version.

W. S. Jevons and the Foundation of Modern Economics

R. D. Collison Black

We hope to go to Bellagio on Monday and stay about three
nights there, then to Lugano . . .

Mrs. HARRIET JEVONS to her sister, Sarah Taylor,
Milan, 28 March 1874

I

IT WOULD have added to the aptness of this occasion if I had been
able to record that 1871 had seen not only the publication of Jevons'
Theory of Political Economy but also a visit by its author to Bellagio.
Yet the fact that there was an untidy gap of some three years between
those two events may serve to bring out the point of view on which
I base this paper. The centenary of Jevons' first statement of his
theory to the British Association was duly commemorated in 1962;[1]
we are meeting now to commemorate another centenary, but one could
perhaps justify a commemoration in 1979, the centenary of the
publication of the second edition of Jevons' *Theory of Political
Economy* (in some respects more definitive and significant than the
first)—or at almost any other date through the seventies.

In other words, while 1871 may form a convenient focal point at
which to celebrate the advent of marginalism, in my view it is not
correct to think of 1871 as "the year of the marginal revolution."
The phrase "marginal revolution" is attractive, and useful if employed with due caution, but so interpreted, it relates to a process
and not to an event comparable with, say, the establishment of the
Paris Commune. That process was neither begun nor ended in 1871,
though it was certainly significantly forwarded. All this is familiar,

R. D. COLLISON BLACK *is Professor of Economics at The Queen's University of
Belfast.*
1. Cf. *Manchester School* 30 (Sept. 1962): 203–73.

and I think hardly controversial, but the popular use of the term "revolution" tends to confine it so much to striking and violent events that it is perhaps worth emphasizing that the dictionary definition includes "fundamental reconstruction," which can be a lengthy process; and it is this with which we are concerned in the history of economic ideas of a century ago.

That process of fundamental reconstruction which transformed political economy into economics had many facets, but in one sense it could be seen as involving a shift from mainly macroeconomic to mainly microeconomic studies. So while we are surveying the whole process broadly, it may also be appropriate to come down to the micro level and to try to see it from the point of view of one of the main participants, W. S. Jevons.

We do not lack assessments of the life and work of Jevons and of his place in the history of economic thought, and these assessments have been made by some of the most eminent economists of our time,[2] so that for me to go over the ground again might result in that negative utility which, according to Jevons himself, "consists in the production of pain."[3] Instead I propose in this paper to attempt three more specific and limited tasks:

(i) An examination of the special qualities which Jevons brought to the study of political economy;

(ii) A consideration of the effect which they may have had in shaping his approach to the subject and the character of his contribution to it, especially the contribution which he made in 1871;

(iii) A comparison of Jevons' expectations concerning the future development of economics with the development which has in fact taken place in the intervening century.

II

"I think there is some fear of the too great influence of authoritative writers in political economy. I protest against deference for any man, whether John Stuart Mill, or Adam Smith, or Aristotle,

2. J. M. Keynes, "William Stanley Jevons, 1835–1882: A Centenary Allocution on His Life and Work as Economist and Statistician," *Journal of the Royal Statistical Society* 99 (1936): 516–48; reprinted in his *Essays in Biography* (1951 ed.), pp. 255–309; L. C. Robbins, "The Place of Jevons in the History of Economic Thought," *Manchester School* 7 (1936): 1–17.

3. Jevons, *The Theory of Political Economy*, ed. R. D. Collison Black, Pelican classics (Harmondsworth, 1970), p. 114; all page references are to this edition.

being allowed to check inquiry" wrote Jevons.[4] This well-known passage, especially when taken in conjunction with the statement which precedes it, that "in the republic of the sciences sedition and even anarchy are beneficial in the long run to the greatest happiness of the greatest number," has given rise to the impression that one of the qualities which Jevons brought to the study of political economy was the quality of being an outsider and a revolutionary—the man with a chip on his shoulder because he found it hard to get his ideas accepted.

The corollary of this proposition is that there were, at the time when Jevons was developing his ideas, insiders; or to put the matter more formally and precisely in the now familiar terminology of Professor T. S. Kuhn[5] that in British political economy there was a scientific community, its center in J. S. Mill, which had established a paradigm (in the shape of the classical theory of value and distribution) which governed their view of the economic world and enabled them to cope with its problems by the puzzle-solving techniques of normal science. However, awareness of anomalies was creating a state of crisis in the subject, giving opportunity for the emergence of revolutionary theories, preparatory to the occurrence of a radical paradigm shift.

How far does the experience of Jevons accord with this interpretation of the situation? In parts it accords with it quite well, in parts rather badly. In fact it seems to me to demonstrate that Kuhn's theory of scientific revolutions is itself a paradigm which is inadequate to explain all the facts.

In the first place, Kuhn's concepts relate to a scientific community whose field of research is not generally accessible to the layman, and whose members essentially report to one another.[6] Yet, as Professors Spengler and Eagly have argued,[7] economics did not attain

4. Jevons, *Theory*, p. 261.
5. Kuhn, *The Structure of Scientific Revolutions* (Chicago, 1962). Cf. A. W. Coats, "Is There a 'Structure of Scientific Revolutions' in Economics?" *Kyklos* 22 (1969): 289–96; M. Bronfenbrenner, "The 'Structure of Revolutions' in Economic Thought," *History of Political Economy* 3, no. 1 (Spring 1971): 136–51.
6. Kuhn, pp. 20–21.
7. J. J. Spengler, "Exogenous and Endogenous Influences in the Formation of Post-1870 Economic Thought," in *Events, Ideology and Economic Theory*, ed. R. V. Eagly (Detroit, 1968); cf. pp. 159–60, 189–90.

to this stage of professionalization until the post-1870 period. According to Kuhn, this would place the subject in a "pre-paradigm" phase; yet most of us would feel inclined to accept that classical political economy had established a paradigm.

In fact the state of economic thought in England from about 1850 to 1870 suggests that a discipline may very well have reached the stage of establishing a paradigm without being fully professionalized. Now an outsider who seeks to introduce new ideas, ultimately leading to a paradigm shift, has two problems—that of getting his ideas published in a reputable form, and that of getting them accepted. It would seem that when a subject is not professionalized, the first of these tasks at least ought to be easier; it is therefore interesting to find that one of the outsider economists of the period held precisely the opposite view.

In his *Recent Political Economy* published in 1867, William Lucas Sargant complained of the fact that England possessed no professional economic journal comparable with the *Journal des Economistes* in France:

> The natural result is an entire discouragement of individual inquiry, for who will work out a new theory, when he has no means of securing public attention? The more original is an author, the less will he be relished by the reading world; unable to appreciate him, and shrinking from the trouble of unlearning the lessons it has acquired; the more dependent therefore is such an author, on the good offices of those who profess to weigh the merits of new publications.
>
> So low has England sunk in an ignorant contempt of innovation in Political Economy, that new principles are not merely condemned: they are even refused a hearing, unless they are put forth by a friend of the reviewer: personal partialities and antipathies have taken the place of discriminating justice. An author, the cut of whose beard is disliked, may publish at his own expense and will not have the poor satisfaction of being abused.[8]

8. W. L. Sargant, *Recent Political Economy* (1867), Introduction, p. v. Sargant (1809–89) was a Birmingham small-arms manufacturer. He wrote a number of economic works which show independence of mind, if not great originality.

Was Jevons one of those who suffered from this state of affairs? The evidence on this point is mixed, but it is noteworthy that his first successes came, not with his *Notice of a General Mathematical Theory of Political Economy*, but with his empirical works—his Statistical Diagrams and *A Serious Fall in the Value of Gold*. This fits interestingly with Sargant's argument, for the *General Mathematical Theory* was a piece which could only be addressed to and understood by an audience of professional economists, whereas the other works were such as could be appreciated by laymen and particularly by businessmen.

It is true that in the case of his statistical diagrams and *A Serious Fall* Jevons had to resort to publication at his own expense, and that he was at first depressed and discouraged by the lack of interest in them;[9] it is true also that one of the first notices which his diagrams received in the *Economist* could be put down to "personal partialities," for it was the work of Richard Holt Hutton, who was related to Jevons by marriage.[10] Nevertheless some of the best notices of Jevons' work came unsolicited, and it was not long until he had achieved recognition beyond his expectations.[11]

So it would appear that it was not only "the cut of an author's beard" which mattered in the literary London of the 1860's; editors and reviewers were not necessarily hostile to a young unknown who had something worthwhile to say. However if the initial difficulties of getting his work published in a reputable form did not prove too serious for Jevons, to have the content of his theories accepted by his peers was another matter. I shall refer to this question again

9. Jevons, *Letters and Journal of W. Stanley Jevons* (1886), pp. 162, 175; and cf. Rosamond Könekamp, "William Stanley Jevons (1835–1882): Some Biographical Notes," *Manchester School* 30 (Sept. 1962): 262–63.

10. This review appeared in the *Economist* 19, no. 1267, 15 Nov. 1862. Richard Holt Hutton (1826–97) was married to a granddaughter of William Roscoe, Jevons' maternal grandfather. Hutton was best known as editor of the *Spectator* and at this time had just begun his long association with Meredith Townsend on that paper. However, he still retained a connection with the *Economist*, of which he had been nominally editor from 1858 until 1861 under the direction first of James Wilson and then of Walter Bagehot. Cf. A. Buchan, *The Spare Chancellor* (London, 1959), p. 127.

11. E.g., the review of the Statistical Diagrams in the *Exchange Magazine* referred to in *Letters and Journal*, p. 178. Cf. also the attention and public praise given to *A Serious Fall* by Cairnes and Fawcett. R. D. Collison Black, "Jevons and Cairnes," *Economica* 27 (Aug. 1960): 214–32.

later in this paper;[12] here I am concerned only to underline the point that there is a distinction between being accepted as a reputable author on a subject and having all one's theories accepted. Some of Jevons' own comments, and some of the interpretations placed on them by others, have tended to obscure this.

There is another attribute which Jevons brought to the study of economics which has not received anything like as much attention, but which I suggest is of considerably greater importance. Jevons was, as Keynes put it, "the first theoretical economist to survey his material with the prying eyes and fertile, controlled imagination of the natural scientist."[13] In this respect he was genuinely one of the "new men"—coming from an intellectual background markedly different to that of the established figures in political economy—and his approach to the subject might therefore be expected to be novel and challenging.

I suggest that it may be more relevant and valuable to look at Jevons, not in relation to the scientific community of economics (an entity whose existence *circa* 1860–70 I presume to question), but in relation to more recognized and recognizable communities in the natural sciences, particularly of chemists, astronomers, and meteorologists. It was in 1858 that Jevons reached the conclusion that "there are plenty of people engaged with physical science, and practical science and arts may be left to look after themselves, but thoroughly to understand the principles of society appears to me now the most cogent business."[14] At this time his training and experience were mainly in applied chemistry, although his personal research had led him into meteorology, "a sort of difficult *scientific exercise* rather than a science itself."[15] In chemistry Jevons had distinguished connections; he had been recommended for his post as assayer in Sydney by his teacher Thomas Graham, professor of chemistry at University College, London, and afterwards master of the Mint. On his return from Australia Jevons was told by Graham that he would have been prepared to recommend him for a post at the Kew Observatory, and

12. Below, end of Sec. III.
13. Keynes, *Essays in Biography*, p. 268.
14. *Letters and Journal*, p. 101.
15. *Ibid.*, p. 89. Cf. Keynes's contention that Jevons "approached the complex economic facts of the real world, both literally and metaphorically, as meteorologist." *Essays in Biography*, p. 267.

in 1862 Graham again offered to place Jevons in a lectureship in natural philosophy at the Andersonian Institution in Glasgow.[16]

Jevons was also strongly influenced by his cousin Harry Roscoe,[17] who was one of Bunsen's research students at Heidelberg and became professor of chemistry at Owens College, Manchester. It was the example of Roscoe which led Jevons towards scientific studies, Roscoe who arranged the reading and publication of his early papers, and Roscoe who was disappointed by his cousin's decision to become a political economist.

These early papers of Jevons were concerned with such problems as the forms of clouds; when Jevons sent copies of them to the great astronomer Sir John F. W. Herschel in 1861, they were favorably received and correspondence between the two men continued over the ensuing decade.[18] So it seems clear that Jevons could have made at the least a respectable career as a practitioner of "normal science" in chemistry or meteorology. He never lost his interest in the natural sciences, and indeed one of the very last papers which he published was on a meteorological topic—"Reflected Rainbows."[19]

On the foundation of this basic training in experimental science Jevons deliberately built a further training in logic and mathematics so that he ultimately acquired a knowledge of scientific method which was both broad and deep. This is abundantly demonstrated in his massive *Principles of Science* (1874), which has largely been ignored by economists, no doubt, as Professor Ernest Nagel has suggested, because it lacks any specific treatment of the methods of social science.[20] However Dr. Wolfe Mays has argued that "there is a close relationship between Jevons' philosophy of the natural sciences and his methodology of the social sciences," and I think it must be accepted that he has made out his case.[21]

16. W. S. Jevons to F. B. Miller, 5 Oct. 1859; Jevons to Henrietta Jevons, 3 March 1862, in unpublished letters in the Jevons Papers.

17. Sir Henry Enfield Roscoe (1833–1915), professor of chemistry at Owens College, Manchester, 1857–85; vice-chancellor of the University of London, 1896–1902; M.P. for Manchester (Southern Division), 1885; privy councillor, 1909.

18. W. S. Jevons to Sir John Herschel, 21 July 1861, in Herschel Papers, Royal Society, London.

19. *Field Naturalist*, Aug. 1882.

20. Nagel, Introduction to the Dover ed. of Jevons, *The Principles of Science* (New York, 1957), pp. lii–liii.

21. W. Mays, "Jevons's Conception of Scientific Method," *Manchester School* 30 (Sept. 1962): 223.

Two particular points made by Mays seem to me of special significance in relation to Jevons' economic work. The first is that "following Boole and De Morgan, he believed that any rational system of ideas could be put into symbolic form. The system could then be operated on according to the laws of logic to produce a chain of deductions. In discussing the logical method to be used in economics, Jevons therefore emphasized its deductive character." Mays goes on to emphasize that the familiar criticism of Jevons as a mathematical economist who knew very little mathematics misses the point that "as far as his formal studies were concerned Jevons was essentially a logician trying to base mathematics on logic." The second point is that "Jevons no doubt under the influence of his meteorological work . . . put considerable emphasis on the study of statistical data in economics."[22]

Both of these points can be explained by the nature of Jevons' early training and interests as a man of science; both have considerable importance in explaining the character of his contribution to economics in general and to economic theory in particular.

III

"The keystone of the whole Theory of Exchange," said Jevons, "and of the principal problems of Economics, lies in this proposition— *The ratio of exchange of any two commodities will be the reciprocal of the ratio of the final degrees of utility of the quantities of commodity available for consumption after the exchange is completed.*"[23]

Now this certainly represented a pathbreaking change in economic theory; and it may be instructive, as Professor Spengler has said, to ask "of the path-breaker, why he elected to break a particular path."[24] Professor Spengler adds that to answer such questions we need adequate biographical information, and in attempting to answer them for Jevons I think we shall realize again the truth of Professor Jaffé's statement: "If we consider carefully a truly original concept, even one couched in austere mathematical symbols, we find that it is inevitably composed of an intricate combination of elements which are derived not only from the discoverer's social, intellectual, and physical

22. Mays, pp. 233, 236, 228.
23. Jevons, *Theory*, p. 139.
24. Spengler, p. 179.

environment, but also from his own personal traits, attitudes and endowments."[25]

In dealing with the question posed above, the distinction, which again we owe to Professor Spengler,[26] between the *core* and the *shell* of economics makes a useful point of departure. Few economists today would question that the concept of economizing behavior is an essential part of the core of their subject, but with the classical economists this was not so. Now, as I have argued elsewhere,[27] what Jevons was attempting to do from 1860 onwards was to formulate and present the "true theory of economy" as "a very contracted science"—and this he himself states clearly as the objective of the *Theory of Political Economy*: "But as all the physical sciences have their basis more or less obviously in the general principles of mechanics, so all branches and divisions of economic science must be pervaded by certain general principles. It is to the investigation of such principles—to the tracing out of the mechanics of self-interest and utility, that this essay has been devoted."[28]

So my contention is that Jevons was really setting out to establish the core of our subject as a science of economizing behavior, and the reasons for his so doing can be found in his intellectual environment and in his personal circumstances. First of all, this is clearly the approach of a man trained in the natural sciences, the element in Jevons' intellectual background which I have stressed. Yet, secondly, it is an approach which grew out of Jevons' solitary years in Australia. Examination of his personal journal and correspondence, particularly during 1858–59, shows that he then thought long and deeply about his own position and prospects in terms of "using life with true economy and effect";[29] his conception of political economy as "a sort of vague mathematics which calculates the causes and effects of man's industry, and shows how it may best be applied" dates from that time also.

Many writers have felt that, as Professor Blaug says, "A change

25. W. Jaffé, "Biography and Economic Analysis," *Western Economic Journal* 3 (Summer 1965): 224.

26. Spengler, p. 187.

27. Black, Introduction to the Pelican Classics Edition of Jevons, *Theory*, pp. 12–13.

28. Jevons, *Theory*, p. 50.

29. W. S. Jevons to Lucy Jevons, 11 Jan. 1858; *Letters and Journal*, p. 99.

of emphasis as drastic as the marginal revolution . . . must surely
have been associated with changes in the institutional structure of
society and with the emergence of new practical problems.''[30] Nothing
of this kind can be readily traced in the circumstances under which
Jevons lived while preparing his theory; but if the interpretation put
forward here is correct, it is unnecessary to look for it. For, as Professor Spengler has argued, a thought system which is based upon
concepts by postulation is much more likely to be impervious to ex-
traneous influences than one which is based on concepts by intuition—
and this is precisely the type of logical thought system which Jevons
was constructing.[31]

If Jevons was attempting to set out the core of economic behavior (as a process of maximizing utility) then it would seem that
the mathematical logic of the process should have been more important to him than the psychological assumptions of hedonism, and
I think that Jevons' own statements are consistent with this view.
On any occasion when he expounded his conception of the changes
which were taking place in economic studies, and his own contributions
to them, he laid primary stress on the mathematical aspects of the
utility concept as involving a functional relationship between variables.[32]

Ross Robertson has indeed suggested that ''the Benthamite approach was thoroughly understood by Jevons and subtly rejected,''
and Wolfe Mays has gone on from this to argue that ''Jevons's statement that economics deals with pleasures and pains would then seem
little else but a *façon de parler*. . . . Jevons is . . . giving an operational
definition of pleasure and pain in terms of our economic transactions.''[33] It would tend to strengthen and complete my own line of

30. Mark Blaug, *Economic Theory in Retrospect*, 2d ed. (1968), p. 5.
31. Spengler, p. 165. Spengler defines concepts by postulation as ''concepts
by intellection, imagination, perception, the meaning of any one of which 'in
whole or in part is designated by the postulates of some specific deductively
formulated theory in which it occurs,' and the use of which in scientific and
philosophic analysis entails the use of formal logical reasoning, deduction and
mathematics.'' Cf. F. S. C. Northrop, *The Logic of the Sciences and the Human-
ities*, chaps. 5 and 13.
32. Cf. ''The Mathematical Theory of Political Economy,'' *Journal of the
Royal Statistical Society* 37 (1874): 478–88, and especially p. 487.
33. Ross M. Robertson, ''Jevons and His Precursors,'' *Econometrica*, July
1951, pp. 233–34; Mays, 240–41. Compare Northrop's firm assertion that ''Jevons'

argument here if I could accept these views; but I do not think that Jevons in the *Theory of Political Economy* "subtly rejected" the Benthamite approach. His economics would have been better if he had —he could, for example, have come much closer to realizing his ideal of a quantitative science of economics if he had dealt simply with the "laws of demand" instead of trying to determine the "laws of utility."[34]

Adherence to Benthamism may well have been a main reason for Jevons' oft-remarked failure to construct a complete and consistent marginal theory of value and distribution. However, there were other reasons for this also. When Jevons was preparing the second edition of his *Theory*, he told Walras: "My idea now is to produce a considerable volume with full references, descriptions and quotations from works on the math-method, also including translations of Cournot's and your works, and with the best abstract I can get of Gossen." He did not carry out this program, and Walras made no attempt to conceal his disappointment at the failure.[35]

Earlier, in 1875, Jevons had promised Walras that in that year he would give papers on mathematical economics to the Political Economy Club and to Section F of the British Association. He gave addresses to both bodies in 1875, but the first was on railway administration and the second on the coal question. This suggests a reason for the failure to live up to the expectations of Walras—Jevons simply was not a one-subject man. Having worked out and published his ideas on the basic "mechanics of utility and self-interest," he was anxious to move on and contribute to some of the many other subdivisions into which he conceived economics must be separated.

It is not the purpose of this article to discuss or evaluate the contributions which Jevons made to subdivisions of economics outside the theory of value and distribution. Yet it is impossible to place his

---

economic theory presupposes a specific philosophical theory" (i.e., Bentham's). Northrop, p. 350.

34. Cf. my note 41 to p. 174 of Jevons, *Theory*. I have attempted to explore the relationships between Jevons' economics and Bentham's utilitarianism somewhat further in the Jevons Centenary Lecture delivered at University College, London, "Jevons, Bentham and De Morgan," *Economica* 39 (May 1972): 119–34.

35. Jaffé, *Correspondence of Léon Walras and Related Papers* (Amsterdam, 1965), 1:599, 645. Walras wrote: "Je vous avouerai franchement que je n'ai pas trouvé que vous ayez fait de cette publication ce qu'il était possible d'en faire. . . ."

contribution to the development of marginalism in proper perspective without referring to them. So it should be remembered that after his first statement of the "true theory of economy" had failed to gain attention, Jevons turned to prosecute his studies in the statistical analysis of monetary problems with considerable success, even while he was devoting much time to the development of his system of logic.

By 1871 Jevons was well established in his chosen profession of social scientist—the Manchester professor traveling to London to read his papers to the [Royal] Statistical Society, to give evidence before parliamentary committees, to be consulted by the chancellor of the Exchequer.[36] It was, then, as an applied economist that his contemporaries knew and respected him, rather than as a theorist; "je vous connaissais de réputation, mais seulement comme auteur de travaux estimés sur la question de la variation des prix et de la dépréciation de la monnaie," wrote Walras to Jevons at the outset of their correspondence. "Je vous savais mathématicien, mais je me figurais que vos applications mathématiques étaient plûtot statistiques qu'économiques."[37] This comment suggests a view of Jevons which may in itself account to some extent for the failure of the *Theory of Political Economy* to gain rapid acceptance. Not only were its contents radically new, but they also came from an unexpected quarter. As the ideas of the marginalists gained ground, Jevons' reputation as a theorist grew; but although he did his share in propagating those ideas, he could not devote the whole of his restless energy and fertile mind to them. Already in 1875 he had begun to investigate "the Solar Period and the Price of Corn," and he had still to write many of the papers which were later collected into *Methods of Social Reform* and *Investigations in Currency and Finance*.

Jevons might well have returned to the core of theory if time had been given him. In the time that was given him, it may be asked, did he maximize the returns from his efforts by spreading them as widely as he did? Perhaps marginalism might have advanced more quickly had he concentrated more narrowly upon it; yet in the last analysis such speculation is surely, in every sense of the word, an impertinence. The history of every science is molded in part by the character of those who advance it, and it was not in the character of Jevons to advance

36. Cf. *Letters and Journal*, pp. 241, 245, 246.
37. Walras to Jevons, 23 mai 1874, in Jaffé, 1:397.

economics otherwise than as he did—by successive attacks on a number of fronts. To be one of the founders of marginalism was only one of his achievements, and in judging those achievements it must be remembered that the span from the time when Jevons presented his first paper to the British Association as a young unknown to the time of his death was just under twenty years. Few economists, indeed few scientists of any sort, can have accomplished so much in so short a lifetime.

IV

We are now perhaps in a position to see Jevons' *Theory of Political Economy* both in the wider perspective of his work in economics as a whole and in the longer perspective of a century of the development of economic thought since. As we look back over that century it may be instructive to consider what Jevons, as one of the participants in the "marginal revolution," thought the future development of economics should be and how far his expectations have been realized.

As is well known and documented, the 1870's were a period of heart searching and stock taking in economic thought,[38] and Jevons took his share in the process. His views on "The Future of Political Economy" are set out in his 1876 inaugural lecture of that title and in the Preface to the second (1879) edition of the *Theory*.[39] From these sources Jevons' specifications for the future shape of economics can readily be put together, and it is obvious that in his view it involved much more than simply the working out of the marginal principle.

Jevons frequently stated his belief in the "complete inductive method," which involved the combination of deductive reasoning with empirical verification. Hence, he was in no doubt that "the present economical state of society cannot possibly be explained by theory alone,"[40] but equally clear that empirical and historical studies alone

38. Cf. T. W. Hutchison, *A Review of Economic Doctrines, 1870–1929* (London, 1953), chap. 1.

39. Jevons, "The Future of Political Economy," Introductory Lecture at the opening of the session 1876–77 at University College, London, Faculty of Arts and Laws. *Fortnightly Review* 20 (Dec. 1876): 617–31, reprinted in *Principles of Economics* (1905), pp. 187–206.

40. *Ibid.*, p. 195.

would be valueless without the aid of deduction. From this followed his well-known prescription for "the present chaotic state of Economics": "Subdivision is the remedy. We must distinguish the empirical element from the abstract theory, from the applied theory, and from the more detailed art of finance and administration. Thus will arise various sciences, such as commercial statistics, the mathematical theory of economics, systematic and descriptive economics, economic sociology, and fiscal science."[41]

The basic theory of economy—all that was attempted in the *Theory of Political Economy*—must be essentially mathematical in character, while the empirical studies would involve the application of statistical method. Professor Spengler has pointed out that "the welding of statistical and mathematico-economic theory did not proceed apace until in or after the late nineteenth century,"[42] but it was certainly envisaged by Jevons in 1871, and he emphasized that "the future progress of economics as a strict science must greatly depend upon our acquiring more accurate notions of the variable quantities concerned in the theory."[43] So Jevons can be seen to have envisaged economics as developing into a strict science or complex of sciences, with a mathematical core and a statistical shell.

Looking back on the *Theory of Political Economy* after a century we may be tempted to echo Keynes's exclamation: "How disappointing are the fruits, now that we have them, of the bright idea of reducing Economics to a mathematical application of the hedonistic calculus of Bentham!"[44] We may reasonably point out the dangers inherent in Jevons' overenthusiastic identification of the theory of economy with elementary mechanics. Was not this sort of thing the cause of that sorry state of affairs now prevailing and recently described by Martin Shubik, in which "with the arrogance that characterizes our profession it is customary to refer to a set of moderately dull exercises on some constructs arising from mediocre, casual utilitarian psychological theorizing as 'the theory of consumer choice' "?[45]

Perhaps it was, but in justice to Jevons we should remember that

41. Jevons, *Theory*, Preface to 2d ed., pp. 49–50.
42. Spengler, p. 173.
43. Jevons, *Theory*, p. 174.
44. Keynes, *Essays in Biography*, p. 155.
45. Shubik, "A Curmudgeon's Guide to Microeconomics," *Journal of Economic Literature* 8 (June 1970): 410.

all he was attempting was a pioneer statement of one, certainly fundamental part of what he envisaged as a highly complex science. Whatever we may say about the marginal revolution, none of us would deny that we have lived through another revolution in economics in the last twenty years; and if we were asked to say in what that revolution consists, we would probably point to the increasing rigor of theory and to the stress on econometric testing of it. If Jevons could be called upon to give his opinion of the economics of 1971, I suspect that he would only express surprise that it has taken us so long to get so far; for are we not now applying those lessons of the need for logic and measurement which he taught? I would contend that these, more than any statement of marginal utility theory, are the true hallmarks of his originality and the true sources of the contribution which Jevons the scientist made to the foundation of modern economic science.[46]

46. In an interesting article reporting on the various commemorations of the centenary of the "birth of Marginal Utility Economics" held in 1971, Dr. P. J. Uitermark has pointed out that some of the main features of the assessment of Jevons presented here are anticipated in S. J. Chapman, *Outlines of Political Economy* (new ed., 1920), pp. 448–49. Chapman there noted that Jevons "realized to the full the technical possibilities of Utilitarianism" and "assimilated research in positive economics to research in the natural sciences." This very concise and well-balanced account of Jevons' contribution to the development of economics does not appear in the original (1911) edition of Chapman's *Outlines* and was unknown to me until Dr. Uitermark sent me a copy of his paper, "De Geschiedenis van de Economie, 1871–1971: Een Verslag," *De Economist* 119, no. 6 (Nov.-Dec. 1971): 719–39.

Léon Walras's Role in the "Marginal Revolution" of the 1870s

William Jaffé

I

ON THE occasion of a centenary, far from being a fault, it is particularly fitting to tell a twice-told tale . . . lest we forget, lest we forget. Although so much has already been written, and well written, by this time about the "marginal revolution"[1] that it is difficult to think of anything new to say, yet there is a danger that we may forget what transpired a hundred years ago in the history of economic theory, because that "revolution" has been so radically transformed and transmuted since its beginnings that all trace of its pristine character tends to fade away in our memories.

The successive and often contradictory reevaluations of the "marginal revolution" of the 1870s leave the historian of economics in the 1970s perplexed, wondering whether it is more appropriate dolefully to commemorate the "marginal revolution" as a disaster or joyfully to celebrate the event as heralding a great leap forward in the progress of economics. If the historian recalls his right role, however, he will do neither, but be guided in his judgment of a Jevons, a Menger, or a Walras by Shakespeare's sage comment, "So our virtues/Lie in the interpretation of the time" (*Coriolanus*, IV, vii).

The assessment of Léon Walras's "virtues" was, however, one thing at one time when the "marginal revolution" was simply inter-

WILLIAM JAFFÉ *is Professor of Economics at York University, Toronto.*

1. Perhaps better called "marginal revolt" or "marginal insurrection," since the "revolution" in standard economics was not an accomplished fact for several decades after the 1870s. Marginalism itself, considered as a mathematically expressed incremental concept, but applied to productivity rather than utility, had made its appearance earlier in von Thünen's *Isolierte Staat*, vol. 2 (1850); see Thünen (1930), pp. 584–87. I shall, nevertheless continue using "marginal revolution" in this paper as a term consecrated by usage which is, after all, just as apposite as "Newtonian revolution" in the history of science. If I enclose the term in quotation marks, it is only to emphasize the obvious, that I am not responsible for the nomenclature.

preted as the overthrow of the labor or cost-of-production theory of value by the marginal utility theory; and it became quite another thing later on when the "marginal revolution" was interpreted as the commencement of model building on a grandiose scale, in which equilibrium is defined as a set of marginal equalities pervading the entire system of exchange, production, capital formation, and money under ideal competitive conditions. The latter-day image being essentially mathematical, the revolution of the 1870s was viewed also as the turning point in the metamorphosis of economics from a branch of intuitively reasoned literary discourse into a rigorous mathematical discipline.

As there is no clear limit to the variety of interpretations that can be placed upon the "marginal revolution" after the event, let us turn to the event itself, viewed as a *marginal utility* innovation, and see how Léon Walras came to take part in it. Then, in the interpretation of *his* time, we may be better able to arrive at a reasonable appraisal of his "virtues."

II

Léon Walras first entered upon the scene as a revolutionary on August 16 and 23, 1873, when he read his paper, "Principe d'une théorie mathématique de l'échange,"[2] in Paris before the Académie des Sciences morales et politiques. It was from beginning to end a daring paper, a clarion call for a new approach to the theory of value and for the transformation of political economy into a mathematical science, issued, moreover, by a mere novice, an "outsider," making his debut as an economic theorist.[3] Loud and clear though

2. Léon Walras [hereinafter referred to as L.W.] (1874a). In the republication of 1883, L.W.'s curves representing the marginal utility (i.e., *rareté*) functions were changed. They had originally been drawn as straight lines and appeared again as straight lines in the 1st ed. of the *Eléments* (Léon Walras, 1874b), but in the 1883 version and subsequent editions of the *Eléments*, they appear curvilinear in form. See Jaffé (1954), pp. 567–68, Collation Note [b] to Lesson 8; and Jaffé (1965a), 2:574, Letter 412, in which the change was announced.

3. In the *Séances et travaux de l'Académie des Sciences morales et politiques* (L.W., 1874a), the paper was listed among the "Communications des savants étrangers," a bitter pill for L.W., who was as much a Frenchman as the academicians, though he did come from a foreign professorial post in Lausanne to deliver his paper. For an account of the reception of the paper by his audience, see Jaffé (1965a), 1:334–36, n. (7) to Letter 232, and for L.W.'s reactions, see ibid., pp. 332–34, Letter 232, and pp. 370–74, Letter 256. Cf. Jaffé (1954), p. 44.

the call was, it fell on hostile, uncomprehending ears. Walras left the meeting, enraged and defiant.

Little did he suspect at the time that he had fellow insurgents of the same ilk, who had, in fact, stolen a march upon him. When he learned shortly afterwards that he was not the very first to have issued a marginal utility manifesto, he was discountenanced; but he need not have been, for his "Principe d'une théorie mathématique de l'échange" possessed an extremely important feature, outlined in high relief, which had been barely hinted at in W. Stanley Jevons's *Theory of Political Economy* or in Carl Menger's *Grundsätze der Volkswirtschaftslehre*, both of 1871. It was this distinguishing feature which placed Léon Walras rather than Jevons or Menger in direct line of filiation with the modern development of economic analysis since the 1930's. What this feature was will appear in the course of the following sketch of Léon Walras's maiden analytical paper of 1873.

The paper opened with a statement of the relation of pure economics to applied economics, pointing out that before we can weigh the relative merits of *laisser-faire, laisser-passer* on grounds of efficiency or justice, we must first investigate "the natural and necessary" consequences of free competition in exchange and production. Given, to start with, certain predetermined quantities of productive services, it will inevitably follow from the free play of competition that, after a while, (i) certain definite quantities of various products will be turned out; (ii) each of the products will have a definite price at each instant of time; and (iii) each of the productive services will also have a definite price at each instant of time. The object of pure theory is then to inquire how these three natural effects of "free competition," i.e., the quantities of products, their prices, and the prices of the productive services, are determined. The answer to this inquiry is found by solving a system of equations in which the three effects of "free competition" appear as unknowns.

The problem seen in this way is, as Walras observed, "extremely vast and complicated," but it can be simplified by considering it in two stages. In the first stage, production is assumed away, so that the problem is reduced to one which Walras enunciated as follows: "Given certain quantities of commodities, to formulate a system of equations of which the prices of the commodities are the roots." This is what the mathematical theory of exchange is all about. Once the first stage has been completed, the way is open to the second stage. Now production is taken into account and the commodities whose quantities were given in advance in the theory of exchange are replaced by products resulting from purchases of productive services in suitable combinations. In the second stage, therefore, the problem becomes, in Walras's words: "Given certain quantities of productive services, to formulate a system of equations which has for its roots: (1) the quantities produced of the products; (2) the prices of these products; and (3) the prices of the productive services."

Thus, in Walras's hands, pure economics assumed the form of what he called a "physico-mathematical" science. He made no claim that this was anything really new. It had long been that sort of a science, as is seen in the writings of the Physiocrats and in the treatises of the English economists from Ricardo to John Stuart Mill. The trouble was that these economists did their mathematical thinking in everyday language, and hence cumbersomely and ineptly. Cournot, according to Walras, was the first to have undertaken to apply mathematics to economics explicitly and competently; and for having shown him the way, Walras expressed his profound gratitude to Cournot. At the same time Walras insisted that in his own work he had followed a line of his own, quite different from that of Cournot. His economics was different in that he took "free competition," which he considered the general case, as his starting point and studied monopoly only as a special case, whereas Cournot had taken monopoly as his starting point and proceeded from there by steps to an analysis of unlimited competition. Walras pointed out also that his mathematics was different in that he relied for his formal demonstrations mainly upon the elementary principles of analytical geometry, whereas Cournot had recourse exclusively to the infinitesimal calculus.

At this point Walras announced that in the remainder of his paper he would confine his attention to the theory of exchange in its simplest conceivable form, where only two commodities are traded for each other. Sections II to IV of the paper read before the Academy were little more than a crisp and crystal clear résumé of Lessons 9 to 13 inclusive of the first edition of the *Eléments*,[4] in which Walras dealt in analytical detail with the problem of price determination in a perfectly competitive market where only two commodities are traded.

4. Corresponding to Lessons 5, 6, and 7 of the definitive edition, L.W. (1874b).

Though the first instalment of the first edition of the *Eléments* had not yet been published (it did not make its appearance until July 1874),[5] by June 1873 Walras already had in hand the proofs of sixty pages embodying his mathematical theory of exchange.[6] In at least one respect the résumé was superior to the *Eléments*: only in his 1873 paper did he explicitly undertake "to define with precision the mechanism of free competition by which we suppose our market to be regulated." It comes out more clearly in the résumé than in the *Eléments* that Walras meant by an ideally perfect competitive market one in which there is no friction or viscosity in the flow of bids and offers to a central point where positive or negative excess demand is eliminated prior to the closing of any contracts. Contracts are then executed at a unique current equilibrium price. The process of elimination of excess demand is normally entrusted in the best-organized markets to brokers, whose procedures are so mechanical that a "calculateur" (a computer!) might have done just as well, though— Walras surmised in 1873—not as quickly.[7]

If that were all Léon Walras had to say in his first analytical paper, it might well have earned for him our praise for having perceived in Cournot's demand function the basis of an elegant reformulation of the old familiar theory of supply and demand, but it would hardly have earned for him a place among the initiators of the "marginal revolution" in our histories of economics. Fortunately, the paper

5. Jaffé (1965a), 1:410–11, Letter 284.
6. Ibid., 1:319, n. (3) to Letter 218.
7. L.W.'s operational definition of the competitive market was further elucidated in a subsequent article, "La bourse, la spéculation et l'agiotage" (1880), and was slightly elaborated upon in an undated manuscript which came to light in 1966 when it was discovered in a forgotten cupboard of the Bibliothèque Cantonale et Universitaire de Lausanne, inside a folder containing L.W.'s long-lost translation of W. S. Jevons's *Theory of Political Economy* (see Jaffé, 1965a, 1:570-72, Letter 410; and pp. 644-48, Letter 465). The published article describes the operations of the Paris stock exchange as precluding not only nonuniformity of price but also any trading at "false prices." "Si la quantité demandée et la quantité offerte sont égales, il y a *prix courant* et l'échange a lieu à ce prix; les titres passent des mains des agents vendeurs à celles des agents acheteurs, ou du moins l'affaire est conclue, sinon réglée. Autrement, l'échange n'a pas lieu." It was because of this characteristic of the *modus operandi* of a well-organized market that L.W. saw no reason to introduce the use of "tickets" (provisional contracts) in his theory of pure exchange, and not because he overlooked trading at "false prices" in this theoretical analysis as I previously suggested (Jaffé, 1967). In the Walrasian perfect market, there is no such phenomenon to take into account. See L.W. (1898), pp. 407–9.

did not end with a bare theory of the competitive market mechanism. It went on to two more sections in which Léon Walras expounded his theory of *rareté*, or, as we should call it, his theory of marginal utility. Section V was headed "How demand curves result from utility and the quantity possessed," and Section VI, "Analytical definition of the exchange of two commodities for each other. *Rareté*: the cause of value in exchange." *Rareté*, for Walras, constitutes the underlying motive force which furnishes the power to run the competitive market mechanism. As Sections V and VI of the paper simply resume Lessons 14 to 18 of the first edition of the *Eléments*,[8] there is no need to repeat the argument here.

There is need, however, to call attention both to the manner in which Léon Walras introduced his marginal utility principles and to the role he assigned to it in his "Principe d'une théorie mathématique de l'échange" and his *Eléments*. It is this, more than anything else, which distinguishes Léon Walras from his corevolutionaries and which made him, rather than Jevons or Menger, the favorite ancestor most frequently honored in the latest developments of economic theory since the 1930s. R. G. D. Allen wrote in 1956, "The analysis of equilibrium of exchange was left by Walras in a form to which only minor glosses need be added."[9]

From the very start, Léon Walras introduced his marginal utility theory immediately into his analysis of market price determination without considering it in any other context. His whole attention was focused on market phenomena and not on consumption. This is evident from the fact that in postulating diminishing marginal utility he said nothing more in his 1873 paper and in the first edition of the *Eléments* than "I submit" ("je pose en fait") or "It must be admitted" ("Il faut admettre")[10] that the intensity of want for an additional unit or fraction of a unit of a commodity decreases as the consumption of that commodity increases. Consumption, however, is only mentioned incidentally. While the driving force in the theory of exchange is, as Walras saw it, the endeavor of all traders to maximize their several satisfactions, it is marketplace satisfactions rather than

8. Corresponding to Lessons 8, 9, and 10 of the defintive edition, L.W. (1874b).
9. Allen (1956), p. 314.
10. L.W. (1874b), §§74–75 of Lesson 14, corresponding to §§74–75 of Lesson 8 of the definitive edition.

dining-room satisfactions[11] which Walras had in mind. His passing allusions to consumption served only to reveal that he was perfectly aware that all trading is done with a view to ultimate consumption and that general experience in consumption influences the trader's market decisions. Walras went no further than this because, in effect, he defined the whole realm of economics in terms of catallactics.[12] He would have overstepped the bounds of a catallactic science had he done more than consider his *rareté* or marginal utility functions as exogenously determined parameters. The apparatus the economist has at his disposal no more fits him to derive these functions from consumption experience than to derive them from their presumed physiological, psychological, or sociological determinants.

This view is, I believe, borne out not only by the general tenor of Walras's argument throughout the *Eléments* in all its editions but also by certain subtleties in phrasing. For example, in his 1873 paper he defined *rareté* as the "intensity of the last want satisfied by the *quantity possessed* of a commodity."[13] In the first edition of the *Eléments* he defined *rareté* more technically as "the derivative of *effective* [i.e., total] *utility* with respect [again] to the *quantity possessed*."[14] It is curious that in the second edition of the *Eléments* (1889), without offering any explanation and without changing anything else in the context, he changed *"quantity possessed"* to read *"quantity consumed"* in these definitions.[15] I suspect he did this more as an accommodation than out of principle, in order to bring his definition into conformity with those of Jevons and Menger with whose writings he had become familiar in the interval between the appearance of the first and second editions of his *Eléments*. In whatever edition we consult the *Eléments*, we find that it is via exchange in the competitive market and by no other process that Walras supposed his traders to achieve the proportionality between *raretés* (or marginal utilities) and prices, given only two sets of exogenously determined parameters: (i) the marginal utility functions of the traders,

---

11. Cf. Stigler (1965), p. 124.

12. Archbishop Richard Whately's term for the Science of Exchanges. Cf. Schumpeter (1954), p. 911.

13. L.W. (1874a), §V, italics in original.

14. L.W. (1874b), §75 of Lesson 14, italics in original.

15. Ibid., §75 of the 2d ed. (1889). Cf. Jaffé (1954), p. 568, Collation Note [c] to Lesson 8.

and (ii) their initial endowments (or initial "quantities possessed").

Locating his marginal utility theory where he did, as an integral part of his theory of the determination of competitive market prices, Walras succeeded far better than either Menger or Jevons in forging a clearly defined analytical link between marginal utility and market price. Analytically, Menger got no further than to demonstrate the relation between given scales of "Bedürfnissbefriedigungen" and the quantities exchanged in the case of two isolated barterers trading horses for cows.[16] Though Menger clearly intended to extend his marginal utility theory to explain price formation in a competitive market, when he finally worked up to the case of "beiderseitiger Concurrenz," the connection between his marginal utility scales and price formation lost its analytical firmness.[17]

Whether Jevons's performance in this respect was superior to Menger's depends upon the interpretation one places on the argument from which Jevons derived his famous "equations of exchange."[18] So vague was Jevons's method of harnessing his "final degree of utility" theory to the determination of prices in a competitive market, that Walras was left with the impression that no such harnessing took place at all. In his famous letter of May 23, 1874, in which he acknowledged Jevons's priority in formulating the concept of marginal utility with mathematical precision, Walras declared that Jevons had missed the opportunity to derive the "equation of effective demand" from considerations of maximum utility, a derivation essential, so Walras contended, to the solution of the problem of the determination of equilibrium price.[19]

If Walras did Jevons less than justice, Edgeworth was inclined to do him more than justice. How can one say, as Edgeworth did, that Jevons gave a lucid description of the working of a perfectly competitive or "open" market which results in the establishment of

16. Menger (1871), pp. 163–67, corresponding to pp. 183–87 of Dingwall and Hoselitz (1950).

17. Ibid., pp. 201–5, corresponding to pp. 216–20 of Dingwall and Hoselitz (1950).

18. Jevons (1871), p. 100 of the 4th ed., corresponding to p. 143 of the Pelican ed.

19. Actually, as Professor Samuel Hollander pointed out to me, "Jevons took prices as *data* during his analysis of exchange, so that he cannot be said to have dealt with price determination at all, though he himself seems to think that he did." S. Hollander to W. Jaffé, 27 July 1971.

a uniform price?[20] Moreover, the illustration by which Jevons introduced his theorem of proportionality between "final degrees of utility" and prices in order to determine "the results of exchange," viz.,[21]

$$\frac{\phi_1(a-x)}{\psi_1 y} = \frac{\phi_2 x}{\psi_2(b-y)} = \frac{y}{x} = \frac{p_1}{p_2}$$

looks for all the world like an example of isolated barter, albeit between "trading bodies."[22] Edgeworth denied this, invoking Bishop Berkeley's "representative particular" in order to show that, though the trading Jevons described is done by a couple of individual dealers, "there is presupposed a class of competitors in the background." Edgeworth's erudite interpretation remains unconvincing. It is by no means evident that Jevons was aware of the implications Edgeworth later ascribed to his argument. All one can say is that Jevons juxtaposed his account of price determination in a perfectly competitive market with the theory of "final degree of utility."[23] It requires an excessively strained interpretation to see in this juxtaposition anything like the analytical integration which we find in Walras.

III

Of special interest to the historian of economic analysis is the question, How did Léon Walras arrive at his particular conception of marginal utility, the distinctive characteristic of which lay, as we have seen, rather in the employment of the idea than in its formulation? Fortunately, Léon Walras left to posterity a mass of documents revealing much of his private mental history.[24] These documents, besides shedding additional light on the genesis of the "marginal revolution," constitute excellent material for a case study of the process of scientific discovery.

20. Edgeworth (1881), p. 109. Rather than lucid, Professor Donald A. Walker regards Jevons's description as "confused, obscure and incomplete." D. A. Walker to W. Jaffé, 10 July 1971, in which Professor Walker announces he is writing a paper on this matter.

21. Black (1970), pp. 22 and 204.

22. Jevons (1871), pp. 88–90 of the 4th ed., corresponding to pp. 135–36 of the Pelican ed.

23. Jevons (1871), pp. 114–18 of the 4th ed., corresponding to pp. 152–55 of the Pelican ed.

24. For a description of the depositories of these documents, see Jaffé (1965a), 1:xii.

The story thus unfolded does not, alas, possess high dramatic qualities. We do not have here a case where a fundamentally novel theory occurred to the discoverer in a single illuminating flash nor one in which the discoverer appears congenitally endowed with serendipity in any extraordinary measure. On the contrary, Léon Walras's path toward his solution of the problem of exchange value was long and tedious. It had been first blazed ineffectually by his father, Auguste Walras, in 1831,[25] and was then trodden and retrodden by Léon, who began in 1859 and got nowhere until 1872. Léon Walras's contribution to the "marginal revolution" was, in fact, the fruit of efforts of two generations of Walrases.

Auguste Walras first turned his mind to the theory of value and to economics generally when, during a brief interval in his early career, he embarked in the late 1820s upon the study of law and became dissatisfied with the juristic conception of property as defined in the Civil Code.[26] Being of a philosophical frame of mind, and no doubt influenced by the attacks of the socialists of his day on the legitimacy of private property, he sought a more logically coherent basis than the socialists had to offer for drawing the line between public property and private property. He then consulted the principal economic treatises, both French and English; and again he was disappointed.[27] The trouble lay in their faulty theories of value, for without a satisfactory theory of value an adequate theory of property was impossible, since nothing is appropriated, whether for public or private use, unless it has value.[28] Neither the English labor or cost-of-production theory of value, nor the French utility theory would do. The true source of value, Auguste Walras argued, is not labor or cost of production or utility, but *rareté*, by which he meant literally scarcity. Only those things that are scarce, that is, limited in quantity as well as possessing

25. Auguste Walras [hereinafter referred to as A.W.] (1831).

26. L.W. (1908), pp. 2–3. For two excellent accounts in English of A.W.'s theory of property and value, see Gray (1931), pp. 333–36; and Howey (1960), pp. 28–32. See also "Avant-propos," A.W. (1831), pp. i-xxiv, corresponding to pp. 53–65 in Leduc (1958).

27. The principal French economists A.W. consulted were J. B. Say, Destutt de Tracy, Charles Ganilh, Nicholas Massias, and Simonde de Sismondi; the English economists, Adam Smith, David Ricardo, James Mill, and John Ramsay McCulloch. See Leduc (1938), p. 303, n. 1; and pp. 308–9, n. 54.

28. A.W. (1831), pp. x-xiii, corresponding to pp. 57–59 in Leduc (1938).

utility, have value; and only to such things are property rights attached.[29]

In order to give an air of precision to the common-sense meaning of the term *rareté* or scarcity, he defined it as the ratio of the number of persons desiring the good, each person being presumed to want no more than a single unit of the good, to the total quantity of the good available.[30] In the course of time, Auguste Walras became aware of a fundamental flaw in his mathematical definition of *rareté*. He wrote to his son Léon on May 18, 1861, that he was troubled by the fact that individuals frequently want more than one unit of a good, depending on their tastes, their age, their sex, their wealth, etc.[31] Since individuals differ from one another in so many respects, we cannot fall back upon the expedient of counting a person wanting, say, two units of a good as two persons and so forth. Auguste Walras now perceived that the first term of the ratio by which he first thought *rareté* could be defined and measured must be meaningless, made up as it is of a sum of incommensurable, non-additive entities. Since this "difficulty," as he called it, renders impossible the establishment of a standard unit of want (*unité de besoin*), Auguste Walras concluded that until such difficulties are surmounted, economics could not become a mathematical science like mechanics, physics, acoustics, and optics.

It was the challenge implicit in his father's conclusion which incited Léon to long labors that eventuated in his marginal utility theory. As Léon was the first to acknowledge, he owed much to his father for having adumbrated the problem,[32] but it is evident that he could not possibly have attained to any conception at all of marginal utility by pursuing Auguste Walras's line of reasoning. Even Auguste Walras's comparison of *rareté* to speed was spoiled as a potentially fruitful hint, when he added, "Just as speed is a ratio of distance covered to the time taken to cover it, so *rareté* is a ratio of the sum of wants to the total supply of goods available to gratify the wants."[33]

29. Ibid., chap. 4, corresponding to pp. 99–112 in Leduc (1938).
30. Ibid., p. 151, corresponding to p. 176 in Leduc (1938). Cf. Howey (1960), p. 31, where the ratio is inverted.
31. [A.W.] (1913), pp. 147–50. For fuller bibliographical information on A.W.'s published letters to L.W., see Jaffé (1965a), 1:19, n. (3) to Letter 1. Cf. Howey (1960), p. 31, and Leduc (1938), p. 306, n. 24.
32. For example in L.W. (1908), p. 172.
33. [A.W.] (1913), pp. 148–49.

If it was not Auguste Walras who directly inspired Léon Walras's discovery of marginal utility, was it anyone else? Surely it was not Cournot, who deliberately backed away from any analysis of the relation of utility to demand.[34] Could it have been Jean Jacques Burlamaqui (1694–1748), a professor of law in Geneva, whose name Léon Walras coupled with that of his father as having furnished the correct solution of the problem of the origin of value?[35]

I cite the obscure Burlamaqui, who does not appear in Schumpeter's encyclopedic *History of Economic Analysis*, rather than a score of others whose names have been made familiar in studies of the prehistory of marginal utility, because Burlamaqui was one of the few early writers on the subject with whose work we may be sure Léon Walras was familiar in his formative years as an economist. Auguste Walras had quoted extensively from the *Elémens du droit naturel*, which was posthumously made up of Burlamaqui's lecture notes[36] and first published in the original Latin in 1754 and in French translation in 1820. The French version found its way into Léon Walras's private library,[37] presumably by inheritance in 1866.

The *Elémens du droit naturel* is of especial significance, not only because Auguste Walras had declared that Burlamaqui's doctrine of value was in every respect like his own[38] but more importantly, from the point of view of tracing the filiation of ideas, because Burlamaqui's chapter "On the Price of Things and Services Traded" (which followed his discussion of property),[39] was essentially a systematic restatement of Samuel von Pufendorf's theory of value enunciated in

34. Cournot (1838), chap. 1, §3, and chap. 4, §21.
35. L.W. (1874b), §155 of Lesson 27, corresponding to §157 of Lesson 16 of the definitive edition.
36. Burlamaqui (1821), Preface of anonymous editor, pp. xvii–xix.
37. Burlamaqui (1821) is listed in an inventory of L.W.'s books drawn up by his daughter, Aline Walras, after his death. The list is contained in two copybooks which were bequeathed to Professor Gaston Leduc, who generously passed them on to me. See Jaffé (1965a), p. xii.
38. "La doctrine de Burlamaqui . . . est la mienne." A.W. (1831), p. 212, corresponding to p. 220 in Leduc (1938).
39. Burlamaqui (1821), part 3, chap. 11, pp. 209–19. Chaps. 8, 9, and 10 deal with property in a manner foreshadowing A.W.'s. How closely Burlamaqui anticipated A.W. on value is seen in the following passage: "Mais l'utilité seule . . . ne suffit pas pour mettre un prix aux choses, il faut encore considérer leur *rareté*, c'est-à-dire la difficulté que l'on a de se procurer ces choses, et qui fait que chacun ne peut s'en procurer aisément autant qu'il en veut" (ibid., p. 212).

De officio hominis et civis in 1675.[40] Thus, Pufendorf's utility-cum-scarcity theory of value and price exerted via Burlamaqui very much the same influence on Auguste Walras as it did via Gershom Carmichael and Francis Hutcheson on Adam Smith, so far as we can judge from Adam Smith's *Lectures on Justice, Police, Revenue and Arms.*[41]

Apparently unaware of Pufendorf's still earlier anticipations of his doctrine of value and property, Auguste Walras looked upon Burlamaqui as his true forerunner. In the *Elémens du droit naturel* he found confirmation of his theory of *rareté* and was, therefore, all the more confident in using it to expose the errors he attributed to Adam Smith and Ricardo of the English school and to Condillac and J. B. Say of the French school.[42] Auguste Walras admitted that the English and French authors whom he attacked had occasionally brought *rareté* into the picture (true, above all, of Condillac),[43] but

40. The following passage from Pufendorf, quoted in W. L. Taylor (1965), p. 63, lies at the origin of Burlamaqui's doctrine (see above, n. 36): *"Hence an increase of value tends to be produced especially by scarcity. . . .* For articles in everyday use prices are raised especially when their *scarcity* is combined with *necessity or want."*

41. Cf. Taylor (1965), chap. 2, pp. 63-72. In Adam Smith's brief discussion, "Of the Natural Wants of Mankind" found in his *Lectures*, he appears also to have apprehended the principle of diminishing utility, which he expressed as follows: "Nothing without variety pleases us. . . . Uniformity tires the mind." Smith (1896), p. 159. See below, n. 44, for Nassau Senior's similar expression of the idea.

42. A.W. (1831), chaps. 12, 13, and 14; and A.W. (1849).

43. A.W. was not entirely just to Condillac. Though at one point Condillac wrote, "La valeur des choses est donc fondée sur leur utilité" (Condillac, 1798, p. 10), he followed this up almost immediately with the corollary, "La valeur des choses croît dans la rareté, et diminue dans l'abondance" (p. 11), exactly A.W.'s thesis. Moreover, Condillac advanced the very argument A.W. later used to attack the English school, "Une chose n'a pas de valeur, parce qu'elle coûte, comme on le suppose, mais elle coûte parce qu'elle a une valeur" (p. 14). Condillac went further and discoursed upon the relationship of utility-cum-scarcity to trading behavior, first in the case of isolated two-party barter, and then in market exchange, where price is determined by demand and supply. Ibid., chap. 2. Though Condillac does not name Turgot in this context, his whole argument reads like an attempt to clarify Turgot's unfinished piece, "Valeurs et monnaies" (1769), where Turgot comes remarkably close to expressing in words the theory of proportionality between marginal utilities and ratios of exchange. See Turgot (1844), 1:85. As L.W.'s private library is known to have contained both Condillac's *Le Commerce et le gouvernement* and the *Œuvres de Turgot* (see above n. 37), these writings may well be regarded as direct sources of inspiration of the work of both Walrases. L.W., however, continued to reflect his father's view that Condillac, like J. B. Say, founded value on utility rather than scarcity. See L.W. (1874b), §155, corresponding to §157 of the definitive edition.

he contended that they did so only parenthetically or too unsystematically, which prevented them from perceiving unequivocally that value has its ultimate source in *rareté* and in nothing else.

For all their penetrating insight into the bearing of scarcity on value and price, neither Burlamaqui, nor Genovesi, nor Turgot, nor Condillac, nor Nassau Senior, all authors whom Léon Walras had apparently read at an early stage,[44] can be said to have offered a likely lead to anything like a rigorous formulation of the theory of marginal utility. They never sharpened their argument to a fine analytical point; their disquisitions on value were even more discursive than those of Auguste Walras. Little more can be claimed for the previous literature which we have reason to believe Léon Walras had consulted before 1874 than that it posed the problem. It did not contain any anticipatory suggestions of the way in which Léon Walras finally solved the problem. We are left, therefore, with no alternative but to search for such suggestions in Léon Walras's manuscripts and worksheets.

IV

We begin with his manuscript entitled "Application des mathématiques à l'économie politique" and designated as "1ère Tentative, 1860."[45] It was a sorry performance which he had the good sense never to submit for publication. The whole effort centered around a

44. L.W. named Nassau Senior along with Antonio Genovesi (1712–1769) as precursory exponents of the doctrine of scarcity. See L.W. (1874b), §159, corresponding to §161 of the definitive edition. Senior had written in 1836, "Of the three conditions of value, utility, transferableness and limitation in supply, the last is by far the most important. The chief sources of its influence on value are two of the most powerful principles of human nature, the love of variety [cf. n. 41 above] and the love of distinction [*pace* Veblen!] . . . . Not only are there limits to the pleasure which commodities of any class can afford, but the pleasure diminishes in a rapidly diminishing ratio long before those limits are reached." Senior (1938), pp. 9–10. As Professor Leduc informs us, A.W. published a review article in 1836 on a French version of Senior's writings which had appeared that year under the title, *Principes fondamentaux de l'économie politique, tirés des leçons édites et inédites de N.W. Senior* par le comte Jean Arrivabene. See Leduc (1938), p. 38 and pp. 309–10, n. 61. A.W.'s article was published in the *Revue Mensuelle d'Economie Politique*, 1836, pp. 359–68. In Genovesi the scarcity doctrine is more implicit than explicit, unsystematically developed and wanting in even a semblance of rigor. See Genovesi (1769), part 2, chap. 1.

45. The manuscript, classified under the mark F.W. V, 1 in the Fonds Walras at the Bibliothèque Cantonale et Universitaire de Lausanne, is described and summarized in Jaffé (1965a), 1:216–17, n. (33) to Letter 148.

labored attempt to assign meaning to the proposition that "the price of things is in inverse ratio to the quantity offered and in direct ratio to the quantity demanded," where quantity offered was defined as the total existing quantity in the possession of the several individuals in the world considered and the quantity demanded as the sum total of their wants or needs. He employed precisely drawn three-dimensional diagrams to illustrate his function, $V = F(q_d, q_0)$, and lost himself in a maze of simple algebra, all in an effort to confute Cournot. Auguste Walras's quasi-mathematical definition of *rareté* upon which his argument was founded led him completely astray. The "1ère Tentative" represented no advance at all toward the goal he was destined eventually to reach.

The next analytical manuscript, also entitled "Application des mathématiques à l'économie politique," but designated as "2ème Tentative, 1869–1870,"[46] is quite different and shows that in the interval, while he was engaged in a succession of occupations and enterprises that left him little leisure for theorizing, he had made considerable progress in shaping the structural pattern of his general equilibrium model. He formulated an equation of exchange[47] which he later used in his *Eléments*,[48] and then proceeded to develop his theory of the mechanism of exchange, first in the case of a two-commodity market, and then in the case of a multi-commodity market, again foreshadowing the *Eléments*.[49] This did not dampen his misconceived resolve, dating from the "1ère Tentative," to prove Cournot wrong in dismissing as meaningless the ratio of the quantity demanded of a commodity to the quantity offered.[50] Léon Walras still clung to his father's idea of *rareté*, which he expressed as the ratio of the utility of a commodity for all consumers taken together to the total

46. The manuscript of the "2ème Tentative" is preserved along with that of the "1ère Tentative" under the same classification mark (see above, n. 45), and is described and summarized in Jaffé (1965a), 1:217–21, continuation of n. (33) to Letter 148. The second and third parts of the "2ème Tentative" reveal recognizable anticipations of the structural features of L.W.'s later theories of production, capital, money, economic progress, national income, and taxation, with which we are not here concerned.

47. The equation, $mv_a = nv_b$, was probably derived from Isnard. See Jaffé (1969), pp. 25–28.

48. L.W. (1874b), §44 in all editions.

49. Ibid., §§ 44 and 108–14. See Jaffé (1965a), pp. 573–74, Collation Note [h] to Lesson 11.

50. Cournot (1838), chap. 4, §20.

quantity of that commodity in existence—though now with a shade less confidence. Reflecting his father's late misgivings, which had been disclosed to him, as we have seen, in 1861, Léon admitted that since the first term of the ratio is a non-linear function of the second, a fixed standard of measure of relative *rareté* is impossible. His tortured algebra was of no avail.

It was this mixed bag of bungled mathematical economics and fruitful insights into a general equilibrium model that Léon Walras brought with him when he arrived in Lausanne in December 1870 to take up his post as professor of economics. There was certainly nothing in that bag which would point to his eventual role as a marginal revolutionist, except his dogged persistence in trying to make sense of his father's *rareté*.

The final manuscript of interest to us in studying Léon Walras's progress toward marginal utility consists of notes he prepared at Lausanne for a series of lectures he undertook to deliver in Geneva in January 1872.[51] Here we can see that even at that late date he still fell far short of the mark. For present purposes, we need only consider the notes for the third, fourth, and fifth lectures, which dealt with utility in the theory of exchange.

At a point where he discussed the demand curve for a given commodity, he enumerated the factors determining the curve as follows: (a) "l'utilité d'extension," which determines the intercept of the demand curve on the quantity axis; (b) "l'utilité d'intensité," which, he said, determines the slope of the demand curve; (c) the total existing quantity of the commodity; and (d) the distribution of the total quantity among the holders of the commodity. He remarked that the second of these factors is imponderable.

Utility came again into his discussion in connection with what he called "price curves." These "price curves" represent demand price as the function of a fixed total quantity offered for sale in the market at whatever price it can fetch. As these fixed total quantities are assigned different values, i.e., as the quantity parameter is shifted, different prices ensue, and thus Walras obtained a special kind of demand curve which he called a "price curve." He subsequently in-

51. This manuscript, entitled "Système des phénomènes économiques," is classified under the mark F.W. V, 1 in Lausanne and is summarized in Jaffé (1965a), 1:293–96, n. (2) to Letter 293.

troduced this concept into the *Eléments*,[52] but made very little of it there, whereas in his Geneva lecture notes of late 1871 he drew from it strange inferences concerning the relationship of utility to the "price function." He named the total area (QOP in Fig. 1, drawn in the Walrasian manner, with price measured on the horizontal axis) under such a curve "virtual utility"; he described as "effective utility" the area of any rectangle (qOpm) inscribed within the curve with one of its corners on the curve and the diagonally opposite corner at the origin; he regarded the mixtilinear triangle (mpP) outside the rectangle and bounded on one side by the price axis as "the quantity of wealth which those who pay [a certain price (Op)], would, if necessary, be willing to yield above and beyond the wealth they actually do sacrifice."

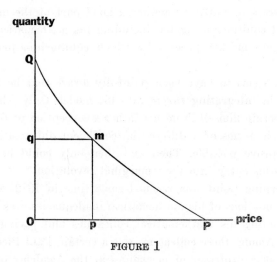

FIGURE 1

What have we here but Dupuit's construction, including Dupuit's consumers' surplus, without any mention of Dupuit's name! This is indeed strange when we remember that in the 1877 instalment of the first edition of the *Eléments*, Walras went to great lengths to demolish Dupuit's theory and to denounce it as "one of the gravest of errors."[53] In after years, Léon Walras and Pareto never tired of anathematizing Dupuit, Alfred Marshall, and Auspitz and Lieben for

52. L.W. (1874b), §152, corresponding to §153 in the definitive edition.
53. Ibid., §§368–70, corresponding to §§385–87 of the definitive edition.

allegedly identifying demand curves with utility curves.[54] In Walras's and Pareto's eyes, this was *the* sin against the Holy Ghost. But, as we have just seen, Walras in his unregenerate days, in 1871, prior to seeing the light, committed the selfsame sin, identifying the utility curve not with an individual's demand curve, but, worse than that, with a market demand curve. At that time, he seemed totally oblivious of the fact that this implied interpersonal comparisons of utility as well as the assumption of the constant marginal utility of whatever it was that was given in exchange for the commodity demanded. Neither of these implications had any place in Walras's definitive version of the marginal utility theory that was to make its first appearance quite soon in the paper he read before the Académie des Sciences morales et politiques in August of 1873. Certainly at the opening of 1872, Léon Walras was still floundering, though he had made progress in putting together a good part of the machinery of his general equilibrium model, including his mathematical theory of the aggregate market process by which equilibrium prices are determined.

Walras seems to have been painfully aware that he had not yet succeeded in integrating *rareté* into his model. Only when he managed to liberate himself from his father's conception of *rareté* and to redefine it in terms of a differential coefficient did a satisfactory integration prove possible. Then and then only could he be said to have made his entry into the "marginal revolution."

The turning point was reached some time in 1872. Walras, who was quite conscious of his mathematical inadequacies, was in the habit of buttonholing his mathematical colleagues and plying them with questions. Among these colleagues was a certain Paul Piccard (1844–1920?), then a professor of mechanics at the Academy of Lausanne. We do not know exactly how Léon Walras framed his question, but it appears from a letter he wrote to Piccard after the event[55] that the question had something to do with the derivation of demand curves from considerations of utility and quantity. That this was very probably the case is clear from an undated manuscript signed by Paul

54. Jaffé (1965a), 2:343–47, Letter 913; pp. 421–23, n. (3) to Letter 990; pp. 485–87, Letter 1051; and pp. 488–89, Letter 1052. See also Pareto (1906), p. 585, §56 of the Appendix; and Pareto (1960) 1:373, Letter 162, and 3:60–63, Letter 561.

55. Jaffé (1965a), 1:345–47, Letter 239.

Piccard and found in a sheaf of Walras's papers all from the year 1872.[56] This manuscript contained an answer to just such a question.

What Piccard did was to furnish Léon Walras with the simplest analytical tools required for establishing the condition of maximum satisfaction for a trader. Piccard's exposition was on an extremely elementary level, probably in deference to Walras's limited mathematical attainments at this time. The demonstration was practically all geometrical; only the conclusions were translated into analytical symbols. Starting with two negatively inclined marginal utility curves, which Piccard called the "courbes de besoin" of a given trader for commodities (A) and (B) respectively, and assigning to the trader a certain quantity of (A) and no (B), he supposed a given price of (A) in terms of (B) to be current in the market and asked what our trader would do under the circumstances to improve his situation as measured by the sum of bounded areas under the curves. Piccard pointed out that the sum of the bounded areas is maximized, subject to the condition now known as the budget constraint, when exchange is carried to the point where the last small increment of area under the trader's marginal utility curve of commodity (B) is equal to the corresponding last small decrement of area under the trader's marginal utility curve of commodity (A). Piccard, after translating into symbols the dimensions of the small areas relinquished and acquired at the critical point where maximization of the trader's satisfaction is achieved, then stated what was really a first-order condition of equilibrium for the trader, namely, equality between the marginal utility of the amount of (B) acquired and the marginal utility of the balance of (A) retained multiplied by the reciprocal of the price of (A) in terms of (B). In order to reduce the equation to one containing only two variables, the quantity of (B) acquired was expressed as the product of the quantity of (A) given up multiplied by its price in terms of (B), thus:[57]

$$\psi(A_0 p_a) = \frac{1}{p_a} \phi(Q_a - a_0)$$

56. Ibid., 1:309–11, n. (4) to Letter 211, where the manuscript is described and the text published in full.

57. In this equation, Q_a is the trader's original endowment in (A), A_0 is the amount of (A) given up in exchange, p_a is the price of (A) in terms of (B), and ϕ and ψ are the marginal utility functions of commodities (A) and (B) respectively.

So, at least, the equation appears inserted on the manuscript in Walras's hand, to correct a slip in Piccard's demonstration. Piccard concluded, "This equation is none other than that of the required curve, for the only variables it contains are p_a and A_0." Actually, he had derived an offer curve; but since in the two-commodity case, an offer curve of one commodity is derived from the demand curve for the other commodity, it doesn't make any essential difference.

Unquestionably it was from Piccard's mathematical demonstration that Léon Walras distilled his refined and analytically tractable conception of marginal utility. Piccard's method of deriving an individual's demand curve from marginal utility curves furnished Walras with the indispensable clue to his discovery of the fundamental theorem of proportionality of the *raretés* of commodities to their market prices,

$$r_a : r_b : r_c : \ldots \; :: p_a : p_b : p_c \ldots$$

Nevertheless it was truly Léon Walras's discovery,[58] for Piccard's note could hardly have helped him unless he had previously set himself the problem, first suggested by his father, of relating utility-cum-scarcity to the determination of market prices. It is no wonder Walras persisted in calling marginal utility by the inherited term *rareté*, even after he learned of other terms in the literature—if only to mark the origins of the discovery.

How much Auguste Walras's drive was behind this discovery is seen in Léon's retention of his father's slogan, "*rareté* is the cause of value." Now Léon was able to endow the slogan with a semblance of cogency, for both Walrases envisaged the causal nexus in terms of two necessary, but admittedly not sufficient, conditions:[59] universal concomitance and exact proportionality. Walras's theorem established just such a nexus between *raretés* and market prices.

V

On reaching the end of the tale of Léon Walras's tortuous journey to marginal utility, one is left with the nagging question, Why did

58. Cf. Walker (1970), p. 688. In my judgment, Professor Walker is inclined to underestimate the credit due to L.W. for the discovery and to overestimate that due to Piccard.

59. A.W. (1849), in Leduc (1938), p. 330. Cf. Jaffé (1954), p. 512, n. (3) to Lesson 10.

Léon Walras have to wait until Piccard, a professor of mechanics and not an economist at all, pointed the way? The answer, I believe, lies in Léon Walras's inadequate mathematical training. Though in his youth he had taken special mathematical courses in preparation for the entrance examinations of the famed Polytechnic School of Paris, and though, after twice failing these examinations, he was finally admitted upon examination to the Paris School of Mines, he still knew nothing about the extreme values of functions.[60] His secondary-school education had equipped him with a fair knowledge of algebra and analytical geometry, but only the vaguest notions of the calculus. After that, as he himself later acknowledged,[61] he spent his time reading about the history of the calculus instead of working out its problems. He could hardly have learned anything more at the School of Mines, where he was a student in name only—in order to give himself an acceptable status in the eyes of his parents while he dabbled in novel writing.

The fault, however, was not entirely his. In Léon Walras's youth the teaching of the calculus was in an underdeveloped stage. We know, for example that in the 1830's, when Cournot was asked to give a course of lectures on the differential calculus at Lyons, so novel did the subject appear that auditors flocked to the lecture hall in large numbers, only to dwindle to ten as the successive topics treated became too difficult for the untutored to follow.[62] No wonder, for the only pertinent books available were advanced treatises on the differential and integral calculus which, being intended for specialists, slurred over demonstrations of the elementary principles. In the absence of textbooks designed for beginners, systematic teaching of the subject was quite impossible. It was not until 1860 that the first introductory calculus textbook[63] appeared in France for the benefit of students primarily interested in applications.

60. This is evident from a manuscript dated "4 décembre 1853" which I have recently (1966) identified as L.W.'s, though it was misclassified in the Fonds Walras among A.W.'s paper under the mark F.W. VI. Written at the time he was studying for his entrance examinations, it was an elaborate exercise in "The Decomposition of Rational Functions into Partial Fractions," but shows no clear understanding of the theory of maxima and minima.
61. See L.W.'s "Notice autobiographique" in Jaffé (1965a), p. 2.
62. Cournot (1913), pp. 155–56.
63. Haton de la Goupillière (1860). See Jaffé (1965a), 1:528, n. (3) to Letter 372, for a quotation from Haton de la Goupillière's "Avant-propos."

This suggests a hypothesis or, let us say, until further evidence is accumulated about the teaching of the calculus in countries other than France, a surmise which may help explain not only why it took so long for economic theorists to formulate the marginal utility principle but also why in the early 1870s three discoverers independently hit upon very much the same solution of the same age-old problem. Only then had Newton's and Leibnitz's inventions begun to trickle down to the classroom. When a knowledge of the calculus ceased to be an esoteric attribute of pure mathematicians and physicists, when it became generally one of the intellectual attainments of educated persons whose schooling was not exclusively literary, then economists within the wider circle of the mathematically cultivated, pondering upon the confused efforts of the past to relate utility to price, might quite spontaneously perceive the calculus way out of the confusion. At least, that was the way found by Jevons and Léon Walras.

We cannot be sure that Carl Menger furnishes a counterexample until we know something about his education, or at least whether he had been exposed to the calculus. Von Hayek assures us that "there is no reason to believe that he [Menger] lacked either the technical equipment or the inclination [toward mathematics]."[64] Unless we are prepared to dismiss out of hand the possibility of intellectual osmosis, we cannot ignore the fact that Carl Menger's brothers were intensely interested in mathematics. Consequently, it is not altogether unlikely that also in Menger's case the discovery of marginal utility may have been suggested by the calculus.

VI

What conclusions can be drawn from the above worm's-eye view of the "marginal revolution," disclosing but a small corner of the spectacle? Does serious attention to the details of Walras's life here recounted distort rather than illuminate an understanding of his scientific work, as, it seems, Professor Stigler[65] would have us believe?

64. F. A. von Hayek, biographical introduction to Menger (1871), L.S.E. Reprint, p. ix. Carl Menger, however, objected in principle to the use of mathematics as a research tool or as a fundamental method in economics, though he granted that it might serve as a convenient mode of demonstration or exposition. See Jaffé (1965a), 1:768, Letter 566; and 2:2-6, Letter 602.

65. Stigler (1970), p. 426. Professor Stigler asks the question, "What relevance have the details of a man's personal life to the nature of his sci-

Does it not rather throw a more penetrating light on the significance of Walras's contribution when it is seen how he fitted his newly found marginal utility principle into his slowly unfolding general equilibrium scheme? Does this not also make it more apparent that whatever the weaknesses and defects of the marginal utility principle may be, whether we have abiding faith in subjective motivation or abjure it in favor of its outward and visible signs, Léon Walras's role in the "marginal revolution" was clearly to delineate the need[66] and the place in a general equilibrium model for some such power-generating engine to activate the market mechanism? Does not the biographical narrative of Léon Walras's awesome voyage of discovery of marginal utility in terms of a differential coefficient reveal the voyage as an academic adventure, directed in large part by prevailing pedagogic winds? Does this not, at the same time, broaden the context of W. Stark's and Mark Blaug's relativist-absolutist dichotomy[67] by

---

entific work?'' He answers that "biography distorts rather than illuminates the understanding of scientific work," and, presumably alluding to my article on "Biography and Economic Analysis" (Jaffé 1965b), cites me as having recently given "the opposite answer." If Professor Stigler is inveighing against the fallacy of the *argumentum ad hominem*, he is undoubtedly right and there is no opposition between our views. Just as "the personal history of Gauss is entirely irrelevant to the question of the adequacy of his proof that every equation has a root" (Cohen and Nagel, 1934, p. 380), so also the personal views and actions of Knut Wicksell in matters of marriage, blasphemy, and national defense have nothing to do with the adequacy of his theory of capital and interest. It would be inadmissible to employ the biographical data of a discoverer to establish or negate the logical coherence of his novel theoretical model or its econometric correspondence with reality. But surely the historian of economics, *qua* historian, would be derelict in his duty if he confined himself to evaluating past theories on general analytical and empirical grounds, without investigating the *genesis* of these theories, thinking of the past in terms of the past and critically exploiting all the pertinent documentary evidence available. For an answer to the question of the relevance of biographical data to the performance of the specifically historical tasks of the historian of economics, Professor Stigler need not have gone far afield. His colleague, Professor Milton Friedman, provided a succinct and hardly contestable answer long before mine appeared when he wrote: "Progress in positive economics will require not only the testing and elaboration of existing hypotheses but also the construction of new hypotheses. On this problem there is little to say on a formal level. The construction of hypotheses is a creative act of inspiration, intuition, invention; its essence is the vision of something new in familiar material. The process must be discussed in psychological, not logical, categories; *studied in autobiographies and biographies*, not treatises on scientific method; and promoted by maxim and example, not syllogism or theorem." Friedman (1953), pp. 42–43; my italics.

66. E. J. Mishan would say there is no such need. See Mishan (1961).
67. Stark (1944), p. 1, and Blaug (1968), pp. 1–8.

relating Léon Walras's discovery to contemporary intellectual conditions, including the contemporary memory of things past, as well
as to external events? Does not the same narrative, starting with
Auguste Walras's search for a passage leading from the stormy waters
of the early socialist denunciations of property to some solid analytical
ground for socialist goals, dispose of the absurd myth that marginal
utility was expressly invented to refute the Marxian labor theory of
value? Does not a reexamination of Léon Walras's 1873 paper hinting
at an extension of the application of the marginal utility principle to
the theory of production, which he later carried out in the *Eléments*
(along with its extension, in the end, to capital formation and money-
holding) help us perceive that a salient achievement, for better or
worse, of the "marginal revolution" was its shifting of emphasis away
from production considered as a wealth-increasing process to production considered as an aspect of exchange, away from a preoccupation
with distributive shares toward a preoccupation with the allocation
of resources? Herein, indeed, in the interpretation of the time, his time
and ours, Léon Walras's "virtues" lie. Whether such "virtues" are
admirable or not is another question.[68]

REFERENCES

Allen, R. G. D. *Mathematical Economics*. London: Macmillan, 1956.

Black, R. D. Collison, ed. *The Theory of Political Economy* by W.
Stanley Jevons. Harmondsworth, Middlesex: Pelican Books, 1970.

Blaug, Mark. *Economic Theory in Retrospect*. 2d ed. Homewood, Ill.:
Irwin, 1968.

Burlamaqui, Jean Jacques. *Elémens du droit naturel*. Nouvelle édi-
tion. Paris: Delestre-Boulage, 1821.

Cohen, Morris R., and Ernest Nagel. *Introduction to Logic and Scientific Method*. New York: Harcourt Brace, 1934.

Condillac, Etienne Bonnot de. *Le Commerce et le gouvernement*.
Œuvres de Condillac, vol. 4. Paris: Ch. Houel, 1798.

Cournot, Augustin. *Recherches sur les principes mathématiques de la
théorie des richesses*. Paris: Hachette, 1838. Reprint edited by

68. For support of research leading to this paper, I am indebted to the National Science Foundation under Grants GS-1516 and GS-1997 and to North-
western University. I am also indebted to my colleague, Professor Thomas T.
Sekine, to Professor Samuel Hollander, and to Professor Donald A. Walker, for
valuable comments and suggestions.

Georges Lutfalla. Paris: Marcel Rivière, 1938. English translation by Nathaniel T. Bacon, edited by Irving Fisher. New York: Macmillan, 1927.

———. *Souvenirs (1760–1860)*. Edited by E. P. Bottinelli Paris: Hachette, 1913.

Dingwall, James, and F. Bert Hoselitz, eds. and transs. *Principles of Economics* by Carl Menger. Glencoe, Ill.: Free Press, 1950.

Edgeworth, F. Y. *Mathematical Psychics*. London: Kegan Paul, 1881. Series of Reprints of Scarce Tracts, no. 10. London: London School of Economics, 1932.

Friedman, Milton. *Essays in Positive Economics*. Chicago: University of Chicago Press, 1953.

Genovesi, Antonio. *Lezioni di commercio o sia d'economia civile* (1765). New Edition. Bassano, 1769.

Gray, Alexander. *The Development of Economic Doctrine*. London: Longmans, Green, 1931.

Haton de la Goupillière, J. N. *Eléments de calcul infinitésimal*. Paris: Mallet-Bachelier, 1860.

Howey, R. S. *The Rise of the Marginal Utility School; 1870–1889*. Lawrence: University of Kansas Press, 1960.

Jaffé, William, ed. and trans. *Elements of Pure Economics* by Léon Walras. Translated from the definitive edition (1926). London and Homewood, Ill.: Allen and Unwin, and Irwin, 1954. (Reprints of Economic Classics. New York: Augustus M. Kelley, 1969).

———, ed. *Correspondence of Léon Walras and Related Papers*. 3 vols. Amsterdam: North Holland (for Royal Netherlands Academy of Sciences and Letters), 1965. (*a*).

———. "Biography and Economic Analysis." *Western Economic Journal* 3 (Summer 1965): 223–32. (*b*).

———. "Walras's Theory of *Tâtonnement*: A Critique of Recent Interpretations." *Journal of Political Economy* 75 (Feb. 1967): 1–19.

———. "A. N. Isnard, Progenitor of the Walrasian General Equilibrium Model." *History of Political Economy* 1 (Spring 1969): 19–43.

Jevons, W. Stanley. *The Theory of Political Economy*. London: Macmillan, 1871. 4th ed., edited by H. Stanley Jevons. London: Macmillan, 1924. For the Pelican edition, see Black (1970).

Leduc, Gaston, ed. *De la nature de la richesse et de l'origine de la valeur* by Auguste Walras. Paris: Alcan, 1938.

Menger, Carl. *Grundsätze der Volkswirtschaftslehre*. Vienna: Braumüller, 1871. Series of Reprints of Scarce Tracts, no. 17. London: London School of Economics, 1934. For the English translation, see Dingwall and Hoselitz (1950).

Mishan, E. J. "Theories of Consumer's Behavior: A Cynical View." *Economica*, n.s. 28 (Feb. 1961): 1–11.

Pareto, Vilfredo. *Manuel d'économie politique*. Paris: Giard [1909].

———. *Lettere a Maffeo Pantaleoni*. 3 vols. Edited by Gabriele de Rosa. Rome: Banca Nazionale del Lavoro, 1960.

Schumpeter, Joseph A. *History of Economic Analysis*. New York: Oxford University Press, 1954.

Smith, Adam. *Lectures on Justice, Police, Revenue and Arms*. Oxford: Clarendon Press, 1896.

Stark, W. *The History of Economics in Its Relation to Social Development*. New York: Oxford University Press, 1944.

Stigler, George J. *Essays in the History of Economics*. Chicago and London: University of Chicago Press, 1965.

———. Review of *The Evolution of Modern Economic Theory* by Lord Robbins. *Economica* 37 (Nov. 1970): 425–26.

Taylor, W. L. *Francis Hutcheson and David Hume as Predecessors of Adam Smith*. Durham, N. C.: Duke Univesrity Press, 1965.

Thünen, Johann Heinrich von. *Der isolierte Staat*. Edited by Heinrich Waentig. Jena: Fischer, 1930.

Turgot, Anne Robert Jacques. "Valeurs et monnaies" (1769). *Œuvres de Turgot*. Edited by W. Eugène Daire, 1: 75–93. Paris: Guillaumin, 1844.

Walker, Donald A. "Léon Walras in the Light of His Correspondence and Related Papers." *Journal of Political Economy* 78 (July/Aug. 1970): 685–701.

Walras, Auguste. *De la nature de la richesse et de l'origine de la valeur*. Paris: Johanneau, 1831. For the Leduc edition, see Leduc (1938).

———. *Mémoire sur l'origine de la valeur d'échange*. Paris: Typographie Panckoucke, 1849. Republished as appendix in Leduc (1938), pp. 316–43.

[Walras, Auguste]. "Lettres inédites de et à Léon Walras." *La Révolution de 1848* 10 (1913): 138–56.

Walras, Léon. "Principe d'une théorie mathématique de l'échange."
Séances et travaux de l'Académie des Sciences morales et politiques,
Jan. 1874, vol. 101 of the Collection, 33d Year of the New Series,
part 1, pp. 97–116; first republished in the *Journal des Economistes,*
April/June 1874, 3d ser. 34, no. 100:5–31; republished again with
minor revisions in the *Théorie mathématique de la richesse sociale*
(Lausanne: Corbaz, 1883), pp. 7–25. Italian version: "Principio
d'una teoria matematica dello scambio," translated by Gerolamo
Boccardo in the *Biblioteca dell'Economista,* 3d ser. 2:1293–1301.
Turin: Unione tipografica, 1878. German version: "Prinzip einer
mathematischen Theorie des Tausches," translated by Ludwig von
Winterfeld, in *Mathematische Theorie der Preisbestimmung der
wirtschaftlichen Güter: Vier Denkschriften,* pp. 1–17. Stuttgart:
Enke, 1881. (a).

———. *Eléments d'économie politique pure.* 1st ed. (in two instal-
ments), Lausanne: Corbaz, 1874–77; 2d ed., Lausanne: Rouge,
1889; 3d ed., Lausanne: Rouge, 1896; 4th ed., Lausanne: Rouge,
1900: definitive ed. (published posthumously), 1926. Reprinted
Paris: Pichon and Durand-Auzias, 1952. For English translation,
see Jaffé (1954).

———. "La bourse, la spéculation et l'agiotage." *Bibliothèque Universelle et Revue Suisse,* 3d Period, 5 (March 1880): 452–76; and
6 (April 1880): 66–94. Republished in L.W. (1898), pp. 401–45.

———. *Théorie mathématique de la richesse sociale.* Lausanne: Corbaz,
1883.

———. *Etudes d'économie politique appliquée,* 1st ed., Lausanne:
Rouge, 1898; 2d ed., Paris: Pichon and Durand-Auzias, 1936, edited
by G. Leduc. The pagination is the same in both editions.

———. "Un initiateur en économie politique, A. A. Walras." *Revue
du Mois* 6 (1908): 170–83.

Vilfredo Pareto and Marginalism

Vincent J. Tarascio

PANTALEONI once observed that the history of science is not a piece of machinery whose construction and principles of action we know: "History is written by men, and accordingly I think the criteria governing history of science are disputable. Every change in criteria, of course, modifies judgment."[1] Pantaleoni's thoughts are particularly relevant to discussions concerning the "marginal revolution." Whether or not the advent of marginalism in our discipline can be called revolutionary depends, to a great extent, on how one views its origins, as well as its impact upon economic science and thought.

The problem of origins is extremely complex. There appear to have been many currents and crosscurrents, endogenous and exogenous to economics, all of which influenced the development of marginalism in varying degrees.[2] Marginalism, then, serves as an excellent example of a situation quite common in historical studies where the identification and description of an event is a much more simple task than accounting for its existence.[3]

The term "marginal revolution" may lead to the impression that the acceptance of the idea of marginal utility came quickly. Such an impression would be erroneous. As Professor Howey has argued:

VINCENT J. TARASCIO *is Professor of Economics at the University of North Carolina at Chapel Hill.*

1. M. Pantaleoni, "Vilfredo Pareto," *Economic Journal* 33 (Sept. 1923): 431.

2. As Professor Blaug, *Economic Theory in Retrospect* (Homewood, Ill., 1968), p. 304, has pointed out: "The historical explanations that have been advanced fall roughly into four classes: (1) an autonomous intellectual development within the discipline of economics; (2) the product of philosophical currents; (3) the product of definite institutional changes in the economy; and (4) a counterblast to socialism, particularly to Marxism."

3. Aside from the intrinsic complexities, there are complexities of another kind which arise when a particular phenomenon is analyzed. There are many ways in which to view the subject of analysis. For instance, the four historical explanations of marginalism mentioned in note 2 above really deal with quite different aspects of marginalism—objective, philosophical, institutional, and ideological. Which of these explanations is most appropriate depends upon the purpose of the study. Even a synthesis of all these aspects does not render a complete picture, since we are always dealing with abstractions.

The idea penetrated the thinking of economists most slowly, and had to win its victories, one by one, over inertia and, less frequently, over active opposition. The Marginal Utility School emerged at the end of twenty years but throughout this period [1870–1890], *and for a long time thereafter* [my italics], the idea of marginal utility stood alongside the older views as a new but minor variant of economic thought.[4]

It seems that the advent of marginalism was revolutionary not so much in terms of time, i.e., the rapidity with which marginalism took hold, but in its implications for economics. Marginalism manifested itself not only in methods of analysis but also in the scope and definition of economics. In this sense there is little doubt that marginalism revolutionized economic thought. Nevertheless, the process involved a very long time, and the contributions of various writers differed along the way. The first shots were fired by Jevons, Menger, and Walras in the 1870's, but the battle was still being fought by Pareto in 1897, when he felt it necessary to defend the "new theories of economics": "Several criticisms of a work [*Cours d'économie politique*, 1897] that I have recently published have shown me that certain points of view from which the new economic theories can be considered have not been thoroughly understood."[5]

Pareto's role in the marginal revolution went beyond a mere defense of the theories of his predecessors. His own contributions to economic theory are well known, and there is no need to repeat them here.[6] But what is generally overlooked is the fact that his contributions stemmed from a conscious effort which reflected his views on methodology and method. Actually, Pareto fought several battles simultaneously throughout his career with (1) the German historical school in defense of theory, (2) the "literary" economists in defense of mathematical economics, (3) the "Marshallians," as an advocate of general equilibrium analysis, and (4) those with a hankering for

---

4. R. S. Howey, *The Rise of the Marginal Utility School* (Lawrence, Kans., 1960), pp. i-ii.

5. Vilfredo Pareto, "The New Theories of Economics," *Journal of Political Economy* 5 (Sept. 1897): 585.

6. Perhaps the least-known works on Pareto are a collection of papers published in the *Giornali degli Economisti* 64 (Jan.-Feb. 1924): 1–143, by M. Pantaleoni, E. Barone, V. Ricci, L. Amoroso, A. de Pietri-Tonelli, G. Del Vecchio, M. Fanno, V. Gobbi, G. Borgatta, R. Benini, G. Prato, R. Michels, E. Ciccotti, G. Mortara, F. Vinci, P. Zugaro, and others.

metaphysics. Some of these battles involved individuals within the marginalist camp, while other battles involved those antagonistic to marginalism. In almost every case, the basis for controversy was more methodological than doctrinal.

The purpose of this article is to examine those parts of Pareto's methodology which are relevant to marginalism. Although I have dealt with Pareto's methodological approach to economics elsewhere, I have not related his views specifically to his economic theories.[7]

Utility and Value

In economics the materials with which Pareto worked were only partially his own. He was influenced by Cournot, Jevons, and Walras. In addition, according to Pantaleoni, his work on utility theory would not have been what it was without Edgeworth and Irving Fisher.[8] Nevertheless, the "new economic theories" had a much broader meaning for Pareto than that usually associated with the "marginal utility school." In a doctrinal perspective, marginal utility theory can be viewed as a revolt against cost-of-production theories of value. In this sense, the marginal revolution was a revolution in value theory. On the other hand, marginal utility theory also represented the general use of maximization techniques in economic analysis. The doctrinal and analytical aspects and their implications are logically distinct. Pareto was a firm supporter of the "new economic theories" only in a qualified way, namely, he gave greater weight to the analytical than to the doctrinal aspects of the theories.

As concerns the doctrinal aspects, he was often critical of the views of his contemporaries. To begin, there was the matter of the "cause of value," a result of earlier polemics, which preoccupied the minds of many of his contemporaries. For instance, according to Pareto, Walras affirmed "to be certain that *rareté* (ophelimity) is the reason of value in exchange."[9] Pareto believed that by arguing that *rareté* was the reason for value in exchange, Walras was merely committing

7. Vincent J. Tarascio, *Pareto's Methodological Approach to Economics: A Study in the History of Some Scientific Aspects of Economic Thought* (Chapel Hill, N. C., 1968).

8. Pantaleoni, "Vilfredo Pareto," p. 584.

9. Vilfredo Pareto, *Manuale d'economia politica* (Milano, 1906), chap. 3, §227, pp. 235–36.

a methodological error similar to those who argued in favor of cost-of-production theories of value. Instead, Pareto refused to argue in favor of either. He viewed the problem of value in terms of the functional interdependency concept:

> If one thinks in terms of tastes, production being given, then the value in exchange is determined exclusively by tastes; and hence, the cause of value is ophelimity [utility]. On the other hand, for one who thinks in terms of obstacles [production], the cause of value is the cost of production. If with obstacles one stops to consider only labor, then the cause of value is exclusively in labor. Thus it was with Marx—in his theory of value other conditions were eliminated such that values depended only on labor.[10]

"Value," then, could take on any meaning, depending upon which conditions one wishes to consider. For Pareto, the prevailing definition of "exchange value" had "the serious defect of suggesting that exchange value is something objective, a property of things. . . ."[11] All this was reminiscent of a metaphysical stage of all sciences:

> In the early stages of every science there is apt to be a good deal of reasoning about terms rather than things themselves. This method of procedure, however, is not entirely erroneous. Words are often the depositories of the experiences of men, and so long as a new-born science has not succeeded in accumulating for itself a sufficient aggregate of direct experiences it may find it advantageous to have recourse to a common fund of experiences more or less vaguely represented by words.[12]

Nevertheless, there are "disadvantages attached to the vagueness of experience such as is given by everyday words."[31] With usage, mental concepts become "real entities" so that individuals tend to attach a significance to them far beyond their importance for science. The matter of "value" is one such example. One result is that many con-

10. Ibid., §225, p. 234.
11. Vilfredo Pareto, "Economie mathématique," *Encyclopédie des Sciences mathématiques*, tome 1, vol. 4, fasc. 4 (Paris, 1911). Translated as "Mathematical Economics," *International Economic Papers* 5 (1955): 59, n. 6.
12. Pareto, "New Theories of Economics," p. 497.
13. Ibid.

troversies in economics over that term were a waste of time. For this reason, Pareto attempted to avoid the use of the term: "I do my whole lecture course on political economy without using the term value, and I only mention it when I touch on the history of doctrines."[14]

From what has been said thus far regarding Pareto's views on "value," it might appear that he was merely quibbling about the metaphysical nature of terms used in economics. To some extent this is correct. On the other hand, and what is more important, the discussion serves as an introduction to a very important conclusion regarding the purpose of the "new economic theories." To use Pareto's words, "there are people who think that the new economic theories have been produced to explain value. Far from it! I am looking for something very different from the metaphysical reason of value."[15] If the purpose of the "new theories" was not to explain value, then what was it? Pareto's answer was simply, "I look for a theory which may include and present economic facts. For my part, I know only a system of equations of pure economics as being capable of attaining that end, just in the same way that the system of equations of celestial mechanics explains and represents the movements of celestial bodies. I have no other reason for accepting the theories of pure economics."[16] The whole matter of "value" takes on a different meaning when viewed in the perspective of a system of equations which depicts general equilibrium. With the aid of mathematics, one can establish the equations which express the interdependence of all the apparently unrelated phenomena one wishes to consider.[17] Not only are discussions concerning *the cause* of "value" shown to be misleading, but the argument that the "new theories" are designed to explain "value" reflects a rather narrow view of the range of their applicability and significance.

In summary, for Pareto, the importance of the "new theories" of economics was not so much in their ability to explain "value" as in

14. Vilfredo Pareto, "Sul principio economico," *Giornale degli Economisti* 22 (Feb. 1901): 131–38. Translated as "On the Economic Principle," *International Economic Papers* 3 (1953): 207.

15. Ibid.

16. Ibid.

17. Vilfredo Pareto, "Sul fenomeno economico. Lettera a Benedetto Croce," *Giornale degli Economisti* 21 (Aug. 1900): 139–62. Translated as "On the Economic Phenomenon," *International Economic Papers* 3 (1953): 184.

their ability to relate a great deal of economic phenomena with the use of a rather simple hypothesis—the hedonistic hypothesis. *Pure economics*, through analogy with the other sciences, draws many consequences from one or very few principles by deduction.[18] According to Pareto, the hedonistic hypothesis of the marginal utility school had been tried out, and the results of utility theory tended to agree with observed behavior. Therefore it was a useful hypothesis, even though it represented an application of the general observation of the utilitarians that men try to obtain the maximum pleasure with the minimum pain.[19] Although Pareto departed from many of his contemporaries on the subject of value, he was appreciative of the importance of marginal utility theory for economic analysis. Nevertheless, even here he felt there was room for "improvement," a point to which I shall now turn.

The Hedonistic Hypothesis and Pareto's Axiom of Choice

The more common view of Pareto's contribution to utility theory is that, through the use of monotonic transformations (index functions), he was able to avoid the necessity for cardinal measures of utility.[20] Hence the cardinal utility theory of the "marginal utility school" was replaced by an ordinal theory of utility. This view reveals only a part of a more general problem which concerned Pareto. Let us begin, as a starting point, with what is more or less known and then proceed to the less familiar.

As is well known, the hedonistic hypothesis suffered an important limitation from the point of view of empirical science—it required that utility be measurable. This requirement was particularly troublesome to Pareto:

> Subsequently it seemed to me that one could go one step further. I was worried about that *pleasure* and that *pain* which had to be measured, because in reality, nobody is capable of measuring pleasure.[21]

18. Ibid., p. 183.
19. Ibid.
20. For instance, regarding Pareto's contribution to utility theory see Joseph Schumpeter, "Vilfredo Pareto (1848–1923)," *Quarterly Journal of Economics* 63 (May 1949): 162–63.
21. Pareto, "On the Economic Phenomenon," p. 183.

In addition, there was also a definitional and logical problem involved in the hedonistic hypothesis:

> Here are two lines of reasoning: 1) "So-and-So gets more pleasure out of A than out of B. He therefore chooses A and from that fact certain equations follow. 2) So-and-So chooses A, and from this certain equations follow."[22]

The first statement contains a word which is not well defined, i.e., pleasure:

> One must either give a definition of it independently of the fact of choice (and in this case it is necesssary to prove the first proposition, and I do not know if this has been done, . . .), or, as has been done in reality, one makes that pleasure depend on choice. In this case the first proposition is a tautology. In either case, therefore, one should exclude it; either because it is doubtful and causes difficulties . . . or because it is useless.[23]

For the reasons contained in the above citation, Pareto substituted "the material fact of choice"[24] in place of the hedonistic hypothesis. The axiom of choice was all that was necessary; considerations of pleasure and pain were superfluous for his purpose.

There are other advantages to working with the axiom of choice instead of the hedonistic hypothesis. Firstly, it broadens the scope of (utility) theory, while at the same time avoiding motivational considerations:

> Whether I have chosen it [Rhine wine] because I prefer Rhine wine, or because the doctor has ordered it and I dislike ordinary wine, or because I want to drink a bottle with a friend who likes Rhine wine, or for any other reason; all this does not matter. I stop at the fact [of choice].[25]

Secondly, a choice between two wines does not require that such a choice be a calculated one, as would be the case with the hedonistic

22. Ibid., p. 190.
23. Ibid., p. 191.
24. Ibid., p. 190.
25. Ibid., p. 191.

hypothesis.[26] All that is necessary is consistency (transitivity), in which case the choices "would change only if human nature, tastes, and customs were to change."[27]

The axiom of choice does not necessarily preclude subjective considerations relating to the environment in which a choice situation takes place. Uncertainty is one example. The philosopher Croce was critical of Pareto's axiom of choice because in a choice situation the individual actor would be faced with different states of nature. He argued that one could not imagine himself under different conditions at the same moment, concluding, "Fancy has its laws and does not allow the imagination of what is unimaginable."[28] Pareto's answer to Croce's critique was that in order to make a potential choice it was not necessary to imagine oneself in different circumstances at the same time. Usually, choice situations involve successive comparisons until a choice is made. For instance good A is compared with B then B with A and so on until an actual choice is made. What is more important, Pareto argued that potential choices are always based on *expected* utility, on the *concept* of the goods to be consumed, not the real fact of consumption, which is ex-post. Hence stochastic elements are present, but with experience (repeated trials) their influence diminishes:

> When I eat an orange, I shall have the feeling that there is a difference between the pleasure I had imagined and one I experience, and the memory of such a sensation will be an element in modifying future choices. This is one of the reasons why economic theories come near the truth only so far as oft-repeated facts, and not [single] choices or exceptional facts, are concerned.[29]

Pareto's discussion of expected utility was suggestive of later "dynamic" utility theories based on learning theory: within the framework of stimulus-response analysis, which is represented in the theory of choice as a sequence of replicative static decision situations, the

26. Ibid., p. 189.
27. Ibid., p. 191.
28. Benedetto Croce, "Replica all'articolo del Professore Pareto," *Giornale degli Economisti* 22 (Feb. 1901): 121–30. Translated as "On the Economic Principle," *International Economic Papers* 3 (1953): 201.
29. Pareto, "On the Economic Principle," p. 206.

individual is assumed to converge towards maximizing behavior.[30]

In the above discussion regarding potential choices, Pareto resorts to examples involving utility. This might appear to involve a contradiction, in view of his tendency to argue in favor of the axiom of choice rather than the hedonistic hypothesis. However Pareto distinguished between subjective and objective considerations. His desire to substitute the axiom of choice for the hedonistic hypothesis was based on *objective* considerations, i.e., scientific grounds, whereas he never denied the importance of the *subjective* elements of utility, i.e., involving the individual actors.[31] The failure to grasp this distinction has led some writers to believe that Pareto experienced difficulty in "disentangling himself entirely from old utility theory."[32] The point is that Pareto never intended to "disentangle" himself from the subjective aspects of utility theory. This point becomes quite clear in his *sociology*.[33]

In his pure economics, Pareto's primary interest was in the objective aspects. Hence his emphasis on "choice." Indeed, he went so far as to define *pure* economics as the science of choice: "I do not have the slightest difficulty in justifying the assertion that pure economics is concerned only with the choices which fall on things the quantities of which are variable and susceptible of measurement."[34] This definition applied only to *pure* economics in contradistinction to applied economics, which included institutional factors. Pareto's conception of pure economics was that it involved a study of objective

30. The more recent works of Hart, Marschak, Wald, and Luce represent this line of reasoning. Cf. James Murphy and Vincent J. Tarascio, "Uncertainty, Learning, and Dynamic Utility Theory," presented at the winter meetings of the Econometric Society, Detroit, 1970.

31. For a discussion of Pareto's distinction between objective, subjective, and utility aspects of a proposition see Vincent J. Tarascio, *Pareto's Methodological Approach to Economics*, p. 95.

32. Schumpeter, p. 163.

33. In his sociology, Pareto pointed out that in cases of uncertainty individuals resort to *subjective* probabilities in choice situations. Even though objective probabilities (as one finds in cases involving risk) are not possible in many situations, this does not preclude subjective probabilities. The latter do not necessarily involve cardinal numbers, but an ordinal ranking is sufficient. Pareto, *Trattato di sociologia generale* (Florence, 1916), translated into English as *The Mind and Society* by Arthur Livingston (New York, 1935) I, §§553–65, pp. 334–42. The works of Ramsey, von Neumann and Morgenstern, Savage, and de Finetti follow this line of reasoning in varying degrees.

34. Pareto, "On the Economic Phenomenon," p. 188.

factors, i.e., the relationship between economic quantities, without reference to the individual (subjective factors) either in terms of motivation or normative implications: "the individual may disappear; we do not need him any longer in order to determine economic eqilibrium."[35] This is a rather remarkable statement in view of the individualistic (and subjective) orientations of the marginal utility theorists. But Pareto recognized that, within the scope of existing marginal utility theory, the individual was redundant, insofar as one means by the term a human being rather than an element in a system. Georgescu-Roegen describes the situation aptly, pointing out that

> for a science of man to exclude altogether man from the picture is a patent incongruity. Nevertheless, standard economics takes special pride in operating with a man-less picture. As Pareto overtly claimed, once we have determined the means at the disposal of the individual and obtained "a photograph of his tastes—the individual may disappear." The individual is thus reduced to a mere subscript of the ophelimity function $\phi_i(X)$. The logic is perfect: man is not an economic agent simply because there is no economic process. There is only a jig-saw puzzle of fitting given means to given ends, which requires a computer not an agent.[36]

Although Georgescu-Roegen appears to be critical of Pareto in the above citation, the fact of the matter is that Pareto was quick to see that the "marginal revolution" transformed *pure* economics to a "man-less science," to use Georgescu-Roegen's words. Pareto merely removed the façade to expose so-called "economic man" of *pure* economics for what he was—neither economic nor man. In other words, a logical implication of marginal utility theory was a more general mathematical marginalism, with all its advantages and shortcomings. These advantages and shortcomings will be brought out in the following sections.

Tastes and Obstacles

The "marginal revolution" brought with it a refinement of the

35. Pareto, "Mathematical Economics," p. 61.
36. Nicholas Georgescu-Roegen, *Analytical Economics* (Cambridge, Mass., 1966), p. 104.

idea of equilibrium, as well as its widespread use in economic analysis. The refinement consisted largely of the mathematical determination of static equilibrium and a study of stability conditions. The idea was extended to include the individual, the firm, the market, and finally general economic equilibrium.

There are many ways to approach a study of economic equilibrium. One may begin with the concepts derived from immediate (subjective) experience. These concepts may include "prices," "capital," etc., as well as the institutional environment in which these "phenomena" are said to occur, i.e., markets, etc. These concepts may also consist of various types of economic processes such as consumption, production, and distribution. In Walras's *Elements*, we find a study of exchange, production, and capitalization, the latter two added to the first as restrictive assumptions are relaxed.[37] The central focus is the individual, as a demander of goods and supplier of factor services. The entrepreneur is also there, but behind the scenes; he buys factor services and produces goods. The "objective functions" are utility maximization and profit maximization for the consumer and entrepreneur, respectively.

Another way to approach the study of equilibrium is to replace those concepts drawn from immediate (subjective) experience by simpler, less complex concepts, in order to permit a more rigorous study of equilibrium. This process of abstraction, in order to achieve a greater degree of generality, has been characteristic of all the physical sciences. Perhaps the most succinct introduction to Pareto's version of general equilibrium is contained in the following sentence: "Science proceeds by replacing the relationships between human concepts (which relationships are the first to occur to us) by relationships between things."[38] Hence if one wishes to investigate the reciprocal relations which determine the economic equilibrium, many of the concepts used in "ordinary reasoning" can be dispensed with by developing a perfectly general mathematical logic of systems.

37. Léon Walras, *Eléments d'économie politique pure* (Paris, 1926), trans. William Jaffé as *Elements of Pure Economics* (Homewood, Ill., 1954). This repetition in Walras may appear redundant to anyone concerned more with mathematical elegance than with economic content. On the other hand, a student can probably learn more economics in Walras's *Elements* than in Pareto's *Manuale*. The *Manuale* is more useful to those who have mastered the *Elements*.
38. Pareto, "On the Economic Phenomenon," p. 196.

Such a system may deal with undefined "things" which are subject to certain restrictions. As Schumpeter has pointed out, Walras and all the marginal utility theorists were "trying to solve the problems that in ultimate logic reduce to only one: all their problems—not only the problems of production—are problems in the transformation of economic quantities and formally alike, the difference consisting merely in different restrictions to which economic action is subject in different fields."[39]

In Pareto's case, a greater degree of generality was achieved through his conception of an equilibrium resulting from the contrast of "tastes" and "obstacles."[40] The tastes are the "forces" that impel the individual to action. The obstacles are the constraints imposed upon the system. These constraints may be defined in various ways. A study of them gives rise not only to theories of exchange, production, capitalization, etc., but, more generally, to almost any form of "relations which can be imagined."[41] Nevertheless, Pareto pointed out as a practical matter, "we must, by observation of correct cases, select those of particular interest to us."[42]

In Pareto's system, production, exchange, consumption, and distribution no longer exist as distinctions. Amoroso points out that "there does not exist in real life a distinction in things corresponding to this distinction of words . . . all economic problems are included in the general conditions of equilibrium."[43] Pareto, mapped out a very general theory of economic equilibrium in mathematical terms. In fact, so general that the system of equations which resulted was not new to him:

Let us go back to the equations which determine equilibrium. In seeing them somebody—and it might be the writer—made the observation . . . "These equations do not seem new to me, I know them well, they are old friends. They are the equations of rational mechanics." This is why pure economics is a sort of mechanics or akin to mechanics.[44]

39. Schumpeter, p. 158.
40. Cf. Pareto, *Manuale*, chaps. 4 and 5.
41. Pareto, "Mathematical Economics," p. 65.
42. Ibid.
43. Luigi Amoroso, "Vilfredo Pareto," *Econometrica* 6 (Jan. 1938): 6.
44. Pareto, "On the Economic Phenomenon," p. 185.

The analogy with rational mechanics goes beyond the equations themselves. The concept of marginal utility corresponds to "forces" in mechanics. According to Pareto, given the axiom of choice, "that something is no longer there. However, mechanics can be studied leaving aside the concept of forces."[45] In pure economics, one turns to the equations themselves; hence, according to Amoroso, "the position of equilibrium was determined just as soon as a function (index) was known, which, with the sign of its derivatives, would indicate the direction of the movement."[46] In terms of equilibrium theory, Pareto's contribution to the "marginal revolution" was the extension of marginalism through the use of index functions, while at the same time demonstrating mathematically that ultimately the problems that marginal utility theorists were attempting to solve were very similar to problems in mechanics. Hence *pure* economics dealt with the *mechanical* aspects of economics. This point deserves further clarification, since a great deal of misunderstanding has existed regarding the alleged mechanistic characteristics of the marginal revolution.

Pure Economics, Applied Economics, and Policy

Until now, I have discussed Pareto's contributions to theory, or what was referred to as "pure economics" by Pareto and some of his contemporaries. For Pareto, pure economics dealt with a "tiny slice of economics," namely, that which lends itself to quantitative analysis:

> This is how economics has become, in part, mathematics; from the moment it began to discuss quantities and to establish relations between the variations of these quantities it found itself within the realm of mathematics.[47]

The quantities and relations studied in pure economics represented more or less "mechanical phenomena." Pure economics was, by analogy to other sciences, a part of economics which dealt with mechanical aspects:

> Anatomy studies many things, among which are the movements of the bone structure through the actions of muscles. On reaching this special study, a man who knows mechanics

45. Ibid.
46. Amoroso, p. 5.
47. Pareto, "On the Economic Phenomenon," p. 182.

will say: "But this is the theory about levers. It is useless for you anatomists to re-make a theory that has been known for so many centuries." This part of anatomy—let us call it X anatomy, to be clear—is a mechanical one.[48]

The analogy of pure economics with mechanics does not end with the similarity of the equation systems. There are also normative and methodological implications. As concerns the normative implications, an economist interested in pure economics need not concern himself with normative aspects of economics. Again by analogy with other sciences:

> One man kicks another. In this phenomenon there is a part which is not only similar to but indeed identical with a mechanical phenomenon, that is to say, the movement of the foot, the balance of the man, etc., are exclusively mechanical phenomena. Yet they lead finally to an act that is without doubt subject to approval or disapproval. Why therefore, should that part of the economic phenomenon which is similar to a mechanical phenomenon, not lead equally to a fact subject to approval or disapproval?[49]

Pareto admits that in his example above, there is something besides the pure mechanical fact; in economic phenomena there is also something else besides that studied by pure economics. This will always be the case, since, because of the complexity of concrete economic phenomena, we labor under subjective difficulties. Therefore, we "divide it [the concrete phenomenon] into more or less arbitrary parts and this division, or analysis, is the basis of the various sciences."[50]

Because pure economics deals only with the mechanical aspects of economic phenomena, its ability to solve concrete cases is very restricted. Again by analogy with other sciences, applied economics takes account of complexities which are ignored in pure theory:

> A profound error, of which unfortunately certain mathematical economists are not innocent, is to imagine that mathematical economics can directly solve the problems of practical

48. Ibid., p. 186.
49. Ibid.
50. Ibid.

economics. This is not the case. Mathematical economics is only one of the many parts which, united by synthesis, can provide a solution of practical problems. It bears the same relation to them as theoretical mechanics does to problems of applied mechanics . . .[51]

Pareto often used the term "incomplete synthesis" to refer to the propensity of economists to attempt to solve concrete problems solely on the basis of pure theory.[52] For Pareto, pure theory would always be limited in its ability to deal with concrete problems, because of its very nature:

> In working out theories in economics it is an illusion to believe that we get any closer to the concrete by starting with the laws of supply and demand than we do by starting with the "utility" of early economists, or with "marginal utility," the "rarity," or the "ophelimity," of more recent economists. Whatever we do we are resorting to abstractions and we cannot do otherwise.[53]

What is important for my purposes, Pareto called attention to the limitations of marginalism for solving concrete problems. The limitation was largely the consequence of its *mechanical* nature. The mechanical nature of pure economics was seen by Pareto not as a "fault" (contrary to many critics of marginalism), but merely as a limitation which could be resolved by (1) taking into account complexities through a process of successive approximations (at the theoretical level), (2) considering the effects of institutional factors, i.e., market structure, etc. (applied economics), and (3) a synthesis of the respective social sciences (sociology). Pareto worked in all these areas above, but he undoubtedly attached the greatest importance to (3):

> For the past ten years I have been perpetually repeating that in order to study a phenomenon, one must first separate out

51. Pareto, "Mathematical Economics," pp. 88–89.
52. Philip Wicksteed was one such example cited by Pareto. He believed he had solved the concrete problem of distribution on the basis of a simple mathematical "proof," i.e., the marginal productivity theory. Later Wicksteed realized his error of "incomplete synthesis." Cf. Wicksteed, *Common Sense of Political Economy* (London, 1933), p. 815 n.
53. Pareto, *Mind and Society*, IV, §2409, pp. 1734–35.

its elements, analyze, and then, in order to solve a concrete case, one must bring together the conclusions of the various sciences and make a synthesis.[54]

He argued that human action is essentially synthetical in nature; *homo œconomicus, homo ethicus, homo religiosus* exist only as abstractions, since concrete human action involves some combination of them.[55]

What Pareto worked with in pure economics was the theory of static equilibrium. What movements occurred were movements or tendencies towards a state of equilibrium. The external forces were tastes and obstacles, and these are the only ones explicitly considered in the *Manuale*. Pareto realized that, in reality, the system moves continuously under the action of internal and external forces. The internal forces, largely non-economic, influence the external forces so that economic dynamics really merges into sociology.[56]

Pareto's Sociology

Pareto's sociology is extremely complex, and I shall not attempt an exhaustive analysis or even an outline.[57] Instead, I shall focus attention on those parts of it which are of particular interest in terms of the marginal revolution.[58]

Pareto, as mentioned above, stressed the limitations of "pure economics" for solving concrete problems. His sociology serves as an example of the type of "synthesis" he had in mind when dealing with concrete problems. Pareto's sociology can be viewed as an "economic sociology," not so much because there is a great deal of economics contained in it as because it represents a logical develop-

54. Pareto, "On the Economic Phenomenon," p. 186.
55. Pareto, *Manuale*, chap. 1, §15, p. 11. For a more detailed discussion of Pareto's view on scope see Vincent J. Tarascio, *Pareto's Methodological Approach to Economics*, chap. 4.
56. This definition of dynamics is at variance with the so-called mechanical dynamics of today, where the time path from one equilibrium to another is studied.
57. Pareto's sociological theory is contained in the *Trattato*. For adaptations and illustration of the theory see *Fatti e teorie* (Florence, 1920) and *Transformazione della democrazia* (Milan, 1921).
58. This is done with some reservation because in discussing only a part, indeed a small part, of Pareto's sociology, I shall be presenting a very incomplete picture of a very complex work. The reader should keep this in mind.

ment from pure economics to policy. Because policy involves politics, his sociology is a sociology of the political process. Also, Pareto was an economist turned sociologist, and he brought to sociology many of the concepts characteristic of his economics. The best example is his sociological "utility" theory.[59]

In his sociology, Pareto defines "utility" as satisfactions deriving from *all* sources, both economic and non-economic, in contradistinction to ophelimity, which represented satisfactions derived only from economic sources. He then assumes that the individual actors in the social system have some conception of what is good or beneficial for themselves and others in the system. In other words, each individual has a subjective welfare function. Each individual in the system assigns weights to the utilities of others, as he imagines them. For every individual there exists an ideal state which renders his subjective welfare function at a maximum. Since individuals' conceptions of what is good for themselves and others differ, i.e., they are heterogeneous, the likelihood of the existence of a social state which satisfies all members in the system is extremely small. In other words, the internal constraints in the system are such that there is no solution to the system of differential equations. Nevertheless society possesses some degree of cohesiveness. The reason it does so is that individuals are willing to submit themselves to a higher authority—say government.

Pareto begins by assuming that the government's political welfare function is given; the government assigns coefficients to the utility functions of all individuals, to the benefit of some and the detriment of others. In other words Pareto was calling attention to the differential effects of *all* policy. Later, Pareto "endogenizes" government into the system; he turns to the analysis of the political process. The political process is viewed as the reciprocal attempts of governments and individuals (and groups) to transform each other's welfare functions into their own. The dynamic element in the system is ideology (derivations).[60]

Pareto then defines an all-inclusive Pareto *social* optimum. An

59. Cf. Pareto, *The Mind and Society*, II, §§ 2105–55, pp. 1452–1500.
60. For a detailed and more rigorous presentation of Pareto's utility theory sketched out above, see Vincent J. Tarascio, "Paretian Welfare Theory: Some Neglected Aspects," *Journal of Political Economy* 77 (Jan.-Feb. 1969): 1–20.

important implication of the dual welfare criteria is that the conditions of Pareto *social* optimum may not be consistent with those of a Pareto *economic* optimum.[61] Indeed, it would be surprising if the case were otherwise, for in concrete reality there are other factors in addition to considerations of efficiency which influence goals and policy—equity considerations, for instance.

Pareto's sociological "utility" and welfare theory represented a pioneering effort to carry the "marginal revolution" beyond the boundaries of economics. Through his application of the marginal principle to the analysis of the political process, he demonstrated the generality of that principle. Also he argued that what had been assumed to be essentially qualitative phenomena did lend themselves to quantitative analysis. To use Pareto's words, "From what we have been showing it also follows that the problem of utility [in sociology] is quantitative and not qualitative, as is commonly believed."[62]

Pareto's sociology also represented a counterweight to the mechanistic nature of his pure economics. In pure economics, individuals are constrained to act in a particular way. The parameters at the individual level were prices, tastes (given utility functions), and technology (given production functions). A change in any of these resulted in a new configuration of equilibrium. The ability of individuals to influence each other or to act collectively to alter the parameters in the system (i.e., through interpersonal interaction) is assumed away. In reality, individuals do act collectively to alter conditions in order to maximize their interests (say wages and profits) either privately or politically. Not only is this propensity, and its economic consequences, recognized in Pareto's sociology, but it becomes a central theme; the political process is examined in such a general way that an important part of the sociology becomes an analysis of interpersonal interaction (in contrast to the impersonal interaction characteristic of pure economics). The former type of interaction involves subjective and dynamic considerations, while the latter focuses attention on objective and static aspects.[63] In Pareto's

61. Hence Pareto anticipated so-called theories of the "second best."
62. Pareto, *The Mind and Society*, IV, §2155, p. 1500.
63. It is true that in economics we speak of "subjective" utility, but this means nothing more than assuming that the individual knows what is best for

pure economics, economic man resembles a mechanical man. This is the point Pareto was making when he stated, "For the determination of equilibrium, the individual can be replaced just as well by curves."[64] In his sociology, Pareto was dealing with synthetical man, whose actions stem from economic, political, ethical, etc., motives. These motives represent a complex of sentiments and interests.

An important consequence of the marginal revolution was the narrowing scope of economics. Pareto was not alone in his concern regarding the narrow scope of pure economics. In turning to sociology, Pareto was more or less in the tradition of economic sociologists such as Marx, Weber, Veblen, and later, Schumpeter. Others of his contemporaries, such as Walras and Marshall, used somewhat different approaches. Walras's trilogy consisted of pure economics, applied economics, and social economics. Marshall's *Principles* was a kind of applied sociology. The works of all the above writers represented either an implicit or an explicit recognition of (if not concern for) the limitations of pure economics for dealing with concrete problems.

Conclusion

For Pareto, the "marginal revolution" represented an advance in economic science not so much because of the doctrines of the marginal utility economists as, to a great extent, because of the analytical (marginal) techniques they employed. As concerns the former, he showed that some concepts—"value," "marginal utility," etc.—were superfluous for science. Also he carried the conception of economic equilibrium to a higher level of generality in order to examine the properties of the system. All of these efforts represented an extension of the principle of marginalism within economics while at the same time suppressing what he believed to be metaphysical elements. He also introduced marginalism into sociology. In summary, the significance of Pareto's contribution to the "marginal revolution" was that he went beyond its characteristic doctrines, and by doing so, he led economics in a direction of greater theoretical generality. Hence his theoretical work represented the link between the early marginalists (marginal utility theorists) and modern economic theory.

himself. One implication of the assumption is that it *avoids* the problem of subjective uncertainty, a problem which Pareto faced up to in his sociology.
    64. Pareto, "Mathematical Economics," p. 62.

In his sociology, Pareto distinguished between the subjective, objective, and utility aspects of problems being investigated. The first is with reference to the individual actor and his perceptions; the second is from the point of view of positive science; the third involves judgments regarding what is "beneficial" or "good" both subjectively and objectively. These distinctions are also relevant to discussions of the "marginal revolution." In this article I have focused on subjective factors, i.e., Pareto's role.

The objective considerations of the "marginal revolution" may suggest the relative imperviousness of economics to external influence, even though weight is given to external influences.[65] Finally, the utility aspects of marginalism involve a judgment as to whether economics has benefited or suffered a detriment as a consequence of the "marginal revolution." It appears that economics gained a rigor, but has suffered a loss in scope. Pareto was well aware of this when he stressed the need for "synthesis."

To the extent that the "marginal revolution" has colored our view of the world, and I believe it has, it involves an ethics and a mystique. As Croce recognized, the fundamental character of the "marginal revolution" could be reduced to four conceptions: "The *mechanical*, the *hedonistic*, the *technological*, and the *egoistic*."[66] Today, on the hundredth anniversary of the "marginal revolution," the fundamental character of microeconomic theory remains the same as that of the "marginal revolution."

65. Cf. J. J. Spengler, "Exogenous and Endogenous Influences in the Formation of Post-1870 Economic Thought," *Events, Ideology and Economic Theory*, ed. R. V. Eagly (Detroit, 1968), pp. 167–69; George Stigler, *Essays in the History of Economics* (Chicago, 1965), p. 22.
66. Croce, p. 173.

To What Extent Was the Austrian School Marginalist?

Erich Streissler

N o LESS an authority than T. W. Hutchison has stressed, "What was important in marginal utility was the adjective rather than the noun."[1] The theoreticians of subjective value were marginalists first and economists of utility second. According to Mark Blaug[2] "the essence of the economic problem" for the marginalists after 1870 (or, as I would prefer to call it, for the Neoclassical Departure) was to search for the conditions under which given productive services were allocated with optimal results among competitive uses, optimal in the sense of maximizing consumers' satisfaction. This ruled out consideration of the effects of increases in the quantity and quality of resources, as well as the dynamic expansion of wants—effects that the classical economists had regarded as the sine qua non of improvements in economic welfare. I would add that by the very logic of the maximization problem, all true neoclassical economics is economics under certainty, the static framework of analysis being closely linked to the plausibility of the implied assumption of full information. Finally, marginalism in its essence is a decision theory; in the language of mathematical programing it focuses on the objective function first, on the choice variables second, and on the restraints not at all.

In all these senses the Austrians were not marginalist. Or, to put this central thesis of my article more cautiously, marginalism was not the essence of their endeavor; it remained—*pace* Hutchison—*an adjective, not the noun.* Marginalism is introduced in the middle of Menger's *Grundsätze*, but it is for this very reason not central to,

ERICH STREISSLER *is Professor of Economics and Econometrics at the University of Vienna.*

1. T. W. Hutchison, according to M. Blaug, *Economic Theory in Retrospect*, 2d ed. (Homewood, Ill., 1968), p. 299.
2. Ibid.

not the keystone[3] of, this very logical construction. Or, to put it in Menger's own words, it was "not *merely* [!] his endeavor to create a unified theory of price."[4]

Menger's book is a conscious complement to Adam Smith's *Wealth of Nations* and for this reason it is not static, but concerned with economic progress. It is intended to elucidate the change *in the range and in the quality of goods*. It is an investigation of the restraints of economic action, or rather the *change of the restraints* through a change in the choice variables (and not primarily an investigation of objective function in economics), to such an extent that Menger thought it necessary to stress this aspect as the sole object of economic theorizing.[5] And it is, above all, basically an *information theory*, economic theory under *uncertainty* and not under *certainty*. Because of these aspects the Austrians always stressed, and stressed rightly, I think, that they were *the* school of *subjective* value, a school apart.

It is easy to refute this statement of mine by pointing to numerous counterexamples among the very large group of economists emanating from Austria. Therefore we have to turn first to the question, *Who were "the Austrians"?* Who was their most important author? Some give the palm to Friedrich von Wieser, either because of his sociological insights or because he shows greatest conformity to the general neoclassical (or marginalist) tradition.[6] Some rank Eugen Böhm von Bawerk above the rest because of his lasting mark on one aspect of economic theory.[7] But those who see the most signal contribution to economics in a wealth of seminal ideas and even more

3. As T. W. Hutchison stresses, to my mind wrongly, in spite of his sympathetic understanding founded on solid research. *A Review of Economic Doctrines, 1870–1929* (Oxford, 1953), p. 141.

4. C. Menger, *Grundsätze der Volkswirtschaftslehre* (Vienna, 1871), p. 10. The English version, sometimes quoted below, is *Principles of Economics*, trans. J. Dingwall and B. F. Hoselitz, ed. F. H. Knight (Glencoe, Ill., 1950).

5. Menger, *Grundsätze*, p. ix: "Die theoretische Volkswirtschaftslehre beschäftigt sich . . . mit den *Bedingungen*, unter welchen die Menschen die auf die Befriedigung ihrer Bedürfnisse gerichtete vorsorgliche Thätigkeit entfalten."

6. Lord Robbins to my mind tends towards this evaluation in his *Evolution of Modern Economic Theory* (London, 1970), p. 204. Wieser's law of costs is called "the keystone, as it were, of the whole edifice of the subjective theory of value," a claim somewhat sweeping both as to content and as to assignment of authorship.

7. This seems to be the hierarchy of esteem of Sir John Hicks.

in an original and unique *vision* of the economy, as Hayek[8] or I myself would do, will rank Carl Menger far above the rest.

This is not merely a question of personal taste; it is a question of facts. Menger—given, of course, the personality that he was—had *the status, the institutional position to enforce at least initial concurrence with his opinions* and thus became the pivot on whom the school turned. He became associate professor at the University of Vienna in 1873 and full professor in 1879. From that moment on, in the context of the university system then prevalent, there fell upon him the main responsibility not only for the teaching of economic theory but above all for the *recruitment of academic teachers* in theoretical economics. His nearly unlimited authority would find a check only in his colleague, the incumbent of the chair of economic policy. Fortunately this colleague was at first his paternal friend Lorenz von Stein, twenty-five years his senior, about to retire, and anyway more interested in the theory of public administration than in economics; and then he had the right to select even his colleague, his choice falling after two short interregna on a near-pupil and certainly a great admirer, Eugen Philippović von Philippsberg. As the incumbent of the chair in the capital of Austria, and therefore of the capital chair in Austria, he shared in theory, but not to a significant extent in practice, the right of admittance of Austrians to the academic profession in economics with the full professors of economics at other Austrian universities. And what this right entailed is expressed to a nicety by the still valid, though of course now defunct, statute of the University of Freiburg in Germany which declares that the professor admits to the doctoral course "only his closest intimates and real pupils"; if true for the doctorate, how much more so for the *Habilitation*, the final "degree" admitting to academic teaching! It was therefore usual in the *Habilitationsschrift* to quote the Master copiously, to paraphrase Him and if He liked the variations on His theme, even to dedicate the finished work to Menger.[9] One can well

8. Hayek says of the Austrian School: "Its fundamental ideas belong fully and wholly to Carl Menger." Einleitung to *Carl Menger, Gesammelte Werke*, ed. F. A. von Hayek, 2d ed. (Tübingen, 1970), 1:v.

9. J. von Komorzynski, *Der Werth in der isolirten Wirtschaft* (Vienna, 1889), is dedicated to Menger, "Dem [!] Professor der Nationalökonomie an der k. k. Universität zu Wien." (Interestingly enough, his later book of 1903, *Die Nationalökonomische Lehre vom Credit*, is dedicated to Böhm-Bawerk, who had

imagine His Excellency[10] perusing the latest homage to his greatness and finding that the little effort showed sound judgment, that the "young man" quoted perspicaciously, and that he was therefore worthy to enter the fold. It was good not to fall out with His Excellency even after having become an (unpaid!) university lecturer; for universities electing to a chair might very well take his advice. And once one became professor oneself, independence had not come yet; for one started as an associate professor and before one ascended to the august rank of a *full* professor, the Emperor might again consult His Excellency. It was thus not just common social background —again a result of the system, all the Austrians being lawyers (or rather jurists), most of them closely connected with the civil service, and about half of them nobles—it was not just this social background which unified the Austrians; it was the direct "influence," or perhaps better, the grip of Menger which enforced cohesion. Menger, even more than founder of a school, was the apex of a social system! The Austrians were by necessity the Menger school, as Hayek stressed.[11] I shall therefore try to sketch the position towards marginalism of the Austrian School *under the reign of Menger*, a reign which lasted from 1879 to 1903. I shall found my remarks mainly on Menger's writings and on those *Habilitationsschriften*—much too little known internationally—which were written, especially in the 1880's, under his immediate supervision or at least in close dependence upon him. For Menger embodied the unique Austrian tradition, and he was the least marginalist of all the Austrians. *The further his pupils escaped him, the more marginalist they became, precisely because they escaped him, precisely because they assimilated other traditions.*

In a symposium stressing these other traditions in separate con-

---

surpassed Menger in the hierarchy by that date.) Similarly R. Schüller, *Die klassische Nationalökonomie und ihre Gegner* (Berlin, 1895), is also dedicated to Menger. G. Gross, *Die Lehre vom Unternehmergewinn* (Leipzig, 1884), cites Menger on page 1. H. von Schullern-Schrattenhofen, in *Untersuchungen über Begriff und Wesen der Grundrente* (Leipzig, 1889), cites Menger on the second page of his book (p. 4) and then copiously. This is very revealing, as Schullern passed his *Habilitation* with Böhm-Bawerk in Innsbruck. (Böhm first appears on page 8 and then in another eleven footnotes, the distant Menger netting only five.) Numerous other examples could be added.

10. It is slight exaggeration to call Menger "His Excellency," as he did not become a Geheimrat until 1900, after his period of greatest immediate influence.

11. F. A. von Hayek, s.v. "Wiener Schule," in *Handwörterbuch der Sozialwissenschaften* (Stuttgart-Tübingen-Göttingen, 1962), vol. 12.

tributions, I think it is my duty to stress the particularly Austrian tradition. And in the nineteenth century, that was Menger pure and simple, Menger, who is to a large extent now forgotten precisely because in the reign of his successors in Vienna, the co-reign of Wieser (1903–24) and Böhm-Bawerk (1904–14)—the latter predominating during his lifetime—much of what was genuinely Menger's tradition got lost. In Menger's view his successors were, during the latter part of their lives, backsliders, especially Böhm-Bawerk, whose famous theory of capital and interest he judged to be "one of the greatest errors ever committed."[12] The long-lived Menger charged Böhm-Bawerk even in his obituary: "Böhm incorporated into his exposition of the theory of value numerous elements of past doctrine!"[13] As Böhm-Bawerk once told Schumpeter, well characterizing the university system of the day: "Science progresses through the old professors' dying off."[14] Unfortunately, in the case of Menger it was for once, I believe, retrogression. For Menger, who started marginalism in Austria, went beyond it at the same time, and to him, and I think also to us, his ideas beyond marginalism were the most precious. Menger is uniquely great because he surpassed marginalism at the same time that he created it; for as a pure marginalist he was certainly not the equal of Walras.[15]

As I have said, Menger's *Grundsätze* was an attempt to sketch a theory of economic development. The fifth paragraph of the initial chapter, to which this whole programmatic exposition leads, is entitled "The Causes of Progress in Human Welfare." There Menger states what is really, I believe, the central thesis of the book: It is not so much the division of labor, that is to say, a feature of the productive process, that increases welfare, but the constant widening of the range of goods and the improvement of their quality, i.e., changes in the productive output. Even the division of labor itself is a consequence of the increase in the range of commodities, which

---

12. J. A. Schumpeter, *History of Economic Analysis* (New York, 1954), p. 847, n. 8.

13. *Carl Menger, Gesammelte Werke*, 3:303. Menger there qualifies Böhm's missionary role for the theory of subjective value by the derogatory aside, ending in an exclamation mark, which is translated above.

14. Schumpeter, *History*, p. 850.

15. It is just because he admired Walras so much that Schumpeter is such a bad guide to the real Austrian achievement, which has always been in complete contrast to Walras.

makes it all the more "necessary and economic."[16] This is Mengerian "technical progress," the change of commodities (and, in a narrower sense, also of wants),[17] *product innovation*, to be contrasted with Marxian "technical progress" (that full development of classical ideas), the *process innovation* of an immutable product. It is thus in the true tradition of Menger that Schumpeter's treatment of technical progress is so much more inclusive than Marxian or modern neoclassical treatment. Notice, furthermore, that Menger usually speaks of the "quality and quantity" of goods and discusses quality in extenso in two long paragraphs.[18] Even this first statement thus shows that Mengerian goods are three-dimensional: they have *quantity*, *quality*, and *variety* as separate dimensions of dynamic change.

Lest we be chided by His Excellency from the grave for backsliding into an objective theory, we must not understand Mengerian technical progress as a change of *things*; it is above all a change of informational content, a change in *our* understanding. It is the "increasing understanding of the causal connections between things and human welfare"[19] which alone constitutes the correct "subjective value" view of progress. Menger wrote the remarkable sentence, "the quantities of consumption goods at human disposal are limited only by the extent of human knowledge."[20] For instance, advances in agricultural chemistry make agricultural produce much less scarce and on the other hand impart value to minerals up to then thought worthless, an object lesson impressed forcefully on German minds with the start of potassium mining in Thuringia in the 1860's.[21] Such "progress in perception"[22] also increases our wants; so Menger expressly speaks of a "capacity of human needs for *infinite* growth."[23]

Numerous further instances could be given of Menger's constant

16. Menger, *Grundsätze*, p. 28; Engl. trans., p. 73.

17. This vision may have owed something to one of Menger's own teachers, or rather to the supervisor of his own *Habilitation* soon to be his elder colleague, Lorenz von Stein.

18. Menger, *Grundsätze*, pp. 114–19; and pp. 66 f.

19. Ibid., p. 25.

20. Ibid., p. 29.

21. Menger, *Grundsätze*, p. 25, mentions mineral salts in agricultural chemistry.

22. Ibid., p. 62.

23. Ibid., p. 38, Engl. trans., p. 83.

stress on problems of information. Goods are defined as early as page 3 by the perception of their usefulness, and utility is *perceived* utility —in italics! What does entrepreneurial activity consist of? First and foremost of the dissemination of "information about the economic situation."[24] It will not seem surprising that this information-theory approach frequently leads Menger to illustrate his remarks on the production process by examples from the creation of human capital, for instance, the training of teachers well in advance of an educational need. Finally, Menger was quite positive that the creation of good will in enterprises increased the wealth of an economy, not only private wealth but also the sum total of social wealth; though here, for once, he did not say that this was because of a decrease in economic "frictions," a decrease in decisional effort, a creation of stable information channels.[25]

To the three dimensions of goods so far discussed—quantity, quality, and variety—we have thus to add *informational content*, variable over time and, at any given moment, over individuals. Because of the interindividual differences in information, Menger was chary of all aggregation,[26] especially of capital. He would have thoroughly enjoyed Gorman's proof[27] that for this very reason capital is indeed not amenable to an exact aggregation.

The stress on informational content is one of the respects in which Menger was very modern; but it was the one in which he found fewest followers. Schumpeter, of course, in the middle generation of the Austrians, built, on this cornerstone, combined with the Marxian notion of the progressive entrepreneur, his famous theory of innovation. Hayek, who in the third generation of Austrians is the economist closest to Menger's thought, has turned his attention since 1945[28] in-

24. Ibid., p. 137; Engl. trans., p. 162; the German text does not make it clear whether they have to inform others or themselves.

25. This is one of the points in which he considered Böhm-Bawerk's concept of capital much too objective. See especially *Grundsätze*, pp. 5 ff.

26. He discusses the aggregation of national wealth in an admirable passage (p. 75), rejecting it both for other unnamed reasons and because of "opposing interests." He accepts national wealth, and thus aggregates, however, as concepts for limited objectives.

27. W. M. Gorman, "Measuring the Quantity of Fixed Factors," in *Value, Capital and Growth: Papers in Honour of Sir John Hicks*, ed. J. N. Wolfe (Edinburgh, 1968), pp. 141 ff.

28. F. A. von Hayek, "The Use of Knowledge in Society," *American Economic Review*, vol. 35 (1945).

creasingly towards economic problems of information transmission and information content. But the first generation ignored this aspect of Menger's thought. Böhm-Bawerk, for instance, denied that the good will of firms increased wealth, a denial on which Menger still chided him in his obituary.[29] While Menger expressly states that the amount of information available to an individual, his "knowledge of business life."[30] increases his bargaining power and can thus modify resulting prices in his favor, Wieser is dense enough to state in one of *his* key passages that though entrepreneurs are better informed than consumers, they still have no influence on price whatsoever![31]

Mengerian man thus knows little about the present, though, interesting enough, he is constantly trying to *increase* his knowledge, creating *social institutions* to gather information, empowering growing droves of middlemen to act on his behalf. Still less than about the present does he know about the future. Again and again Menger stresses the *time dimension* of goods and the amount of *uncertainty* this entails. Just as Keynes was intrigued by the existence of the speculative motive, so Menger was the herald of *precautionary balances* in real[32] and monetary terms. "Indeed even among the goods of the poorest people, I believe some goods will be found that are expected to be utilized only in unforeseen contingencies."[33] And even money, Menger thought, is mainly held for opportunities which in fact do not

29. See *Carl Menger, Gesammelte Werke*, 3:301, where Menger charges Böhm with "augenfällige[n] Künstlichkeit der theoretischen Konstruktion" and "des Widerspruches, in welchem Böhm's Grundauffassung zur Erfahrung steht." Menger's views on good will were, as Professor Coats has reminded me, close to those of John R. Commons. See Commons, *Institutional Economics* (1934; reprint ed., Madison, Wis., 1959), 2:668 f. It is remarkable that Menger, the founder of one of the neoclassical schools, was very close to the Institutionalists, and not only on this point.

30. Menger, *Grundsätze*, p. 177; Engl. trans., p. 195.

31. F. von Wieser, *Über den Ursprung und die Hauptgesetze des wirtschaftlichen Werthes* (Vienna, 1884), p. 169: "[Die Producenten haben] selbstverständlich . . . ausser in den Fällen des Monopols, keine Macht über die Preise. . . . Der Werth wird von den Producenten nicht vorausbestimmt, sondern nur vorausgewusst." Contrast this passage with Menger, *Grundsätze*, p. 211 n. On the overtones of historical evaluation in this position of Wieser, see E. Streissler, "Structural Economic Thought: On the Significance of the Austrian School Today," *Zeitschrift für Nationalökonomie* 29 (1969): 237 ff., at §5, pp. 256 ff.

32. Menger, *Grundsätze*, p. 37, names a medicine chest and fire extinguishers as examples of precautionary stocks.

33. Ibid.; Engl. trans., p. 82.

materialize.[34] Finally the lack of knowledge about the future attains
its full significance because of the high complementarity of commodities, which makes it so very difficult to synchronize plans.[35]
The idea of the essential uncertainty of the future was much more
readily taken up by Menger's successors than the stress placed on the
defective information in the present. It was Böhm-Bawerk, and not
Keynes, as is sometimes stated, who presented a full-fledged theory
of certainty equivalents[36] in his *Habilitationsschrift* of 1881 and who
suggested the Neumann-Morgenstern utility measurement, the comparison between a certain occurrence and a lottery ticket.[37] It was,
however, already Menger, and not Böhm-Bawerk, who stressed the
myopic estimation of future wants, the defective telescopic faculty
of man.[38] Menger's ideas on uncertainty proved still vigorous among
Austrian authors in the thirties and forties. Morgenstern's famous
Sherlock Holmes/Moriarty example would have proved very much
to His Excellency's liking. And Menger also gave the first tentative
suggestions—with numerous graphic examples, for instance, from
town planning—for the advisability of perspective planning relative
to future wants. Or may one even say of sequential planning,[39] an
idea which, as everyone knows, was introduced into statistics by
Abraham Wald?

Why, if the time dimension loomed so large in his thought, was
Menger so cross with Böhm-Bawerk's theory of capital, that "greatest

34. Menger in his article "Geld" says, in translation: "The amount of money
which is used in actual payments constitutes only a part, and indeed a relatively
small part, of the cash necessary to a people, and . . . another part is held (in
order that the economy may function without friction) in the form of various reserves as a security against uncertain payments, which in many cases in fact are
never realized." Menger, s. v. "Geld," in *HdStw.*, 3d ed. (1909); reprinted in
Gesammelte Werke, 4:109 f.

35. Menger, *Grundsätze*, pp. 14 ff., 40 ff., esp. p. 43.

36. E. Böhm von Bawerk, *Rechte und Verhältnisse vom Standpunkte der Volks-
wirtschaftlichen Güterlehre* (Innsbruck, 1881), p. 88. His central sentence is:
"Wir reduziren mit einem Worte alle Nutzens-*Möglichkeiten* auf *Gewissheit*,
und stellen die Kompensation dadurch her, dass wir dasjenige, was wir an der
Wahrscheinlichkeit des erwarteten Nutzens hinzufügen mussten, um sie zur
Gewissheit zu erhöhen, von seiner *Grösse* oder seinem *Werthe* in Abzug bringen."

37. Ibid., pp. 86–89.

38. Menger, *Grundsätze*, p. 122: "Die Menschen [lassen] sich leicht verleiten
. . . vorübergehende intensive Genüsse höher zu achten, als ihre dauernde Wohl-
fahrt."

39. Ibid., p. 39.

error ever committed''? I think it was on the one hand because Böhm's analysis was much *too one-dimensional* for Menger, in whose own vision everything immediately ramified in some five to ten dimensions. Menger would describe the accumulation of capital as an increase in the range of capital goods and an ever-increasing complexity of the web of complementarities, while Böhm unified capital by the concept of the period of production. (The so-called Austrian theory of the cycle, on the other hand, fully derives from Menger, who develops it for fortuitous, though not for regular, changes in demand.[40] He is supported by an even fuller treatment from Komorzynski.)[41] Böhm tried to determine *the* rate of interest while Menger has a theory of the determinants of the price of labor, of rent, and of capital goods, but not of interest: in his view, interest was not a homogeneous quantity. There was possibly, though he never said so, a theory of ''own-rates'' and certainly a theory of profits. But for Menger most decidedly no theory of the *general level* of profits or of the general level of interest existed.[42] Profits and interest depended much too much on subjective influences to make the concept of their level meaningful. Furthermore Menger believed that profits depended to a great extent on the various *degrees of monopoly*—and he saw monopolies everywhere. Böhm on the other hand, had presented a theory of interest in terms of perfect competition. In fact it is quite clear in reading Menger that Menger was the first great economist who pictured, as a further important dimension of his thought, the world as one of *imperfect competition.* I need hardly remind you once more of his constant stress on changes in the quality of goods, an essential idea in the theory of imperfect competition. Even more important, his whole chapter on price theory introduces *monopoly theory* as the *general theory,* argues that monopoly is much more prevalent than is commonly realized by pointing to the single artisan or grocer in a village,[43] and expressly states that even the competitor has a limited power to fix prices,[44] which places such a com-

40. Ibid., pp. 15 f., with an example from the supply crisis of cotton during the American Civil War.

41. Komorzynski, *Der Werth in der isolirten Wirtschaft,* pp. 32–50.

42. See especially the article Menger wrote before the publication of Böhm's central book in order to fend off Böhm's impending attack. C. Menger ''Zur Theorie des Kapitals'' (1888), in *Gesammelte Werke,* 3:135 ff., esp. pp. 182 f.

43. Menger, *Grundsätze,* pp. 201 f.

44. Ibid., pp. 206 ff., esp. p. 211 n.

petitor firmly in the fold of imperfect competition. Alas, in this vision, too, he found no followers, Wieser in particular being enamored of perfect competition.[45]

Not only was Böhm-Bawerk's theory of capital too one-dimensional for Menger; it was also *too technical*. To introduce technical terms meant treating with the archenemy in an unforgivable way. Menger simply did not believe that laws of production, if they existed at all, had anything to do with economics;[46] and Böhm had postulated a law of decreasing technical productivity of roundaboutness (as we now know, an idea not wholly thought through). Some authors have even credited Menger with having postulated a law of increasing roundaboutness himself.[47] But that is not correct. In fact it is instructive to see where Menger differed from Böhm in this respect. Menger states in one place that a more roundabout technique chosen in production has to be more productive than a less roundabout technique discarded.[48] But this is an axiom of choice with a positive interest rate (discussed in this passage), not a technical law. And in general he speaks of the progressive extension of the *planning horizon* ever further into the future,[49] a subjective concept completely different from the mainly technical idea of an increase in the period of production.

Finally we have to consider Menger's most radical departure from generally received economic ideas: he did not suppose that one and the same good had at a given moment of time *everywhere the same price*; and still less that it had the same price at neighboring moments of time. Menger wrote a long chapter on the marketability of commodities (we would nowadays say their varying degrees of *liquidity*), a chapter which is the prelude to monetary theory and where money is appropriately introduced as the commodity of highest liquidity.[50]

45. With Wieser, in contrast to Menger, monopoly is a negligible exception. See, *Über den Ursprung*, p. 169 and passim.
46. Menger, *Grundsätze*, p. 120, culminates in the sentence: "Im practischen Leben [fragt] Niemand nach der Geschichte der Entstehung eines Gutes."
47. Hayek, in his "Einleitung" to *Carl Mengers Gesammelte Werke*, 1:xv, correctly claims for Menger only "his distinct anticipation of the Böhm-Bawerkian doctrine of the underestimation of future wants" (pp. 122 and 127–28).
48. Menger, *Grundsätze*, p. 136.
49. Ibid., p. 127.
50. Menger calls liquidity "Absatzfähigkeit der Waaren," to which a whole section of the book, chap. 7, § 2, pp. 233–49, is devoted. This section is justified on its first page, p. 233, as follows: "Auch ist es ja klar, dass die bisher noch

(In the concept of liquidity and the stress on precautionary balances, in fact in his whole monetary theory, Menger is very close to Keynes. No wonder; both Menger and Keynes, by the time he wrote the *General Theory*, had received formative experiences from the stock exchange.) In markets that are not well-ordered, price tends to vary much,[51] Menger emphasizes, a problem which becomes particularly glaring if the value of a commodity has first to be estimated in a time-consuming way, as with real estate and factories.[52] But even the well-ordered market determines only price limits. Within these limits —and it is suggested in the quantitative illustrations that they are wide[53]—prices are determined by a *bargaining process*. A decisive term used by Menger to describe the determination of price, a term avidly taken up by many of his followers, is *price conflict* (Preiskampf).[54] He stresses that a divergence between demand and supply prices is ''a general feature of the economy,''[55] an idea which he took from stock-exchange quotations. Finally he is explicit on the point that *exchange* as such is *not costless*,[56] a fact which again militates against a unique equilibrium price.

That a lack of full determination of price was much to the fore in Menger's mind can also be seen through the *Habilitationsschriften* of the 1880's. Gross,[57] for example, presented a complex bargaining theory of profit determination, especially stressing interest bar-

---

immer controverse Lehre über den Ursprung des Geldes, des absatzfähigsten aller Güter, in den hier einschlägigen Untersuchungen allein ihre volle und befriedigende Begründung finden kann.''

51. Menger, *Grundsätze*, p. 241.

52. Ibid., p. 248.

53. Ibid., pp. 177 f., 80–100; 30–80 on p. 184; on the following pages successively more individuals are introduced demanding the commodity in question, always above 10 percent. Even in the example of competition, p. 204:50 to 60!

54. Ibid., p. 177. G. Gross and Schullern-Schrattenhofen frequently use this term.

55. Ibid., p. 174.

56. Ibid., p. 170.

57. G. Gross, *Die Lehre vom Unternehmergewinn* (Leipzig, 1885). Gross's explanation of the manifold determinants of profit in a multidimensional bargaining process was certainly much closer to Menger's ideal of conformity to the ''Auffassung des gemeinen Lebens'' than Böhm-Bawerk's theory, which—interestingly enough—the theoretician Menger, who was much closer to the best tradition of the Historical School than he thought, and much closer than his followers, considered too theoretical. Gross, being a railway director, of course knew what he was talking about.

gains[58]—wage bargains being, according to him, so well understood
that a short treatment is deemed sufficient;[59] Schullern-Schrattenhofen[60] wrote on the bargaining elements in rent determination; and
so on. In these books Menger's term *price conflict* is widely used as a
descriptive term.

We can now collect our strands of thought. Menger had incorporated into his founding volume *practically all the ideas which
make the application of the marginal calculus difficult and hazy*; and
by his express refusal to recognize a unique and determinate market
price he even discarded the main prop that supports marginalism.
The law of markets was in the later Austrian School very appropriately
termed *Wieser's law of the equalization of price* (Gesetz des Preissaus-
gleiches); and even this term is rather evocative of a *process* leading
to equilibrium, not of equilibrium itself. Menger, on the other hand,
could not even conceive of equilibrium as anything precisely describable.[61] His economics in its substantive content was disequi-

58. Gross, pp. 132–36. Menger's and his followers' theoretical ideas on bargaining owe much to Hermann and to Schäffle, the latter being Menger's immediate predecessor in the chair at Vienna University. F. B. W. von Hermann,
Staatswirthschaftliche Untersuchungen (Munich, 1832; 2d ed., 1870), who is
merely followed by Schäffle, is very explicit that ''der Preis [wird] keineswegs
durch die Kosten allein bestimmt . . . , wie Ricardo und seine Schüler lehren''
(p. 429). He presents a price theory depending on the different elements of
supply and demand. Demand and supply, it is suggested, determine the *limits*
within which the price will lie. For instance, relative to demand, he speaks, on
p. 428, of ''die obere Gränze, über die sie [viz., the quantity of goods forming
the price] nicht steigen kann.''

59. Gross, p. 145: ''Die Gründe, welche die *Minimal-* und *Maximalgrenze* des
gemeinen Arbeitslohnes bestimmen, sind so vielfach und so gründlich erörtert
worden, dass wir glauben, uns hier ganz kurz fassen zu können.'' He then treats
the subject in twenty pages (!), giving particular attention to the remuneration
of qualified and white-collar labor and studying managerial remuneration.

60. Schullern-Schrattenhofen, *Untersuchungen*, e.g., his conclusions on p. 31
or on p. 93.

61. I differ from F. Machlup, ''Equilibrium and Disequilibrium: Misplaced
Concreteness and Disguised Politics,'' *Economic Journal* 68 (1958): 1 ff., esp.
pp. 4 f., that every economic model has to start out and to end with an equilibrium
position. Machlup, in fact, implicitly assumes that all economic processes can be
represented by very special mathematical models, and furthermore that adjustment speeds tend to be high. I use the term ''disequilibrium economics'' in the
precise sense that prices are thought to be, not point variables, but subject to
a distribution; and that in spite of tendencies towards uniformity of price there
are sufficient tendencies towards divergence to keep the coefficient of variation
of price approximately constant over time. Such a model might be termed an
equilibrium model relative to the variance or the coefficient of variation of price,
but disequilibrium economics relative to prices themselves.

librium economics.[62]

If Menger did not believe in equilibrium, how is it possible that we find in his founding treatise all the laws of the determination of price and especially of the determination of the prices of productive inputs? Menger would have replied that he had to show the fundamental causes that determined economic processes. It is perhaps best to put this contrast in exact mathematical language: Menger did not try to outline the equilibrium points, the solutions of a set of differential equations; he tried to sketch the whole force map. Formally the two descriptions of a system of differential equations are, of course, identical. But their uses, their interpretations are different. Menger wanted to sketch the *forces leading towards equilibrium* while leaving it undecided how quickly equilibrium tends to be approached and how closely it is approximated. He wrote the revealing sentence that individuals "will endeavor to attain clarity . . . [only to that] degree of exactness that is sufficient for the practical success of their activity."[63] If individuals do not need to be overprecise, why should the economist try to be so in describing their decision processes? And if Menger's treatment of the maximization problem in production is sometimes criticized as somewhat sketchy, I am sure it was purposely so. Komorzynski states explicitly that a precise specification of the productive inputs into commodities is in general impossible.[64] Menger did not believe that the input-output relationship even in the sense of a production function is a fixed datum; rather, the relationship between inputs and outputs is tenuous and haphazard.

Menger, it is true, also knew a *tâtonnement* process. But it is most instructive to contrast his *tâtonnement* with that of Walras. Mengerian man has first to gather copious amounts of information about the state of the world, an effort undertaken especially by merchants and

62. Misled by E. Kauder, *A History of Marginal Utility Theory* (Princeton, 1956), p. 100, I formerly thought Menger had announced his dissent from Walras's central positions to the latter by writing him: "A conformity does not exist between us. There is an analogy of concepts in a few points, but not in the decisive questions." This (free) translation of a passage in Menger's letter to Walras of 27 Jan. 1887 is, however, misconstrued by Kauder. It refers to Gossen (!) in relation to Menger, not to Walras. See W. Jaffé, *Correspondence of Léon Walras and Related Papers* (Amsterdam, 1965), 2:176, Letter 765.

63. Menger, *Grundsätze*, p. 39; Engl. trans., p. 84.

64. Komorzynski, *Der Werth in der isolirten Wirthschaft*, pp. 9-11, 14.

industrialists.[65] But even these cut their efforts short. The task would become insupportably difficult if goods were not *standardized,* if institutions for gathering information, like the stock exchange, were not created, and if a numerous class of middlemen did not come into existence whose sole purpose it is to improve the *tâtonnement* process. Thus the device of the auctioneer also appears in Menger; but here the auctioneer is real, a broad social class. By and by we gain ever better insight into the true equilibrium state (here there is an optimistic note in Menger) though part of the real gain of the *tâtonnement* process is said to lie in a realistic representation of the true degree of risk.[66] Thus Menger's *tâtonnement* is a social process and a most laborious one to boot. One might, perhaps, condense the contrast between Menger and Walras thus: *Walras's tâtonnement takes a minute;*[67] *Menger's tâtonnement takes a century!* Needless to say, with Menger we are most of the time out of equilibrium in the sense that the equilibrium price has not yet been found.

Menger's lack of belief in the appropriateness of equilibrium analysis also explains his lack of belief in the expediency of using mathematics. It must be stressed that he came from a mathematically minded family so that the explanation of his behavior by lack of mathematical training does not really hold water. Rather, the then prevalent mathematics, calculus, was useful only in the description of equilibrium situations, and Menger was not interested in these. It is only today that we have the mathematical tools to treat the kind of problem Menger set himself: topology, the theory of graphs, some of the more complex ideas in the theory of differential equations, and above all, the explicit introduction of probability distributions as in the theory of stochastic processes.

Schumpeter once wrote " 'subjective' theory must always appeal to 'objective' facts [data] if it is to produce concrete results."[68] Menger faced this dilemma squarely. He wrote a completely subjective theory; and that meant that he eschewed deriving concrete results.

65. Menger, *Grundsätze,* p. 46.
66. Ibid., pp. 241–49.
67. L. Walras, *Eléments d'économie politique pure* (Lausanne, 1874), p. 69: "On peut voir, sur de grands marchés fonctionnant même sans courtiers ni crieurs, le prix courant d'équilibre se déterminer en quelques minutes [!], et des quantités considérables de marchandise s'échanger à ce prix en deux ou trois quarts d'heure."
68. Schumpeter, *History,* p. 911.

He was content to show all the manifold dimensions of causation in the economic field. In his view the final outcome of all these forces at work could not be fully described. And that is the basic failure of his theory: he ended in doubt and not in positive theorems.

There was, for instance, one basic decision problem which he did not attack: If there is no such thing as a level of the rate of interest or the rate of profit, how is the problem of recruitment into entrepreneurial occupations to be solved? How do people know whether one type of industry is more promising than another?[69] Presumably Menger thought that occupations are chosen purely in a social context, Jews being born as entrepreneurs or doctors and Catholics of the lower aristocracy as civil servants or officers. But even for his own Austria this is not a wholly satisfactory picture. Menger's analysis, as Viner[70] points out, is in fact altogether devoid of supply functions of a long-run kind and to a certain extent also of a short-run kind. He never considers the variations of services from a given stock—for instance, the supply of labor services. Thus, when we wish to continue his suggestions nowadays, we have to give ourselves a push and jump a little beyond Menger's paralysing scepticism. We can, for example, use the concept of an equilibrium distribution of events which themselves are not equilibria. Then, with the much more refined tools of the present-day economist at our command, we are able to derive useful theorems from the manifold suggestions which Menger has left us.

69. G. J. Stigler, in *Production and Distribution Theories* (New York, 1949), p. 148, puts his finger with nicety on this weakest point in Menger: ''Menger's preoccupation with directly consumable goods probably plays a part in the fundamental defect in his theory—the complete neglect of costs—but a more important explanation lies in his failure to realize the continuity of production.''

70. J. Viner, ''Schumpeter's *History of Economic Analysis*,'' in his *The Long View and the Short: Studies in Economic Theory and Policy* (Glencoe, Ill., 1958), p. 363.

The "Marginal Revolution" and the Decline and Fall of English Classical Political Economy

T. W. Hutchison

I

THE "marginal revolution" is a capacious term comprising some highly heterogeneous elements: *three* such elements if one starts from the famous trinity of Jevons, Menger, and Walras; or *two*, highly disparate, elements if one contrasts simply what happened to economic theory in England with what happened on the Continent. In Vienna and Lausanne what happened was the systematic deployment (though not the first original discovery) of the marginal concept, followed over the succeeding two or three decades by a great period of constructive development, *but without any fundamental overturning or rejection of the central theories of value and distribution previously prevalent in those parts.* It may seem, therefore, to be stretching the overworked term "revolution" pretty far to apply it to what happened in Vienna or Lausanne (or on the Continent). In England, on the other hand, there had been the long domination of an orthodox body of doctrine comprising method and policy as well as theory and including, in particular, theories regarding labor, value, and wages (analytically linked in their simplifying assumptions) which had long been impervious to intellectual influences from abroad. The rejection in the late sixties and early seventies of these central theories of value and wages, by Jevons and others of a new cohort or generation of economists, which was accompanied by a more widespread questioning of orthodox methods and policy principles, was a pretty sudden and rapid one. This might well be described as the destructive phase of a "revolution," though the constructive phase was slow in getting under way and only followed after a long time-lag.

These are the arguments we are elaborating in the present article.

T. W. HUTCHISON *is Mitsui Professor of Economics at the University of Birmingham.*

II

In order to describe, assess, or explain (to the extent that "explanation" is possible) what happened with regard to economic theory in 1871 and the years either side, it seems essential to distinguish between the state of economic theory with its prevailing orthodoxies in the leading Continental countries in the 1860's and early '70's, on the one hand, and the peculiar and very different position in Britain, on the other. The history of economic thought in the first half or three-quarters of the nineteenth century was and still is often portrayed in very Anglo-centric terms, as though the theories which achieved for so long in Britain such an extraordinary dominance and authority, perhaps unique in the history of the subject, enjoyed a similar hold and authority elsewhere in Europe. This was not the case. The contexts and backgrounds from which Jevons' *Theory*, Menger's *Grundsätze*, and Walras's *Eléments* emerged differed significantly, at any rate as between the first-named and the other two. Of course, in the broadest and most general terms all three faced the same fundamental questions of the determinants of value, prices, and incomes, and all inherited the same answers which had come down from a common Western tradition extending from Aristotle to Adam Smith. But in the nineteenth century the theories of value and distribution had developed pretty differently in Britain as contrasted with the rest of western Europe. Moreover, in the middle decades of the nineteenth century, say from the late forties to the late sixties, there was very little communication, regarding economic theory, between the economists of Britain and those of the Continent.[1] There

1. "Insularity and Cosmopolitanism in Economic Ideas, 1870–1914," *Papers and Proceedings of the American Economic Association*, May 1955, pp. 1 ff. Neither on the import nor on the export side were there any significant movements of ideas, in or out of Britain, regarding economic theory, between the late forties and the late sixties, except perhaps for the influx of Comteist and historical ideas in the late sixties, which were of methodological rather than theoretical significance. An example of English insularity or the rejection of *imports* into England is furnished by J. E. Cairnes, as the last of the "classical" economists. As Professor S. G. Checkland put it: "Cairnes had no doubt that political economy was essentially an English business, and that contemporary French and German ideas were scarcely worthy of notice." *Manchester School*, May 1951, p. 149. Checkland cites Cairnes's claim that "every great step in the progress of economic science (I do not think an important exception can be named) has been won by English thinkers." *Essays on Political Economy* (1873), p. 232. Also regarding the absence of imports into England, F. W. Taussig wrote: "The insular condition of social and political speculation in Great Britain in the

was no world market, nor even a Western European Common Market in economic theorizing, and the British market was dominated by a monopolistically inclined orthodoxy—indeed, for a time almost by a single monopolist. Jevons, Menger, and Walras reached their results by differing routes, with differing degrees of indebtedness to differing sets of predecessors. In particular, they had to contend with very different prevailing theoretical doctrines, or orthodoxies. So there is a considerable element of coincidence in the publication of Jevons' and Menger's books coming in the same year. On the other hand, it could be argued that the marginal concept and the marginal utility idea were of such basic significance that they were bound to come through sometime and that the increasing occurrence in isolated publications in different countries of the marginal concept, and of its application to utility, made a coincidence in dates inevitable sooner or later. However, the apples were not ripening on a single international tree, but on separate national trees, and there was no significant communication until after they had been separately picked—when, in fact, international communication began between Jevons and Walras in 1874. Certainly there were important reasons, as we shall discuss later, why 1870 or '71 was an appropriate moment for Jevons' *Theory* to appear in England if it was to make an impact or be seen subsequently as marking a kind of breakthrough. But this hardly applies to Menger's *Grundsätze*, which in a sense might have appeared in

---

middle of the century, and the stagnation of economic thought in particular, prevented any breath of influence from reaching English thinkers. The Germans went their way, unnoticed by their English-speaking contemporaries. . . . The French never were much influenced by Ricardo.'' *Wages and Capital* (1896; reprint ed., 1932), p. 266.

Regarding *exports from* England Bagehot observed: ''Political Economy, as it was taught by Ricardo, . . . has remained insular. I do not mean that it was not often read and understood; of course it was so, though it was often misread and misunderstood. But it never at all reigned abroad as it reigns here.'' *Economic Studies* (1879; new ed., 1895), p. 4. Marshall also, in 1897, wrote of the classical theories being mostly ''bad sailors; and if they were met with in other lands, they generally had a languishing air as though they had not recovered from sea-sickness.'' *Memorials of Alfred Marshall*, ed. A. C. Pigou (1925), p. 295. Earlier (1876) Jevons had observed regarding English exports to France: ''Foreign economists, such as De Laveleye, Courcelle-Seneuil, Cournot, Walras and others have taken a course almost entirely independent of the predominant English school.'' *Principles of Economics* (1905), p. 190. In his essay below in this volume, Professor Piero Barucci notes regarding Italy in the latter part of the nineteenth century: ''Economic classicism counted only a handful of followers. Ricardo was still rarely read and little understood.''

Germany or Austria at any moment in the previous decade or so, like Gossen's *Entwicklung* or Mangoldt's *Grundriss*.[2]

Menger's *Grundsätze* certainly marks an important beginning, unlike, to the same extent, Jevons' *Theory*, which can be said to mark an end as well as, and as much as, a beginning. Menger's work marks very definitively the foundation of the Austrian School, with its long and remarkable history. Though the Austrian School is not as homogeneous and monolithic an entity as it is sometimes treated as being, it can be said to possess certain common family features which can mainly be traced to the *Grundsätze*. What made the breakthrough for Menger and his *Grundsätze*, transforming the work from being simply another extremely distinguished but isolated exposition of the marginal utility idea, was the almost immediate adherence of two brilliant and very prolific disciples in Wieser and Böhm-Bawerk, though it was more than a decade before these two were ready to publish their major contributions.

In Menger's *Grundsätze* (though the *term* is not used) the very careful and precise elaboration of the marginal concept is the key technical or analytical contribution, being applied from the start both to consumers' goods and services and to producers' goods and services, establishing, at least in outline, much of the complete pattern of marginal microeconomic analysis. But although Menger does have a paragraph or two attacking cost-of-production theories in terms similar to Jevons' well-known passage on "bygones," he was certainly not rebelling, as Jevons was in England, against a powerfully entrenched orthodox theory of value and distribution which had given little, and certainly much too little, scope to utility, demand, and consumers' wants. Nor was Menger confronted, regarding the theory of distribution, by the wages-fund and natural-wage theories, which were the prevailing orthodoxies for Jevons, and which Jevons attacked alongside the labor and cost-of-production theory of value. Menger did not even think it necessary to mention the wages-fund and natural-wage theories. The wages-fund theory had been demolished by Hermann in 1832 and never gained significant support in Germany.[3] Nor did the Ricardian natural-wage doctrine. Thus the link

2. Mangoldt's *Grundriss* should certainly be ranked with the three celebrated works of 1871 and 1874, and perhaps *above* two of them.

3. F. W. Taussig, *Wages and Capital* (1896; reprinted ed. 1932), pp. 266 ff.,

between wages or distribution and productivity and (ultimately) consumer demand was not suppressed in Germany as it had been in the "English" theory. Therefore Menger's basically unified approach to the valuation of final consumers' goods and of factors of production was not in itself a fundamentally novel or unorthodox departure, but was in harmony with the prevailing approach. What was novel, and of the greatest technical importance, was simply the introduction, analysis, and application of the marginal concept.

Anyhow, Menger, as he himself originally proclaimed in his Preface of 1871, was following out ideas developed most recently by German predecessors. He certainly contributed a fundamental and vital concept, one that advanced decisively a tradition of value theory, starting from utility or human wants, which can be traced back to Aristotle (whom Menger frequently cites as an authority both in the *Grundsätze* and later in the *Untersuchungen*).[4] When, therefore, he felt aggrieved at the very restricted interest in his pathbreaking ideas in Germany, this was not because a ruling orthodoxy with

explains that "the radical objection," to the wages-fund doctrine of Hermann and his followers is that "Capital, after all, is not the real source from which wages are paid. That real source is the income of those who buy the products made by labourers, or, briefly, the income of consumers." Marshall (1885) also noted (perhaps with a touch of chauvinism) that "the French and German economists, though on the whole they had not done nearly so much good work as the English, have never given any countenance to the doctrine that there is a determinate wages fund." *Principles of Economics*, ed. Guillebaud (1961), 2:606.

4. Menger emphasizes in his preface to the *Grundsätze* that "the reform of the most important principles of our science here attempted is therefore built upon a foundation laid by previous work that was produced almost entirely by the industry of German scholars." *Principles of Economics*, trans. J. Dingwall and B. F. Hoselitz (1950), p. 49. The index to the *Grundsätze* contains most of the great names in the European utility tradition from Aristotle onwards, including the great eighteenth-century theorists Galiani, Condillac, Genovesi, and Beccaria, with J. B. Say and Auguste Walras from nineteenth-century France, and from among Menger's more immediate German forerunners, K. H. Rau, Hermann, and Mangoldt.

Later Wieser, also, in the preface to *Natural Value* emphasizes how much "Menger is indebted to the German school of political economists. . . . It may be said that, in great part, the German school long ago formulated the conceptions, leaving us only the task of filling them out by adequate observations. . . . The new value theory . . . is in truth fulfillment of what German theory had long demanded." Wieser cites as forerunners of the marginal utility analysis, or of the Austrian or Mengerian version of it, "all those who have derived value from utility," listing most of those mentioned above from Menger's index and adding the very interesting name of Daniel Bernoulli. *Natural Value*, trans. C. A. Malloch (1893), pp. xxxii–xxxiv.

regard to value (and wage) theory was too strongly entrenched, or because it was regarded, in the famous words of John Stuart Mill, that "happily, there is nothing in the laws of value which remains for the present or any future writer to clear up; the theory of the subject is complete."[5] Moreover, if Menger's ideas did not at once make much headway, or as much as he had hoped, in spite of his immediately acquiring such brilliant disciples and expositors, it was because there had come to be very little interest throughout much of Germany in the advance and refinement of economic theory of any kind (which was the reason for Menger's explosion against the German historical economists in his *Untersuchungen* twelve years later, and for the subsequent *Methodenstreit*).

III

The theories of the English school were scarcely more influential in France in the middle of the nineteenth century than they were in Germany and Austria. Léon Walras started from a tradition of French economic theory which emphasized the role of utility and scarcity in the determination of value. This went back to Condillac and in particular to J. B. Say (whom Schumpeter describes as Walras's "true predecessor"). Say not only emphasized the role of utility in value but based the explanation of the incomes to factors on their productivity. More directly, Walras was indebted to his father and Cournot. As Schumpeter says: "He paid conventional respect to A. Smith. The rest of the great Englishmen meant little to him."[6]
Walras was indeed something of a rebel and felt himself almost

5. *Principles of Political Economy*, ed. W. J. Ashley (1909), p. 436. It is true that in the introduction by Menger's son to the posthumous second edition of the *Grundsätze* (1923), there is a quotation (undated) from the notes of Menger senior maintaining that he had "set himself the task of countering the theories of Adam Smith which he saw to be erroneous," and that as regards himself and Jevons, "we both stood in strict opposition to Smith's theory" (pp. vii–viii). This is one of those puzzles in Menger's writings—there are a number in the *Untersuchungen*—which are very difficult to interpret owing to the obscurity enveloping Menger's early intellectual development and the main influences acting on him. To counter or come out in opposition to the theories of Adam Smith in Germany and Austria in the 1860's had about as much or as little significance as today to counter or to come out in opposition to the theories of Keynes in Chicago.
6. J. A. Schumpeter, *History of Economic Analysis* (1954), p. 828. As Professor G. J. Stigler puts it: "Say's approach was fundamentally much more modern than that of his English contemporaries." *Essays in the History of Economics* (1965), p. 304.

an outcast. But what he was rebelling against was not orthodox theories of value and distribution, but, first, the particular kind of extreme laissez-faire policy dogmas prevailing in France, and, secondly, the rejection of mathematics by those whom he described as the "mandarins" of French economic orthodoxy, in whose citadels he had not been able to find employment. Walras certainly did not have to start by contending against an entrenched theoretical orthodoxy on value and distribution, such as was represented in Britain by the wages-fund theory, the labor and cost-of-production theory of value, and the natural-wage theory. Walras rightly describes these theories as those of "the English school." They were part neither of the tradition he built upon nor of the orthodoxies with which he contended. But here and there in the *Eléments* he turns aside for a page or two in order to criticize them. Indeed he recognizes that "the efforts of the English school to develop a theory of rent, wages and interest were far more sustained and thorough than those of the various French schools," emphasizing "the order and continuity of development and the enduring quality of the English doctrine."[7] Sustained, thorough, and orderly the "English" doctrines may well have been, but they seemed to Walras to suffer from a certain fundamental error as compared with the traditional French (and German) approach.

On the subject of value Walras writes:

> The science of economics offers three major solutions to the problem of the origin of value. The first, that of Adam Smith, Ricardo and McCulloch, is the English solution, which traces the origin of value to *labour*. This solution is too narrow, because it fails to attribute value to things which, in fact, do have value. The second solution, that of Condillac and J. B. Say, is the French solution, which traces the origin of value to *utility*. This solution is too broad, because it attributes value to things which, in fact, have no value. Finally, the third solution, that of Burlamaqui and my father, A. A. Walras, traces the origin of value to *scarcity* [*rareté*]. This is the correct solution.[8]

7. *Elements of Pure Economics*, trans. W. Jaffé (1954), p. 398.
8. Ibid., p. 201. The "scarcity" tradition stems from the same, originally Aristotelian, source as the "utility" tradition, coming down through the "nat-

Walras's distinction between his second and third solutions owes much to his eagerness to differentiate his position from that of French orthodoxy, which mainly followed J. B. Say. For both of the French or Continental solutions, though distinguished by Walras, recognize the role of utility and demand not adequately provided for in the "English" theory.

On distribution Walras, after expounding the marginal productivity theory, turns aside to demolish the "English" theories. He recognizes, by way of contrast that "J. B. Say had a tolerably clear and accurate idea of the combination of the three productive services in the process of production. The terminology he employed was good; we have therefore adopted it ourselves."[9] This is almost the highest possible praise from Walras. When he discusses briefly "the English theory of wages," as enunciated by J. S. Mill, and in particular the wages-fund theory, he dismisses as "nothing but a long and tedious quibble" one of Mill's essential fundamental propositions to the effect that to purchase produce is not to employ labor. On the other hand Walras later pays tribute to Jevons who "wrote ten remarkable pages at the close of the preface to his second edition (pp. xlviii–lvii), in which he clearly stated that the formula of the English school, in any case the school of Ricardo and Mill, must be reversed, for the prices of productive services are determined by the prices of their products and not the other way round."[10]

---

ural law" school, and notably through Pufendorf, to Carmichael and Hutcheson. Walras cites Burlamaqui, whose ideas descend directly from this great school.

9. Ibid., p. 425. The contrast is especially marked between Walras's treatment of J. B. Say's distribution theory and that of J. E. Cairnes, representing the "English" viewpoint: "Thus he [J. B. Say] tells us that rent, interest, and wages are all perfectly analogous; each giving the measure of utility which the productive agency (of which each respectively is the reward) subserves in production. Rent, according to this theory, does not depend on the different costs at which, owing to the physical qualities of the soil, agricultural produce is raised, nor profit on the cost of labour, nor wages on demand and supply, but each on the utility of the functions which land, capital, and labour respectively perform in the creation of the ultimate product. Thus the distinct economic laws which regulate the distribution of wealth amongst the proprietors of these three productive agencies are confounded, in order to introduce a *moral* argument in defence of the existing structure of society, and to place the three classes of landlords, capitalists, and labourers on the same footing of social convenience and equity." Cairnes, *Character and Logical Method of Political Economy*, 2d ed. (1875), p. 14.

10. Walras, *Éléments*, p. 45. See also p. 385, where Walras attributes to Jevons "the germ" of the marginal productivity analysis in chaps. 6 and 7 of his

IV

The note of challenge and revolt against the central theories of the dominant orthodoxy, described by Jevons as "the Ricardo-Mill Economics,"[11] is prominently featured throughout his *Theory* and at once emphasized on the first pages of his original preface. We have just seen how irrelevant such a note of revolt against the prevailing central theories of value and distribution would have been for Menger and Walras, who confronted no dominant, authoritative textbook proclaiming "completeness" (with nothing "for the present or any future writer to clear up") for a treatment of value which gave such an inadequate role to demand and the final consumer.

It must be emphasized, next, that Jevons' call to revolt was not an isolated, individual challenge against the prevailing theories, although it was the first of Jevons' public writings in which he proclaimed this kind of protest (his paper of 1862 had simply stated "a Theory of Economy" without any criticism of or challenge to other theories). Jevons, in fact, in 1871 was giving a weighty and spirited shove to a bandwagon of revolt which had begun to roll two or three years previously. In 1862 his paper had made no impact, but by 1870 he saw that the time was ripe for a fundamental revolt against the prevailing orthodoxies, which was, in fact, under way. For in the late sixties a series of attacks had begun on the central body of orthodox theory, notably on the wages-fund theory, but more broadly on the method and policy conclusions of the dominant English school of thought.

In fact in the space of a few years in the late sixties and early seventies the Ricardo-Mill system of theory underwent a remarkably

---

Theory. Walras is only prepared to agree to a very soft version of the Malthusian theory and strongly rejects the harder sorts of policy conclusion derived from it (p. 388).

11. *Theory of Political Economy,* 4th ed. (1931), p. li. Jevons here "insists" on a view which "will overthrow many of the principal doctrines of the Ricardo-Mill Economics." Finding an apposite description for the enemy to be "overthrown" ("The Mercantile System," "Ricardo-Mill Economics," "Classical Theory") is an essential element of a successful attempt at "revolution," probably more important than simply the statement of some fundamentally new idea. Jevons' 1862 paper had, of course, contained no attack on dominant theories and was disregarded. Similarly what made Keynes' *General Theory* "revolutionary" was not so much any other new developments in his own ideas since the *Treatise* of six years previously, but the identification of "Classical" theory as a formidable and ubiquitous enemy to be overthrown.

sudden and rapid collapse of credibility and confidence, considering
how long and authoritative had been its dominance in Britain. In view
of the rapidity and central importance of the change in ideas, what
took place in Britain might not unreasonably be described as a "revolution," though mainly in a destructive, negative sense:[12] there was
much less agreement between the rebels regarding what should replace the orthodox theories than that these theories should be rejected.
For nearly two decades there was in Britain a somewhat confused
interregnum. But in this negative sense the term "revolution" may
be justifiable, even though some aspects or components of the orthodox
system survived the attacks, some never were attacked, and a sort
of pious counterrevolutionary restoration or retention of some of the
"classical" terminology and concepts was subsequently undertaken
by Marshall.

The collapse in confidence seems to have been common to and
more or less simultaneous among both the handful of competent con-
tributors to economic theorizing and the wider "educated class" of
the general reviews. The upheaval beginning in the late sixties and the
watershed of the seventies were, of course, concerned with policy and
method as well as theory. Clearly, after the extension of the franchise
in 1867, fundamental new departures in policy would probably have
to be considered sooner or later. Regarding method, however, the his-

12. Many indications of a general breakdown in confidence, among both economists and the wider interested public, in the prevailing orthodoxies can be cited
from economic writings in the early and middle seventies. For a number of these
see T. W. Hutchison, *Review of Economic Doctrines, 1870–1929* (1953), p. 6.
There were, for example, the well-known words of Walter Bagehot, writing in the
middle seventies of Political Economy: "It lies rather dead in the public mind.
Not only does it not excite the same interest as formerly but there is not exactly
the same confidence in it." *Economic Studies,* new ed. (1895), p. 3. In 1876 Jevons
found that "respect for the names of Ricardo and Mill seems no longer to preserve unanimity. . . . We find the state of the science to be almost chaotic."
Principles of Economics (1905), pp. 190–91. In 1877 Sir Francis Galton was leading an attempt to exclude political economy from the British Association. See
"Considerations Adverse to the Maintenance of Section F," *Journal of the Royal
Statistical Society,* Sept. 1877, p. 468. Regarding attitudes to policy there is the
evidence of Lord Milner about the Oxford of 1872–76, years "marked by a very
striking change in the social and political philosophy of the place, a change which
has subsequently reproduced itself on the larger stage of the world. When I went
up, the Laisser faire theory still held the field. All the recognized authorities were
'orthodox' economists of the old school. But within ten years the few men who
still held the old doctrines in their extreme rigidity had come to be regarded as
curiosities." Introduction to Toynbee's *Lectures on the Industrial Revolution*
(1908), p. xxv.

torical and Comteist attacks, though in due course largely repulsed, contributed to the uncertainty and loss of confidence. As regards the central theoretical structure, some of the main pillars seemed to have lost the ability, if they ever had it, to bear the weight of generalization which they had previously been assumed to be capable of sustaining.

The main outlines of what happened to political economy in England at this time were quite clearly and it seems quite accurately described by Henry Sidgwick at the beginning of his *Principles* (1883). He wrote as someone reasonably detached, nicely combining a certain perspective with some first-hand acquaintance, while the scrupulous quality, balance, and fairness of his judgment hardly ought to need emphasis. Sidgwick's opening words describe how in England (c. 1863) ''some twenty years ago, both the Theory of Political Economy in its main outlines, and the most important practical applications of it, were considered as finally settled by the great majority of educated persons in England.''[13] He goes on to maintain that ''comparatively little notice was taken'' of the attacks of the middle sixties, such as Frederic Harrison's Comteist diatribes, the criticisms of MacLeod, and Longe's refutation of the wages-fund theory (1866), and then concludes: ''In 1871, however, these halcyon days of Political Economy had passed away. Their termination was of course not abrupt; but so far as any date can be fixed for it, I should place it at the appearance of Mill's notice of Mr. Thornton's book *On Labour* in the *Fortnightly Review* of March, 1869.'' So,

13. Sidgwick, *Principles of Political Economy* (1883), p. 1. After citing McCulloch's earlier confidence that ''the errors with which the science was formerly infected are fast disappearing'' and Torrens' prophecy that ''twenty years hence there will scarcely exist a doubt respecting any of its more fundamental principles,'' Sidgwick quotes the following remarkable passage from the *Edinburgh Review* (1861) to indicate how strong was the authority of the orthodox doctrines in the early sixties: ''Political Economy is the only moral science in which definitions of fundamental terms sufficiently accurate to obtain general currency amongst all persons conversant with the subject have yet been produced. The consequence has been that the conclusions of those who understand the science are accepted and acted on with a degree of confidence which is felt in regard to no other speculations that deal with human affairs. Political Economists can appeal to the only test which really measures the truth of a science—success—with as much confidence as astronomers. The source of their success has been that they have succeeded in affixing a precise meaning to words which had for ages been used by millions who attached to them vivid but not definite notions, such as wages, profits, capital, value, rent, and many others of the same kind.'' *Edinburgh Review*, Oct. 1861, p. 465.

classical orthodoxy was already crumbling when, as Sidgwick puts it, "a second shock was given in 1871 by the publication of Professor Jevons' *Theory of Political Economy.*"

Sidgwick attributed the supreme authority of and confidence in the orthodox theories in the fifties and early sixties to two causes: (i) the prosperity that had (in due course) followed on the abolition of the Corn Laws, and (ii) the impressive mastery of J. S. Mill's lucid and authoritative exposition of the principles of the subject.

As regards the first "cause," *there was certainly little in the way of major policy challenge in the fifties—unlike the earlier decades of the century.* The framework of the free-market, free-trade economy had been established in the thirties and forties. This seemed to have been followed in the fifties and early sixties by a convincing measure of fairly widespread prosperity, and so the conclusion seemed plausible, at any rate for the wider public, that the major policy problems of political economy had been solved, if not for all time, at any rate for the foreseeable future.[14] Moreover, the theories of the subject, having borne fruit in such successful policies, might thereby be considered to have received a convincing general corroboration.

Secondly, with regard to the dominance of J. S. Mill and his *Principles*, it is not always realized how near he was to literally monopolizing the British market in economic ideas at this time. Marx's snide remark about Mill's eminence being due to the flatness of the surrounding landscape has a certain hard truth when one looks at the vital dates of the leading or near-leading economists in England in the nineteenth century. There was a comparatively large and distinguished cohort born about fifteen years before Mill, including McCulloch, Torrens and Senior, who were naturally beginning to fade away by the middle fifties. There were, however, very few born for

14. This kind of presumption may be behind the view, several times expressed in the seventies, that in political economy "the great work has been done," as Robert Lowe said (1876); or as Cairnes had put it (1870): "It is not denied that the science has done some good, only it is thought that its task is pretty well fulfilled." *Essays on Political Economy* (1873), p. 240. Checkland writes of the "apparent exhaustion of application." He cites Jowett's belief that, "with the exception of the field of distribution, 'Political Economy, like Benthamism has done its works,'" and Gladstone's view that "the application of economics to public policy was almost complete." "Economic Opinion in England as Jevons Found It," *Manchester School*, May 1951, pp. 417–18.

about the next quarter century, that is, within about a dozen years either side of Mill.[15]

In the middle and late sixties, however, a new cohort of writers, all under forty in 1865, born about twenty years or more after Mill, were beginning to assert themselves. The most important members of this new cohort were Cliffe Leslie, Fleeming Jenkin, Bagehot, and Jevons, who all rejected the central Ricardo-Mill theories of value and distribution. Of those who had a significant theoretical contribution to make, only J. E. Cairnes,[16] born slightly earlier, was left on the other side, and his attempts at defending the Ricardo-Mill orthodoxy can be said only to have weakened its position, either by the extent of the concessions he made (on the wages-fund doctrine and by the "non-competing groups" analysis) or by the extremity of his hard-line Mal-

15. In his fascinating pioneer paper "Statistical Studies in the History of Economic Thought," *Essays in the History of Economics* (1965), pp. 31 ff., Stigler lists 56 "important English economists" born between 1712 and 1861, that is, at an average rate of nearly 4 per decade. So one is dealing with pretty small numbers in attempting to distinguish changes and transitions in economics, and even smaller in contributions to economic theory or analysis, for the Stigler list includes a fair proportion of historical and statistical economists. Obviously, also, there are some rather marginal inclusions and omissions which might be suggested, but we shall follow strictly the Stigler list. This shows a remarkable fluctuation in the birth-rates relevant to the period with which we are concerned:

(1) The 11-year period 1787–97 (inclusive) is extremely prolific, with 13 births, against what would be an "average" of about 4. These are Hodgskin, Whately, McCulloch, Senior, Torrens, Jones, Bailey, Joplin, Lloyd, Wakefield, Scrope, Porter, and Babbage, almost a quarter of the entire list.

(2) Then for 22 years (1798–1819 inclusive) there is a "great depression," with only 3 births altogether, compared with an "average" of about 9—Longfield, J. S. Mill, and W. T. Thornton.

(3) From 1820 the birthrate recovers again, with 7, including Cairnes, Bagehot, and Leslie, in the 1820's, and 4 more, all highly distinguished, in the 1830's—Giffen, F. Jenkin, Jevons, and Sidgwick.

These quantitative observations are not put forward in order to explain Mill's extreme preeminence, but in order to underline the literal fact of it. In, say, 1852 there were only three "important" English economists between the ages of 32 and 55—the other two being Longfield and W. T. Thornton. Longfield had long previously completed his main contributions, while Thornton was to have a crucial date with Mill in 1869.

Stigler also gives a column stating the year of his economists' major publication in economics, *or* the mean year of their range of publications. The 1830's figure very frequently, with ten entries, and there are four more by 1844. From 1845 to 1865 (inclusive) the only entries are J. S. Mill (1848), Newmarch (1858), and W. T. Thornton (1860). But in 1866 we get Leslie and Cairnes, in 1868 Bagehot, and in 1870 Jenkin and Jevons.

16. Henry Fawcett might be added to Cairnes as a surviving defender of English "classical" orthodoxy; but Stigler finds him "an easy exclusion" from his list of "important" English economists, and we accept this judgment.

thusian gloom.[17] It was the emergence of this new group of economists, with important critical or constructive contributions to make
to economic theorizing, who all rejected the central theories of value
and wages of "the Ricardo-Mill Economics," which makes a comparatively brief span of years in the late sixties and early seventies
so important a turning point in the history of economic theory in
England.

<h2 style="text-align:center">V</h2>

We would like to emphasize that in his *Theory* Jevons attacks the
central pillars of the Ricardo-Mill theory of distribution, as well as
the theory of value; and that in any case, because of the logical and
conceptual links between the two, the attack on the one implied an
attack on the other. In the Preface to the first edition of his *Theory*
Jevons at once joins the assault on the wages-fund doctrine (already
launched in the later sixties by Longe, Thornton, Leslie, and Jenkin).[18]
In the second edition he goes on to demand that we "cast ourselves
free from the Wage-Fund Theory, the Cost of Production doctrine
of Value, the Natural Rate of Wages, and other misleading or false
Ricardian doctrines."[19]

It is often insisted that in contrast with their close unification
in fully developed marginal analysis, in the English or "classical"
system, the theories of value and distribution were "separate" or not
analytically connected. Certainly they were not unified in the same
close-knit way. But the Ricardian labor-cost theory of value and the
theory of natural wages and, in a looser sense, the wages-fund theory,
were closely linked by common assumptions or simplifications. If,
possibly partly because of changing economic conditions or "environmental" factors, these simplifications came to seem less plausible or
justifiable, then *both* the Ricardo-Mill theory of value and that of
wages or distribution were being rejected as general explanations of

17. See Taussig, *Wages and Capital*, pp. 263–65, for Cairnes's retreat on the
wages-fund doctrine.
18. For Cliffe Leslie on the wages-fund doctrine, see his *Essays in Political
and Moral Philosophy* (undated), p. 43, in his review of Cairnes' *Leading Principles*. For Fleeming Jenkin's rejection of "this fallacy," see his essay of 1870
"The Laws of Supply and Demand," in *The Graphic Representation of the Laws
of Supply and Demand and Other Essays on Political Economy*, reprint ed. (1931),
p. 94, and also his paper on trade unions (1868), ibid., pp. 8–14.
19. Jevons, *Theory of Political Economy*, 4th ed. (1931), pp. vi, xiv.

the workings of actual goods and labor markets, as these had in fact become.

Jevons clearly perceived this interdependence in his call to revolt against the prevailing orthodoxy. Moreover, although he did not elaborate the marginal productivity analysis, he strongly asserted its basic principle in insisting that distribution to the factors must be explained by their contribution to production, an idea suppressed in the "classical" or, at any rate, the Ricardo-Mill theories. Jevons expressed the idea in the "Concluding Remarks" in the first edition of the *Theory* and, as recognized by Walras, with great force at the end of the Preface to the second edition. He also sees that although this productivity type of explanation or "the true theory of wages," is "not new as regards the French school, it is new, or at any rate renewed, as regards our English Schools of Economics."[20]

The wages-fund and natural-wage theories both failed to link wages with productivity—a link which would in turn have pointed towards a greater emphasis on final, consumer demand. The common assumption, alike in the labor-cost theory of value, the natural-wage theory, and, to a lesser extent, the wages-fund theory, was that it was empirically justifiable to assume that "labor" was broadly and generally homogeneous, or that different types or qualities were reducible to a common homogeneous "labor" by some stable scale. This was the necessary basis both for a labor-cost theory being justifiable and for a theory of a general "natural wage," or even a significant general average wage, being a reasonably adequate approximation. This simplification is assumed by Mill at the outset of his chapter, "Of Wages," (II. xi. 1.) where he begins by claiming that it is "convenient" to "proceed in the first instance as if there was no other kind of labour than common unskilled labour of the average degree of hardness and disagreeableness."[21]

20. Ibid., pp. 269–70 and p. xiv. As Professor R. D. C. Black points out, it seems to involve some misconception of Jevons' thought to look for a unified approach to the analysis of distribution in his chapters in the *Theory* on rent, labor, and capital, in which there is undoubtedly "a certain asymmetry of treatment." It is unjustifiable to conclude from this asymmetry that Jevons did not clearly discern the marginal productivity principle, though he did not work it out. There are clear suggestions of the outline of a general marginal productivity approach both in the later chapters of the *Theory* and in the Introduction to the second edition, as Walras maintained. See the Pelican Classics edition by R. D. C. Black of W. S. Jevons, *Theory of Political Economy* (1970), pp. 17–19.

21. Mill, *Principles of Political Economy*, ed. Ashley (1909), p. 343.

In one of his crucial passages Ricardo (opening Section II of the first chapter of his *Principles*) had written:

> In speaking, however, of labour, as being the foundation of all value, and the relative quantity of labour as almost exclusively determining the relative value of commodities, I must not be supposed to be inattentive to the different qualities of labour, and the difficulty of comparing an hour's or day's labour, in one employment, with the same duration of labour in another. The estimation in which different qualities of labour are held, comes soon to be adjusted in the market with sufficient precision for all practical purposes, and depends much on the comparative skill of the labourer, and intensity of the labour performed. *The scale, when once formed, is liable to little variation.* If a day's labour of a working jeweller be more valuable than a day's labour of a common labourer, it has long ago been adjusted, and placed in its proper position in the scale of value.[22]

This is what Jevons emphatically rejected in the much-quoted concluding paragraph of his chapter on the Theory of Exchange:

> But it is easy to go too far in considering labour as the regulator of value; it is equally to be remembered that labour is itself of unequal value. Ricardo by a violent assumption, founded his theory of value on quantities of labour considered as one uniform thing. He was aware that labour differs infinitely in quality and efficiency, so that each kind is consequently paid at a higher or lower rate of wages. He regarded these difficulties as disturbing circumstances which would have to be allowed for; but his theory rests on the assumed equality of labour. This theory rests on a wholly different ground. I

22. *Principles of Political Economy and Taxation*, in *Works of David Ricardo* (1951), 1:20 (italics added). See also Mill's *Principles*, book III, chap. 4, and J. E. Cairnes, *Some Leading Principles of Political Economy* (1874), pp. 87–88. As Stigler expounds Ricardo: ''The wages of labor are also diverse, varying with skill, cost of education, and the like. Yet the occupational wage structure is very stable, so we may treat a skilled laborer as (say) three unskilled laborers if the former's wage is three times that of unskilled labor. Thus the expenditure on wages may be taken as proportional to the number of 'equivalent unskilled' laborers. (Ricardo should also have specified that the occupational structure of laborers is stable).'' *Essays in the History of Economics*, p. 188; see also p. 330.

hold labour to be *essentially variable, so that its value must be determined by the value of the produce, not the value of the produce by that of the labour.*[23]

Jevons was not alone at this time in attacking this central simplification of the Ricardo-Mill value and distribution theory. Walter Bagehot in his chapter on cost of production quotes *exactly* the passage cited above from Ricardo and goes on to emphasize why this simplification had become less plausible in the fifty years since Ricardo wrote:

And fifty years ago, when manufactures grew but slowly, and when the arts were comparatively stationary, this mode of speaking may not have been wholly incorrect—at any rate was not perfectly false. But nowadays the different skill used in different employments varies incessantly; it tends to increase with every improvement in quality; it tends to diminish with every improvement in machinery. Even between the same employment at different times it is difficult to compare it, and between two different employments it is impossible to compare it.[24]

Actually J. S. Mill, apparently without fully realizing the implications, and J. E. Cairnes, more explicitly, had introduced a fatal qualification to the Ricardian simplification regarding the homogeneity of labor, in their concept of "non-competing groups." Indeed Cairnes conceded that in "no inconsiderable proportion of all the exchanges which take place within such a country as this" value cannot be explained by cost of production, and that the demand side, in the form of the principle of reciprocal demand, has to be invoked (as in J. S. Mill's theory of international values):

Therefore, the action of cost of production in regulating value is by no means as extensively prevalent, even within the limits of the same country, as the current theory would lead us to suppose. The same commodity follows the law of cost of production in some exchanges and does not follow it in others;

23. Jevons, *Theory*, pp. 165–66 (italics in the original).
24. Bagehot, *Economic Studies*, ed. R. H. Hutton (1895), p. 262.

nor is it true that the value of any commodity conforms to the principle of cost in all exchanges.[25]

In fact the exceptions to the Ricardo-Mill theory were now becoming more important than the general case and the general explanation. As Jevons subsequently wrote to Foxwell (14 November 1879):

Cairnes professedly supports the theory [of the wages fund], but his arguments really tend against it in a deadly manner. He cannot stop at any non-competing groups, and his ideas followed out lead to entire rejection of the theory.[26]

25. Cairnes, *Some Leading Principles of Political Economy* (1874), p. 80. In this part of my argument I am much indebted to the paper by K. J. Arrow and D. A. Starrett ''Cost- and Demand-Theoretical Approaches to the Theory of Price Determination,'' read to the Symposium at the University of Vienna (June 1971) celebrating the centenary of Carl Menger's *Grundsätze*. Arrow and Starrett write: ''Apart from the problem of capital, the classical structure gradually faced new challenges, partly due to more detailed study of the real world, partly due to changes in that world. By the middle of the nineteenth century, the course of real wages was certainly inconsistent with any subsistence theory. The value placed by the market on labor could not be explained by its cost of production; the most natural alternative was to explain wages by the productivity of labor, an explanation only useful if labor was intrinsically scarce. In short, labor had to be treated like land. Also, the only explanation of relative wages in a classical model was Smith's doctrine of equalizing differences, due to unpleasantness, riskiness, and the like. Individuals were supposed to have equal abilities but were not indifferent among alternative jobs. But this is already a multi-factor model; not only raw labor but also willingness to do unpleasant work or to engage in risk-bearing are scarce primary factors. Further, the most casual observation of the world suggested that equalizing differences were an inadequate explanation of relative wages; it was frequently remarked that the most highly paid positions were the most, not the least preferred. When Cairnes started talking about 'non-competing groups,' the classical model was completely vitiated. The multiplicity of primary factors required a new theory. The great founders of the neoclassical school, Carl Menger, W. S. Jevons, and Léon Walras, and their precursors, A. A. Cournot and H. H. Gossen, understood the glaring omission of demand from the classical model. They took as an expository point of departure a model which was the polar opposite of the classical, the model of pure exchange.'' Arrow and Starrett conclude that what ''led to the downfall of the classical theory'' was ''the failure to explain either absolute or relative wages.'' We would add that this failure rapidly came to a head in the late sixties and early seventies. The suggestion by Arrow and Starrett regarding changing ''environmental'' conditions may be noted, though we would suggest that the theory of ''structure'' which met its downfall might be described as the ''Ricardo-Mill'' rather than the ''classical'' theory.

26. *Letters and Journal of W. S. Jevons*, ed. Harriet A. Jevons (1886), p. 408. See also S. G. Checkland, in *Manchester School*, May 1951, p. 164.

VI

Let us now look in rather more detail at the collapse of two main pillars of the Ricardo-Mill distribution theory, (i) the wages-fund doctrine and (ii) the natural-wage theory. We are concerned to emphasize the common elements in the inadequacies of these wage theories and the inadequacy of the Ricardo-Mill value theory.

(i) The extent and suddeness of the collapse of confidence in the prevailing orthodoxies was most prominently exhibited with regard to the wages-fund doctrine in the late sixties and early seventies. F. D. Longe's *Refutation* in 1866 was slightly too early to make an impact. But Cliffe Leslie and Fleeming Jenkin (both 1868) were followed by W. T. Thornton (1869), who extracted the capitulation from Mill, which Sidgwick saw as the critical episode in the collapse of confidence in "classical," or Ricardo-Mill, political economy. We would emphasize that we are not *necessarily* insisting that the wages-fund doctrine was totally untenable or should have been abandoned as completely as it was by Mill and others. It may be that the consensus of the time should be considered wrong. But there is no question in which direction the consensus then pointed, and it was a consensus led by some of the ablest economists of that or any other date.[27] In the seventies, as Schumpeter puts it "killing the wages fund became a favourite sport."[28] We have seen Jevons continuing the attack along with his general challenge to the Ricardo-Mill value theory and the natural-wage theory. Cairnes (1874) seems to have regarded himself as attempting a defense, but in doing so emptied the doctrine of almost all its earlier content and got listed by Jevons along with those who had abandoned it.[29] Reviewing Cairnes's *Leading Principles*, Cliffe Leslie emphasized the interdependence between the Ricardo-Mill theories of wages and of value:

> The doctrine of cost of production involves the whole theory of wages and profit: and an immense superstructure which has been built on what Mr. Cairnes would call the orthodox theory,

27. As Marshall put it in 1885: "Twelve years ago England possessed perhaps the ablest set of economists that there have ever been at one time." *Memorials of Alfred Marshall*, ed. Pigou, p. 152. This seems to put the classical epoch, or its various phases, in their place.

28. Schumpeter, *History of Economic Analysis*, p. 671.

29. Jevons, *Theory*, 4th ed., p. xliv.

must stand or fall with that theory. The subject may conveniently be approached by an examination of the doctrine of "the Wages Fund" and an "average rate of wages," for which Mr. Cairnes contends.[30]

Later there was the well-known work of F. A. Walker (1876) and further attacks by such a varied range of economists as Ingram, Toynbee, Rogers, Henry George, and Sidgwick. After Cairnes' dubious effort the wages-fund doctrine was only maintained at the level of the successive editions of Fawcett's *Manual*. Certainly there was nothing very elaborate to put in its place, except for what Cannan calls "the produce-less-deductions" theory of wages,[31] which did, however, point towards the marginal productivity analysis.

(ii) The other part of the Ricardo-Mill distribution theory, and the third of the three basic Ricardo-Mill doctrines from which Jevons demanded that economists "cast themselves free," was "the theory of a natural rate of wages, that which is just sufficient to support the labourer." Jevons added: "I altogether question the existence of such a rate. . . . I am inclined, therefore, to reject altogether the current doctrines as to the rate of wages."[32]

The theory of the natural rate of wages is a direct implication of the hard-line version of the Malthusian population doctrine. It is, of course, highly confusing to refer to "the" Malthusian population doctrine. There was a whole spectrum of Malthusian population doctrines and Malthus himself moved to and fro along this spectrum. At the extreme soft end was a completely empty generalization, predicting simply that anything might happen—"a perfect example of a tautology masquerading as a theory."[33] At the hard end—from which the natural-wage doctrine derives—there was perhaps the most sweeping, weighty, and consequential empirical generalization ever put forward

30. Leslie, *Essays*, p. 43.
31. E. Cannan, *A Review of Economic Theory* (1929), p. 356.
32. Jevons, *Theory*, p. 269. Jevons continues: "Even if the theory held true of any one class of labourers separately, there is the additional difficulty that we have to account for the very different rates which prevail in different trades. It is impossible that we should accept for ever Ricardo's sweeping simplification of the subject, that there is a natural ordinary rate of wages for common labour, and that all higher rates are merely exceptional instances, to be explained away on other grounds." Jevons later insisted that "rates of wages are governed by the same formal laws as rents" (p. xlvii).
33. M. Blaug, *Economic Theory in Retrospect*, 2d ed. (1968), p. 73.

in the history of economic theory, a proposition which had the most drastic implications for wages, living standards, and economic and social policies.

The hard and soft Malthusian propositions are utterly different in their meanings and implications, and it is thoroughly confusing to try to discuss the extent of support for, or the decline of, "the" Malthusian doctrine without distinguishing between them.[34] The different propositions were upheld by different people for different, though partly concurrent, periods of time. In between the hard and the soft extremes was a range of propositions of varied and often rather hazy content depending on the precise interpretation of the various particular qualifications introduced by different writers. It is sometimes difficult enough to pin down at all precisely just what any one author understood by his version of the Malthusian doctrine. To generalize about groups of writers or about general changes in support is almost impossible in terms of "the" Malthusian doctrine.

Ricardo and J. S. Mill took a line well towards the hard end of the spectrum, and *their distribution model had content only to the extent that it could derive this from a hard, empirical Malthusian proposition.*[35] Although the hard-line doctrine had been rejected by

34. Walter Bagehot summed up the crucial and wide difference between the hard and soft Malthusian theories in his dictum: "In its first form the *Essay on Population* was conclusive as an argument, only it was based on untrue facts; in its second form it was based on true facts, but it was inconclusive as an argument." *Economic Studies*, ed. R. H. Hutton, new ed. (1895), p. 179.

35. Schumpeter emphasizes the essential role of the hard Malthusian doctrine in the Ricardian model: "The theory of rent having fulfilled its only purpose, which is to get rid of another variable in our equation, we are left, on the margin of production, with one equation and two variables—still a hopeless business. But, so it occurred to Ricardo, wages are not really a variable either, at least not within that equation. He thought he knew, from external considerations, what they will be in the long run: here the old Quesnay theory comes in, reinforced by Malthus' law of population." *History of Economic Analysis*, p. 569. See also Stigler's essay "The Ricardian Theory of Value and Distribution," in *Essays in the History of Economics*, pp. 156 ff., esp. pp. 157, 169, and 172. Stigler emphasizes that the subsistence level *has* to have stability if the theory is to have any significance. It could indeed be argued that Mill's treatment of the population doctrine is not as consistently hard as Ricardo's. Certainly Mill expresses, here and there, more rather vague hopes about a distant future. But the logic of the Ricardian model, as he restated it, demanded the hard Malthusian doctrine that, as Mill himself put it, "It is but rarely that improvements in the labouring classes do anything more than give a temporary margin, speedily filled up by an increase of their numbers." *Principles*, ed. Ashley, p. 161. For J. E. Cairnes' hard-line discussion, see his *Some Leading Principles of Political Economy*, pp. 332–48.

such "classical" soft-liners as Senior, McCulloch, and Torrens—and by many others—*it was, therefore, still firmly entrenched in the ortho-dox theorizing of the sixties in the dominant, authoritative text of J. S. Mill and in texts of his disciples Cairnes and Fawcett.*[36] Jevons and the others of the new wave of economists of the late sixties and early seventies were not attacking a defunct Aunt Sally. But after their attacks, apart briefly from Cairnes and Fawcett, *no economist of note attempted to resurrect a hard-line Malthusian doctrine*, at any rate in Britain.[37] Softer Malthusian propositions continued to be

36. As Mark Blaug puts it: "In John Stuart Mill's *Principles* (1848) the Malthusian theory of population became, once again, the key to the Ricardian theory of distribution. In his effort to restore Malthus' arguments Mill indeed effected something of a counterrevolution." "The Empirical Content of Ri-cardian Economics," *Journal of Political Economy*, Feb. 1956, p. 48. Blaug ascribes the failure to last of the first comprehensive rejection, in the 1830's, of the hard Malthusian doctrine, to the fact that no one had any other theory of wages to put in its place. It is true that in the thirties no one *in England* did have any alternative wage theory, though there was Longfield in Dublin and J. B. Say and Hermann on the Continent. But by the seventies this was not true, even in insular England, when the hard version of the Malthusian doctrine was rejected (for the second time) by almost all the leading economists. On this occasion, though the replacement was not worked out, Jevons pointed quite clear-ly to the lines on which a new distribution theory could be developed in terms of marginal productivity. There was also by the 70's a much weightier body of empirical evidence refuting the hard-line doctrine (weighty enough, though it might be said, the evidence had been forty years before).

37. There is an important "environmental" reason (suggested by Professor A. W. Coats at the Bellagio meeting) which could have contributed much to the final elimination of the hard (but not the soft) Malthusian doctrine, around 1870. This is the first rapid growth at this time of large food imports from out-side Europe. The hard-line doctrine depended not only on the constant pressure of population, but also on the narrow limits for expanding the food supply. Professor W. H. B. Court has written of "a revolution in the British trade in foodstuffs. This took place with surprising suddenness. In ten years, between 1868 and 1878, the United Kingdom ceased to grow the greater part of the wheat she consumed and began to take from abroad nearly one-half instead of one-seventh of the meat which she needed. This was the beginning of a bulk im-portation of foodstuffs upon which the national standard of living was to depend in future." *A Concise Economic History of Britain* (1964), p. 201. Professor R. S. Sayers emphasizes the same point: "When the U.S.A. settled down after its Civil War (1861–5), that country became a major source of cheap wheat for the English market. Total imports into Britain rose from about 1 million tons in the late fifties to 3 to 4 million tons in the early eighties, and half of this came from the United States. Imports from the United States alone, that is to say, nearly equalled home production." *Economic Change in England, 1880–1939* (1967), p. 108.

It was just this development that J. S. Mill went on denying the likelihood of, in successive editions of the *Principles*, even up to when it was beginning to happen. Regarding Australia and the U.S.A., Mill argues: "Their agriculture has

maintained. Though the extreme form of soft-line Malthusian proposition was without empirical or predictive content, simply amounting to the use of a set of terms and concepts, or a taxonomy of "checks," there were soft (though not so extremely soft) Malthusian propositions, not altogether empty empirically, which implied or consisted of rather vague general maxims or warnings to beware of excessively rapid population increases. It was allegiance to this kind of tenuous generalization, as well as to some of the Malthusian terminology and concepts, that was implied by the lip service that continued to be paid to "the Malthusian doctrine."

When Jevons insisted that he had no doubt of the "truth and vast importance" of "the doctrine of population," but dismissed it because "it forms no part of the direct problem of Economics," it was

---

to provide for their own expanding numbers, as well as for those of the importing countries. They must, therefore, from the nature of the case, be rapidly driven if not to less fertile, at least what is equivalent, to remoter and less accessible lands, and to modes of cultivation like those of old countries, less productive in proportion to labour and expense" (I. XIII. 3). Again (in IV. IV. 8): "The principal fund at present available for supplying this country with a yearly increasing importation of food, is that portion of the annual savings of America which has heretofore been applied to increasing the manufacturing establishments of the United States, and which free trade in corn may possibly divert from that purpose to growing food for our market. This limited source of supply, unless great improvements take place in agriculture, cannot be expected to keep pace with the growing demand of so rapidly increasing a population as that of Great Britain."

In his edition of Mill's *Principles*, W. J. Ashley, by way of comment on Mill's rather pessimistic predictions, gives an interesting table of the percentages of the population fed from home-grown corn: 1831–35, 96%; 1856–60, 71.9%; 1881–85, 26.4%. It would be strange to assume that economists, from the early seventies onwards, had no inkling of the great development of overseas food supplies and the consequent falsification of the basic assumptions of the Ricardo-Mill model. In fact, by the middle seventies, Bagehot was recognizing that political economy "does not teach that of necessity there will be, as time goes on, a greater and greater difficulty in providing for the increase of mankind. . . . That augmentation of difficulty will not arise, first, because some of the inhabitants of old countries can emigrate to new countries, where people may increase as fast as they can; secondly, *because those emigrants produce more than they want in bare subsistence, and can send home a surplus to those who remain behind*; thirdly, because even in the old countries the growing improvement in the arts of production is likely, at least, to counterbalance the inevitable difficulty of a gradual resort to less favoured and fertile soils." *Economic Studies*, p. 124 (italics added). By 1881–82 Toynbee was recognizing in his *Lectures* that Malthus could not "foresee the great importation of food which would take place in later times. . . . Now, we import one half of our food, and pay for it with our manufactures." *Lectures on the Industrial Revolution* (1894), p. 112.

obviously a soft-line doctrine that he was brushing aside.[38] It is easy to exclude a doctrine that has nothing to say about wages or anything much else and is, indeed, empty of empirical content. Certainly Jevons was seeking to focus attention on the allocation problem as central to economics and to concentrate on allocation "given a certain population," as he puts it. But it would have been impossible to exclude from the concerns of economists a hard-line Malthusian proposition, with its vast implications for wages, living standards, and policy possibilities, *unless*, of course, it was regarded as demonstrably and finally falsified and devoid of all empirical validity. Jevons was contributing to the final rejection and abandonment *by economists* in England of hard-line Malthusianism when he demanded that economists "cast themselves free" from the Ricardo-Mill theory of the natural wage.

Sidgwick and Marshall later kept alive a decidedly softish version of the Malthusian theory, which, though extensively and imprecisely qualified and difficult to test, was not completely devoid of all predictive content.[39] Somewhat belatedly, indeed, Marshall (1893) recognized that a decisive break with the earlier hard-line doctrine had taken place. He spoke of "a change . . . which separates the economics of this generation from the economics of the past." What Marshall, who was of about the same generation as Jevons, then held to separate the economics of the earlier decades of the century from that in the later decades (a transformation which, he held, had not even then penetrated the current literature on the Poor Law) was acceptance of the doctrine: "If you tax the rich, and give money to the working classes, the result will be that the working classes will increase in number, and the result will be you will have lowered wages in the next generation."[40]

38. Jevons, *Theory*, p. 266. As Fleeming Jenkin wrote (1870), obviously of the soft version: "The Malthusian Law, true as it is, gives no help in determining what profit a capitalist will expect, or what comfort a labourer will expect; because, in fact, it gives no help in determining the cost of production either of labour or of anything else." Jevons could calmly dismiss a doctrine of population which "gave no help" in determining cost of production, wages, "or anything else." But he could not have dismissed from economics any doctrine which *did* give such help. F. Jenkin, *The Graphic Representation of the Laws of Supply and Demand and Other Essays*, reprint ed. (1931), p. 98.

39. See Sidgwick, *Principles of Political Economy*, pp. 147–57; and A. and M. P. Marshall, *The Economics of Industry*, chap. 5.

40. *Official Papers* (1926), p. 225. Marshall explains the rejection of the older views—valid in their day—by changes in the social environment: "It seems to me

Marshall had tried to play down the change in value theory, and the challenge to orthodoxy, launched by Jevons. At least we would agree that the "change" regarding the theory of wages (and population) is in some way, of wider significance, at any rate in policy terms. But what must be emphasized is that the "change" in wage theory and the "change" in value theory, in England, were closely linked, both temporally and logically or analytically. Temporally, it was the challenge of Jevons on the natural-wage theory, developed alongside his final utility theory of value, together with other attacks in the late sixties and early seventies by economists of the same new cohort or generation as Jevons, which constituted the final and decisive rejection, from which it never recovered as it had previously, of the hard-line Malthusian doctrine, till then firmly entrenched in J. S. Mill's *Principles* and supported by Cairnes and Fawcett. Logically and analytically, the same oversimplified concept of "labor" and "wages" was involved in *both* the Ricardo-Mill natural-wage and population doctrine *and* the labor cost-of-production value theory. To replace this common weak link, Jevons called for a much more decisive role for consumer demand and utility in value theory, and for productivity in wage and distribution theory, both of which had always been acknowledged in the leading French and German writers. On the Continent, where no such overturning of existing theories was necessary, the theories of value and distribution were sharpened and refined by the new marginal concept and entered on a long period of constructive development at the two centers led by Menger and Walras.

English "classical" political economy has received much more intensive treatment by historians of economic thought than any other period or episode. But its decline and fall from a position of almost unique authority and dominance has been given comparatively very little examination. We have here a case, almost unparalleled in the history of economic theory, of the comparatively sudden abandonment of a central theoretical core which had long and authoritatively prevailed as an established orthodoxy. The overworked term "rev-

that whenever I read Poor Law literature of today I am taken back to the beginning of the century; everything that is said about economics has the flavour of that old time. Statements which were true then, taking account of the conditions of the working classes and of the state of wealth, are reproduced and made the basis of arguments which seem to me to be not valid now."

olution'' does not seem far-fetched in describing this process in England in the late sixties and early seventies. But if the term ''revolution'' is only to be applied where one authoritative regime is replaced more or less immediately by another authoritative regime, then we cannot speak of a revolution occurring in England in or around 1871, and certainly it seems difficult to describe what happened on the Continent as revolutionary. But if the first negative or destructive phase, by itself, can be described as revolutionary, then it would be difficult to point to a more clear-cut and important example in the history of economic thought.

What Jevons called for, in his *Theory of Political Economy*, was that English economists should abandon the peculiar insular eccentricities of their natural-wage, labor cost-of-production, and wages-fund theories and rejoin the mainstream of western European thinking. Of course some of the leading ideas of English classical orthodoxy survived into the new period, but only those which it had always shared in common with French and German theorists. For example, the deductive method survived the historical and Comteist attacks, although these had contributed to the uncertainty and upheaval of the seventies. The assumption of competition as the general, ''normal'' case survived, although the new marginal analysis was much better equipped to deal with non-competitive markets, and its development had been much stimulated by those concerned with the growing problems of public monopolies.[41] The Turgot-Smith saving and investing analysis and J. B. Say's concepts of aggregate demand and supply largely survived. The rent analysis can also be said *to some extent* to have survived; but its generalization in the marginal productivity treatment really involved its wholesale transformation. Marshall, of course, was to carry through something of a restoration of some of the English ''classical'' concepts and terms, though this hardly amounted to more than a façade. As Schumpeter says:

> No unbiased reader can fail to perceive . . . that Marshall's theoretical structure, barring its technical superiority and various developments of detail, is fundamentally the same as that of Jevons, Menger, and especially Walras, but that the rooms in this new house are unnecessarily cluttered up with

41. T. W. Hutchison, *A Review of Economic Doctrines, 1870–1929*, pp. 16–17.

Ricardian heirlooms, which receive emphasis quite out of proportion to their operational importance.[42]

And of course it should be added, that according to Marshall's own record, it was just at the beginning of what we would claim to be the critical revolutionary period, though publication was delayed for nearly a quarter of a century, that with the aid of Cournot and Thünen, his "main position as to the theory of value and distribution was practically completed in the years 1867 to 1870."[43]

However, it may at least be agreed that the Marshallian regime, in spite of his discovery of and debts to Continental writers, for some decades not unsuccessfully revived something of the earlier Anglican insularity and the orthodox dominance of the single book. For a time, through much of the first quarter of this century, separate "schools," notably in Cambridge, Vienna, and Lausanne, survived with their particular peculiarities of terminology and assumptions, before in the second quarter merging into a general, cosmopolitan North American and western European melting pot. It was, of course, in Marxist economic theorizing that some of the old ideas and concepts of English "classical" orthodoxy continued a form of existence. Certainly, in the economic regimes of eastern Europe, claiming somewhat questionably to be following out the economic theories of Marx, the neglect of consumer demand, utility, and choice of the earlier English theories had a twentieth-century practical, political counterpart.[44]

42. Schumpeter, *History of Economic Analysis*, p. 837.
43. *Memorials of Alfred Marshall*, ed. Pigou, p. 416. So Marshall can be regarded as a member of the new cohort of economists which came to the front in the late sixties and which rejected some of the central theories of the Ricardo-Mill orthodoxy (except for the somewhat older Cairnes).
44. This article represents a complete rewriting of the paper delivered at the Bellagio Conference and owes much to the discussion there.

The Marginal Revolution and Concern with Economic Growth

Joseph J. Spengler

The leading idea behind all sciences in the nineteenth century was that of development.

WALTER EUCKEN

We are living in an age of growth.

J. R. HICKS

Now join and sing the Words of Mill,
  The Words of Stuart Mill
And if you have a Soul to save,
  Then he can save it still.

STEPHEN LEACOCK

THIS ESSAY deals with what the post-1860 marginalists had to say about economic growth and development, about change in economic structure and the behavior of per capita output. Since it is assumed that marginalism does not represent a complete break with the past in Kuhn's paradigmatic sense,[1] it is in order to touch briefly upon approaches to economic development in vogue prior to the ascendancy of the marginalists. These approaches may be grouped under four heads: (1) Classical, (2) Early Marginalist, (3) Historical, and (4) Marxist. We write of concern with economic growth, since what was said could hardly be described as a theory of economic growth.

JOSEPH J. SPENGLER *is James B. Duke Professor of Economics at Duke University.*

  1. See T. S. Kuhn, *The Structure of Scientific Revolutions* (Chicago, 1962); A. W. Coats, "Is There a 'Structure of Scientific Revolutions' in Economics?" *Kyklos* 22 (1969): 289-96. Coats believes only the Keynesian revolution to be unique. For a thoroughgoing account, see Emil Kauder, *A History of Marginal Utility Theory* (Princeton, 1965); also his "Intellectual and Political Roots of the Older Austrian School" *Zeitschrift für Nationalökonomie* 17, no. 4 (1958): 411-25. See also G. J. Stigler, *Production and Distribution Theories* (New York, 1948), and T. W. Hutchison, *A Review of Economic Doctrines, 1870-1929* (Oxford, 1953).

The elements entering into these four approaches may be categorized as follows:[2] (a) those bearing upon growth and/or development at the aggregative or individual level (i.e., population movements, formation and allocation of both physical and non-physical or personal capital, together with division of labor and increasing returns); (b) sources of physical constraint upon growth (i.e., finiteness of the available stock of land and natural resources); and (c) factors which, though serving at times to check growth, might be made more favorable to growth (i.e., a society's institutional parameters, which may be described as economic, political, or social in character). The course of growth therefore was found to depend upon the degree to which (a) might more than offset (b), at times as a result of improvement in a society's social parameters—included under (c)—which strengthened (a). How (c) was dealt with reflected the philosophical orientation of authors, in particular whether key institutions were condemned, as by writers of anarchistic persuasion,[3] or the state was viewed as merely an agent of society[4] or as an all-inclusive societal organism.[5]

I. Pre-1860 Growth Theory

There follow brief accounts of pre-1860 discussion of economic growth found in representative writings of classical, earlier marginalist, earlier historical, and earlier socialist writers.

(1) *Classical.* Despite Ricardo's concern with functional distribution, the main emphasis of the members of the classical school was upon economic development, an emphasis originating in Adam Smith's *Wealth of Nations*, a work designed in part to demonstrate the shortcomings of the growth policies put forward by mercantilist writers.[6] Their approach was mainly from the supply side. A partial

2. Lord Robbins approaches economic development somewhat differently, examining it under the heads of population and returns, accumulation and effective demand, education and the growth of knowledge, organization and policy, and the role of money. See his *The Theory of Economic Development in the History of Economic Thought* (New York, 1968).

3. E.g., see William Godwin, *Enquiry Concerning Political Justice* (London, 1793).

4. E.g., see R. M. MacIver, *The Web of Government* (New York, 1947).

5. E.g., see F. W. Coker, *Organismic Theory of the State* (New York, 1910).

6. See my ''Adam Smith's Theory of Economic Growth,'' *Southern Economic Journal* 25 (1959): 397–415; 26 (1959): 1–12. On mercantilist growth theory

exception was Malthus's *Principles of Political Economy*, the author
of which included among the various factors affecting economic
growth the possibility that demand might prove deficient, a possibility
denied implicitly by Adam Smith and explicitly by J. B. Say and
James Mill as well as by others who had complete faith in the
essentially homeostatic and optimally self-adjusting character of the
economy. We may, however, look upon the views of J. S. Mill as
representing the final views of the classical school, no longer wholly
describable as "magnificent dynamics." He was (except for Henry
Fawcett and J. E. Cairnes) the last of the school and the one who
(according to Hicks) "killed the old Growth Economics and paved
the way for the Static Epoch which was to follow."[7]

Large portions of J. S. Mill's *Principles* were devoted to economic
development.[8] In Book I he described the requisites of production,
division of labor and cooperation, and the "laws" of increase of
labor, capital, and the yield of land. In Book IV he described the circumstances underlying the progress of societies in wealth, capital,
population, and improvements. He drew attention to non-economic
sources of backwardness (e.g., despotic government, unsuitable customs
and institutions) responsible for the depressed condition of Asia.
He was much concerned lest unrestricted population growth consume
the fruits of progress, but he did look upon emigration as a temporary
palliative. As with Smith, so with Mill, land was the ultimate limitational factor, replaceable only in part by capital, itself often in
short supply; whence a comfortable Stationary State represented the
best of the options available—perhaps so, even given access to foreign
produce as in Marshall's time. Mill recognized the importance of
education, science, and the state of the arts, though he believed that
the state could play only a minor role in economic development.

and classical growth theory, see papers in *Theories of Economic Growth*, ed.
Bert F. Hoselitz (Glencoe, Ill., 1960); also Lord Robbins.

7. See J. R. Hicks, "Growth and Anti-Growth," *Oxford Economic Papers*
18 (1966), p. 260; William Baumol, *Economic Dynamics* (New York, 1959),
chap. 2. See also H. Myint's interpretation in his *Theories of Welfare Economics*
(Cambridge, 1948), Part I.

8. I have described Mill's views in Spengler, "John Stuart Mill on Economic
Development," in Hoselitz, *Theories of Economic Growth*, pp. 113–54. See also
Lord Robbins, *Theory*, and "On A Certain Ambiguity in the Conception of Sta-
tionary Equilibrium," *Economic Journal* 40 (1930): 194–214; A. Marshall,
Principles of Economics, ed. C. W. Guillebaud (London, 1961), 2:50–51, 59; 1:xv.

What Mill had to say bears some resemblance to what some present-day authors say, though they do not yet anticipate an ideal stationary state as the best men can hope for.

(2) *Early Marginalists*. With the partial exception of W. F. Lloyd, the early marginalists did not center their analysis so effectively upon the derivation of the value of something from the marginal utility of its services as did the Austrian and other later marginalists. The early writers did, however, reason administratively in marginal terms.[9] I have chosen M. Longfield (1802–84) and H. von Thünen (1783–1850) to represent views on growth put forward by earlier nineteenth-century marginalists, rather than Senior, Dupuit, Gossen, Lloyd, or Cournot, though the approach of Gossen and in some degree that of Lloyd had more in common with that of the marginalists of the 1870's than the others here named. Von Thünen was credited with stimulating J. B. Clark and A. Marshall and with giving rise to location theory. Cournot's use of marginal analysis was slow to be appreciated.[10]

Of the elements entering into Longfield's observations bearing upon economic development (e.g., division of labor, improvements), most striking are the effects of capital formation and the resulting decline in the interest rate, among them lengthening of the planning-time horizon, extension of durable investment, improvements in agriculture, and stimulus to better management, education, and cleanliness.[11] Increasing division of labor consequent upon growth of population increased output, especially of manufactured articles "consumed by the poor," and thus partly offset possible increases in the cost of food.[12] External trade too could ease population pressure, in part by substituting for emigration.[13] In sum, a number of co-

9. On the early marginalists see Kauder, *History*; R. S. Howey, *The Rise of the Marginal Utility School, 1870-1889* (Lawrence, Kans., 1960); G. J. Stigler, *Essays in the History of Economics* (Chicago, 1965), chap. 5.

10. A. A. Cournot, best known for his marginalist approach to pricing under various degrees of competition, was not concerned with economic growth in his earliest work though he did deal with somewhat related matter in his *Principes de la théorie des richesses* (Paris, 1863), bk. IV, and pp. 311–50, 386–96.

11. M. Longfield, *Lectures on Political Economy* (1834; reprint ed., London, 1931), pp. 228–35. The "principle of saving" was "a much stronger motive to exertion than the desire to spend." Ibid., p. 266.

12. Ibid., Lecture V and pp. 233, 235–39, 252–53, also pp. 236–39 on institutions.

13. Ibid., pp. 239–41.

operating circumstances, among them good institutions, could conduce to economic development.

Von Thünen differed from contemporary and later marginalists in his greater emphasis upon the role of space than upon that of time—in the organization of economic activity in a rural economy dominated by horse transport and hence unlike the essentially manufacturing economy of which Alfred Weber wrote. His concern was the optimal location of economic activities, mainly agricultural, under model conditions which, he pointed out, differed somewhat from real conditions, *inter alia* the wealth-reducing effect of restrictions on trade.[14] In a static isolated state, taxation of agriculture absorbed capital and thus curbed the growth of agriculture and population; in a slowly progressing state, it slowed the rate of progress.[15] In his posthumous notes,[16] von Thünen pointed to the role of human capital, to the effect of population growth upon land use, to how increase in the price of grain and land rent was associated with industrial, urban, and transport development, and to how the development of rail systems was increasing economic interdependence and the value of products of interior regions. He pointed also to interrelations between industrial progress, agriculture, the order and distribution of towns, and the nature of industry. He remarked the productivity-increasing effects of education and drew attention to both economies of agglomeration and the stimulus to population growth occasioned by high wages and to capital formation by high interest rates as in the United States. Elsewhere in this work von Thünen dealt with the contribution of education and with the formation of capital and its impact upon its own marginal yield and that of labor. He also sought to show that the "natural" wage (i.e., the geometrical mean of the subsistence needs of a worker and his product) met a number of criteria and maximized national revenue.[17]

14. *Der isolierte Staat*, trans. C. M. Wartenberg, as *Von Thünen's Isolated State* (1826, 1850, 1876), ed. Peter Hall (London, 1966), pp. 7–160 on the model, and 161-96 on "Comparison of the Isolated State with Reality."
15. Ibid., pp. 197–214.
16. Ibid., pp. 261–98.
17. Ibid., pp. 225–58. This thesis is developed in the second part of *The Isolated State*, trans. Bernard W. Dempsey, S.J., as *The Frontier Wage* (Chicago, 1960); Dempsey's analysis occupies pp. 1–186 of the volume. See also H. D. Dickinson, "Von Thünen's Economics," *Economic Journal* 79 (Dec. 1969): 894–902; Colin Clark, "Von Thünen's Isolated State," *Oxford Economic Papers* 19 (1967):

(3) *Historical*. Representative of an historical approach are
Simonde de Sismondi (1773–1848), Friedrich List (1789–1846), and
Wilhelm Roscher (1817–1894). Sismondi drew attention mainly to
problems associated with industrialization, while List pointed to the
alleged need for the state to intervene in such wise as to accelerate
economic transformation in late-developing states. Roscher examined
development from an historical point of view; he along with List
"began the tradition of historicism in economics," Hayek observes.[18]

Sismondi's views, relevant in the present context and subsequently influential, were put forward in his *Nouveaux principes d'économie
politique* (Paris, 1819) which appeared sixteen years after the appearance of his much more Smithian *De la richesse commerciale*
(Geneva, 1803).[19] Having drawn attention to supposed adverse con-
comitants of the industrial revolution (e.g., emergence of a proletariat
and a class struggle, underpayment of wage earners, loss of worker
interest in the prosperity of industry, a weakening of controls on
population growth, an unhappy environment for workers, displace-
ment of farmer cultivators, etc.) and its failure to assure man's
beneficent development, Sismondi suggested the need for a slowing
down of the rate of social transformation, together with state intervention and reforms to prevent or cushion evils associated with a
too rapid rate of socioeconomic change (e.g., labor-protecting legislation, abolition of child labor, minimum wages, social insurance for
workers, profit sharing, small-scale agriculture). In sum, Sismondi
believed, the benefits of social progress would be more evenly distributed and greater were socioeconomic transformation to proceed
somewhat less rapidly than he found it to be doing.

Friedrich List (1784–1846), among the economical writers who
made use of a stage theory of economic development (as did many

370–77; B. F. Kiker, "Von Thünen on Human Capital," ibid., 21 (1969): 339–
43.

18. F. A. Hayek, *The Counter-Revolution of Science* (Glencoe, Ill., 1952),
pp. 125, 205. On the genesis of both historicism and a planned approach, see ibid.,
pt. 2.

19. For summaries of Sismondi's views see Mao-Lan Tuan, *Simonde de
Sismondi as an Economist* (New York, 1927); E. Halévy, *Sismondi* (Paris, 1933).
See also Henryk Grossman, "The Evolutionist Revolt Against Classical Eco-
nomics," *Journal of Political Economy* 51 (1943): 381–96, 506–22; Thomas
Sowell, "Sismondi: A Neglected Pioneer," *History of Political Economy* 4 (1972):
62.

under the influence of the eighteenth-century concept of progress),[20] utilized such theory as a basis for a policy of temporary state intervention designed to accelerate development in countries with an economic potential. He had in mind Germany, which, he believed, lagged in the development of manufactures, the growth-generating *primum mobile*, in part because he believed (unlike William Playfair and Thorstein Veblen) that early starters tended to enjoy an increasing differential advantage over latecomers.[21] What was indicated was protection of native manufacturing, together with free importation of agricultural products and raw materials, until a nation's manufactures had been developed to a stage where they could meet foreign competition and the nation could safely undertake to benefit from the advantages associated with general freedom of trade.

What Roscher, most catholic, eclectic, and learned of the earlier German historical economists,[22] had to say pertinent to growth is much more descriptive than analytical in character; his purpose was to examine each "politico-economical fact" within the framework of the whole economy and "national life" of a people and to allow adequate weight to such important elements as the "ideals" regnant at any time.[23] He directed attention mainly to economic elements, but with subdued reference to stages in development and to so-called laws of development of the sort associated with the historical school and descended from those that had flourished already in the evolutionary climate of opinion of the preceding century.[24]

In his account of "production" Roscher identified factors that affect production (e.g., external nature, "taste for labor," "capital,"

20. Stage theories are discussed in Hoselitz, pp. 193–238. They are criticized by Walter Eucken in *The Foundations of Economics*, trans. T. W. Hutchison (London, 1950), pt. II.

21. List, *The National System of Political Economy*, trans. S. P. Lloyd (London, 1885), pp. 107 ff., 156–63, 419–20. See also Carl Brinkman, *Friedrich List* (Berlin, 1949).

22. The first edition of W. Roscher's *System der Volkswirtschaft* was completed in 1854. I depend on the translation of the 13th ed. by J. L. Lalor, as *Principles of Political Economy*, 2 vols. (New York, 1878).

23. Ibid., I, p. 126 and note.

24. For samples of eighteenth-century evolutionary thought, of which illustrations are also to be found in literature of the Graeco-Roman world, see J. S. Slotkin, ed., *Readings in Early Anthropology* (Chicago, 1965), chap. 6. Carl Menger deals with Roscher and others of the "historical school" in his *Problems of Economics and Sociology*, esp. pp. 178–92, discussed below. See also Hoselitz, esp. p. 208.

division and cooperation of labor, economies of scale, uses to which
potentially productive agents are put, institutional structure, mon-
etization of exchange).[25] He took note also of long-run empirical
trends, such as the effect of advancing "civilization" on rent, prices,
price structure, interclass relations, and as the impact of price
revolutions.[26] He treated factors influencing the international distribution of capital[27] as well as those underlying capital formation
(e.g., degree of interclass harmony, distribution of income, and
factors conducing to prodigality and extravagance).[28] At the same
time he observed that growth of consumption must keep pace with
increase in productive capacity, since otherwise commercial crises
would result and growth-producing forces would be weakened.[29] He
noted also that while prodigality was destructive of capital, the
process of saving, if not accompanied by a compensating process of
expenditure, might retard the formation of capital.[30] In an appendix
prepared for his American edition he put forward a qualified defense
of temporary protection for industries with potential.[31]

(4) *Socialist.* While developmental as well as utopian philosophy
is to be found in the pre-Marxist and utopian socialists[32]—much
more given to economic planning than their Marxist successors—
economic growth received greater attention at the hands of Marx and
Engels, against whose value theory Böhm-Bawerk in particular later
directed criticism. In the *Communist Manifesto* (1848), Marx and
Engels advanced a stage theory and the view that the time was at
hand for the Proletariat to emancipate the exploited class from op-
pression by the Bourgeoisie; they also listed measures designed to wrest
capital and control from the Bourgeoisie, a list Engels later described
(in the Preface to the 1872 German edition) as requiring modifica-

25. Roscher, *Principles,* bk. I, also §214.
26. Ibid., §§115, 130, 140–41, 156–57, 201–02.
27. Ibid., §187.
28. Ibid., §§205, 222–23, 230–33, 229.
29. Ibid., §§213–15.
30. Ibid., §§218–23, 230–31, and 233 on the limited usefulness of "luxury."
31. See ibid., app. III, §§1, 6–9, and §5 on the tendency of protectionism to
increase the importance of the progressive elements in the social structure, a view
later developed by Pareto. Roscher made less use of stages than did List. See
Hoselitz, p. 208 n.
32. E.g., see Hayek, pt. II; Frederick Engels, *Socialism, Utopian and Scientific*
(1883; Chicago, 1918); E. Halévy, *The Era of Tyrannies* (New York, 1965), pp.
21–104.

tion. Marx's general view is indicated in the Preface to his *Critique of Political Economy* (1859), where the legal forms of the relations of production, after having favored the material forces of production, are said to have become fetters upon them and in need of replacement by "new higher relations of production" in keeping with existing "material conditions." This view appears again in *Das Kapital*,[33] where the concentration of capital is described as giving rise to a "monopoly of capital" which

> becomes a fetter upon the mode of production, which has sprung up and flourished along with, and under it. Centralisation of the means of production and socialisation of labour at last reach a point where they become incompatible with their capitalist integument. This integument is burst asunder. The knell of capitalist private property sounds. The expropriators are expropriated.[34]

II. The Marginalists

The marginalists selected for consideration are those with whose names the marginalist revolution is identified, Jevons, the Austrians (Menger, von Wieser, and Böhm-Bawerk), and Léon Walras. With this revolution a number of changes in emphasis took place, all associated with the establishment of marginal utility as the key to economic analysis and the corresponding elevation of the process of imputation and of the derivation of the demand for sources of services from that for services as such. (1) The conception of costs was transformed into one emphasizing alternatives or opportunities forgone with the result that so-called "real" obstacles (e.g., pain, irksomeness, even past costs or "bygones") were described as of little or no relevance. (2) Demand, choosing, and choice were thrust to the fore, with the result that *futurity* and *expectations* became the overriding orientations of man's economic behavior. (3) Corollary to (2) is a more explicit emphasis upon elements in economic contexts which are relatively variable and hence susceptible of manipulation and change under the guidance of choice. (4) Insofar as choice and futurity were made to rule, the so-called rational aspects of man's behavior

33. Marx, *Capital*, vol. 1 (Chicago, 1906), chap. 32.
34. Ibid., p. 837.

were emphasized and the role of motivation was sharpened. (5) Economics became a subjective science, one concerned in the main with what might be called the content of the mind and hence with "information" and how the many minds constituting a community continually adjusted and readjusted to each other and thereby generated equilibria and what amounted to stability-facilitating institutions.

All these changes led the marginalists under consideration to deal with growth and development somewhat differently than the authors treated in Section I above. They agreed with those authors who played down the role of the state and with each other on at least two points. (a) The rate of economic growth, being essentially the resultant of the uses to which inputs were directed, was viewed more explicitly as the product of conscious individual decisions and choices and less as an automatic outcome of the surplus-producing propensity of the economic mechanism.[35] (b) Since the total output of a society's variable agents of production was seen to be conditioned by the degree to which inputs were so distributed among uses as to equalize the productivity at the margin of members of each category of variable inputs, optimizing the allocation of these inputs was inferred to be a determinant of gross and net national product. Whence whatever stood in the way of such optimization (e.g., monopoly) became a limitation upon the size of output. In what follows attention will not be devoted to (a) and (b), since all marginalists had to take them into account, but to other views bearing upon economic growth.

Explicit emphasis upon economic development was not so prominent in the systems of the post-1860 marginalists as in those of earlier writers, but they did emphasize allocation, the disposition of resources, and choosing between present and future. Moreover, they explicitly recognized that the rate of growth necessarily varied with the degree to which decisions under (a) were future-oriented rather than virtually present-oriented. The marginalists also recognized the constraining influence of limitational factors extant in man's physical environment.

We shall now examine in order the views on economic growth—

35. This statement is not always borne out. For example, J. B. Clark distinguished "capital" from "capital-goods" and treated the former as virtually self-replacing and growing. *The Distribution of Wealth* (New York, 1399), chap. 9, esp. pp. 126 ff.

views not often well integrated into the framework of post-1860 marginalism—of Jevons, the Austrians, and L. Walras. Only passing notice will be given the views of those who followed in the steps of the originators. Of course, were Marshall included, it would appear that there was greater continuity between the classical past and the marginalist present, for he was more disposed to recognize arguments of his classical predecessors than were the marginalists.[36]

W. S. Jevons

Of the originators of the marginalist revolution of the 1870's, W. S. Jevons (1835–82) was the most empirical in his approach to scientific questions. Moreover, it was this empiricism which seems to have given rise to the considerable interest which he manifested in the prospective economic growth of the British economy, manifested perhaps in his statement that growth could go on continuously in the absence of limitational factors.[37] There is little immediately apposite to growth in *The Theory of Political Economy* (1871), devoted as it was to a treatment of this subject in a manner analogous to that of "Statical Mechanics" and the "laws of Equilibrium of a lever as determined by the principle of virtual velocities."[38] He did say that economic dynamics remained to be developed, and he noted that the theory of population, "no part of the direct problem of Economy," was as scientific as the facts then permitted.[39] The "great problem of Economy" was allocation, so to employ a given population with given resources "as to maximize the utility of the produce."[40] Hence he sometimes but not always treated technological change as of essentially exogenous origin, whereas he looked upon the emergence

36. See also Lord Robbins, pp. 14–15 and 170–71 on the "marginal revolution" and the contribution of the marginal method itself to rejecting an all-or-nothing approach and choosing within a range of options.

37. On Jevons' work see R. D. C. Black, "Jevons and Cairnes," *Economica* 27 (Aug. 1960): 214–32; and papers by Black, R. Könekamp, and W. Mays, in *Manchester School of Economic Studies* 30 (Sept. 1962): 203–50; J. M. Keynes, "William Stanley Jevons," *Journal of the Royal Statistical Society* 99 (1936): 516–48, 554–55; E. W. Eckard, *Economics of W. S. Jevons* (Washington, 1940). See below at notes 50 and 51 on his proposition that growth might be continuous and free of constraints.

38. Jevons, *Theory*, p. viii.

39. Ibid., pp. vi, viii-ix, 254–55. Cp. Jevons' evaluation in 1876 of Malthus's views, reprinted in his unfinished *Principles of Economics*, with a preface by Henry Higgs (London, 1905), pp. 192–93.

40. Jevons, *Theory*, p. 255.

of wants of an ever "higher character" as internal to an economy.[41] Such change in wants and consumption in turn modified the range within which international trade was advantageous to a country.[42]

Jevons dealt indirectly with growth phenomena in several of his lesser works. Thus he noted the importance of division of labor, but he denied Smith's close connection of it with inventions; he referred instead to "economic conditions which favour the promotion of science" and invention, among them modes of "supporting and requiting scientific labours."[43] And he added that economic and demographic growth were increasing the need for governmental regulation of the economy and the usefulness of "community of consumption" (e.g., public goods).[44]

Having examined the impact of the rise of prices in the wake of gold discoveries, Jevons concluded that though there had been "individual cases of hardship," the "fall in the value of gold" had had "a most powerfully beneficial effect. It loosens the country, as nothing else could, from its old bonds of debt and habit. It throws increased rewards before all who are making and acquiring wealth, somewhat at the expense of those who are enjoying acquired wealth. It excites the active and skilful classes of the community to new exertions...."[45] His empiricism and his utilitarianism are evident in his examination

41. This treatment of wants is taken from T. E. Banfield and could be viewed as anticipatory of Marshall's treatment of wants and activities. See Jevons, *Theory*, pp. 46–51; Cp. A. Marshall, *Principles of Economics* (London, 1920), bk. III. On authors who influenced Jevons see R. M. Robertson, "Jevons and His Precursors," *Econometrica* 19 (July 1951): 229–49. Jevons condemned wasteful luxury in his unfinished *Principles of Economics*, pp. 44–48. Cp. ibid., pp. 21–35 on consumption. "The oatmeal diet of the Scotch must have contributed towards creating their character of invincible energy and sound intellect." Ibid., p. 32. On Marshall's treatment of wants and activities see Talcott Parsons, *The Structure of Social Action* (New York, 1937), chap. 4.

42. Jevons, *Theory*, pp. 186–90.

43. Jevons, *Principles*, pp. 90–103. "Knowledge . . . is not consumed at all" by use. Ibid., p. 97. "Travelling by balloons or aeronautic machines is in all probability chimerical" and unlikely to "supersede railway trains." Ibid., p. 94.

44. Ibid., pp. 202–6. On limitations of laissez-faire, see ibid., pp. 204–5.

45. Jevons, *A Serious Fall in the Value of Gold Ascertained and Its Social Effects Set Forth* (London, 1863), chap. 4, esp. p. 62. He denied that creditors or annuitants had equitable claims to relief. Ibid., pp. C2–65. He described "gold-digging," however, as a "dead loss of labour" from a collective point of view, a wrong comparable to a Government's depreciating its currency. Ibid., p. 67. Elsewhere he advocated allowing the amount of paper currency "to vary according to the natural laws of supply and demand." *Money and the Mechanism of Exchange* (1875), 3d ed. (London, 1893), p. 312.

of the role of the state respecting employer-employee relations; this role must be arrived at experimentally and in light of its "total utilitarian results."[46] He opposed, in keeping with his marginal tenets, both licensure and trade-union control of access to employment, for the benefits thereby achieved were sought and obtained by a few at the expense of the many.[47]

In *The Coal Question*[48] Jevons dealt with economic growth far more than in other of his works, though as an empiricist rather than as a marginalist. This work reflected the importance which he (like von Liebig) attached to the "economy of power" and hence to natural resources whence power was derived and to implications of limitations present in man's environment.[49] In England the overriding source of power was coal, a source for which there was no prospect of a suitable substitute, particularly one that would conserve England's "peculiar industrial supremacy" in the world economy. Coal was "the mainspring of modern material civilization" and "the chief agent in almost every improvement or discovery in the arts which the present age brings forth." Hence, should this agent become weaker, "so far, then, as our wealth and progress depend upon the superior command of coal we must not only cease to progress as before—we must begin a retrograde career." The "natural law of social growth," of uniform progress, characteristic of organic nature found itself held in check by inorganic nature, in the present instance, coal, given

46. Jevons, *The State in Relation to Labour* (London, 1882), pp. 23 ff., 164–66; also pp. 48–49 on consumer protection and chap. 3 on the factory acts. See also his *Methods of Social Reform* (London, 1883), pp. 266–367, on the short-comings of government ownership and/or operation of public utilities and the absence of competition.

47. Jevons, *The State*, chap. 4, esp. pp. 98–109, 119, 165. Great care needed to be exercised lest registration of practitioners (e.g., medical) create a partial monopoly. Ibid., pp. 99, 119–24.

48. Jevons, *The Coal Question*, 3d ed., ed. A. W. Flux (London, 1906); my references are to this. The first edition appeared in 1865 and was revised in 1866. Jevons' son, H. S. Jevons, continued aspects of his father's study in *The British Coal Trade* (London, 1915). In his preface to the 3d edition, Flux corrected misunderstandings of Jevons' argument.

49. In 1876 Jevons observed that "the enormous wealth of the United States has been created by the freedom and energy of internal trade acting upon natural resources of unexampled richness. . . . Their wealth would be far greater still were external commerce in the States as free as internal commerce." *Principles*, p. 187

that food imports had temporarily removed constraints flowing from the limited supply of land.[50]

Jevons rested his tentative projection of future British coal consumption on the basis of continuing growth of a population, unchecked by dearth of food, together with continuing growth of coal exports and of per capita consumption of coal stimulated by invention (which Hearn in *Plutology* had described as cumulative).[51] Such projected growth could not persist, however, since the cost of extracting coal would begin steadily to increase long before the nation's coal reserves had been exhausted.

> We cannot long continue our present rate of progress. The first check to our growing prosperity, however, must render our population excessive. Emigration may relieve it, and by exciting increased trade tend to keep up our progress; but after a time we must sink down into poverty, adopting wholly new habits, or else witness a constant annual exodus of the youth of the country.[52]
>
> The rapid growth of our great towns . . . is a matter of very serious concern as regards the future. *I do not say that the failure of our coal-mines will be the only possible check.* Changes here, or in other parts of the world, may, even before the failure of our mines, reduce us to a stationary condition, and bring upon us at an earlier period the sufferings and dangers incident to our position. But such a grievous change, if it does not come before, must come when our mines have reached a certain depth.[53]

He did not anticipate adequate relief through importation of coal, "our peculiar energy."[54] Nor did he believe that Britain's population

---

50. Jevons, *Coal Question*, chap. 1, p. 1; this chapter was the preface to the author's first edition. Ibid., p. xxv. See also ibid., chaps. 7-9. As late as 1901 Henry Adams, a well-informed observer, described western Europe as "one great empire . . . ruled by one great emperor—Coal." *The Education of Henry Adams*, Modern Library ed. (1931), p. 415.

51. Jevons, *Coal Question*, chaps. 9-12.

52. Ibid., p. 11. Jevons attributed the emigration of the 1850's and 1860's to external allurements rather than to rising population pressure in Britain. Ibid., pp. 220-22, 230-32, 418-24.

53. Ibid., p. 232.

54. Ibid., p. 9, also chap. 13.

pressure could be effectively and continuously relieved through emigration; for eventually the populations of the United States and other countries would have become large enough to permit transformation of their economies into effective competitors with Britain that would further weaken her economy.[55]

Jevons did not propose a way out, nor apparently did he suppose that Britain would become transformed into a comfortable "stationary state" of the sort described by Mill. Taxation of coal exports which, though growing, were small compared with domestic consumption, was not practicable; nor was taxation of domestic coal consumption or other forms of interference within the exportation or the consumption of coal. He did propose paying off the national debt on the ground that, as the price of coal rose, taxation for debt service would fall.[56] In sum, Britain's economic progress was destined to slacken, and her economy eventually to contract.[57] The alternatives facing Britain were unattractive.

> When our main-spring is here run down, our fires burnt out, may we not look for an increasing flame of civilisation elsewhere[?]. . . . Britain may contract to her former littleness . . . . But our name and race, our language, history, and literature, our love of freedom, and our instincts of self-government, will live in a worldwide sphere . . . If we lavishly and boldly push forward in the creation of our riches, both material and intellectual, it is hard to over-estimate the pitch of beneficial influence to which we may attain in the present. *But the maintenance of such a position is physically impossible. We have to make the momentous choice between brief but true greatness and longer continued mediocrity.*[58]

P. H. Wicksteed

Despite the later work of Edgeworth and others, marginalism in the refined Austrian sense never thrived in British economics, nourished as it was by the concerns and approaches of Mill, Sidgwick,

55. Ibid., chap. 16.
56. Ibid., chap. 17; also chap. 11 on the cost in coal of British transport. J. S. Mill endorsed Jevons' view on paying off the debt. Eckard, chap. 4.
57. Ibid., chap. 12.
58. Ibid., pp. 459–60; italics are in the original.

and others. However, were one to select that British author who made the most effective and persuasive use of marginalism, one would almost certainly choose P. H. Wicksteed (1844–1927). For he, more than any other British economist, made marginal utility the fulcrum of analytical economics and disregarded so-called real costs which continued to be assigned importance by Alfred Marshall and others. Wicksteed did not deal with economic growth as such. He did, however, touch upon it implicitly in his pointing to the need for factors to be mobile and for an economy to be flexible if it was exposed to essentially exogenous sources of change (e.g., invention, opening of new trade routes, changing wants).[59] Only then would resources be optimally employed, given the pattern of wants. In his exposition more than in that of the other marginalists (except Walras), the underlying framework of comparative statics is evident. More or less growth would ensue, his argument implies, accordingly as the ends sought, the ideas of "worth," called for more or less growth. Resources would contribute to growth, given that as the objective, commensurately with how well they were administered.[60]

Austrian Marginalists

(a) The major concern with growth evident in the work of Carl Menger[61] (1841–1921) consists in his theory of the evolution of economic and economy-related institutions. In the preface to his major work, *Grundsätze der Volkswirtschaftslehre* (1871),[62] he declared "economic theory" to be "concerned, not with practical rules for economic activity, but with the *conditions* under which men engage in provident activity directed to the satisfaction of their needs"—with

59. Philip H. Wicksteed, *The Common Sense of Political Economy* (1910), ed. Lionel Robbins (London, 1933), pp. 14–16, 22–23.

60. Ibid., pp. 344–47, also chap. 5 on laws of returns.

61. According to J. A. Schumpeter, Menger belonged among the top ten economists, from Marx on, because he revolutionized economic theory with "a new explanatory principle." See *Ten Great Economists from Marx to Keynes* (New York, 1951), pp. 89–90. See also Hutchison, chaps. 9–11.

62. I make use of C. Menger, *Principles of Economics*, trans. James Dingwall and Bert F. Hoselitz (Glencoe, Ill., 1950). A posthumous second edition appeared in Vienna in 1923. On the climate of opinion environing the Austrians see the works of Kauder, cited above in note 1, and Eucken, *Foundations*, pp. 58–60, 324. See also A. R. Sweezy, "The Interpretation of Subjective Value Theory in the Writings of the Austrian Economists," *Review of Economic Studies* 1 (June 1934): 176–85.

the laws of "phenomena that condition the outcome of the economic
activity of men and are entirely independent of the human will."
These allowed much scope for man's activities and his progress in
civilization.

In his discussion of the "causes of progress in human welfare"
Menger denied that "division of labor" could be "designated as the
most important cause of the economic progress of mankind." Such
progress was the result rather of man's "increasing understanding of the causal connections between things and human welfare" and
of his "increasing control of the less proximate conditions responsible
for human welfare."[63] Obstacles to progress (e.g., uncertainty, stu-
pidity, monopoly, limits on marketability) were weakened by the
"progress of civilization,"[64] the growth of human knowledge, and
increase in the availability of goods of a lower order and hence of the
opportunity to engage in more roundabout production.[65]

Productivity-favoring institutions could and did come into existence
spontaneously and without state or other collective intervention.
The institution of money, so essential to the extension of the division
of labor, was a case in point. "There were elements in the situation
that everywhere led men inevitably, without the need for a special
arrangement or even government compulsion, to a state of affairs in
which this difficulty was completely overcome."[66] Menger goes on
to explain how "*each* economizing individual becomes increasingly
more aware of his economic interest" and the need to engage in
exchange to meet his requirements. "He is led by this *interest,
without any agreement, without legislative compulsion, and even
without regard to public interest*, to give his commodities in exchange
for other, more saleable commodities, even if he does not need them
for any immediate consumption purpose." Certain of these goods are
observed to be more salable and become, "under the powerful influence of *custom*, acceptable to everyone in trade," and hence capable
of serving as money.[67] Money thus "is not an invention of the state.

63. Menger, *Principles*, pp. 71–74, 161, 236–37; also 67, 70 on causality, 83
on futurity, and 239 on specialization. In his article above in this volume Professor
Erich Streissler develops more fully Menger's view as depicted in this paragraph.
64. Ibid., pp. 53, 74, 89, 103.
65. Ibid., pp. 73–74, 152–56.
66. Ibid., pp. 258–59.
67. Ibid., pp. 259, 260, also 320.

It is not the product of a legislative act. Even the sanction of political authority is not necessary for its existence."[68] Menger develops this view further in his analysis of the methodology of social science, where he shows that money, like other social institutions, is "the unintended result, . . . the unplanned outcome of specifically *individual* efforts of members of a society."[69]

In his later work, after rejecting the regnant theory of analogy between social phenomena and natural organisms,[70] Menger goes on to examine "those social phenomena which are not a product of agreement or of positive legislation, but are unintended results of historical development." Money is but one of a number of instances. "Law, language, the state, money, markets, all these social structures in their various empirical forms and in their constant change are to no small extent the unintended result of social development. The prices of goods, interest rates, ground rents, wages, and a thousand other phenomena of social life in general and of economy in particular exhibit the same peculiarity."[71]

Given his analysis of the origin of economic institutions, Menger could not assign importance to the role of the state or to collective planning. He could, as he did, point to such institutions as the "common law" as highly conducive to the "common good."[72] He could also point to the confusion involved in the notion of "an ethical orientation of economics"[73] and in misinterpretation of the nature of economics and the object of its study.[74]

(b) Friedrich von Wieser (1851–1926) who, together with E.

68. Ibid., pp. 261–62.
69. C. Menger, *Problems of Economics and Sociology* (Urbana, Ill., 1963), pp. 152–55, esp. p. 155. The German original, here translated by F. J. Nock, with an introduction by Louis Schneider, was entitled *Untersuchungen über die Methode der Socialwissenschaften und der Politischen Ökonomie inbesondere* (Leipzig, 1883). Schneider discusses at length Menger's theory of the spontaneous origin of institutions, in part following F. A. Hayek's analysis. See Schneider's introduction in *Problems*, pp. 4–19.
70. Menger, *Problems*, bk. III, chap. 1. See ibid., pp. 25, 74–81, for a critique of the view that "economic phenomena are to be treated only in connection with the total social and political development of nations." See also ibid., pp. 42, 45–46, 53, 69–70.
71. Ibid., p. 147, also 155–59, 226–27; 230–31; also bk. III, chap. 2 as a whole. See also Menger, *Principles*, pp. 216–17 on "competition" and 269 ff. on markets.
72. Menger, *Problems*, p. 234.
73. Ibid., p. 237.
74. Ibid., passim.

Böhm-Bawerk (1851–1914), most effectively continued and developed the work of Menger, devoted virtually no attention to economic growth in his unnoticed first book or in his more widely known second book.[75] Proceeding from the origin of value to exchange value and the process of imputation, von Wieser sought to correct Menger's alleged error in generalizing from the imputation of value at the consumer level to that at the producer level.[76] He then subjected to criticism not only the "socialist theory of value" but also Ricardo's treatment of rent and von Thünen's calculation of the return to capital.[77] It may be said, therefore, that his definition of costs (in opportunity terms) and his attempt to determine the productive contribution of factors (among them capital) contributed to understanding of the efficiency with which factors could be allocated among uses. It may also be said that his development in Book VI of E. Sax's attempt[78] to extend marginal analysis to the public economy contributed to use of private-economy yardsticks, together with a cost-benefit approach, in connection with various public undertakings, among them release of a country's potential beyond the current developmental capacity of private enterprise.[79] Von Wieser noted, however, that application of the theory of value in the public economy was handicapped by the vagueness of value in the national economy and by the need to consider "other than merely economic facts."[80]

More attention was devoted to matters connected with economic growth in von Wieser's *Theorie der gesellschaftlichen Wirtschaft* (1914).[81] Herein he adopts Menger's explanation of complicated

75. F. von Wieser, *Der natürliche Werth* (1889), trans. C. A. Malloch as *Natural Value*, together with a preface and analysis by William Smart (London, 1893).

76. Ibid., bk. III, chaps. 4–8. For discussions of von Wieser's approach see W. L. Valk, *The Principles of Wages* (London, 1928), and *Production, Pricing and Unemployment in the Static State* (London, 1937). On Wieser's critique of Menger's alleged deficiencies, see Stigler, *Production and Distribution Theories*, pp. 164–69.

77. Wieser, *Natural Value*, pp. 64–66, 78–81, 114–23, 129–31, 161–64.

78. E. Sax, *Grundlegung der theoretischen Staatswirtschaft* (1887).

79. v. Wieser, *Natural Value*, pp. 223–29.

80. Ibid., pp. 229–31, 241–43.

81. F. von Wieser, *Social Economics*, trans. A. F. Hinrichs, with preface by W. C. Mitchell (New York, 1927). Mitchell contrasts this work with Wieser's *Natural Value* in Mitchell, *The Backward Art of Spending Money* (New York, 1937), chap. 12.

social institutions as "unintended social results of individual-technical factors."[82] He also emphasizes the need on the part of the theorist to draw on his "practical consciousness of economic relations," on that "wealth of experiences which are common property of all" and accessible to all "without resort to special scientific instruments."[83] There is in the *Theorie* a sense of change as in Menger's work, but less of optimism than in Menger's work.

It was essential, therefore, for the theorist to take into account the emergence under capitalism of concentrations of economic power which interfere with that "well regulated balanced competition" required to make self-interest subservient "to the general welfare." Whence "economic society" can no longer be treated as a "sum of individuals" and "modern economic theory requires for its completion a more profound theory of society" as well as a "theory of state economy" and allowance for "the economy of the world."[84] He compared the emergence of "modern mammoth industries . . . under capitalistic leadership" to the accomplishment of "modern empires, now almost complete" under "dynastic leadership," and observed that the latter made possible the growth of "mammoth capital," of "capitalistic despotism," with its restraint of the "freedom" of all but an elite and its abolition of "the freedom of the oppressed."[85] Solution lay in continuing evolution, since the prevailing order had grown because it had fulfilled "the intent of the economy" and would dissolve in time, under new leadership and with the discovery of "new paths . . . in the community of exchange." Despotism would not disappear, however, even under socialism, unless "the masses [were] sufficiently strong to offer resistance to the prevailing leaders."[86]

Von Wieser argued that economic science must accommodate itself to repudiation of the classical doctrine of non-intervention and the "theorem that private freedom guarantees the attainable maximum of social utility."[87] It was the "capitalistic compelling forces which

82. v. Wieser, *Social Economics*, p. 163, also p. 162.
83. Ibid., pp. 3–5. Wieser, Mitchell (pp. 252–54) points out, studied human behavior, economic planning and otherwise, "from inside the human being."
84. v. Wieser, *Social Economics*, pp. 11–12.
85. Ibid., pp. 401–6.
86. Ibid., pp. 407–8.
87. Ibid., p. 409.

disfigure the social spirit of the economy from which they arose" and against which the protection of the state was required, presumably because, in the absence of these forces, one would find in the private sector the appropriate kind of activity, exchange relations, and valuation.[88] While there was no need for "change of the common, economic, legal order," there was need for such action by the state as would be appropriate to doing away with "the profits of mammoth capital" which were largely "unearned winnings." Protective and related legislation for workers was indicated as well, since labor organizations as such could only partially countervail "capitalistic power" and might even on occasion become subservient to this power. Even so, since experience with the curbing of organizations and powers remained limited, more experience was required before adequate policies could be developed. It was to be expected, however, that "social egoism," "theoretical enquiry," and relevant "practical experience" would in time give rise to proper means.[89]

Von Wieser touched in passing upon various growth-related elements such as time-preference, limits to growth, inflation, capital formation, technical arts, economies of scale, and size of state and industry.[90] The presence of what today are called "externalities" might warrant state intervention in the developmental process.[91] The state gave unity to the economy, guarding "the social legal order" and protecting "common interests against conflicting private interests";[92] it could also, when necessary, guard the developmental interests of the nation's economy within the world economy.[93] It is correct to say, however, that such interventionist role as von Wieser assigned the state was directed more to the prevention of inequities than to the fomenting of economic development as such.

(c) Böhm-Bawerk may be described as putting forward a theory of growth in his *Positive Theory of Capital* (1888), a sequel to his *Capital and Interest* (1884), wherein he reviewed and assessed opin-

88. Ibid., pp. 413, 415, also 425–34 on valuation and on how exchange value in the private sector helps guide the state in its actions based on use value.
89. Ibid., pp. 413–16, also 456–62.
90. Ibid., pp. 39, 72, 74, 290, 298, 356, 391, 401, 403.
91. Ibid., pp. 427–29.
92. Ibid., p. 437.
93. Ibid., pp. 456–62.

ions respecting interest.[94] In this essentially deductive theory,[95] "capital" played the dynamic role, but with man and nature—the "technical elements of production," "the primary productive powers"—constituting the foundation of man's productive activities. Moreover, since the natural agents were in limited supply and hence imposed physical constraints upon production, man was under compulsion to make economical use of these agents, which in Böhm's system more than in Jevons's consisted of land.

> All that we get in production is the result of two, and only two, elementary productive powers—Nature and Labour. . . . What nature by herself does, and what man does along with her—these form the double source from which all our goods come, and the only source from which they can come. . . . Limited technical elements must be treated with consideration, must be saved, must be fully utilised . . . . They form the specifically *economic* natural endowment of man. Since all, or at least almost all, limited gifts and energies of nature are connected with land, we may, without much danger, take Land . . . as the representative of this economic natural endowment.[96]

The exertions of labor "form the counterpart" to the uses of land. "Labour has almost entirely an economical character" because "the very extensive claims put forward by human needs" outweigh the physical strength of labor and the capacity of labor to exercise its "powers." So we are warned "to economise our labour."[97]

Man can transform the original factors or elements or powers into "goods for human consumption" in one of two ways. He

94. In what follows I have used William Smart's translations and the three-volume *Capital and Interest*, trans. G. D. Huncke and H. F. Sennholz (South Holland, Ill.: Libertarian Press, 1959); this set includes the *Positive Theory*, *Capital and Interest*, and *Further Essays on Capital and Interest*. On Böhm-Bawerk's relation to classical and neoclassical theory see R. E. Kuenne, *Eugen von Böhm-Bawerk* (New York, 1971), pp. 1-10.

95. Böhm-Bawerk was critical of the historical school of economists in general and of their views on capital and interest in particular. On his general critique see "The Historical vs. the Deductive Method in Political Economy," *Annals of the American Academy of Political and Social Science* 1 (1891): 244–71, and "The Austrian Economists," ibid., pp. 361–84; also "The Ultimate Standard of Value," ibid. 5 (1895): 149–208.

96. Böhm-Bawerk, *The Positive Theory*, trans. William Smart (1891; New York, 1923), bk. II, chap. 2, pp. 79–80.

97. Ibid., pp. 80–81.

may combine the economical productive powers with one another,—or with activities of free natural powers,—in such a
way that the desired good immediately emerges as the result of
the combination. . . . Or he may take a roundabout way, and,
with the element at his command, may make, first, another
good, and then, with its assistance, the good he wishes.

The second indirect approach is technically more productive, but, as
a rule, it entails the ''sacrifice of time'' and imposes the need to wait
until the results of more fruitful ''roundabout ways'' become available. Moreover, ''on the whole . . . every lengthening of the roundabout process is accompanied by a further increase in the technical
result,'' but ''as a rule, . . . in a smaller proportion.'' Sometimes ''a
new invention'' will shorten the roundabout process, though usually
it lengthens it and, if used, involves ''a greater number of intermediate
products, or . . . investment of capital''—a longer ''average period''
of production.[98]

Having described ''capital'' as ''an aggregate of products destined, not for immediate consumption or use, but to serve as means
of acquisition,'' as ''stored-up valuable natural power, . . . the
medium through which the two original productive powers exert their
instrumentality,'' Böhm-Bawerk insisted that capital was ''not an
independent factor,'' not ''independently productive,'' in the sense
that some part of a productive result was attributable to it and hence
not to labor and nature.[99] Increase in a community's ''stock of capital,'' essential to the more effective use of the original factors, required that it give up enough of the consumption which it might
have enjoyed and devote its productive powers both to keeping the
current stock intact and to adding to this stock.[100]

A community's disposition to add to its stock of capital and make
production more roundabout reflected the comparative roles played
in its economic life by ''present'' and ''future.'' ''Our economical

98. Ibid., pp. 81–89. Anticipating the controversies of the 1930's over the
meaning of this period, Böhm-Bawerk described remote inputs as of negligible
significance. Ibid., p. 90. Elsewhere he argues that inventions which lengthen
the customary period of production are ''more numerous than those that entail
a shortening.'' *Further Essays*, pp. 24–33, esp. p. 24; also pp. 53–56 on the
selection of options. See also Kuenne, *Böhm-Bawerk*, pp. 44–63, 68–71.

99. Böhm-Bawerk, *Positive Theory*, pp. 59, 95, 99.

100. Ibid., p. 100–18, 124–25.

conduct has exceedingly little reference to the present, but is, almost entirely, taken up with the future.''[101] In Book V Böhm-Bawerk sought to show why most men set the subjective use value of present goods above that of similar future goods and how the market accentuated this difference. As a country's wealth increased, however, production became more roundabout and the length of the production period increased, subject to the constraint imposed by the agio ruling between present and future goods, an agio essentially independent of economic organization.[102]

Near the close of this study Böhm-Bawerk drew together the factors upon which the interest rate supposedly depends and thus identified most of the conditions upon which growth of average and aggregate output depended. Of decisive importance were ''the amount of the National Subsistence Fund'' (i.e., ''the stock of wealth accumulated in a community''), ''the number of producers to be provided for out of the same,'' and what we shall call the productiveness of capital at the margin.[103] The rate at which capital was formed (presumably given the rate of interest) varied inversely with the extent of and desire for consumption loans and with the number of landowners and members of the rentier class who could live comfortably on their rents and interest and hence not be under pressure to be economically active. Capital formation varied directly also with how thrifty and economical of habit a nation (including receivers of rent and interest) was. Increase in the ratio of population to capital reduced average output and could affect savings adversely. The ''discovery of new and more productive methods of production, outlets, business opportunities, etc.'' tended to make ''surplus returns'' higher than they would have been otherwise, and their loss to reduce these returns.[104] Interest itself was thus a universal phenomenon, one manifest under all modes of economic organization and hence not eliminable through socialist or other revolutionary measures. By implication, therefore, as later Soviet experience demonstrated, interest

101. Ibid., p. 238.
102. Ibid., bk. VI, chaps. 5–10.
103. Ibid., pp. 410, 420, also 393–94. On greater roundaboutness and ''more capital per capita,'' see *Further Essays*, pp. 57–63.
104. Böhm-Bawerk, *Positive Theory*, bk. VII, chaps. 4–5, esp. pp. 393–94, 401–02, 410–12, 420.

would have to be taken into account in all plans for growth and, if abolished in one of its guises, would reappear in others.

Böhm-Bawerk, always a critic of socialism, stressed the universality of economic behavior, of economic response to given constraints, and hence of the preferability of a competitive to a non-competitive regime. In a later work he therefore criticized the thesis that the share of the product going to a factor of production was determined by the force or "social power" exerted by the men standing behind the factor in question.[105] He pointed out that the price of a factor can be influenced only within the range set by actual supply and demand conditions, by the alternatives open to (say) an employer of labor and to workers (whose alternatives, e.g., are very limited in densely populated countries). Moreover, when one party achieves advantage, a corrective response may be set in motion by the self-interest of the disadvantaged party. While personal distribution could be influenced by "power," functional distribution could be influenced only within narrow limits if at all. Growth as such was not treated, but it was noted that upward pressure on wages tended to check the extension of roundaboutness. Nor is growth referred to in Böhm-Bawerk's critique of Marx, at the close of which he declared that the Marxian system had "no abiding future," though there would be "a socialism" after Marx as there had been before Marx.[106]

Léon Walras

Economic development received little direct attention from Léon Walras, though he was alert to technical progress; a number of his observations are indirectly relevant, however—e.g., his inclusion of "leisure" in income, his treatment of enterprise and production, his somewhat qualified defense of the competitive system, and his inclusion of "personal faculties" under capital.[107] He was concerned

105. Böhm-Bawerk, "Macht oder ökonomisches Gesetz," *Zeitschrift für Volkswirtschaft, Sozialpolitik und Verwaltung* 23 (Dec. 1914): 205–71. There was considerable discussion of "force versus economic law" in Austria and Germany early in this century. See F. Zeuthen, *Problems of Monopoly and Economic Warfare* (London, 1930), pp. 145–50. V. Pareto dealt with the impact of political conditions on the economy.

106. Böhm-Bawerk, *Karl Marx and the Close of His System*, ed. Paul M. Sweezy (New York, 1949). Included in this edition are R. Hilferding's and L. von Bortkiewicz's critiques of Böhm-Bawerk's critique.

107. I have used William Jaffé's classic translation of Walras's principal

mainly with four problems: exchange, production, capital formation, and circulation.

Walras dealt with growth in connection with "progress." He described "progress" as "a diminution in the intensities of last wants satisfied, i.e., in the *raretés* of final products, in a country with an increasing population." The possibility of progress therefore depended "on technical progress" (additions, modifications, and replacements of technical coefficients of production) and "*economic progress*" (substitution within a given technical framework). Progress thus was subject to limits, since an augmentable source of services, say "capital-services," could be substituted for a non-augmentable source of services (e.g., "land-services") only within limits, limits which presumably could be reduced but not eliminated by "technical progress."[108] In general, since population tended to increase, whereas the land available for cultivation was ultimately fixed by the limitedness of its amount and of man's capacity to utilize inferior land, progress depended upon man's capacity to save and increase his capital and substitute its services for those of land.[109] Walras consequently rejected the view which he attributed to Ricardo and J. S. Mill, that a large number of goods (those "procured by labour") could "be multiplied without limit," for inputs which were limited in supply entered into all goods in some degree.[110]

Limits on the multiplication of products constrained not only progress but also population. For, given their limits, "*raretés* could fall to a certain point so long as population remained the same; or *raretés* could only fall so far if population itself increased up to a certain point. If, however, there is no definite limit to the multi-

work, *Elements of Pure Economics* (London, 1954). I have not drawn on Walras's extensive correspondence, edited by Professor Jaffé, and make only passing reference to Walras's *Etudes d'économie sociale* and *Etudes d'économie politique appliquée*, both edited by G. Leduc (Paris, 1936). For Walras's reference to leisure see *Elements*, pp. 215, 379–80; on free competition, Lessons 22, 41; on enterprise and production, Lessons 17–22; and on "personal faculties" or capital, §§237, 319–21.

108. Walras, *Elements*, Lesson 36, §§323–24, also 327–28, 170–75 on land, capital, and raw materials.

109. Ibid., §§327–29, also 355, 361; also *Etudes*, 2:281–85. See also W. D. Montgomery, "An Interpretation of Walras' Theory of Capital as a Model of Economic Growth," *History of Political Economy* 3 (1971): 278. This appeared after the present paper was completed.

110. Walras, *Elements*, §§342–43, 348–49, also 329.

plication of products, there can be no definite limit to the possibility
of progress."[111] Land being limited in amount, however, it conditioned the response of the structure of prices to population growth.

> In a progressive economy, the price of labour (wages) remain-
> ing substantially unchanged, the price of land-services (rent)
> will rise appreciably and the price of capital-services (the
> interest charge) will fall appreciably .... The price of capital
> goods proper remaining constant, the price of personal facul-
> ties will rise in proportion to the fall in the rate of net income
> [return on capital], and the price of land will rise both by
> reason of the fall in the rate of net income and by reason
> of the rise in rent.[112]

A "progressive rise in the value of land and its services" thus demonstrated, along "with the expansion of capital and population, the
essential characteristics of economic progress."[113] While real wages
tend to rise, Walras's analysis implied that the degree of improvement, if any, depends upon the composition of the worker's consumption budget.[114]

Walras was more interested in economic reform than were the
Austrians, believing that pure theory could be applied in the formation of policy.[115] His emphasis, however, was not upon growth but upon
making the competitive system work, upon preventing the concentration of wealth and power, and upon so combining state intervention
with private enterprise as to make the economy function optimally.
Given these results one may infer, presumably, that he believed
"progress" would be optimal.

III. AFTERMATH

Every school of economists asks questions about some aspects of
economic behavior, generally to the neglect of other aspects, and it

111. Ibid., §324, also §329.
112. Ibid., §§332, 334. Italics are in the original.
113. Ibid., §335.
114. Ibid., §331. For Walras's views on the "social question" in France and
the situation of England, see his Etudes, 1:475–85.
115. See Etudes in which Walras deals with the production and distribution
of wealth. See also M. Boson, Léon Walras, fondateur de la politique économique
scientifique (Paris, 1951); also Hutchison, pp. 210–15.

asks these in certain ways. The marginalists qua marginalists viewed the economic world from inside man through the medium of themselves rather than from outside man through the medium of his self-revealing behavior. Thus M. Pantaleoni, representative of marginalism in Italy, described economic science as consisting "of the laws of wealth systematically deduced from the hypothesis that men are actuated exclusively by the desire to realise the fullest possible satisfaction of their wants, with the least possible individual sacrifice."[116] The initiators of the marginal revolution therefore put less direct stress upon economic growth than did their predecessors, though in the belief that action in keeping with their principles would assure progress if men wanted it.

The marginalists differed in respect of the attention they gave to growth-oriented views. Jevons was an exception, probably because he was an empiricist, not free of classical considerations, and immediately concerned with man's welfare. The marginalists did not really neglect the population problem, mainly because they believed that capital would grow with sufficient rapidity to countervail population growth and prove substitutable enough for essentially non-augmentable natural agents whose limitational role the classical school in particular had stressed. As a rule, they did not inquire if a low or zero rate of population growth was to be preferred. This statement is not true of some of the later marginalists, Wicksell in particular, who upon mastering the marginalist as well as alternative approaches, were free to concern themselves with contemporary problems. Presumably the marginalists assumed that if, as seemed likely, the tastes of populations became more future-oriented, the derived demand for future-oriented goods and services would rise, with the result that output per head would eventually increase. This kind of outcome presumably was most likely in a free-enterprise economy, one quite free of governmental intervention—a mode of economic organization that marginalism was well suited to defend.

The marginalist revolution was by no means without effect upon growth theory.[117] For, although A. Marshall and J. B. Clark traced their emphasis upon marginal productivity to von Thünen, the pro-

---

116. M. Pantaleoni, *Pure Economics* (1889; London, 1898), p. 3.
117. On later marginalists see Howey and the works cited in note 1 above.

ductivity-oriented climate of opinion generated by the Austrians must have contributed as well to the development and popularization of the Cobb-Douglas and related forms of the production function (three decades after Knut Wicksell anticipated it)[118] and hence to the identification and measurement of the main immediate sources of economic output. The emergence of linear programing and (perhaps) of game theory probably was fostered by the marginalist way of thinking. Of the originators of the marginal revolution, Böhm-Bawerk probably generated most growth-oriented influence. His emphasis upon the varyingly roundabout nature of the productive process also inspired the so-called neo-Austrian approach to the trade cycle, with its recognition of the disruptive and probably inflationary impact upon the continuity of economic activity occasioned by efforts to form investment goods at a higher rate than is compatible with the rate of voluntary saving.[119]

Recently several theories have been put forward, the skeleton of which is of Austrian genesis. For example, J. R. Hicks has advanced what he calls a "neo-Austrian growth theory" which "fixes attention on time-sequence" and facilitates "dealing with transitions" such as may accompany a change in technique. He shows how, somewhat after the manner of Hayek's *Prices and Production*, the introduction of a more roundabout process may not be carried through if not enough resources are diverted from consumption.[120] Cochrane and Kiker have shown, as Gary S. Becker suggested in 1967, that the Austrian approach, especially as developed by Böhm-Bawerk, is quite relevant to the study of human capital, now considered a very important source of growth.[121] Böhm-Bawerk's analysis of investment has occasionally stimulated discussion which bears somewhat upon productivity and

118. Wicksell, *Lectures on Political Economy* (1901; London, 1934), pp. 203–6; this was a successor to his *Value, Capital and Rent* (1892; London, 1903) in which the influence of marginalism is pronounced. See also Carl G. Uhr, *Economic Doctrines of Knut Wicksell* (Berkeley, Calif., 1960).

119. For a clear statement see F. A. Hayek, *Prices and Production* (New York, 1932). See also Lionel Robbins, *The Great Depression* (London, 1934), chap. 3; also G. Haberler, *Prosperity and Depression* (New York, 1946), chap. 2, also pp. 326 ff.

120. "A Neo-Austrian Growth Theory," *Economic Journal* 80 (June 1970): 257–81, esp. 275–79.

121. J. L. Cochrane and B. F. Kiker, "An 'Austrian' Approach to the Theory of Investment in Human Beings," *Southern Economic Journal* 36 (April 1970): 385–89.

growth.[122] Jevons, more than the Austrians, stressed the subjective character of cost.[123]

122. E.g., see R. E. Kuenne, ''The Technological Superiority of Present Goods,'' *Zeitschrift für Nationalökonomie* 22 (Oct. 1962): 271–77; R. Dorfman, ''A Graphical Exposition of Böhm-Bawerk's Interest Theory,'' *Review of Economic Studies* 26 (Feb. 1959): 153–58.

123. E.g., see C. W. Nolder, ''Jevons on Cost,'' *Southern Economic Journal* 39 (July 1972): 113–15.

Marginalism and Marxism

Ronald L. Meek

M ARGINALISM and Marxism may seem at first sight a very stale subject for debate, of interest only to antiquarians and the celebrators
of centenaries. What possible good can it do, it may be asked, to
discuss the relation between two theoretical systems which were first
put forward a whole century ago, and neither of which anybody today
accepts without considerable qualification? We do not bother to discuss the bimetallism-versus-monometallism issue today: why then
"Marginalism and Marxism"? There are two justificatory points, I
think, which can be usefully made before we start our task.

First, Marxism is much more than a mere collection of economic
doctrines which can be *compared* with those of marginalism: it contains within itself a set of broad *interpretative* criteria, of a highly
idiosyncratic character, which were designed to evaluate and explain
the origin of other theories. This does not mean, however, that there
is only one unique "Marxist" interpretation of, say, marginalism,
which is faithfully accepted by all Marxists and regarded by them as
valid for all time. The Marxist canons of criticism are sufficiently
broad to allow of several different interpretations, all of which can
properly be said to be "Marxist" in character. Also, it is obvious that
the spirit in which these interpretative principles are applied may
vary considerably. At some times and places they may be applied in
a vulgar, dogmatic way; at others in a sophisticated, flexible way.
In our own time, "Marxism" is no longer necessarily tied up, as it
was in the years between the wars, with the defense of the day-to-day
political and economic policies of a large modern state. The decline
of Stalinism in the USSR has made it possible for the modern generation of Marxists to be much more free and adventurous in their
use of Marx's canons of criticism. Thus the reapplication of these
canons to the problem of the origin and nature of marginalism need

RONALD L. MEEK *is Professor of Economics at Leicester University.*

not necessarily yield the same old conclusions: there may well be
something new to be discovered.

Second, it is not only Marxism which has developed and changed.
Marginalism, too, has altered over the years. The essential point here
is so simple that it is easy to overlook it. When a new doctrine like
marginalism first appears, a Marxist critic of it is necessarily limited
in his available points of reference. He is bound to interpret it in
relation only to the older doctrines which it has succeeded in replacing, and the immediate needs which it appears to serve. As it
develops and changes over time, however, and possibly comes to serve
new needs unforeseen by its founders, the Marxist critic acquires new
points of reference. He can now look back at the doctrines of the
founders with the benefit of hindsight, and what he now sees may
well be rather different from what he saw before.

Let us begin by discussing a feature of marginalism[1] which all
Marxists, whether with or without this hindsight, have always claimed
is *a*, if not *the*, leading characteristic of the doctrine. This is the way
in which it in effect set the seal upon that crucial historical process of
abstraction from the socioeconomic relations between men as producers
which began in theoretical economics in the years following Ricardo's
death.

This point has now been made so often by Marxist—and other—
historians of economic thought that it is unnecessary to do more here
than summarize it very briefly. The classical economists, broadly speaking, believed that if the phenomena of the market were to be fully
understood, the analyst must begin by "penetrating below the surface" of these phenomena to the underlying relations between men
in their capacity as producers, which in the last resort could be said
to determine their market relations. The classical labor theory of value
was in essence an analytical embodiment of this methodological principle; and the classical theories of distribution, which laid much
stress on the class relationships between the recipients of factor incomes, were also closely bound up with it. In the years after Ricardo's
death, however, a fairly rapid retreat from this attitude began, at any

1. From the Marxist point of view, the word "marginalism" is really something of a misnomer, since it relates more to the *method* of the doctrines concerned than to their *content*. "Subjectivism" would perhaps be a better word.
Cf. Oscar Lange, *Political Economy*, vol. 1, trans. A. H. Walker (New York,
1963), p. 235 n.

rate in more orthodox circles. In value theory the new trend was marked in particular by the emergence of a subjective theory of value based in one way or another upon "utility," and in distribution theory by what Schumpeter calls the "prevailing tendency to get away from . . . the class connotation of the categories of economic types."[2]

The so-called "marginal revolution" set the seal upon this development in a distinctive and decisive way. The new starting-point became, not the socioeconomic relations between men as producers, but the psychological relation between men and finished goods. Jevons proclaimed that his theory "presumes to investigate the condition of a mind, and bases upon this investigation the whole of Economics."[3] Menger emphasized again and again "the importance of understanding the causal relation between goods and the satisfaction of human needs."[4] And both these authors in one way or another embodied this new methodological principle in the proposition that, as Walras put it, "*rareté* is the cause of value in exchange."[5] "The theory of exchange based on the proportionality of prices to *intensities of the last wants satisfied*," wrote Walras, ". . . constitutes the very foundation of the whole edifice of economics."[6] It was in this striking way, then, that the primary focus of attention in the theory of value was shifted from the relations between men as producers to the relations between men and goods. And in the new theory of distribution which gradually developed, quite largely on the basis of

2. J. A. Schumpeter, *History of Economic Analysis* (London, 1954), p. 552.
3. W. S. Jevons, *The Theory of Political Economy*, 4th ed. (London, 1931), p. 15.
4. Carl Menger, *Principles of Economics*, trans. J. Dingwall and B. F. Hoselitz (Glencoe, Ill., 1950), p. 58.
5. Léon Walras, *Elements of Pure Economics*, trans. W. Jaffé (London, 1954), p. 145. I think it is going a little too far to describe this proposition, as Professor Jaffé does, as "simply a . . . pious restatement of his father's doctrine" and "no more than an *obiter dictum*" (ibid., pp. 512–13). It is true, of course, as Jaffé in effect states, that in the context of Walras's general equilibrium theory as such the psychological relation between men and finished goods is only one of the elements in the market process as a whole; and that it is in a sense meaningless to ask, when confronted with a formal statement of the interconnections between *rareté*, cost of production, and value, which is *the* cause and which are the effects. But if we are going to lay any stress at all on Walras's doctrine of "maximum satisfaction"—which Walras himself would surely have wanted us to do—it seems improper to regard his notion that "*rareté* is the cause of value" as a mere excrescence upon the main body of his doctrine.
6. Ibid., p. 44. This statement appeared in the preface to the fourth edition of the *Elements* (1900).

the inspired hints of the three founders themselves, the tendency was in the same general direction—towards the notion that the socio-economic relations between the classes which supplied land, labor, and capital had nothing *essentially* to do with the respective rewards which the market process afforded them.

Marxists were bound to see this abstraction from the relations of production as representing a "scientific" retreat, just as the marginalists were bound to see it as a "scientific" advance. The trouble was that in the debate which ensued between the two schools it was very difficult to separate real, substantive issues from purely semantic ones. Marxist critiques of marginalism are studded with comparisons between the "superficial" mode of approach which confines itself to the sphere of market exchange and the "scientific" mode which "penetrates through" to the real social forces lying beneath the surface. Marginalist literature, similarly, is full of references to the "superficial" character of analyses which do not "recede to"—i.e., penetrate through to—utility,[7] and to the "scientific" necessity of separating out the "purely economic" relations from those others (mainly "political") with which they happen to be associated in the actual world.[8] Much of this, on both sides, is pure semantics. It has taken us all a long time to realize that we do not get very far by merely pinning derogatory labels on our opponents' work, and that the real proof of puddings of this sort must always be in the eating.

Associated with this abstraction by the marginalists from the relations of production, Marxists have always maintained, were certain elements of "apologetics" and "ideological illusion." These are very sinister-sounding words; in juxtaposition, they tend to conjure up a picture of a conscious conspiracy to further the interests of the bourgeosie by glossing over certain crucially important aspects of capitalist reality. Possibly there have been some Marxists who have believed that this did actually happen, but they have in fact been very few. Three points may be made in this connection.

In the first place, the marginal revolution was hardly a conspiracy, and certainly not a conscious one. Schumpeter was correct

7. Cf. Jevons, *Theory*, p. xxxi: "His [Cournot's] investigation has little relation to the contents of this work, because Cournot does not *recede* to any theory of utility, but commences with the *phenomenal* laws of supply and demand" (my italics).

8. Cf. Schumpeter, p. 551.

enough, at any rate up to a point, in saying that the new theories *emerged* as "a purely analytical affair without reference to practical questions."[9] It is true that they emerged, at any rate in large part, by way of reaction to the prevailing labor and cost theories of value, and that the founders were very well aware of the dangerous uses which were currently being made of these theories in certain quarters.[10] But this was hardly a *major* preoccupation among the founders, however much it may have become so among some of their followers.

In the second place, there is the question of whether and in what sense the doctrines did in fact "further the interests of the bourgeoisie." They were certainly used explicitly by at least one of the founders to defend free competition; and Walras was probably correct in claiming that his was the first real *proof* of the beneficence of free competition which had ever been attempted.[11] Among the successors and popularizers, of course, this kind of use—or misuse— became much more frequent. Some at least of the successors were obviously more anxious than the founders had been to use the new theories to attack Marxism. Wieser's *Natural Value*, for example, was in intention and effect a sustained polemic against the Marxian and Rodbertian systems; and the marginal productivity theory of distribution, when it eventually emerged in its more or less complete form, was widely and consciously used—in particular by J. B. Clark —to attack the Marxian exploitation theory. In the face of such facts as these, it is not really relevant to argue, as Schumpeter does, that there was nothing in the new theories to serve apologetics any better than the older theories. *In good logic*, it is true, no political or ethical conclusions could in fact be drawn from them—but that is hardly the point. The fact remains that it took a long time for this to be realized, and that apologetic use *was* extensively made of them during this period, and is still—even if less frequently—being made of them today. It is also true, of course, that equalitarian conclusions were occasionally drawn from marginal utility theory, notably (albeit rather disastrously) by Pigou, and that George Bernard Shaw tried to

9. Ibid., p. 888.

10. Cf., for example, Menger's comments in chap. 3, sec. E, of his *Principles of Economics*, pp. 165–74. See also Jevons' "primer" of *Political Economy* (London, 1878), pp. 5–6 and 10–11.

11. Walras, p. 256.

build what Engels called a "vulgar socialism"[12] on the basis of the work of Jevons and Menger. But surely such uses were aberrant, and quite apart from the mainstream. Mrs. Robinson no doubt goes rather too far in claiming that "the whole point of *utility* was to justify *laisser faire*,"[13] but it would be even more misguided to claim that it was not in fact very often put to this use.

In the third place, there is the question of whether the new theories did in fact encourage economists to gloss over important aspects of capitalist reality. In a certain sense, there is no doubt that they did. Leaving aside their general abstraction from socioeconomic production relations, which the marginalists expressly or implicitly claimed to be irrelevant to the central economic problem, the fact remains that during the period dominated by the marginalists there was a tendency to remove from the agenda, or at any rate to relegate to a low position on it, certain important problems—notably those of development and the underemployment of resources, and (to a lesser extent) monopoly—which were of great practical importance by any standards, and which constituted the very subject matter of Marxian economics. Associated with this, in most cases, was the conspicuous absence of any concrete specification about technological change, and the habitual assumption that entrepreneurs were essentially an equilibrating rather than a disequilibrating force[14]—a feature which constituted one of the major differences between marginalism and Marxism.

Something more must be said about this third point before we leave it. It can be quite plausibly argued that the omission or soft-pedaling of such problems was in no way apologetic or reprehensible—that the new men, having decided that a fresh start was necessary with a radically new approach, simply *began* with the particular problem to which this new approach could most directly and readily be applied, i.e., the static problem of scarcity, so admirably defined by Jevons in the "Concluding Remarks" to his *Theory of Political Economy*.[15] This, it may be said, was never intended to be anything more than a beginning; one had to learn to walk in the new direction before one could run in it. Jevons himself, after all, believed that

12. Engels' comment occurs in his preface to vol. 3 of Marx's *Capital*.
13. Joan Robinson, *Economic Philosophy* (London, 1962), p. 52.
14. Cf. Leo Rogin, *The Meaning and Validity of Economic Theory* (New York, 1965), pp. 431 and 443–44.
15. Jevons, *Theory*, p. 267. The relevant part of his statement is quoted below.

"dynamical branches of the Science of Economy may remain to be developed"[16] and had no hesitation in using his theory of capital to throw light on the doctrine of the falling tendency of the rate of profit;[17] Walras attempted, however unsatisfactorily, to "dynamize" his theory; and Menger was quite prepared to agree that the establishment of "laws of development" in economics was "per se by no means unjustified," even if "still quite secondary."[18] In the light of these facts, I am now not sure that the one or two rather tentative attempts I have myself made to interpret the rise of marginalism in terms of the emergence of the problem of scarcity in the real world were really very persuasive. One *can* talk here, of course, about Mill's belief that the stationary state was just around the corner; about Jevons' curious propensity to view coal and even paper as limited;[19] about the Great Depression and the accompanying tendency among economists to regard capitalism as having ended its growth process;[20] and so on. But the hints about this which I have at various times flung out in footnotes have never been taken up—and perhaps rightly not. The idea that economics must always necessarily be confined to the economics of scarcity was not really an inherent part of the new philosophy. What requires explanation is not only the fact that the founders concentrated on scarcity, but also—and more importantly—why so many members of the new school, having as it were cut their teeth on the scarcity problem, were unable to transcend it, thereby often giving the impression that they were unconcerned with those great problems of capitalist reality which worried the man in the street.

Let us now change our perspective, and look back at the rise of marginalism with the benefit of that hindsight which I spoke of earlier. If we do this, what leaps to the eye is a certain feature of contemporary reality which marginalism did not gloss over, but which on the contrary it for the first time fully enshrined in economic theory. This was, quite simply, the more or less universal prevalence, in all

16. Ibid., p. vii.
17. Ibid., pp. 253–54.
18. Carl Menger, *Problems of Economics and Sociology*, trans. F. J. Nock (Urbana, Ill., 1963), p. 119.
19. And also—as Professor Coats did at the Bellagio Conference—about the contrast which must have struck Jevons very forcibly between the great empty spaces of Australia and the narrow boundaries of Britain.
20. Cf. Wesley C. Mitchell, *Lecture Notes* (New York, 1949), vol. 2, p. 59.

spheres of economic activity and among all economic agents, of what Weber called "the spirit of capitalism," reflected in marginalist doctrine by the extension of the principle of economic rationality to cover the behavior of households as well as that of firms.

This is a point emphasized by Oscar Lange in Volume I of his remarkable textbook, *Political Economy*, first published in Poland in 1959. The principle of economic rationality, says Lange, asserts simply that if we want to attain the maximum degree of realization of an end we must *either* use our given means with maximum efficiency *or* attain our given end with a minimum outlay of means. This principle, which seems so obvious to us today—and which was indeed first adumbrated by Quesnay two centuries ago—is in fact something which is historically conditioned and which emerges very slowly (both in reality and in the reflection of this reality in theory) until capitalism arrives on the historical scene and speeds it up. Prior to this, economic activity tends to be largely traditional and customary in character, rather than "rational" in the relevant sense—however much it may have been undermined by the arrival of what Marx called "commodity production" and money exchange. With the eventual arrival of capitalism, however, "rational" behavior comes to prevail in the sphere of gainful activity—particularly of course in the individual capitalist enterprise, the scene *par excellence* of "rational" calculation. But *household* activity, generally speaking, still tends (at any rate for a certain period) to retain much of its former traditional and customary character. Only when the "spirit of capitalism" has become all-pervasive does it begin to appear plausible to assume that household activity, too, is "rational" in the relevant sense.[21]

From this point of view, then, the significance of marginalism lies precisely in its assumption that household activity, as well as the activity of capitalist firms, is conducted in accordance with rational, maximizing principles—meaning by this, as Lange puts it, that there is a uniform aim which is the object of maximization and which integrates all the particular aims which correspond to different needs.[22] In most of the earlier marginalist models, the thing that was assumed to be maximized by households was of course "utility," conceived on

21. Cf. Lange, *Principles*, 1:148–72 and 250–52. See in particular p. 251: "The essence of the subjectivist trend . . . consists in the fact that it treats household activity as behavior according to the economic principle."

22. Ibid., p. 253.

a more or less hedonistic basis. "To satisfy our wants to the utmost with the least effort," wrote Jevons, "—to procure the greatest amount of what is desirable at the expense of the least that is undesirable—in other words, *to maximise pleasure*, is the problem of Economics";[23] and he clearly regarded it as an "inevitable tendency of human nature" that individual consumers should behave in accordance with this principle.[24] Later, however, this "utility" which consumers were assumed to maximize came to be interpreted in a broader way which Lange calls "praxiological," meaning by this that "utility" was conceived as "a degree of realization of the aim of economic activity, independent of the nature of the aim."[25] We are all familiar with the major landmarks in this historical transition from "utility" to "preference." The important point about it, from the viewpoint of the present discussion, is that when the change takes place, marginalism is in effect transformed into a kind of logic of rational economic choice. And the generality of this logic is of course increased further when, as with Robbins and von Mises, "economics" comes to be defined as the study of *any* kind of human behavior governed by the principle of economic rationality, thereby being reduced in effect to a mere branch of the general study of the logic of rational activity as such—i.e., of praxiology.

This last stage in the development of the marginalist trend is of course condemned by Lange, as implying the final self-liquidation of political economy. It is not of course that Lange objects to praxiology as such: on the contrary, his chapter "The Principle of Economic Rationality" in *Political Economy* is full of its praises, and two of its branches in particular—operations research and programing (in the broad sense)—are recognized by him to be of exceptional and growing importance in relation to the economics of control, especially under socialism. What he really objects to is that the marginalist trend should in the final outcome have led political economy into becoming a mere *branch* of praxiology. Political economy, he believes, should properly be an independent science, to which praxiology (especially its programing constituent) should be no more than an auxiliary—an important auxiliary, no doubt, but an auxiliary none

23. Jevons, *Theory*, p. 37.
24. Cf. ibid., pp. 59 and 95.
25. Lange, *Principles*, 1:235.

the less. Look what a fearful fate awaits you, Lange is saying, if you are unwise enough to abstract from the relations of production instead of making them your starting point. Praxiology will then become not your servant, but your master.

But this is hardly the whole of the story, and from the point of view of our present discussion Lange's account stops short of the real denouement. It would be quite wrong to see the marginalist trend as leading *only* to the Robbins–von Mises dead end. Marginalism, with its emphasis on the general principle of economic rationality and on the special importance of *consumer* rationality, directly inspired (or at any rate paved the way for) certain other very different and much more significant developments. I am thinking here, of course, particularly of welfare economics. Most of the partial welfare economics of Marshall was directly based on the concept of marginal utility; and the general welfare economics which we teach today owes a great deal to the inspiration of marginalism—as well as, of course, to the brilliant analysis of general equilibrium made by one of its founders. As early as Pareto and Barone it became apparent that the principles of economic rationality which had been one of the main concerns of the earlier marginalist writers could be used not only as a basis for understanding what actually happened in a free enterprise system, and not only as a basis for checking the rationality of such a system, but also as a basis for deciding what ought to be *made* to happen under a controlled system. And the development of programing was hardly an independent development either: it emerged precisely in order to deal with the problem of the guidance of rational action in cases to which for one reason or another the marginal calculus was not applicable.

The fact that the marginalist doctrine, so often used in earlier days to justify free competition, has developed in such a way that it now serves as a basis for the economics of control should not surprise us unduly. Welfare propositions in fact lay at the very heart of marginalism, right from the beginning. The starting point of every economy, says Menger, is "the goods directly available to economic subjects." The ultimate goal of all human economy is "to assure the satisfaction of our direct needs." What we can do to maintain our life and well-being is to travel the road from this starting point to this goal "in as *suitable* a way as possible, i.e., in our case, in as *economic* a way as possible.'' Under such circumstances "only *one* road can be the *most suitable*. . . . In other words, if economic humans under given conditions want to assure the satisfaction of their needs as completely as possible, only *one* road prescribed exactly by the economic situation leads from the strictly determined starting point to the just as strictly determined goal of economy.''[26] And Jevons, somewhat similarly, describes "the problem of Economics" in the following words: "Given, a certain population, with various needs and powers of production, in possession of certain lands and other sources of material: required, the mode of employing their labour which will maximise the utility of the produce.''[27] The clear implication of such statements as these—which do not by any means stand alone—is that a solution of "the problem of Economics" must necessarily involve a formal description of the "most suitable road" from means to end—i.e., the formulation of optimum conditions for maximizing welfare. And propositions of this type were of course frequently put forward by the founders. Given the aims and preconceptions of the latter, however, it was inevitable that these propositions should have been mixed up with others of a different type, relating to what would in fact happen in markets of a certain kind given certain assumptions about individual motivation. The result is that it is often difficult to decide whether a particular marginalist proposition relates to what *ought* to happen, to what actually *does* happen, or to what *would* happen if (for example) the individuals concerned tried to maximize their net satisfactions. The welfare rules were there, however, and in time, when the need arose, it was not too difficult to abstract them from their free-enterprise integument, develop them, and put them to uses which would have surprised and shocked their original propounders.[28]

The marginalist trend, then, which began in such bitter opposition to Marxism, has in the end resulted in the production of a congeries of theories, concepts, and techniques which have become an indispensable auxiliary to Marxism—and an auxiliary, moreover, whose importance increases, rather than diminishes, as measures of central control over the economy are widened in scope. The great

26. Menger, *Problems*, pp. 216–18.
27. Jevons, *Theory*, p. 267.
28. Not Menger, perhaps: see his very interesting and prescient remarks on the economics of socialism in *Problems*, p. 212.

question today, indeed, is whether, at any rate in a socialist economy, this end product of marginalism ought properly to be regarded not as a mere auxiliary to Marxism but rather as its successor.

The point here is that Marxian political economy, like the classical systems out of which it grew, was concerned in the main to make generalizations about the economic regularities and tendencies which were characteristic of a market economy. These regularities and tendencies, it was assumed, emerged as a kind of unintended net resultant of the interaction of the independent buying and selling activities of millions of individual economic agents. Thus the generalizations at which this political economy arrived could be presented as *laws*, which were conceived as operating objectively, autonomously, and independently of human will and consciousness, like the laws of the physical sciences.

Under socialism, however, the scope of operation of economic "laws" of this traditional type—and therefore the applicability of any of the traditional systems of political economy—must necessarily be greatly reduced. There will still of course be numerous *technical* "laws" to be taken account of in the business of production; certain "laws" of consumer behavior will no doubt still be relevant; and certain classical and Marxian generalizations about the processes of social change may still up to a point be applicable. But is not that just about as far as it goes? When it comes down to really basic things like the allocation of resources, the pattern of prices, and the strategy of overall development, can one under socialism really speak of the existence of "laws," operating independently of human will and consciousness, *of the type which classical and Marxian political economy were specifically designed to deal with?* Those who have claimed that such "laws" do in fact still operate under socialism (e.g., Stalin) seem to me to have really said nothing more than that there are certain basic economic realities which the planners have to take proper account of if they want to avoid getting into a mess. And Marxian political economy cannot give us *very* much help in taking account of them; it is precisely here that we have to bring in welfare economics, programing, operations research, cybernetics, etc.—i.e., the whole panoply of praxiological principles which, as we have seen, is the end product not of the Marxian but of the marginalist trend.

What is the moral of all this? That marginalist economics is a more useful guide to action in a socialist economy than Marxian economics? That all roads lead, not to Rome, but to the economics of control? Both of these, up to a point, I suppose—but also one rather more specific and less stereotyped one. The important point about marginalism is that it was based on the notion of a general principle of economic rationality which embraced both the profit-maximizing activities of firms and the utility-maximizing (or preference-maximizing) activities of consumers, but in which the former were made in an important sense secondary and subordinate to the latter. For an economics of control appropriate to a rational and democratic age to emerge, the existence of a principle of this type was a *sine qua non*. And such a principle was not available anywhere else. In particular, it was not available in Marxian economics. Marx and Engels had, it is true, sketched out the general nature of the allocation problem under socialism a dozen times—the problem of the comparison of the "useful effects" of goods with one another and with the quantity of labor required for their production, they used to call it—but for various worthy reasons they had never attempted to specify the conditions of a rational solution of this problem. Thus the principles of rationality and associated techniques employed by the marginalists were the only ones available when the need for an economics of control arose in practice. It mattered not that these principles had originally been used to explain—and often to defend—what actually happened under competitive capitalism. With or without—more usually without—the appropriate "Marxian" modifications, they were snapped up and used as a guide to what ought to happen in a controlled economy. So the final moral, perhaps, is that the devil not only *can* quote Scripture for his purpose, but *will* do so when the need is urgent and there is nothing else ready to hand.

The Spread of Marginalism in Italy, 1871–1890

Piero Barucci

I

To most economists, marginalism in Italy appears, apart from Maffeo Pantaleoni, to be connected with the names of V. Pareto, E. Barone, A. De Viti de Marco, L. Einaudi, and L. Amoroso, whose works are practically all later than 1890. Yet—as I will try to demonstrate—by 1890 marginalism in Italy had already reached its maturity; by this time it had completed its first steps.

In 1871 Italy was going through a delicate moment in its political and economic development. During its first decade of life, the young kingdom had to overcome serious difficulties. Now, at the beginning of the 1870's, the future seemed less uncertain, though all the problems ushered in by the national political unification in 1861 were still unsolved. The point is that Italy reached political unity and began to be confronted by the ensuing economic problems in a period when the leading countries of western Europe, England and France, small Belgium and Germany, were experiencing rapid economic progress. The differences already existing in 1861 between Italy and those countries inevitably tended to increase. The initial economic backwardness, the comparison with the other quickly developing countries, and the ruinous financial position of the new kingdom appeared at that moment—just after the very first years of understandable enthusiasm—to be a combination of reasons liable to induce deep disheartenment even in those who had been the leaders in achieving political unity. All this appeared particularly evident in 1866, a dramatic year in the life of the new-born united state, when (May 1) the *corso forzoso* was introduced by which the government decreed the inconvertibility of banknotes.

PIERO BARUCCI *is Professor of the History of Economic Doctrines at the University of Florence.*

II

The message of Menger, Jevons, and Walras, which was both a method and a subtle theoretical doctrine, found the Italian economists almost prostrate in meditation of the problems of their own country. When one notes that during the twenty years from 1865 to 1885 (the interim between Francesco Ferrara and Maffeo Pantaleoni) Italian economic thought did not succeed in producing any really outstanding theoretician, one cannot help but underline the influences played by the problems of the country's political unification on the development of economic thought itself.

Direct political engagement eventually consumed the best energies of Italian economists. To mention only the best known, it must be remembered that F. Ferrara, A. Scialoja, A. Messedaglia, F. Lampertico, G. Boccardo, and M. Minghetti held repeated governmental appointments or became members of the Italian parliament.[1] And most of them, both the well-known and the less significant economists, were attracted irresistibly by concrete problems. Consequently, these were not the richest years for pure theory. Any evaluation of Italian economic thought around 1870 must acknowledge that its basic aim was to answer the question of how to attain economic unity. Confirmation of this is provided by the dispute which suddenly broke out among Italian economists in 1874, the so-called "controversy between the two schools." The main difference between the schools con-

1. On these authors, and in general on Italian economic thought during this period, one can still refer to the old writings by A. Loria in *Dictionary of Political Economy*, ed. R. H. I. Palgrave, art. "Italian School of Economics" (vol. 2), later republished in translation in the volume *Verso la giustizia sociale* (Milan, 1908), pp. 76 ff., as well as the well-known volume by L. Cossa, *Introduzione allo studio della economia politica* (Milan, 1892), pp. 519 ff.; Engl. trans. L. Dyer, 1893. Among the most recent writings, we will mention A. Fanfani and G. Barbieri, "Le scienze economiche e sociali dal 1865 al 1889," in the volume *Un secolo di progresso scientifico italiano, 1839–1939* (Rome, 1940), Società per il progresso delle scienze, 6:239–55; G. Palomba, "Le dottrine economiche," in *Cento anni di vita italiana, 1848–1948*, ed. C. Barbagallo (Milan, 1949), 2:251–74; G. Barbieri, "Gli economisti italiani nel primo secolo dell'Unità nazionale," first in *L'economia italiana dal 1861 al 1961* (Milan, 1961), later in G. Barbieri, *Saggi di storia del pensiero economico* (Verona, 1965), pp. 211–60; A. Bertolino, *Il pensiero economico italiano dal Risorgimento nazionale ai nostri giorni* (Lisbon, 1954); A. Macchioro, "Marxismo ed economia politica fra XIX e XX secolo," *Rivista Storica del Socialismo*, Jan.-April 1966, republished in the volume *Studi di storia del pensiero economico* (Milan, 1970); F. Duchini, "L'evoluzione del pensiero economico," in the issue of *Vita e Pensiero*, no. 12 (1970), *1870–1970: La presenza dei cattolici nella vita culturale italiana*, pp. 98–110.

cerned the extent to which the State should take over the economic decisions of private citizens.

In the early seventies, theoretical economics in Italy was languishing. The last "Forewords" by Francesco Ferrara to volumes in the *Biblioteca dell'Economista*[2] go back to 1866. Ferrarism, even though it could count quite a few followers, occupying the majority of Italian university chairs, seemed by then to be in the hands of mere reiterators. Economic classicism counted only a handful of followers. Ricardo was still rarely read and little understood.[3] From the chair in Pavia which he had held since 1858, Luigi Cossa had already started breeding a generation of economists who had in common perhaps only a great respect for historical research, to which many of them devoted their efforts. The eclecticism of the master helped to train economists who later followed the most divergent paths. Among them, Vito Cusumano, who was sent to Germany to complete his studies under Wagner and Engel, represented the intermediate element through which so-called *Kathedersozialismus*, academic socialism, made its official appearance in Italy.[4] The positions of the German "vincolisti" (protectionists), with their criticism of individualism and Adam Smith's liberalism, became extremely popular in Italy within a few months, and Cusumano's writings were not only read but widely disseminated through an ample series of publications. The main reason why these ideas met so ready a reception in Italy during these years, as well as so virulent a reaction, must be sought in the fact that they were diffused at a moment when the prevailing liberalist policy was seriously debated on all levels, and especially on a strictly political level.

This climate of opinion explains the violent critical attitude taken

2. Ferrara edited the first two series of the *Biblioteca dell'Economista*. Concerning the significance of these writings by Ferrara, see F. Caffé, "Il Ferrara delle Prefazioni," in *Bancaria*, 1957, pp. 885–87.

3. An exception in this picture is E. Nazzani, whose essays, *Saggi di economia politica*, gathered into a volume in 1881 (Milan), after being published individually beginning with 1872, are an example of keen theoretical discussion of some typically Ricardian themes.

4. V. Cusumano, "Sulla condizione attuale degli studi economici in Germania," *Archivio Giuridico* (Bologna), vol. 11, nos. 2–4 (1873). These articles were later gathered in a small volume which was published under the same title (Bologna, 1873). After revising and widely integrating them with new sections, Cusumano published the articles again in the volume *Le scuole economiche della Germania in rapporto alla questione sociale* (Naples, 1875).

by F. Ferrara, who was then considered, both by friends and opponents, to be the leading Italian authority in the realm of economic research. Ferrera had no doubt: "Economic science" was that of the "school of liberalism," that of the "disciples of Smith, Say, and Bastiat."[5] Starting from this assumption, he attacked all Italian economists who disagreed with him, in particular Nazzani, Toniolo, Cusumano, Cossa, Scialoja, Messedaglia, and Lampertico. He accused them of having "daydreamed of an actual canonization of the State." This conviction inspired his appeal for a closing of the ranks of "veterans of Smithian economy," almost as if the enemy were at the gate. Ferrara's article had the unfortunate effect of dividing contemporary Italian economists immediately into different camps violently opposed to each other. His authority and his polemical vehemence contributed to a rigid crystallization into groups of scholars who were themselves perhaps by no means eager to transform a scientific discussion into a political and ideological row. But given that climate of opinion, any attempt to damp the fires of controversy was bound to have limited success.

The division emerged in September 1874, and those responsible were on one side Ferrara and on the other especially Luzzatti and Lampertico. On Ferrara's initiative the Adam Smith Society was formed in Florence in September 1874, with its official paper the Florentine weekly *L'Economista*.[6] Almost simultaneously with the constitution of the Adam Smith Society, a circular letter dated 11 September 1874 was issued from Padua and signed by Antonio Scialoja, Luigi Cossa, Luigi Luzzatti, and Fedele Lampertico. The journal of the "Lombard-Venetian" group became *L'Economista d'Italia* published in Rome; but in a short time the group, which had formed an Association for the Development of Economic Studies, after the Milan Congress (4 to 6 January 1875), started the well-known Padua Series of the *Giornale degli Economisti*, which was first published in April 1875 under the direction of E. Forti (publication was discontinued in 1878).

5. F. Ferrara, "Il germanesimo economico in Italia," in *Nuova Antologia* 26 (Aug. 1874): 985.
6. "La società Adamo Smith e la circolare di Padova," *L'Economista*, 24 Sept. 1874, p. 561.

III

What clearly appears, even from the position of men like Cossa and Boccardo, who tried to remain somewhat detached from this controversy, is the fact that economic science in Italy was more and more, compared with the other sciences, taking on "a somewhat encyclopaedic character." For reasons I have been unable to discover, the publisher of the *Biblioteca dell'Economista* transferred responsibility for it from Ferrara, a thoroughbred theoretician, to G. Boccardo, an eclectic author with a limited scientific reputation who was unable to give a decisive new impulse to Italian economic thought.[7] The effect of this change was soon felt. The main feature of the program of the new series of the *Biblioteca dell'Economista* was a prelude to a collection of works which established an artificial cohabitation of Spencer and Marx, Whewell and Schäffle, Walras and Owen, Henry George and Jevons, Schönberg and Quetelet, Cairnes, Brentano, and Roscher in order to make available to Italian readers the most recent developments in German research. This was immediately noted by *L'Economista*, which interpreted the change as abandonment of "classical" tradition and an acceptance of the *Kathedersozialisten*.[8] Indeed, the third series of the *Biblioteca dell'Economista* published the works of the German academic socialists together with the classical authors of sociology and socialism. Among more strictly economic works, it gave special prominence to problems of method. *On the whole, marginalism was a complete intruder.*

Boccardo's decision to translate such a pair of authors as Jevons and Walras must be explained. There are two main reasons: one, to be mentioned later, is completely casual; the other rests on a misunderstanding and must be exposed at once.[9] These works were translated as examples of mathematics applied to economics. It is not

---

7. Among Ferrara's papers, still extant at the Bank of Italy and awaiting publication, there is no trace of the reasons for this transfer of the *Biblioteca dell'Economista* to Boccardo. I am grateful for this information to Professor F. Caffé of the Università di Roma.

8. See *Rivista Bibliografica*, 31 Oct. 1875, p. 556.

9. The judgment of R. S. Howey, *The Rise of the Marginal Utility School, 1870–1889* (Lawrence, Kans., 1960), p. 205, according to which Boccardo's translation "came as a result of his tolerant attitude toward dissenters, however, rather than from an especial appreciation that he had for the work of the members of the Marginal Utility School," should be shared for its second part rather than for its first.

by chance, indeed, that the volume containing translations of Jevons and Walras also included the famous "Memoirs" by W. Whewell concerning the system of Ricardo, and Quetelet's *Social Physics and Anthropometry.*

On the other hand, Boccardo's Foreword to the volume was entitled "On the Application of Quantitative Methods to Economic, Statistical and Social Sciences." For the author of the prefatory pages, indeed, the new element consisted only in the use of mathematics in political economy: he did not grasp in any way the possible connection between the new marginal utility theory, the use of the mathematical technique, and the theory of exchange.[10] In other words, Jevons and Walras entered Italy without any demonstration of their actual theoretical features, in a rather misleading form.[11]

IV

The history of marginalism in Italy begins with a name unknown in the development of economic thought, that of Marc Monnier, and proceeds through an Italian economist of slight significance, Alberto Errera. Thanks to Walras's *Correspondence* in the masterly edition of William Jaffé, the fundamental steps of Walras's entrance into the Italian economists' world can be traced. On 12 March 1874, that is, even before the publication of his "Mémoire" in the *Journal des Economistes,*[12] Walras wrote to Marc Monnier—a poet and man

10. This has been remarked by Howey, p. 259.

11. However, if Boccardo had grasped the real elements of novelty in these works, he could easily have produced a translation of Menger too. In fact Menger had to wait a long time before being appropriately known in Italy. Menger's *Grundsätze* was translated through the efforts of M. Pantaleoni and was published as a *supplemento* to the *Giornale degli Economisti* for the years 1906–7. It was later published in book form (Imola, 1909). Pantaleoni prepared a short foreword. Italian economists also had an exceptional introduction to the works of Jevons and Walras in the latter's long article in the *Giornale degli Economisti,* "A New Branch of Mathematics: On the Application of Mathematics to Political Economy," year 2, vol. 3, no. 1 (April 1876): 1–40. On this article, which was published only in Italian, see W. Jaffé's indications in *Correspondence of Léon Walras,* 3 vols. (Amsterdam, 1965) 1:344, n. 2.

12. It is, as is well known, the paper "Principe d'une théorie mathématique de l'échange," which was read by Walras in Paris at the Académie des Sciences morales et politiques during the two sessions 16 and 23 Aug. 1873. The paper was later published in *Séances et travaux de l'Académie des Sciences morales et politiques,* Jan. 1874, vol. 101 of the Collection, n.s. 33d year, pt. 1, pp. 97–116, and was then republished in the *Journal des Economistes,* 3d ser., vol. 34, no. 100 (April–June 1874), pp. 5–21.

of letters who was then professor of comparative literature at the Academy of Geneva—asking him "les noms des hommes qui ont, en Italie, une chaire d'économie politique: ceux des directeurs de recueils italiens compétents,"[13] to whom he intended to submit a copy of his article on the theory of exchange. Monnier replied mentioning the names of A. Scialoja and A. Errera, and it was with the latter that Walras immediately corresponded.

Errera was a promoter of Walras in Italy, and in this respect—but only in this respect—he was Walras's equal. Through him, Walras was able to submit his booklet to some of the leading contemporary Italian economists,[14] and consequently he became known in Italy much earlier, and possibly better, than elsewhere. The correspondence between Walras and Errera is one of the oddest in the entire history of economic thought. Although he was not always truthful,[15] by constant flatteries Errera became Walras's official representative in Italy and was so successful in propagating Walras's work that he asked Walras to perform the same task for his writings in Switzerland and France. There is something pathetic in this relation of mutual help established between the two. At any rate, Walras, when preparing his résumés both of the paper "Principe" and of his Eléments, made sure that the Italian interpretations of this thought were authentic to the highest degree.

Errera is important in the history of marginalism in Italy for two further reasons. By bringing Walras in contact with Boccardo he promoted the Italian translation of some of Walras's fundamental writings;[16] and he indirectly constituted the connecting link through

13. Cf. Jaffé, Correspondence, 1:250–51.

14. From the correspondence of Walras, it seems possible to infer that the memoir of 1873 was sent to some twenty people in Italy, among whom were Messedaglia, Bodio, Montanari, Cossa, Lampertico, Scialoja, Boccardo, and Minghetti. It seems that the pamphlet was not sent to F. Ferrara, to whom Walras was later to send a copy of his Eléments.

15. It seems impossibile, for instance, that already in March 1874 Errera had read Walras's memoir, as he says (letter of 23 March, in Jaffé, Correspondence, 1:367), just as what he states in the same letter does not seem to be true, according to which Walras would have been already known "for a long time" in Italy.

16. The history of the translation of Walras into Italian is quite complex, although by now W. Jaffé has completely reconstructed it in his footnotes to Volume 1 of the Correspondence. In all likelihood, the proposal to translate the "Principe" (1873) was contained in the first letter written by Walras to Errera, which has not been recovered. A hint can be found in the reply to this letter by

which Jevons, too, penetrated Italian economic culture,[17] so that his *Theory* was translated as early as 1875.[18]

V

When Walras referred to Italy as the country where he had met the most satisfactory recognition, he meant something else: namely, that all Italian reviews of his early works were produced by Alberto Errera or due to him.[19] In view of their critical evaluation it is

the Italian scholar (his letter of 23 March 1874), while explicit evidence appears in his letter dated 8 April 1874. Boccardo, in his letter dated 30 Dec. 1874, expressed to Walras his desire to have the first volume of his *Eléments d'économie pure* translated into Italian. This resulted in a dense exchange of letters, through which it is possible to realize the anxiety of Boccardo to have Walras known to Italian economists, as well as Walras's desire to overcome any difficulty in the carrying out of this purpose. Walras, however, did not want to have only the first volume of his *Eléments* translated, nor could he grant the permission for the translation, the rights of which belonged to his Swiss publisher, who was asking for translation royalties. Boccardo could not wait for the publication of the second volume of the *Eléments*, which would delay too long the complete publication of a volume the foreword of which had already been written at the end of 1874 (indeed, the volume was published in fascicles of 16 pages each). Walras then decided to have translated into Italian, besides the memoir of 1873, three more memoirs delivered in 1875 and 1876 at the Waldesian Society of Natural Sciences at Lausanne. They were published in Italian under the title *Teoria matematica della ricchezza sociale*, in *Biblioteca dell'Economista*, 3d ser., vol. 2 (Turin, 1878), with a short introduction by Walras in which the four memoirs were described as an actual summary of the two volumes of the *Eléments*. See in particular Letters nos. 324, 327, 330, 342, 343, 348, 349, 366, 371, 391, and 392, as well as the comprehensive notes by W. Jaffé, in *Correspondence*.

17. Indeed, it was Walras who suggested Errera's name to Jevons in order to obtain a proper diffusion of his *Theory* also in Italy. Cf. the letter of 29 July 1874, *Correspondence*, pp. 413–14. Later (letter of 24 Sept. 1874) he also mentioned the names of L. Bodio, A. Messedaglia, and F. Ferrara, and finally those of Cusumano, Basile, and Cognetti de Martiis (letters of 29 Nov. 1874). In the already published letters of Walras and Jevons, and those of Jevons addressed to Italian economists, still unpublished, which I was able to consult through the kindness of Professor R. D. Collison Black, I have not found a basis for reconstructing the way in which Jevons established contact with Boccardo and then Cossa. All that is known for sure is that Jevons was informed about the translation of the *Theory* being prepared by Boccardo, towards the end of 1874. Cf. *Letters and Journal of W. Stanley Jevons*, ed. Harriet A. Jevons (London, 1886), p. 329, Jevons to J. d'Aulnis de Bourouill, 23 Dec. 1874.

18. Cf. Jaffé, *Correspondence*, 1:491–92, Walras to Boccardo, 22 Dec. 1875. A hint of the theory of *final degree of utility* had already appeared in L. Cossa, *L'economia dei popoli e degli stati di Fedele Lampertico*, a memoir delivered in the R. Lombard Institute of Sciences and Letters on 12 March 1874, reprinted in L. Cossa, *Saggi di Economia Politica* (Milan, 1878), p. 144. There is some probability that this is one of the earliest Italian quotations of Jevons' *Theory*.

19. These reviews, presented in chronological order, are the following: G. A.

advisable to distinguish the reviews due to two mathematicians, who certainly were not familiar with economic thinking (G. A. Zanon and A. Zambelli) from those due to scholars of economic problems, even though they were not theoretical economists (A. Errera and A. Basile). The reviews by Zanon and Zambelli were concerned only with the theory of exchange, and we know now that they were revised (and Zanon's even corrected) by Walras himself before being published.[20] Certainly both authors took advantage of a comprehensive résumé sent by Walras to Errera which concerned his memoir of 1873.[21] This is confirmed by the fact that the two articles are rather similar. Both seek to explain Walras's theory of exchange, but they had the merit of introducing Italian economists to a rigorously mathematical handling of economics and presenting some clearly marginalist schemes.

The long review by A. Basile is a choice example of how it is possible to assemble a large number of words without any clear meaning when reviewing a work which is hardly understood. Actually, the article is merely a condemnation of the use of mathematics in economics, and there is no hint of marginalism.

A different value should be assigned to Errera's review of the *Eléments*, which must be rated a clear and correct exposition of the first volume of that work. Errera's article can be divided into four parts: (i) an exposition of Walras's idea of wealth, (ii) an introduction to the mathematical theory of exchange, considering only two goods, (iii) illustration of the same theory considering n goods, and (iv) short hints of Walras's conception of money. Quite a few details lead us to assume that actually Errera was translating into Italian a résumé prepared by Walras. There is a clear evidence of this in

---

Zanon, ''Sulla teoria matematica dello scambio del prof. L. Walras,'' *Rassegna di Agricoltura, Industria e Commercio* 2 (July 1874): 217–23; A. Errera, ''Rassegna bibliografica di opere di Economia Politica e di Diritto Industriale,'' *Rivista Europea* 3, no. 2 (July 1874): 315–35 (on Walras, see pp. 19-20 of the abstract); A. Basile, ''Il metodo matematico nell'economia politica: *Eléments d'économie politique pure* par Léon Walras,'' *L'Economista d'Italia*, no. 40 (4 Oct. 1874): 518–20, and no. 42 (18 Oct. 1874): 543–45; A. Errera, ''Appunto bibliografico: *Eléments d'économie politique pure* par Léon Walras,'' an abstract from *La Perseveranza* (Milan, 1875); A. Zambelli, *La teoria matematica dello scambio del Signor Leone Walras* (Padua, 1876).

20. Cf. Jaffé, *Correspondence*, 1:388–89 and 409, respectively Walras to Errera, 5 May 1874, and Errera to Walras, 10 June 1874.

21. Cf. ibid., 1:264, Walras to Errera, 25 April 1874, and pp. 345–47.

Part (ii).[22] But we also know that Walras volunteered to write the usual summary of the entire first volume of the *Eléments* for Errera, which he sent on 5 August 1874.[23] Given this fact and knowing the limitations of Errera's mathematical knowledge, we may assume that the central and most important part of this review should be attributed to Walras. It is therefore correct to say that about 1875 Walras was known in Italy, but what was not known was the theoretical significance of the new school of which the author himself had become a member. This means that marginalism did not enter Italy via Walras: on the contrary it entered via Jevons, thanks both to the friendly association between Jevons and Cossa—resulting in the translation of Jevons' *Primer* into Italian (Milan, 1879) and Cossa's *Guida* into English (London, 1890)—and to the fact that the actual promoter of marginalism in Italy, Maffeo Pantaleoni, publicized the English current, namely, that of Jevons.

VI

This came about, practically, in 1883 with Pantaleoni's application of Jevons' analytical tools.[24] The problem Pantaleoni set himself was that of discovering the criteria followed ''by the average intelligence comprised in Parliament'' in distributing public funds among different possible uses. The logical instrument capable of solving this problem was located by Pantaleoni in the ''comparative degree of the marginal utilities of the various items of public expenditure.'' Par-

22. It is a translation, almost literal, of the old résumé prepared by Walras for the memoir of 1873 and immediately submitted to Errera. Cf. Jaffé, *Correspondence*, 1:345–47, and A. Errera, ''Appunto bibliografico,'' pp. 6–9 of the abstract.

23. Cf. Jaffé, *Correspondence*, 1:412, Walras to Errera 25 July 1874; Errera to Walras 31 July (p. 415), and Walras to Errera, 5 Aug. (p. 417). I was not able to find this résumé.

24. M. Pantaleoni, ''Contributo alla teoria del riparto delle spese pubbliche,'' *Rassegna Italiana*, 15 Oct. 1883, reprinted in M. Pantaleoni, *Studi di Finanza e di Statistica* (Bologna, 1938); Engl. trans. in *Classics in the Theory of Public Finance*, ed. R. A. Musgrave and A. T. Peacock (London, 1967), pp. 16–27. Pantaleoni is known to have been familiar with Jevons already in his thesis for the degree (1881), published as *Teoria della traslazione dei tributi: Definizione, dinamica e ubiquità della traslazione* (Rome, 1882; reprinted, ed. E. d'Albergo, introd. G. U. Papi, Rome, 1958). There he quoted Jevons extensively, but only as an opponent of the theory of the wages fund. Cf. *Teoria* (ed. 1958), pp. 298 ff. A short but correct exposition of Jevons' theory on the ''final degree of utility'' is also to be found in A. Loria, ''La teoria del valore negli economisti italiani,'' *Archivio Giuridico*, 1882; later in abstract form, Bologna, 1882.

liament presumably tends "to obtain the largest total sum of utility";
accordingly, Parliament iself can "approve or reject any expenditure
only on the basis of a judgment which is the resultant of a complex of
different elements or proportions. These are obtained by arranging
in decreasing order the marginal utilities deriving from the various
expenditures, and then weighing the inherent marginal utilities of
possible expenditures."[25]

The entrance date of marginalism into Italy should thus be set
by Pantaleoni's article on financial theory (1883). It must be immediately remarked, however, that the best use of the new theory
occurred as an attempt to apply the theory of marginal utility to the
activity of the State. It should also be underlined that Menger was
still then almost unknown in Italy, while Walras, after his short-
lived appearance ten years earlier, had undergone a long eclipse.[26]
At any rate, Pantaleoni heralded a movement with deep cultural
roots which is quite easy to explain from the historical viewpoint.
One could term it a reactionary movement: reaction against an
economic culture which was losing the features that distinguished it
from other cultures and was getting drowned in a sea of scattered
publications, dealing with the thousand social problems brought by
the times to the attention of scholars.

The features of "pure economics" are easily detectible in Pantaleoni's *Principii di Economia Pura* (1889), a work which was
destined to become the vademecum of an entire generation of Italian
economists and to represent the *"examination of conscience" of an
an entire economic culture in relation to the new marginalist message.* By now there is general agreement about the *marginalist* origin
and nature of Pantaleoni's *Principii.* His aspiration to build up a
"pure" economics, to be translated into theorems identified through

25. M. Pantaleoni, "Contributo" (1938), pp. 21–22. Pantaleoni there uses
Jevons' theory even to frame the problems of "incomes." A hint, very short but
correct, of this basic contribution by Pantaleoni can be found in James M.
Buchanan, "La Scienza delle Finanze: The Italian Tradition in Fiscal Theory,"
in his *Fiscal Theory and Political Economy: Selected Essays* (Chapel Hill, N. C.,
1960). Cf. p. 31.

26. An important development of Pantaleoni's marginalism is supplied by his
article "Rassegna finanziaria: Osservazioni sulla finanza italiana," *Giornale
degli Economisti* 2 (1887): 165–71. Jevons' and Menger's schemes were used by
Pantaleoni also in his booklet *Teoria della pressione tributaria* (Rome, 1887),
later included in the volume *Studi di Finanza e Statistica* (Bologna, 1938), pp.
78 ff.

the names of those who discovered them, his efforts to reach a correct definition of the so-called *hedonistic* premise, and his subtle analyses of the theory of utility, of the value theory, and finally of the theory of exchange are well known.

Within this research, however, two remarkably interesting characteristics should be underlined: (i) Pantaleoni's marginalism developed along the Gossen-Jennings-Jevons line, and (ii) the same marginalism is—at least in his *Principii*—bitterly critical of the Austrian school, at least critical of Menger and Böhm-Bawerk, the former being rated as a "plagiarist," the latter as a "charlatan."[27]

VII

Simultaneously with Maffeo Pantaleoni, other Italian economists were proceeding towards marginalism during the 1880's. In the fields most relevant to the present article it is clear that Italian economists selected two most significant lines of development: the founding of a "Scienza delle Finanze," and the theory of value.

During the decade of the 1880's, reflection on the problems of the economic conduct of the State led to the foundation of the so-called "Scienza delle Finanze." During that decade the "Scienza delle Finanze" began to acquire the features of an autonomous discipline, trying to identify its specific objective of research. The intention of the authors who followed this path was to use the central principles of economic theory to explain the fiscal action of the State, and in particular, to use the new theory of value for this purpose. In this connection Italian economists played a role of fundamental significance, as has recently been recognized.[28]

Pantaleoni, the real keystone for the acceptance of marginalism in Italy, had himself started as a scholar of financial problems. "Scienza delle Finanze" was the door by which marginalism entered Italy; this is a provisional conclusion, but it is an interesting question whether it is also true of other countries.

27. Pantaleoni to Walras, 12 Aug. 1889. Cf. Jaffé, *Correspondence*, 2:906. For these features of "marginalism" in Pantaleoni, refer to ibid., 2:907; Howey, p. 259; and E. Kauder, *A History of Marginal Utility Theory* (Princeton, 1965), p. 81. It must be said that, in connection with von Wieser, Pantaleoni only had, in his *Principii*, fairly positive judgments. This is a point which deserves attention.
28. Buchanan, "La Scienza delle Finanze," and Musgrave and Peacock, *Classics*, "Introduction."

There is an explanation which can be traced in the works of the
same Italian economists. The theory of value, based on the subjective appreciation of the utility of goods, had prompted many deep
investigations into the nature of needs and the way to satisfy them.
As some of these needs required State intervention, it could be but
a short step to a study of the economic conduct of the State itself,
in the light of the schemes suggested to explain how an individual
distributes a given quantity of goods in order to maximize his utility.
The economic conduct of the State thus involved a dual problem: from
the side of cost, the problem was to distribute the fiscal income so
that each citizen achieved a position of balance between the marginal
disutility of the fiscal toll and the marginal utility of the public
service "produced" by the State; from the side of production of these
public services, the problem was, first, that of distributing the national resources between those managed by the public sphere and
those managed by the private sphere, and secondly, that of distributing the former in such a way as to equal marginal utilities in
all their possible uses.

When E. Sax published his famous work in 1887,[29] he found in
Italy an atmosphere immediately receptive to its spirit, and ready
to appreciate its marginalistic contents.[30] G. Ricca Salerno wished
the "Scienza delle Finanze" to be basically economic and criticized
every conception that would view state taxation activity as capable
of solving problems of "social politics," and this approach opened
the way to the diffusion of Sax's work.[31] In the history of the spread
of marginalism in Italy, this author has a limited but distinctive place.
His role is certainly less important than Pantaleoni's, but quite independent. By this I mean that Ricca Salerno proceeded along his
path and arrived at his "meeting" with Sax by following his own personal track. He does not seem to have been directly influenced by the

29. E. Sax, *Grundlegung der theoretischen Staatswirtschaft* (Vienna, 1887).
30. I do not know in which month of 1887 Sax's work was published, and I
was not able to ascertain the delay in publication of the *Giornale degli Economisti*
in that period. It must be remarked, however, that G. Ricca Salerno, in an article
entitled "Nuove dottrine sistematiche nella Scienza delle Finanze," *Giornale degli
Economisti*, 1887, no. 4:376–402, made a few references to this work, and some
of them are fairly comprehensive.
31. G. Ricca Salerno, "Nuove dottrine"; and "Dell'imposta progressiva
secondo alcune recenti dottrine tedesche," *Giornale degli Economisti* (Padua),
year 5, vol. 7, no. 3 (June 1878), p. 284.

works of Jevons, Menger, or Walras; rather, it appears that he had gone through his own evolution by way of a work of completely internal reconsideration, in relation to the "Scienza delle Finanze."

Two different lines of reflection were therefore summing their cumulative effects, in the years 1887 to 1889, and resulted in a kind of explosion of marginalism in Italy. The magical year of "Scienza delle Finanze," in Italy was, however, 1888, when Ricca Salerno summarized the scientific position of this discipline in a *Manuale* which was published in the same collection as Pantaleoni's *Principii*, and in which De Viti de Marco made his reputation with a work that is, by now, a classic.[32] Ricca Salerno's work was one of introduction of the "most significant results of scientific research upon finance" (as the author himself states); De Viti's, on the contrary, clearly revealed originality. Its validity is twofold, consisting in a methodological deepening of the theoretical features of the "Scienza delle Finanze" and in defining certain logical aspects of the State.

In particular, De Viti, by considering the State as "a large industry" the aims of which are the satisfaction of community requirements through a specifically productive activity, affirmed that the State, just like individuals, is subject to the principle of "minimum means." The theory of value, which is for him the marginalist theory, forms the background of his entire study, but never appears in an open way, since it is smothered in the author's concern with laying the foundation of a modern "Scienza delle Finanze."

The seeds of this implication, for which Ricca Salerno and De Viti de Marco were responsible, were to sprout shortly afterwards, first in the writings of A. Zorli and A. Graziani[33] and later, in 1890, in two strictly theoretical volumes, one due to A. Conigliani[34] and the other to U. Mazzola.[35] From the marginalist viewpoint Conigliani's volume

32. G. Ricca Salerno, *Scienza delle Finanze* (Florence, 1888). This work was published in the collection of Manuali of the publisher G. Barbera; and A. De Viti de Marco, *Il carattere teorico dell'economia finanziaria* (Rome, 1888).

33. A. Zorli, *La scienza dei tributi in rapporto alle recenti teorie economiche* (Bologna, 1889); and A. Graziani, "Di alcune questioni intorno alla natura e agli effetti economici delle imposte," *Studi Senesi,* 1889, pp. 209–83. While Zorli's work has a prevailing methodological setting, that of Graziani contains quite a few examples of use of marginalistic schemes, presented with balance and critical accuracy.

34. C. A. Conigliani, *Teoria generale degli effetti economici delle imposte: Saggio di economia para* (Milan, 1890).

35. U. Mazzola, *I dati scientifici della finanza pubblica* (Rome, 1890).

is a jewel. Investigating the "effects produced in economic life, both individual and social, by the changes in taxation," the author starts from the "individual's subjective evaluations of his position." On this foundation, he examines the above-mentioned effects within a scheme which is constantly and clearly marginalistic. The same scheme is evidenced by Mazzola's volume, which is far better known[36] than that of Conigliani. In a few years, then, marginalism in Italy had definitely asserted itself, to the point of making original contributions to the "Scienza delle Finanze" which are still considered first class.

VIII

The debate on the theory of value, on the other hand, was progressing amidst many difficulties. Here Ferrara's inheritance was exceedingly cumbersome. In particular, his theory of reproduction cost lent itself to various interpretations. It was meant to be a critical reply to Ricardo's labor theory of value, in which Ferrera did not see any element of subjectiveness. With his reproduction cost he intended to work out a theory of value which took into account both the element of cost and that of utility of goods. The value of a good would be, in this way, the comparison between the utility attributed by a subject to the good itself and the cost he thinks he would have to incur to reproduce the good. Indeed, this theory emphasized the fact of *utility* of goods, as has recently been recognized.[37] But this was not understood by the few followers of Ferrara then writing on economics.

A few isolated attempts[38] to elaborate the theory of value, and a disconnection from the opposition—obsolete by then—between value-cost and value-cost of reproduction, must be considered, however, almost as a moment of transition before the second phase of the actual introduction of marginalism in Italy (the first consisting in Errera's efforts to gain recognition for Walras). This "second stage" encompasses the years from 1886 to 1890. It was ushered in by the now well-known *Memoria*

36. Chapter 9 of this volume was recently translated into English by E. Henderson and included in Musgrave and Peacock, *Classics*, pp. 37–47.

37. J. M. Buchanan, "La Scienza delle Finanze," pp. 27 ff., and in particular, F. Caffé, *Politica economica: Sistematica e tecniche di analisi* (Turin, 1966), 1:60 ff.

38. See, for instance, A. De Johannis, "Analisi psicologica e economica del valore: Studio," an abstract from *Ateneo Veneto* (Venice, 1883); and A. Ciccone, *Del valore d'uso e del valore di scambio: Considerazioni* (Naples, 1884).

of G. B. Antonelli,[39] and it came to an end with Pantaleoni's *Principii*. On the many implications of Antonelli's writings, and their significance in the history of mathematical economics, there seems to be today a general agreement among economists from many countries. In particular, it has been emphasized that Antonelli's contribution was among the first in economic literature to use determinants, and the very first to handle the problem of so-called integrability in utility theory. In the history of marginalism in Italy, however, Antonelli's writing has probably less importance than might be supposed. By this I do not mean at all to deny Antonelli's contribution to the improvement of the theory of instantaneous exchange, or his contribution to the development of mathematical economics. But in view of the aims of our investigation, it must be kept in mind that Antonelli's writing (i) is a personal reconsideration of only one part of marginalistic literature, namely, the one patently mathematical (Jevons, Walras, and Launhardt), (ii) is restricted to dealing with utility theory only, and (iii) does not underline the revolutionary character of the utility theory of value, either by calling direct attention to it or by capturing its historical meaning. It is the work of an engineer of great keenness who faces this problem as an isolated one without realizing the flow of ideas to which the problem belongs. Little wonder, then, if this contribution remained unknown for a long time and if its influence on contemporary economic literature was almost nil.

From this viewpoint, a far greater influence was that of A. Graziani, who contributed to the dissemination of marginalist ideas in Italy in a series of writings (for example, it was through him that Böhm-Bawerk and von Wieser became known in Italy), both in their implications for financial problems and in respect of the central theoretical meaning of the theory of value[40] (in actual fact the latter

---

39. G. B. Antonelli, *Sulla teoria matematica della Economia politica* (Pisa, 1886), reprinted in *Giornale degli Economisti*, 1951, pp. 235–63, and in W. J. Baumol and S. M. Goldfeld, *Precursors in Mathematical Economics: An Anthology* (London, 1968), pp. 33–39. On Antonelli, see G. Demaria, "G. B. Antonelli, economista matematico ignorato," *Giornale degli Economisti*, 1951, pp. 223–31; and G. Ricci, "Commento alla memoria di G. B. Antonelli dell'anno 1886, 'Sulla teoria matematica dell'economia politica,'" *Giornale degli Economisti*, 1951, pp. 264–97 and 344–85.

40. Besides the already cited *Intorno all'aumento progressivo delle spese pubbliche*, and "Di alcune questioni," let us recall Graziani's "Appunti minimi sulla legge del valore," *Studi Senesi*, 1888, pp. 11–13, and *Storia critica della teoria del valore in Italia* (Milan, 1889), as well as his translation of Sax, "Gli ultimi

was the problem to which Italian economists of the time were devoting their reflection). With Pantaleoni's work, and with the more critical, yet well informed work of A. Graziani, it seemed that the utility theory of value was by then taking the upper hand. The supporters of "reproduction cost" appeared by then a scanty minority, nor at that time were there visible any convinced and vigorous followers of the labor theory of value.[41]

Yet in 1890 the marginalistic theory was vigorously criticized in Italy by three authors from three different standpoints. Valenti, in a comprehensive monograph on the theory of value,[42] after an ample and correct exposition of the theory of Jevons, Menger, and Böhm-Bawerk, remarked that the problem of economic theory cannot be that of taking refuge in investigating the psychological behavior of consumers: it has to explain "why the minor part of value goes to the advantage of those who toil to produce it, and the major part is added to the wealth of those who are already largely provided with it and who have contributed less to determine it with their own work." In this way, he was proposing a return to the "principle of Ricardo," which always remains "the pivot of the theory of value," and the only one capable of answering the kind of question asked.

The critical remarks set forth by Alessio in a very brilliant monograph were of a different kind.[43] In particular, he believed marginalism was incapable of explaining the problems of man as a community member, since it was characterized by a markedly individualistic approach; and he believed that it was difficult to define exactly the idea of "fruition," and that the "law of decrease of enjoyments" was not sufficiently general.

But the most radical and the sternest criticism to which marginalism was then subjected in Italy came from Loria.[44] This author, who was

progressi della Scienza Economica," *Studi Senesi*, 1888, pp. 160–192, which is a sharp review of the different theories of value, ending up in favor of the marginalistic one. Although his position was eclectic, G. Supino also carried on with spreading the knowledge of the most recent contributions of marginalists. Cf. "La teoria del valore e la legge del minimo mezzo," *Giornale degli Economisti*, 1889, pp. 424–49.

41. A timid supporter of Ricardo seems to be A. Montanari, *Contributo alla storia del valore negli scrittori italiani* (Milan, 1889), p. 133.

42. G. Valenti, *La teoria del valore: Saggio* (Rome, 1890).

43. G. Alessio, *Studi sulla teorica del valore nel cambio interno* (Turin, 1890).

44. A. Loria, "La scuola austriaca nell'economia politica," *Nuova Antologia*,

already famous in Italy for certain heterodox works which fell midway between a somewhat sentimental socialism and positivistic evolutionism, immediately grasped "the fundamental character of the Austrian school," identifying it with the "pretension of bringing every economic phenomenon back to the principle of utility." According to him, this was a "prejudiced" way to approach "economic phenomena," since "utility is nothing but a relation between product and man, a psychic evaporation of the latter, a nebulous nimbus crowning real matter. Utility is related to goods, as the shadow to the body." Hence the Austrian school would be dealing with "shadows," not with bodies: it would replace with a "ghost" the "real object," which was the problem of "product distribution."

Loria's indictment at this point is just a little emphatic, and as is often the case with him, it assumes the character of a social indictment. The "Austrian school" is accused of having distracted the attention of economists from contemporary social problems and confined them to the discussion of abstract problems. Indeed, this explains its success. "The English school," Loria observes, "with its deep analysis, had submitted to a merciless criticism some redistribution phenomena, such as real-estate revenues, and had opened the way to a destructive analysis of the most hidden phenomena in the distribution of wealth." But when faced with these conclusions, the "classical school had halted, almost terrified by the consequence" of its own analysis. That is why now nobody had dared to retrace the old path, which would have led to "unveiling" the laws regulating the distribution process. By changing the aim of speculative investigation, "the possibility of a deep analysis of social relations" was precluded and "any theoretical threat against the established economic system" was eliminated.

Loria's analysis, although referring to the "Austrian school" only, concerns the entire range of marginalism and is occasionally reminiscent of typical Marxian motives. I have not been able to ascertain whether it is only and completely the product of the author's mind; but it must be noted that, already in 1890, it announces critical themes which were destined to enjoy a very long life.

---

1 April 1890, reprinted in *Verso la giustizia sociale (idee, battaglie, apostoli)*, 2d ed. (Milan, 1908), pp. 164–81.

IX

At this point it should be clear why I have terminated my research at 1890. In this year, when Pantaleoni's *Principii* were already conquering Italy, Italian economists were completely familiar with marginalist ideas. The works of Conigliani and Mazzola almost form the ending moment of a process of *dépuration* of the "Scienza delle Finanze," a process which had taken place under the standard of the purest marginalism. The writings of Valenti, Alessio, and Loria, on the contrary, are the first critical reply to the new trend.

Thus 1890 is a year of decisive significance in the evolution of economic thought in Italy. It is the year in which Pareto began to devote himself completely to economics, and when the *Giornale degli Economisti*, by then edited by A. De Viti de Marco, U. Mazzola, and M. Pantaleoni, became the journal of Italian marginalism and of the most intransigent liberalism. The army of marginalist-liberalists (for this double name is on the banner round which economists rallied in Italy) suddenly grew more numerous; it included among its ranks the most lively and controversial minds and captured the periodical with the highest scientific preeminence. By 1890 "les jeux sont faits" for marginalism in Italy: the ground was fully prepared for the best results by Pareto and Barone; the work which Ferrara had patiently prepared was complete at last.[45]

In comparison with the new movement, the critics of marginalism were scarcely heard. From then onwards, whatever marginalist writings appeared abroad drew immediate attention in Italy (for example, by 1891 Marshall's *Principles* was already quite well known in Italy). To these years dates the meaningful marriage between Edgeworth and the *Giornale degli Economisti*.

Let us sum it up. In terms of publication, marginalism entered Italy exceptionally early. Jevons' *Theory* had already been translated in 1875, while some of Walras's papers were almost immediately translated into Italian. Thanks to an effective advertising campaign, Walras became known through several reviews which were wisely conducted and revised by himself. But on the whole the new scientific trend

---

45. To Ferrara as a forerunner of marginalism in Italy—something quite different from the pioneeristic style in which research of this kind had been carried out before him—attention has recently been called by F. Caffé, *Politica economica*.

was misunderstood and did not gain momentum until the advent of Pantaleoni. This means that in the final analysis, the real and fertile acceptance of the "marginal revolution" took place in Italy almost simultaneously with the other countries.[46]

Of Jevons, Walras, and Menger, the English economist was the first and best known in Italy and his influence was the most consistent. Menger, on the other hand, became known remarkably later and was appreciated only when, through the discovery of Sax, Menger's works were studied again together with those of Böhm-Bawerk and von Wieser. However, I have come to hold the view that although Pantaleoni derived some ideas from Jevons, the Austrian school was the most influential among Italian economists in the period 1886–90. As late as 1890, Walras was still almost unknown in Italy. Apart from a few pages of Alessio, there were only occasional references to Walras's idea of *rareté*, or his theory of exchange. Walras had not yet received in Italy appropriate recognition for his theory of general equilibrium. This was a strange revenge of history against the man who thought he had found in Italy the most positive acceptance. Walras's case, indeed, forms a startling instance of "spontaneous rejection" of a new theory from a body which was not ready to receive it.

The lack of preparation was theoretical and was not so much due to a definite cultural choice veering away from marginalism. This found a receptive soil wherever either *classicism* or *historicism* were weak. In Italy, during the period reviewed, Ricardo's theories had but few and weak followers. Historicism itself, although appearing well equipped in the way of number, had grouped economists only in terms of a controversial reaction against Ferrara and did not succeed in holding a decidedly theoretical standing; accordingly it ended by confining itself to a scattering of political positions.

There remained the followers of Ferrara, who were not much respected as scientists and were more intolerant of any criticism against the theoretical views and the political teachings of their master.

Amid this army of economists, having no deep roots in the field

46. See F. A. Hayek, *The Position of Carl Menger's "Grundsätze" in the History of Economic Thought*, English draft of the paper presented at the Economic Symposium: One Hundred Years of Carl Menger's *Grundsätze*, Vienna, 17–19 June 1971, p. 13 of the lithographed text.

of theory, without a leader of recognized and unanimous authority, and scattered in dubious sociological or widely diversified political positions, Pantaleoni appeared "as the archangel with the flaming sword." He was the right man at the right moment. By 1890, in Italy, marginalism was becoming economics.

Marginalism in Japan

Tamotsu Matsuura

I

THE history of economics in Japan is, for the most part, the history of the introduction of Western economics. Imported economic theory has greatly influenced the Japanese economy through the formulation of economic policies, the results of which are reflected in the economic development attained by Japan during the last century. Furthermore, Western economics has influenced in a general way the world of thought in Japan. It is no exaggeration to say that, by contributing to the formation of fundamental principles in the social sciences, including economics, and broadly speaking, to the Japanese view of the world, this influence has directed Japan toward modernization or westernization. For their part, Japanese economists have contributed significantly to the logical elaboration and practical application of imported (Western) economics, though without creating an indigenous economics.

In this essay, I wish to examine the nature of marginalism in Japan, especially the process of its popularization, and its position in the modern history of economics, considering the work of Japanese economists. In other words, I want to show how marginalism has influenced the world of economic thought in Japan as well as what meaning it has taken on and how it has worked in the actual economy.

II

Japanese industry obtained huge reparations after bringing the Sino-Japanese War (1894–95) and the Russo-Japanese War (1904–5) to victorious conclusions and enlarged the overseas market for its own products and the purchase of materials, with consequent great strides in its progress. This rapid development of modern industries confronted Japan with inevitable and difficult problems, both economic

TAMOTSU MATSUURA *is Professor of Economics in Keio University.*

and social. Above all, as the Japanese economy was then still underdeveloped, the government had to protect infant industries to enable
them to compete with those of more advanced countries. Secondly,
the government was faced with serious labor and social problems
caused by the worsening of laborers' conditions. In these economic and
social circumstances, the government displayed tendencies in favor
of Germany, which had succeeded in breaking out of her under-
development, after the English liberal policy pattern had been adopted
by the most advanced countries.

It was then that the Academic Society of Social Policy of Japan
was founded by the Professors of the Tokyo Imperial University[1] who
had returned from study in Germany, in imitation of the Verein für
Sozialpolitik.[2] Many of Japan's important economists of that time
belonged to this society. They set forth new theories and gained a
dominant influence in the economic world through the activities of the
society. They supported the social policy based on the ideology of the
German historical school. In a word, the aim and task of the society
was to reject the laissez-faire policy, on the one hand, and to cope
with socialism, on the other, and, above all, to adopt and promote
suitable policies toward the economic and social situation in Japan.
This meant that the government had to resolve labor and social problems within the scope of industrial development.

But criticism of the activities of the Academic Society of Social
Policy was voiced, to the effect that the policies carried out by this
society were not scientific and theoretical, but based on some national-
istic supreme orders. It seems to me that the best example to this
purpose is Tokuzo Fukuda's life. After having studied at the Tokyo
Commercial University,[3] he went to Germany and was taught economics of the historical school by K. Bucher and L. Brentano. He
wrote *Die gesellschaftliche und wirtschaftliche Entwicklung in
Japan*[4] with Brentano. After his return to Japan, he taught economics
at the Tokyo Commercial University and became one of the main
members of the Academic Society of Social Policy of Japan. But
later on he gradually changed his opinion and, when he lectured at

1. Now called the University of Tokyo.
2. The Academic Society of Social Policy of Japan was established in 1896.
3. Now called Hitotsubashi University.
4. It was published in 1900, written in German. In 1907 Yoshizo Sakanishi
translated it into Japanese as *Nihon-keizaishi-ron.*

Keio University in 1905, he became a bitter critic of the historical school. At that time his lectures were mainly based on the Marshallian economics of the Cambridge school. He stated that the economics of the historical school had no theory able to replace the classical theory, which had been destroyed by the former, and that the marginal utility theory established by Jevons and Menger had started a new era in economics.

Thus, on the one hand, the economists, who held this kind of society as their own stronghold and maintained the German historical ideology, tried to cope with the situation of the time and succeeded in destroying the laissez-faire policy based on the English classical school; but, on the other hand, they could not formulate any constructive theory to improve Japanese economics as well as its economy.

But we must also consider another fact: as the economists who mainly belonged to the Academic Society of Social Policy were not able to fight, from a theoretical point of view, against socialist economics—especially Marxian economics, which at that time was gaining a firm foothold, partly associated with the rapid growth of the labor class—a new theory was required which could positively stand out against socialist economic theories.

In that situation, an association of workers was organized in 1897, and an association of socialists were created in 1900. In 1901 the Social Democratic Party of Japan was formed, but on the very day of its establishment it was banned by the government. Against this background, labor and social movements, as well as studies of socialism, became popular. In the 1910's the labor movements rapidly gained ground and many severe strikes took place.

The Academic Society of Social Policy could no longer cope with such a strongly rising tide of the labor class and socialism, which was stimulated by the successful Russian Revolution after the First World War.[5] As a result, the members of this society divided into two groups: one included those economists who analyzed the crisis of the contemporary economic system and supported Marxian economics; the other was composed of those economists who criticized Marxian economics and then studied marginal economics.

Modern economic theory appeared in Japan in the role attributed to it by Oskar Lange in his article "Marxian Economics and Modern

5. This society survived until 1923, but its real role was lost toward 1910.

Economic Theory,''[6] that is to say as a good and useful theory for coping with Marxian economics. Even today when in this country we say modern economics, we mean the economics which stands against Marxian economics. Consequently, the world of economics in Japan is neatly divided into two fighting and rival fields, which are almost isolated, without any theoretical communication.

III

The first introduction of marginal utility theory took place through the translation of Jevons' *Primer of Political Economy* (1878). It was published as early as in 1882–84.[7] Then Marshall's *Elements of Economics* (1879) was translated in 1886.[8] The academic level of these early translations was very low. In 1900, at Keio University, some knowledge about marginalism was acquired through Philippović's and Seligman's books, which had been adopted as texts of economics; in fact, the former depended partly upon Böhm-Bawerk's theory of marginal utility, the latter upon J. B. Clark's theory of marginal productivity.

But it seems to me that the real introduction of marginalism, by which I mean its systematic and critical study, was Fukuda's *Lectures on Political Economy*,[9] which was published in 1907–9 and was a book based on his lectures at Keio University and on Marshall's *Principles of Economics*.

There were two eminent economists who were spurred to the study of marginalism by Fukuda's lectures: Shinzo Koizumi of Keio University and Ichiro Nakayama of the Tokyo Commercial University. We shall view first Koizumi's works. He wrote an article, ''Hermann Heinrich Gossen and His Doctrine,'' in 1911,[10] in which he considered Gossen as a forerunner of the marginal revolution. In the following year he wrote another, ''One Section of the History of the

6. In *Review of Economic Studies* (1935).
7. We can find three translations of this book; the first was the work of Genjiro Yasuda in 1882.
8. *Kingyo-rizaigaku*, trans. Korekiyo Takahashi, who later became minister of finance.
9. *Keizaigaku-kogi*, 3 vols.
10. ''Hermann Heinrich Gossen to sono Gakusetsu,'' *Mita Gakkai Zasshi*, vol. 5, no. 1. It introduced R. Liefmann's article in memory of the centenary of Gossen's birth.

Theory of Subjective Value,''[11] in which he compared Gossen's theory with Jevons's and concluded that the latter had no originality in comparison with the former. Then he translated Jevons' *Theory of Political Economy* (1871) in 1913.[12] I think that Koizumi had the object of tracing back the historical origins of marginalism, which had interested him very much through Fukuda's lectures on Marshall's theory.

Among the economists who tried to introduce marginalism, we can find another name besides the two mentioned above, that is, Toshiro Tezuka. He was also a student under Fukuda at the Tokyo Commercial University. Differently from Koizumi, Tezuka succeeded in introducing and settling the economics of the Lausanne School in Japan, which, after that, reached a leading position in the sphere of maginalism in this country. But it is very interesting that his first work, *Study of Gossen* (1920), dealt with the same problem tackled by Koizumi.[13] I think that they undertook to study Gossen because many economists in Japan at that time were still interested in a historical approach, influenced as they were by the German historical school, rather than in a theoretical one.

We cannot neglect another aspect of Koizumi's works, that is, his criticism, which constituted the first theoretical examination in Japan, of the fallacy of the Marxian labor theory of value. It seems that he began this useful controversy about the theory of value in the 1920's. His first article about this problem was ''Labor Theory of Value and the Problem of the Average Rate of Profit: A Criticism of Marxian Labor Theory of Value'' in 1923.[14] I think that through his study of the Ricardian economics, his criticism of Marx became deeper and riper.[15] I mean his criticism that, in the analysis of ''commodity'' outlined at the beginning of *Das Kapital*, Marx

11. ''Shukan-teki Kachiron Enkaku no Issetsu,'' *Mita Gakkai Zasshi*, vol. 6, no. 2.

12. *Keizaigaku Junri*.

13. *Gossen Kenkyu*.

14. ''Rodo-kachi-setsu to Heikin-rijun-ritsu no mondai—Marx no Kachi-gakusetsu nitaisuru Ichi-hihyo,'' *Kaizo*, Feb. 1923.

15. I must notice that, in spite of Koizumi's highly appreciated contribution to the introduction of marginalism, the essence of his works was characterized by his study of Ricardo, whose theory was included in the Marshallian economics; but, very ironically, he was rejected by Jevons, who had been the first to be studied by Koizumi.

verified his labor theory of value according to the principle of the exchange of equivalents, a verification which is inconsistent with the failure of that principle through the discrepancy between value and price of production, caused by the mechanism of the average rate of profit included in the price of production, which was mentioned in the third volume of the same book. In other words, he pointed out that Marx's assertion of realizing the average rate of profit meant abandoning his labor theory of value. Such criticism could have been produced by his studies on the logical development of the classical school. But I do not think that this criticism was conceived by him. It seems to me that it could depend largely upon Böhm-Bawerk's criticism of Marx. But I can say that Koizumi's criticism is considered the first examination of the fallacy of the Marxian economics through the introduction of marginalism in Japan.

I appreciate the fact that his criticism of Marx not only has a historical value in the development of marginalism in Japan but also represents a great contribution to the raising of the academic level of Marxian economics as well as of marginalism in that country. Professor Hajime Kawakami of the Kyoto Imperial University[16] was the first systematic and scientific introducer of Marxian economics. He refuted Koizumi's criticism from the Marxian standpoint and then gave rise to the heated but useful controversies of the 1920's on the validity of Marxian labor theory of value. The controversies were joined by many economists, who examined Marxian economics in every problem and from every point of view. As for Marxian economists, many issues were raised on the valid understanding of the nature of "commodity" at the beginning of *Das Kapital*, of the labor theory of value, and of the exact interpretation of the general Marxian methodology in the same book. These issues shift then to the examination of "rent" discussed by Marxian economics, which became an important key to analyze the history of Japanese capitalism and economic situation. Therefore, we can see that these controversies, started by Koizumi, were very useful in raising the academic level of Marxian economics. On the other hand, on the side of marginalism —which is thoroughly impregnated with the theory of value, especially with the fallacy of Marxian theory—some economists of marginalism made an advance toward the "economics without theory of value,"

16. Now called the University of Kyoto.

which treated and explained economic phenomena through the analysis of quantitative functions. This tendency became stronger and stronger, for economists of marginalism intended to understand economics logically and analytically.

The basis of such controversies was already prepared in the 1910's. In fact, *Das Kapital* was translated in 1920.[17] And we can find the formation of groups for the study and discussion of the theory of value, especially the Marxian theory, in the main universities in Tokyo and Kyoto.

Thus, I can conclude that Fukuda and Koizumi played very important and great roles in the introduction of marginalism in Japan. After them, in the 1920's, the theoretical approach of the economics of marginalism became more substantial in Japan.

IV

Nakayama, another eminent student of Fukuda in the Tokyo Commercial University, wrote in 1922 the article "On the Two Tendencies of Mathematical Economics and Their Tentative Synthesis,"[18] in which he pointed out that, from the viewpoint of the history of economics, there were two tendencies at work in the origins of marginalism: one from Cournot, who aimed at understanding economic phenomena through a functional approach, the other one from Gossen, who studied psychological factors and thereby tried to find a substantial economic value through a causal approach. Nakayama appreciated Walras as the economist who could synthesize these tendencies. Then Nakayama wrote another article, "Two Forms of the Marginal Utility Theory: Austrian School and Lausanne School,"[19] in which his thought on marginalism, expressed in the preceding article, was enlarged and substantiated. Through deeper study he became fully convinced that the analytical approach of the Lausanne School was more eminent than that of the Austrian School. Later on he developed his theory on the basis of the general equilibrium theory of the Lausanne School. In 1927 he went to Germany and studied at the University of Bonn. He reaffirmed his conviction about the general

17. *Shihonron*, trans. Motoyuki Takahata, though only one volume.
18. "Suri-keizaigaku niokeru Futatsu no Keiko to sono Sogo no Kokoromi nitsuite," *Shogaku Tokyu*, vol. 3, no. 2.
19. "Genkai-riyo-setsu no Ni-Keitai—Austria-gakuha to Lausanne-gakuha," *Shogaku Tokyu*, vol. 6, no. 1 (1926).

equilibrium theory when he attended the seminar of J. A. Schumpeter. After his return to Japan, he wrote his first book in 1932, *Methodology of Mathematical Economics*,[20] and then another one in 1933, *Pure Economics*.[21] It should be remembered here that in the same year Tezuka published the translation of the first half of *Eléments d'économie politique pure* (1874) by Walras.[22] These books of Nakayama's followed closely the theoretical system of Schumpeter. *Pure Economics*, for example, owed much of its theoretical part to Schumpeter's *Das Wesen und der Hauptinhalt der theoretischen Nationalökonomie* (1908), and I regret to point out that in this book the part concerning the theory of the economic development is a degeneration from Schumpeter's.[23] His *Methodology of Mathematical Economics* may be appreciated in the sense that he confirmed the significance of the analytical approach of the pure theory of general equilibrium as fundamental and essential to economics. Moreover, he contended that this theoretical system should be supported by positive and statistical studies. From the latter point of view, he wrote in 1935 the article "On the Statistical Method of Measuring Marginal Utility,"[24] following Frisch's *New Method of Measuring Marginal Utility* (1932), making one step toward an econometric approach.

Nakayama's *Pure Economics* became so popular that I can say that through this book the predominance of the analytical approach of the Lausanne School became fixed in the world of marginal economics. Also, we cannot neglect the works of Miyoji Hayakawa on Paretian economics in the popularization of this school.

Yasuma Takata was another important economist contemporary with Nakayama. At the Kyoto Imperial University he studied sociology, and in the 1920's he was one of the anti-Marxists along with Koizumi. His main interest lay in the theory of distribution, especially in the theory of interest. It seems that his first study on the marginal economic theory was Clark's theory of distribution. After that, fol-

20. *Suri-keizaigaku Hohoron*, as the fifth volume, *Keizaigaku no Kiso-riron*, of Kaizosha's series of economics, Keizaigaku Zenshu.
21. *Junsui-keizaigaku*.
22. *Junsui-keizaigaku Yoron*, vol. 1.
23. Cf. Takuma Yasui, "Nakayama Kyoju no Keizaigaku Taikei—*Junsui-keizaigaku* nitsuite" (The Economic System of Prof. Nakayama—About *Pure Economics*), *Keizaigaku Ronshu*, vol. 4, no. 5.
24. "Genkai-riyo no Tokei-teki Sokutei nitsuite," *Nihon Tokei Gakkai Nempo*, no. 3.

lowing the theories of Schumpeter and Oppenheimer, he studied the theory of imputation of the Austrian School and finally reached the general equilibrium theory of the Lausanne School in the conviction that it was the most valid theory among economic theories. He wrote five volumes of *New Lectures on Economics* in 1932,[25] in which his introduction of Paretian preference theory, as the most valid price theory, is highly appreciated. I must notice that in spite of these facts, Takata held stubbornly by the theory of force in the price determination of factors of production. But I think he was fundamentally and substantially an economist of the Lausanne School.

Thus, the works which introduced marginalism were completed by about 1932–33, and its firm position was established as an important analytical approach in the world of economics. We can also find the economics of the Lausanne School in the main current of marginalism in Japan.

Besides this school, theories of other schools were introduced in this decade. Marshall's *Principles of Economics* was completely translated[26] in 1925–26 and, as far as the Austrian economics is concerned, Menger, Böhm-Bawerk, and von Wieser were introduced; but the introduction of this school was not so systematic as in the case of the Lausanne School. The Austrians were introduced only for particular problems, for example, the Austrian economics of interest.

V

Once marginalism was established in Japan, the task of economists became that of refining. Takuma Yasui was the leading representative of such economists. He intended to eliminate internal and logical defects of the general equilibrium theory, which already occupied a leading position in Japanese marginalism.

Yasui began to study economics as a faithful follower of Walras. He wrote two articles, "Pure Economics and Theory of Price: Focusing on Walras" in 1933,[27] and "Theory of Imputation and Theory of Marginal Productivity: Two Problems of Pure Economics"

25. *Keizaigaku Shinron*, 5 vols.; the second volume, *Kakaku no Riron*, is especially important.
26. *Keizaigaku Genri*, trans. Kinnosuke Ohtsuka.
27. "Junsui-keizaigaku to Kakaku no Riron—Léon Walras o-chushin-toshite," *Keizaigaku Ronshu*, vol. 3, no. 9.

in 1934,[28] in which he expounded his fundamental opinion that the theory of production was most important in Walras's economic system of general equilibrium and that the progress of pure economics, therefore, depended upon the development of this theory. He examined in detail the theoretical structure of the general equilibrium theory of production and clarified the point that this theoretical system was composed of the two theories of marginal utility and of marginal productivity. Next, he concluded that even though the former could be the principle on which to construct the demand function of products, it could not be the principle on which to construct the supply function of productive services and added that, using the theory of marginal productivity as a theory for determining variable co-efficients of production as Walras did, one would find it necessary to correct the equations of production because they must be connected with the other equations of the general equilibrium system. In 1936 he wrote another article, "Time Element and Capital Interest: The Wal-rasian Concept of 'Natural Rate of Interest,' "[29] in which, pointing out that a defect of the Walrasian theory was to be found in the theory of capitalization and credit, and accepting the Wicksellian criticism that Walras did not consider the valid significance of the time element to capital interest, he tried to join the Wicksellian theory with the Wal-rasian system. Then he set about making use of contemporary con-tributions in theories on interest toward the construction of dynamic theory.[30] In 1938, Yasui wrote "Money and Economic Equilibrium: A Study on Walrasian Theory of Money,"[31] and in the same year "A Comment of the Equations of Circulation and Money."[32] In these papers he examined the essence of the Walrasian theory of circulation and money which, in spite of Walras's most devoted effort in his late

28. "Kizoku-riron to Genkai–seisanryuku-setsu—Junsui-keizaigaku no Ni-Mondai," *Keizaigaku Ronshu*, vol. 4, no. 4.

29. "Jikan-yoso to Shihon-rishi—Walras niokeru 'Shizen-rishiritsu' no Gainen," *Keizaigaki Ronshu*, vol. 6, no. 9.

30. At the same time as Yasui, Takeyasu Kimura wrote an article, "Seisan Shihon, Shihon-rishi" (Production, Capital and Capital Interest) *Keizaigaku Ron-shu*, vol. 6, no. 4 (1936), in which he expressed the same views stated by Yasui, i.e., that through the Austrian theory of interest the economics of the Lausanne School could be enlarged and strengthened.

31. "Kahei to Keizai Kinko—Walras Kahei-riron no Ichi-Kenkyu," *Keizaigaku Ronshu*, vol. 8, no. 4.

32. "Ryutsu oyobi Kahei no Hoteishiki eno Ichi-Chukai," *Keizaigaku Ronshu*, vol. 8, no. 9.

years and his last contributions, had been neglected. That is to say,
Walras could integrate and synthesize the theories of money and
relative price, on the one hand, looking for the value of money
through the marginal utility theory and, on the other hand, could
join the money function with the theory of capitalization and credit.
At the same time, Takata too examined this part of the Walrasian
theory. But we cannot find any other article on this problem except
those by the two above-mentioned economists. Very recently, however,
Don Patinkin has dealt with it in more detail in his book *Money,
Interest and Prices* (1956).

In 1939 Hicks wrote his *Value and Capital*, which marked an
epoch in the modern history of economics. This book was intended to
absorb the Austrian theory of interest and all the other leading
theories of the 1930's into the Walrasian theoretical system and direct
contemporary economics toward a dynamic one. I think that Yasui's
intention of study was fundamentally the same as Hicks's. In "Equilibrium Analysis and Process Analysis: A Study on Walrasian Theory
of 'Tâtonnement' " in 1940,[33] Yasui examined the stability of market
equilibrium considering the Walrasian theory of *tâtonnement*. This
attempt was quite independent of Hicks's and Samuelson's works.
Since then, a great deal of his efforts have been devoted not only to a
thoroughgoing examination and confrontation with the Hicksian
theoretical system but also to the development of the theory of dynamic stability, established in 1941 by Samuelson,[34] which paved the
way toward a macrodynamics connected with the Keynesian theory. I
regret to say that, because of language obstacles to communication and
of the war, the works by Yasui could not be introduced to economists
outside Japan. But one can see how highly his works were appreciated
by noting the academic activity of some economists, for example
Morishima and Uzawa; for these economists were influenced in their
youth and still are influenced by Yasui's academic research.

As far as the theory of dynamic stability is concerned, I should
notice the works of Shozo Sono, who wrote the article "The Condi-

33. "Kinko Bunseki to Katei Bunseki—Walras Mosaku-riron no Ichi-Kenkyu,"
pts. 1–4, *Keizaigaku Ronshu*, vol. 10, nos. 1–3 and 6.

34. Paul A. Samuelson, "The Stability of Equilibrium: Comparative Statics and
Dynamics," *Econometrica* 9, no. 2 (April 1941).

tion of Stability in the Market Equilibrium" in 1944,[35] in which he created the original theory, following Samuelson.

At this point I would like to mention some works in Japan concerning the problem of the existence of the equilibrium solution proposed and established by A. Wald in 1935. First of all, let us glance at Kei Shibata, who wrote "Examination of the 'Mechanism of Price-forming,' Explained by Mr. Cassel" in 1930[36] in which he criticized the Casselian system. I think he anticipated the same criticism pointed out by von Stackelberg in "Zwei kritische Bemerkungen zur Preistheorie Gustav Cassels" in 1933.[37] It is the critical point of the Casselian equation system of demand and supply for factors of production when it has n unknowns and m equations, if $n < m$, such system becomes overdetermined, and as long as excessive equations are independent, this equilibrium equation system will remain unsatisfied. This criticism is appreciated as having paved the way for Wald's proof of the existence of the equilibrium solution with Neisser's criticism,[38] as opposed to the simple solution way of counting equations and unknowns; i.e., the solution must have an economic meaning, namely, a non-negative condition.

Secondly, let me mention that in 1954 Arrow and Debreu proved clearly and exactly this problem, making use of Kakutani's theorem of a fixed point which was his generalization and a more applicable formulation of Brouwer's theorem. He wrote an article on this theorem, "A Generalization of Brouwer's Fixed Point Theorem" in 1941[39] from a mathematical point of view, because he is a mathematician. I know that in 1935–36 von Neumann, as a mathematical economist, created a prototype of this theorem which he illustrated in "Über ein ökonomisches Gleichungssystem und eine Verallgemeinerung des Fixpunktsatzes."[40] Anyway, we can appreciate the fact that these Japanese efforts were devoted to raising the level of the logical aspect of the economic theory of general equilibrium.

35. "Shijo-Kinko no Antei-Joken," *Keizai Ronso*, vol. 58, nos. 1 and 2.
36. "Cassel-shi no 'Kakaku-keisei no Kiko' no Gimmi," *Keizai Ronso*, vol. 30, no. 6.
37. In *Zeitschrift für Nationalökonomie*, vol. 4 (1933).
38. Hans Neisser, "Lohnhöhe und Beschäftigungsgrad in Marktgleichgewicht," *Weltwirtschaftliches Archiv*, Oct. 1932.
39. In *Duke Mathematical Journal*, vol. 8, no. 3.
40. In *Ergebnisse eines Mathematischen Kolloquiums*, 8.

VI

Let us now examine the economists who criticized the economics of the Lausanne School methodologically and radically from the point of view of different economic theories. It is very interesting that many of them shared the common tendency to criticize the general equilibrium theory as impractical and made use of marginalism as a useful analytical instrument on the confident ideological basis of Marxism, that is, the criticism of capitalism.

To be sure, at that time the economics of the Lausanne School did not monopolize the world of economics in Japan. Above all, during the introduction period of marginalism, the economics of the Cambridge School was treated and discussed a great deal. Since then, many economists have studied it, but we can find very few systematic researchers on this economics to compare with Nakayama and Yasui of the Lausanne School. And I can say the same thing about the economics of the Austrian and Scandinavian schools.[41]

Let us now consider the works of Eiichi Sugimoto. In 1933 he wrote an article, "Collapse of Static Economics,"[42] in which he concluded that the Lausanne School's static theory of general equilibrium had no competence to analyze practical economic problems. And then in

41. By way of example, I think it better to mention only the works of Hideo Aoyama. He studied the theories of economic fluctuation of the Cambridge and the Scandinavian schools, writing many articles on this problem. There is no doubt that especially his researches on Wicksell pave the way for the understanding of Keynesian and post-Keynesian theories, with translations of Wicksell's and other economists' works in the 1930's. I wish to notice, by the way, that Aoyama's *Dokusen no Riron* (Economic Theory of Monopoly) (1937) was an introduction to the theories of monopolistic competition discussed by Chamberlin and Joan Robinson. Let me mention the main translations of the economists of other schools than the Lausanne one at that time.
(1) Marshall's *Industry and Trade* (1919; 4th ed. 1923) was translated as *Sangyo Boeki Ron* by Takeomi Sanuki in 1928.
(2) Menger's *Grundsätze der Volkswirtschaftslehre* (1871; 2d ed. 1923), was translated as *Kokumin-keizaigaku Genri* by Takuma Yasui in 1937.
(3) von Wieser's *Der natürliche Wert* (1889) was translated as *Shizen Kachiron* by Chiyoo Ohyama in 1937.
(4) Böhm-Bawerk's "Zum Abschluss des Marxschen Systems," in *Staatswissenschaftliche Arbeiten: Festgaben für Karl Knies* (1896), was translated as *Marx-Gakusetsu-Taikei no Shuen* by Hachiro Takehara.
(5) Böhm-Bawerk's "Grundzüge der Theorie des wirtschaftlichen Güterwerts," *Jahrbücher für Nationalökonomie und Statistik*, neue Folge, vol. 13 (1886), was translated as *Keizai-teki Zai Kachi no Kiso-Riron* by Moriyoshi Cho in 1932.
42. "Seitai-teki Keizaigaku no Hatan," *Chuo Koron*, Oct. 1933.

1934 he criticized sweepingly Nakayama's *Pure Economics* in his article, "The Development of Pure Economics: On Reading Nakayama's Recent *Pure Economics*."[43] In the same year he contended in his article "The Equilibrium Pricing Process"[44] that, in a search for this process, the kind of Cambridge cobweb theorem was valid and the analytical standpoint of interdependence of the Lausanne School had to be rejected. In another article, "Some Questions on General Equilibrium Theory: About Pareto's Criticism of Marshall,"[45] he contended that Pareto's criticism made a mistake in declaring that Marshall's theory was not dynamic, and he defended Marshall's concept of "elasticity" as a useful analytical instrument for practical economic problems. In 1939 Sugimoto wrote "Developing Process of Economy and Elasticity,"[46] in which, as a useful index, he tried to use the partial coefficients of elasticity among various economic quantities for the analysis of economic structure, because he thought this was not homogeneous but heterogeneous and only the elasticity approach was valid for such analysis. *The Selective Collection of Marshallian Economics*[47] published in 1940, which was composed mainly of these articles, was a comprehensive compilation of his critical essays about the general equilibrium economics, from his standpoint of partial equilibrium and from his study of the Cambridge School, and included the translation of Marshall's *Pure Theory of Foreign Trade and Domestic Values* (1879).

It is important to mention another aspect of Sugimoto's study. He tried to synthesize the two economic systems, marginalism and Marxism, and based his research on the theory that in order to criticize the capitalistic development, Marxian economics should be studied, considering the marginal economic theory as a useful analytical instrument.[48] In Japan this idea is still strong among some economists.

43. "Junsui-keizaigaku no Hatten—Nakayama Jokyoju no Kingyo *Junsui-keizaigaku o Yomite*," *Hitotsubashi Shimbun*, no. 183.

44. "Kinko-Kakaku no Seiritsu-Katei," *Keizaigaku Kenkyu*, no. 3.

45. "Ippan-teki Kinko-riron nitaisuru Jakkan no Gimon—Pareto no Marshall Hihhan ni chinamite," *Keizaigaku Kenkyu*, no. 6.

46. "Keizai-Hatten-Katei to Danryoku-sei," in *Sakanishi Yoshizo Hakushi Kanreki Kinen Rombunshu* (The Collected Papers in Celebration of Dr. Yoshizo Sakanishi's Sixtieth Birthday), April 1939.

47. *Marshall Keisaigaku Senshu.*

48. Cf. Sugimoto's *Kindai-keizaigakushi* (The History of Modern Economics, 1953).

I shall mention another economist of the same type as Sugimoto, namely, Seijiro Kishimoto. He too stood fundamentally for Marxian ideology, but he wanted to create on this foundation an economic system which could outdo as theory the economics of the Lausanne School. It seems that he began the study of economics through the criticism of Schumpeter's economics from the Marxian ideological standpoint. But he criticized analytically Schumpeter's dualism of dynamic and static economies for its unreality. In 1929 he wrote "Schumpeter"[49] and then in 1933 he published his book, *Theories of Distribution*,[50] in which, aiming at the theoretical and methodological criticism of Schumpeter, he studied the theories of distribution of the Austrian School, mainly Böhm-Bawerk's and von Wieser's theories on interest, and emphasized their significance in the development of economics, though disregarding completely the marginal productivity theory of the Lausanne School.

In *Theory of Price*,[51] published in 1940, he discussed the marginal utility and monopolistic price theories and also the cash balance theory of the Cambridge School, but avoided adopting the general equilibrium theory of price. I think that Kishimoto, like Sugimoto, refuted the methodology of the Lausanne School for its impracticability and intended to create a practical economic system which could criticize capitalistic economy.

VII

By way of conclusion, I wish to evaluate the process of the introduction of marginalism in Japan. It seems that its popularization was, in a general way, due to the fact that an economy had the problem of how to adjust demand with a relatively high level of productivity acquired by forced and strong capital accumulation. Prior to marginalism, economists aimed at economic development through rapid capital accumulation, achieved by means of a distribution favorable to capitalists, pointed to by Ricardo; but after the achievement of huge capital accumulation, economists were aware of the predominance of demand over supply in economic problems. They realized the theory of subjective value to be valid; hence they studied the price mech-

49. "Schumpeter," *Shinko Kagaku no Hata nomotoni*, vol. 2, no. 5.
50. *Bumpai no Riron.*
51. *Kakaku no Riron.*

anism of adjusting demand and supply in an economic system, which is the essence of marginalism.

However, there is little evidence that, giving up the aim of economic growth and hoping for the effect of optimum allocation through price mechanism, Japanese economists directed their efforts to introducing the economics of marginalism. In fact, economists in Japan have been dominantly growth-oriented since the modernization of their country. Therefore, we should consider a second factor in the introduction of marginalism in this country; namely, that as the economics of the German historical school, which prevailed in the period of pre-marginalism in Japan, was criticized for not being scientific and theoretical, some economists undertook to introduce another theory to replace it. Above all, any newly introduced theory would be required to stand out positively against Marxian economics. So the economics of marginalism was introduced in Japan.

As a matter of fact, the conflict between marginalism and Marxism still continues, though it is not theoretical but ideological. This is not only due to the fact that the actual economic and social conditions, such as the prewar victory of socialists in the Russian Revolution, the postwar development of Chinese Communism and the incessant and recurrent severe depressions have supported the continuity of Marxian economics, but also due to the original role of marginalism in the introductory period; i.e., it had to cope with Marxism. Under these circumstances, among Japanese economists we can find intellectual efforts to synthesize these two different systems.

I mentioned that the development of marginalism in its logical aspects had an exceptional success in Japan. It seems to me that a scientific system always develops with a freedom to pursue logical perfection. The development of marginalism in Japan is no exception to the rule. It was independent of the motive of introduction and also the actual economic and social problems. This fact can be verified by the efforts of such economists as Yasui.

As marginalism in Japan moved into a phase of deeper study, economics was able to make great progress from its introduction phase through the successive stages of assimilating, mastering, and improving theories and of their practical application to economic policies. It should be noticed that a deep and full comprehension of marginalism, whether such academic activities were aimed at improving the Lausanne School's economics or at delving deeper into the other schools, facilitated the study and understanding of macro-dynamic theory after the Keynesian Revolution and made it possible to apply it properly to economic policies. In postwar Japan, thereby, the theoretical and technical aspects of a high-growth policy could be established. If it had not been for the adequate preparation and experience acquired through the theoretical development of marginalism, I wonder whether Japan would have adapted itself to the present situation. I can say that, even though it may be an indirect effect, the development of marginalism in Japan had a deep economic significance.

In spite of such development of the theoretical aspects of economics, I regret to say that Japanese economists have not created a new and original theory. It seems to me that this is connected with the problem of the relation between Japan's history of social sciences and its intellectual history. Generally speaking, in the West we can find some common intellectual origin in the background of cultural and social sciences of the same period. In other words, contemporary ideas, including scientific ones, stem from the same intellectual trunk. But in this sense, scientific ideas in Japan had no intellectual trunk. First, I can say that the rapid introduction has kept economics separated from Japanese traditional intellectual history. Secondly, individual judgment and interpretation of every introducer, with no common intellectual background in Western economics, have made impossible the formation of a common basis of cultural and social sciences in Japan.

Consequently, this character of the development of Japanese economics has brought about only an improvement in its technical and logical aspects. Such improvement is easier than in other aspects in Japan in the sense that it can be made within the established framework without considering the fundamental ideas. But this work of improvement has set limits to the innovation and creation of a system in itself.

If the critical, creative, and ideological moments of every scientist are not connected with and concentrated on a contemporary intellectual basis, the energy devoted to the creation of new scientific systems will grow weaker and very soon disappear. In other words, in contrast to the West, because criticism in every field of social science in Japan has not been based on the common intellectual trunk, it could not contribute to concentrating and stimulating the intellectual efforts to create a new system. This is the fate of the academic world, characterized by the history of the introduction of doctrines originating from a different intellectual history; and it is also the case of the Japanese academic world of economics.

Marginalism Moves to the New World

Craufurd D. W. Goodwin

Some revolutions of thought transfer well, others badly. As with wine, the capacity to travel does not necessarily reflect the quality of the passenger. This essay offers a few speculations about the movement of the marginal revolution from its European home to the New World.[1] By the term "marginal revolution" is meant in particular two characteristics of the work of the English, Austrian, and French "marginalist" writers: first, a new emphasis on the place of the individual utility function in the theory of price, and second, use of precise incremental analysis for the study of human behavior and markets.

Section I below provides a brief overview of certain well-known features of the diffusion of marginalism in the English-speaking "new countries": the United States, Canada, and Australia. The cast of characters and their respective contributions are not listed; this has been done by others. The main objective is to discern certain forms and patterns in the events.[2] In Section II some characteristics of the emigration of other great revolutions in economic thought are de-

CRAUFURD D. W. GOODWIN *is Professor of Economics at Duke University.*

1. The spread of marginal ideas within Europe itself has been discussed by Professor T. W. Hutchison in "Insularity and Cosmopolitanism in Economic Ideas, 1870–1914," and by others in the session at the 1954 meeting of the American Economic Association entitled "International Flow of Economic Ideas." *American Economic Review* 45 (May 1955): 1–39.

2. For guides through the course of the marginal revolution in the Old and New Worlds see particularly R. S. Howey, *The Rise of the Marginal Utility School, 1870–1889* (Lawrence, Kans., 1960); Joseph Dorfman, *The Economic Mind in American Civilization*, vol. 3 (New York, 1959); Emil Kauder, *A History of Marginal Utility Theory* (Princeton, 1965); and T. W. Hutchison, *A Review of Economic Doctrines, 1870–1929* (Oxford, 1953). My own work on economic ideas in the English-speaking world during this period is as follows: *Canadian Economic Thought* (Durham, N. C., 1961); *Economic Enquiry in Australia* (Durham, N. C., 1966); "Economic Analysis and Development in British West Africa," *Economic Development and Cultural Change* 15 (July 1967): 438–51; "Economic Ideas in the Development of Jamaica," in *The Transfer of Ideas*, ed. C. D. W. Goodwin and I. B. Holley, Jr. (Durham, N. C., 1968), pp. 138–69; and "The Transfer of Economic Ideas in the Commonwealth," in *Economic Systems and Public Policy: Essays in Honor of Calvin Bryce Hoover*, ed. R. S. Smith and F. T. de Vyver (Durham, N. C., 1966), pp. 252–74.

scribed to see whether, by comparison, any generalized hypothesis can be suggested to explain the specific events under review.

I

Before discussing highlights in the transfer of marginalism from the Old World to the New it is helpful to glance at a few relevant aspects of the milieux which exported and imported the ideas and at the mechanisms which facilitated their movement. It is important also to note changes in these phenomena over time.

With respect to the milieu of origin it is significant that for at least the initial decade of the revolution (the 1870's) and to a lesser extent during the second decade (the 1880's) the European revolutionaries remained outside the respectable establishment or central core of their discipline. Jevons, Walras, and Menger, in varying degrees, all attracted the disapproval and disdain of the most prestigious figures in the English- French- and German-speaking intellectual worlds. Cultural colonies, of which the New World was made up at this time, were quick to discern such a climate of metropolitan opinion. By the 1890's, however, this situation had changed significantly and for several reasons: effective publicists and spokesmen such as Marshall and Wieser had been drawn to the marginalist banner; recognizable "schools" of thought had begun to appear to which followers could feel allegiance; a distinct body of "orthodox" doctrine had crystallized in the writings of the masters; and textbooks had become available which presented the new ideas in a form suitable for wide dissemination. The improvement in the respectability of marginalism is symbolized by the radically different positions in the professional hierarchy held by Jevons in the mid-1870's and Marshall in the mid-1890's.

The milieu of the new countries into which marginal ideas flowed also evolved significantly over the revolutionary decades. At the beginning of the 1870's the discipline of political economy had not changed markedly for nearly half a century. The subject was treated as a relatively minor part of "moral science" consisting of certain immutable principles or laws which could be mastered easily by an unsophisticated layman after a minimum of study. As a subject it was thought to be particularly appropriate for eccentric philosophers, clergymen, and lawyers. In colleges and universities lectures were seldom given by specialists and often by anyone for whom there seemed to be insufficient alternative employment; in addition to lawyers and philosophers, the subject was taught by historians, linguists, mathematicians, scientists of all types, and even college presidents. Readings in political economy were mainly from the British classics (including J. B. Say) and from a few derivative and interpretive domestic texts such as in the United States those by Arthur Perry and Amasa Walker. The overall tenor of most writings was optimistic and hortatory. The writings of Bastiat, which were translated, republished, and copied extensively in Australia, Canada, and the United States, caught well the spirit of the times. The dominant characteristic of a free market system, Bastiat claimed, was the presence of "harmonies" whereby all segments of society shared in gains from the division of labor. At the same time society must be ever vigilant against selfish groups (personified in his famous parable by the rapacious candlemakers) who would distort the system for their own good.

More and more before the arrival of marginalism political economy was seen as an important weapon in the defense of laissez-faire. The writings of social evolutionists, and of Herbert Spencer in particular, were welcomed with enthusiasm by many New World economists and social commentators such as William Graham Sumner in the United States and Henry Gyles Turner in Australia. The concept of political economy as a collection of immutable rules for personal behavior, more akin to a catechism than to a science, was strengthened both by this presumed link with biology and by the Common Sense School of philosophy, which stressed the significance of intuitive judgments in human behavior. During this early period political economy drew much of its popular support from the widespread belief that the subject was an important device for the prevention rather than the analysis of economic evil. Economic principles, it was thought, could keep both statesmen and the working classes on the paths of wisdom, especially with respect to commercial and monetary policy where the temptations of ignorance and sin were especially strong.

The marginal revolution, in the New World as in the Old, was both coincident with and a significant part of the professionalization of economic science. During the 1880's economists began to meet together in significant numbers, to form associations, to publish journals, and above all to perceive their field of inquiry as a respectable discipline.

In the United States these developments were typified by the establishment of the American Economic Association in 1885, in Canada by the creation of a strong department of political economy at the University of Toronto in 1888 under William James Ashley, and in Australia by formation of the remarkable Australian Economic Association in 1887.

Little need be said about developments in the non-self-governing English-speaking new countries. Here, after an early familiarity with both mercantilist and classical principles, progress in economic science failed completely to keep up with that in the independent new countries. There are two explanations for this disparity: first, most of the British colonial rulers did not consider modern analytical economics important for people who were not required to govern themselves, and therefore the subject did not receive encouragement in the educational systems. For the governors of dependent territories, economics as a collection of tools rather than as a list of immutable principles had little appeal. Second, the few nationalist leaders in the colonies who gained some acquaintance with the ''new'' economics through imported books or study abroad failed to find much which could be put to immediate use in their political quests; consequently they either ignored the whole field of economics or, like some West African leaders, attempted to construct a body of distinctive institutional social theory in which marginalism had no part.

The media for the transmission of new economic ideas between the Old and New Worlds evolved significantly with the progress of economic science. Before 1870 the most important transmission belts were the books of classical economists for exposition of theoretical principles and the generalist British periodicals such as the *Fortnightly Review* and the *Westminster Review* for policy interpretations. In some cases (e.g., Francis Wayland's text or the newspaper *The Canadian Economist*) local books and periodicals applied imported theory to domestic data and thereby became filters for the reception of ideas. Rarely in the early period did direct communication or visits abroad by prominent economists play a central role in the passage of ideas. In general, it seems fair to say that most classical economists in the metropolis viewed their New World counterparts with mild patronage and, occasionally, alarm. The various letters on policy matters addressed over the years by John Stuart Mill to correspondents in the colonies in response to supposed misinterpretation of his own doctrines epitomize this attitude.

During the early decades of marginalism the means for genuine professional interchange improved dramatically. First of all, universities and professional asssociations in both the New World and the Old began to publish journals which, in most instances, became obligatory reading for all economists writing in English. Second, economists in all countries accepted a responsibility for knowing a minimum amount about developments elsewhere. Manifestations of this change were the number of articles from and about other countries in the journals, news columns in the *Economic Journal* from such regular correspondents as Arthur Duckworth in Australia, and the various missions abroad—formal and informal—conducted by Americans and Englishmen to study the economic systems of other countries. Third, professional friendships blossomed among economists in different countries as never before, symbolized by the mutual admiration and respect which grew between Alfred Marshall and J. B. Clark. Fourth, as the demand for economists grew in the new countries in response to increased interest in the subject, a migration of young teachers took place which included, sometimes, marginalists such as A. W. Flux who settled at McGill University. Finally, and probably of greatest importance, was the young American economist's custom of traveling abroad for postgraduate study. To some extent the travel took place to countries such as Germany where marginalism was not ascendant; but at the very least these students were exposed to marginalist ideas as an object of attack.

The New World marginalist revolutionaries fall roughly into three categories divided both by time and type: (1) unsuccessful early progenitors, (2) synthesizers who picked up and attempted to absorb some of the new ideas within the old traditions, without, in most cases, appreciating fully their revolutionary significance; and (3) true revolutionaries who joined enthusiastically in battle and helped to scale the walls of orthodoxy. The prevailing mood of the marginalists in the first category was of discouragement, frustration, and futility; that of the second was complacent self-congratulation; and that of the third true revolutionary fervor followed by triumphant celebration.

In varying degrees the ideas which lay behind the marginal revolution of the 1870's were present in the new countries long before this revolutionary decade. The seeds of thought lay in arid ground and failed either to germinate or take root. The most obvious sources of marginalist thought were the Ricardian and Benthamite traditions upon which English classical ideas rested and from which the European marginalists drew inspiration. The content of these ideas, including the notions of declining utility and production functions, is well known, and their presentation in the New World was not significantly different from that in the Old except perhaps for the variant of Ricardian doctrine found in Henry George. In the New World, as in the Old, there were marginalist progenitors who went beyond these great traditions and still did not spark a revolution. Attention will be drawn here to three pioneers, not because they were the most creative or influential in themselves, but because they illustrate how in the years before 1870 even the most promising marginal land lay fallow. Or, to change the metaphor, how marginal bread cast upon the waters was simply eaten by the classical fish without so much as a case of indigestion. The fact that all three of these progenitors were more or less Canadian reflects the writer's early research efforts rather than a chauvinist bias.

The first marginalist explorer was the Scotch-Canadian John Rae, who in his remarkable *New Principles of Political Economy* (Boston, 1834) developed what amounted to a marginal theory of capital in which "instruments" of production were ascribed "orders" according to their rates of return (marginal productivities). Rae was an immigrant to Upper Canada who made his living as a schoolteacher. His training and interests were in the natural sciences as much as in political economy, and in later life he was a practicing physician. He prepared a major treatise on the geology of Ontario which was lost before it could be published.[3]

Even in the arithmetic used we find in Rae an appreciation of a declining marginal productivity schedule for capital. Rae recognized that saving ("accumulation") in the presence of constant technology led to construction of instruments with progressively lower rates of return, while invention permitted "augmentation" of capital or, in our terms, an outward shift of the marginal productivity schedule. Rae

3. See R. Warren James, *John Rae: Political Economist*, 2 vols. (Toronto, 1965) for an account of Rae's life and a compilation of his writings.

discerned that the level of saving was controlled by the "effective desire of accumulation" of the savers in society, a force which was environmentally determined. He employed a proto-marginal approach in showing the role of time in establishing equilibrium in the capital market.

The policy implication of Rae's writings had an important influence directly and indirectly in Canada, Australia, and the United States through such admirers as Nassau Senior and John Stuart Mill. But his theoretical innovations received little notice in the New World. After the marginal revolution had settled into respectability, Rae was rediscovered, and prominent European marginalists such as Akerman and Böhm-Bawerk (in the second edition of the *Geschichte*, 1900) paid him homage. The first public recognition of Rae by an important North American marginalist came from Irving Fisher in 1897. Ten years later in 1907, Fisher dedicated *The Rate of Interest* "to the memory of John Rae, who laid the foundations upon which I have endeavored to build."

The second Canadian progenitor of marginalism is J. B. Cherriman, a Cambridge graduate and professor of mathematics and natural philosophy at University College, Toronto.[4] Cherriman's contribution was of a different type from the suggestive theoretical advances of John Rae. Out of the blue in 1857 Cherriman contributed an article to the *Canadian Journal of Industry, Science, and Art*, the organ of the Canadian Institute, on the subject of Cournot's work in economics. In what was perhaps the first recognition in the English-speaking world of Cournot's great work Cherriman described the *Recherches* as the most important and neglected contribution to political economy since the *Wealth of Nations*. With

4. Cherriman was a fellow of St. John's College, Cambridge, before emigrating to Toronto, and he may well have been influenced by attempts to apply mathematics to political economy demonstrated by William Whewell before the Cambridge Philosophical Society. See James Cochrane, "The First Mathematical Ricardian Model," *History of Political Economy* 2 (Fall 1970): 418-31. It is interesting to speculate whether he knew the young Alfred Marshall, another Johnian. The only other writing by Cherriman on economic topics of which I am aware was in support of a decimal currency for Canada in 1852. See my *Canadian Economic Thought*, p. 75. He was remembered as "a man of great ability and attainments" who "revolutionized the teaching of Mathematics in the Province." *The University of Toronto and Its Colleges* (Toronto, 1906), p. 107. He also gained fame as captain of the University Rifle Corps! W. S. Wallace, *History of the University of Toronto* (Toronto, 1927), p. 90.

the aid of long passages which he had translated himself he gave an "outline of the system followed and some of the deduced consequences." Cherriman described Cournot's work as a landmark for at least two reasons. On the one hand it was a pioneering attempt to apply mathematics to political economy: "in that very wide field of research, which we call by the general name of political economy, no mathematician had hitherto ventured to intrude; yet surely no science ever called louder for this aid."[5] On the other hand, Cherriman said, Cournot had also proposed a pathbreaking theory of prices which integrated demand into market analysis and was useful and valid regardless of the state of empirical knowledge about specific consumer preferences. "Although this law of the demand is thus unknown, we are not thereby precluded from reasoning with regard to it, for by well known processes of analysis, properties of a function may be discovered when the function itself is undetermined."[6] Cherriman did not advance beyond the marginalism found in Cournot in any respect; however, he did draw attention to Cournot's system and praised it mightily in the most important literary and scientific forum in Canada. It is significant for our purposes that the effect of Cherriman's paper upon his listeners was like dropping a stone in a deep well.

Simon Newcomb, another Canadian by birth and another mathematician, is generally regarded as the advanced scout of the marginal revolution in the United States. Like both Rae and Cherriman, and despite his participation in the American Economic Association and other professional groups, Newcomb was a relative outsider to the establishment of academic economists in his day. He taught political economy briefly, and he published a textbook in the field, but even he himself viewed his activity in economics as a "hobby." Newcomb's training and background both help to explain his position in the profession and his enthusiasm for marginalism. His education was self-administered and informal, and for this reason he was open to a variety of unusual influences. For example, he listed books on "Phrenology" as among those which most "profoundly influenced" his "mode of

5. "Recherches sur les principes . . . ," *Canadian Journal of Industry, Science, and Art* 8 (1857): 186.
6. Ibid., p. 189.

life.''[7] He was apprenticed to a quack herbalist for a time, and then he went on to a long and distinguished career as a mathematician and astronomer. Newcomb's first look at political economy came at the age of nineteen when he read Say's *Treatise* and found it ''quite a delight . . . to see human affairs treated by scientific methods.'' He was inspired to pursue the subject from dissatisfaction with what he considered to be the unscientific character of Henry Carey's *Principles of Social Science.* ''With every possible predisposition to look favorably on its teachings, I was unable to find anything in them but the prejudiced judgments of a one-sided thinker, fond of brilliant general propositions which really had nothing serious to rest upon either in fact or reason.''[8]

Newcomb was especially discouraged by the small amount of light which contemporary political economy cast upon the pressing monetary and commercial questions of the day. Consequently, when in 1884 he became professor of mathematics and astronomy at Johns Hopkins University, he devoted a substantial portion of his time to filling this void, especially in a form which would be useful to the layman, in a succession of popular works. He said in 1903: ''What I have done has been prompted by the conviction that the greatest social want of the age is the introduction of sound thinking on economic subjects among the masses, not only of our own, but of every other country.''[9]

Newcomb's claim to priority among American marginalists rests on his appreciative and sophisticated review of Jevons' *Theory of Political Economy* in the *North American Review* for April 1872. Newcomb welcomed Jevons as a writer who was likely to make the marginal revolution finally succeed, with respect to both the use of the utility concept and employment of precise mathematical analysis. He wrote:

If we compare Professor Jevons's work with that of Cournot on the same subject, published more than thirty years ago, we cannot but admit that in fertility of method and elegance of treatment it falls far below it. But the latter can be understood

7. Simon Newcomb, *The Reminiscences of an Astronomer* (Boston, 1903), pp. 14–15. See also Loretta M. Dunphy, *Simon Newcomb: His Contribution to Economic Thought* (Washington, 1956).

8. *Reminiscences*, p. 401.

9. Ibid., p. 408.

only by an expert mathematician, and the number of those who are at the same time mathematicians and economists is too small even to perpetuate the knowledge of such a work, so that even in this age Cournot has met the fate of the Atlantides.[10]

In anticipation of Marshall's later price theory Newcomb predicted that Jevons' extreme emphasis on utility as the explanation for both sides of the market would soon be modified by a more thorough incorporaiton of costs in the theory of supply: "we apprehend that the utility of the commodity to the seller or producer will disappear from the equations altogether, and the relation will appear as one between the conditions of production on the one side, and the utility of the commodity to the purchaser on the other."[11] Newcomb incorporated the ideas of Jevons, with some of his own modifications, in his textbook *Principles of Political Economy* (New York, 1886). Just as Irving Fisher remembered John Rae in *The Rate of Interest*, so too Fisher dedicated *The Purchasing Power of Money* to the memory of Simon Newcomb.

Certain generalizations can be suggested about these three marginalist progenitors which may hold also for some of the other forerunners not covered here, such as J. B. Clark in his *New Englander* articles of the 1870's. First, they all came to political economy with backgrounds and training in other fields. Moreover, none was primarily a teacher of the subject, and all had studied it quite incidentally to other activities. Second, none of the three in his day was considered to be in the forefront of the economics profession; in reputation they range from the unknown Cherriman through the misunderstood Rae to the eccentric Newcomb, who was merely tolerated by his economist colleagues. Third, none succeeded in starting a marginal revolution in North America.

From these generalizations at least two tentative conclusions can be drawn. First, some support can be provided from the marginalism case for the thesis that brilliant and innovative thinking often comes from the fringe or intersectoral areas between disciplines—in this instance the region between mathematics, economics, and the natural sciences. Second, in North America as in Europe the ideas of mar-

10. *North American Review* 114 (April 1872): 435.
11. Ibid., p. 438.

ginalists in a variety of forms were present in the air at least thirty-five years before the "revolution" of the 1870's. Most of the analytical problems and the techniques which captivated later marginalists were known at least in outline. What was lacking on both continents, we must conclude, was the proper environment for these ideas to develop and mature.

Two hypotheses may help to explain why the environment was unsatisfactory for the growth of marginalism in the New World before the 1870's. The first is a variant of the theory of Emil Kauder that the association of political economy with moral philosophy, and especially Protestant theology, rendered the subject relatively impervious to marginalism. Where economics was mainly taught and written about by clergymen, as in the United States and Canada, this thesis would seem to have weight. On the one hand the training of the clerical practitioners, so indifferent to mathematics, did not equip them to receive such a technical innovation, while on the other hand their religious doctrine predisposed them toward a cost-of-production theory of value and against the seemingly self-indulgent concept of utility.[12] The second hypothesis is that marginal utility theory (like modern welfare theory) is a luxury good which will be produced only at an advanced stage of economic development. So long as the marginal utilities of all goods are very high, this argument runs, as they must be on the frontier or in underdeveloped countries, it is unreasonable to expect economists to spend their time analyzing the phenomenon of declining utility. There is no simple way to test either of these hypotheses.

The second phase in the transfer of marginalism to North America began in the 1870's, came to a peak in the 1880's, and continued at a reduced level right into the twentieth century. This period witnessed an attempt by economists trained in classical political economy to absorb marginal ideas within the corpus of their thought without making fundamental modifications in their own practices, without acknowledging revolutionary content in the new ideas, and without

12. Professor Kauder developed his thesis in "The Retarded Acceptance of the Marginal Utility Theory," *Quarterly Journal of Economics* 63 (Nov. 1953): 564–75; he refined it in his *A History of the Marginal Utility Theory*. Sharp dissent from the thesis was expressed by John P. Henderson in "The Retarded Acceptance of the Marginal Utility Theory: Comment," *Quarterly Journal of Economics* 69 (Aug. 1955): 465–73, with reply from Kauder, pp. 474–77.

proclaiming the need to follow the paths of inquiry which the marginalists pointed out. This phase can be regarded as a reaction to the initial impact of the marginal revolution by those in the prevailing tradition who saw economics not as a collection of analytical tools but as a body of established principles which were crucially important only when applied to public policy.

When one considers the slight impact that marginalism had upon the state of American economic thought in the 1870's, it seems remarkable that, by Professor Dorfman's report, Jevons' *Theory* ranked tenth among works on economics sold in the United States in 1876. The explanation for this paradox lies in the nature of this second phase of marginalism, whose form is revealed in the pages of contemporary textbooks. In the popular elementary work *Institutes of Economics* (1888) by E. Benjamin Andrews, president of Brown University and formerly professor of political economy at Cornell, an extraordinary eclecticism with respect to economic theory is portrayed. Within the traditional Mill sequence of production, distribution, and exchange, the topic "value" is still accorded less than twenty pages in this 227-page book. But at the same time Andrews acknowledged that "economics is now in transition," and he recommended for extra reading such diverse authorities as Menger, Böhm-Bawerk, Sidgwick, Marshall, Jevons, and J. B. Clark, together with Mill, Cairnes, Roscher, Ingram, Marx, and others. He did not attempt to sort out or reconcile the conflicting views of the different schools represented by these men but, instead, paraphrased them briefly and implied that they all fitted easily within a grand tradition.

Francis Walker in his *Political Economy* (3d ed., 1888), an "advanced" text of the same period, took a similar line. The main conflict in economics which Walker discerned was between the "English School" of theorists, which argued from a set of premises, and the "German School" of economic history, which concerned itself with descriptive studies. Implicitly Walker treated Jevons and Marshall as merely an extension of the "English School," and he categorized their work as distinctly evolutionary rather than revolutionary in significance. Walker viewed himself as something of a mediator among factions, and like Andrews, he avoided the need to reconcile conflict merely by mentioning all sides and minimizing elements of difference. In his chapter "The Theory of Value" Walker gives just about equal time to Cairnes, Senior, Mill, Marshall, and Jevons, with a few facts thrown in from Roscher. Walker was obviously fascinated by the concept of "final utility" on a declining function, but he presented it cleansed of symbols, diagrams, and mathematics. In his eyes there was no marginal revolution at hand.

Other works with a similar eclecticism to that of Andrews and Walker, even though with differing emphases on marginalism, were the texts by Richard T. Ely and Henry Carter Adams.[13]

A number of possible explanations come to mind for the distinctly non-revolutionary character of this second, assimilative stage in the passage of marginalism to the New World. In the United States an estrangement from British scholarly life was occurring during this period and was accelerated by a growing attachment to German thought, epitomized by the stream of postgraduate students attending German universities. The resistance to English ideas seems to have been inspired at least in part by a real or supposed hauteur exhibited toward American scholars by their Anglo-Saxon Old-World brethren. If anything, American sensitivity intensified as the profession grew stronger. It was one thing for the British to be condescending towards a derivative thinker like A. L. Perry or Amasa Walker; it was quite another thing to patronize original minds like Francis Walker and Richard T. Ely. As Ely wrote to Alfred Marshall as late as 1901:

> I could wish that there was a closer connection between American economists and English economists, but I am not sure how strong the desire for this closer connection may be on the part of your people. The few references to American writers would, to be perfectly frank, indicate that the English economists do not esteem their work very highly. I suppose the connection, today, between the German economists and the Americans is closer than that between the American and English writers. I am speaking about the personal connection as much as about the connection of thought.[14]

13. R. T. Ely, *Outlines of Economics*, 1893; H. C. Adams, *Outlines of Lectures Upon Political Economy*, 1881.
14. A. W. Coats, "Alfred Marshall and Richard T. Ely: Some Unpublished Letters," *Economica*, n.s. 28 (1961): 192. Professor Hutchison describes the growth of a distinctly national brand of British marginalism during the 1890's in his "Insularity and Cosmopolitanism in Economic Ideas, 1870–1914," p. 13.

The resentment against English scholarship in America may have been manifested, to some extent, in resistance to marginalism, at least until Austrian works became readily available in translation in the 1890's.

The force of historicism as an impediment to marginalism is difficult to judge. There was no critic of marginal economics on historical grounds in the New World equal, say, to Laveleye in Belgium or Ingram in the British Isles, but the works of the sceptical foreign historians were imported and did have influence. Moreover, the growth of enthusiasm for the historical method nurtured by Germanic training began in America in the 1870's at a time when it probably drew intellectual resources away from marginal economics, both among the devotees of history such as Francis Walker, and the critics such as William Graham Sumner. Professor Dorfman has noted that ultimately "the German-trained contingent was the first to welcome Jevons' theory as a part of the new economics (Clark attributed his own version of marginal utility to the inspiration of his German teacher, Karl Knies), but they had hardly intended that economics should be restricted to this doctrine."[15]

A second explanation for the assimilation stage of marginalism in the New World was the incapacity of most domestic economists to understand even the simplest mathematics. Without the intellectual equipment to understand the more complex parts of works by Jevons or Menger, let alone Wicksteed and Walras, they tended to interpret these writings as mere elaborations of Cairnes and Senior. Only with the appearance of prominent New World economists who were also competent mathematicians, and with the publication of such important non-mathematical works as Marshall's *Principles* and the Austrian writings in translation did the true "revolutionary" character of this literature become clear.

Yet a third explanation for the assimilation stage is the intense preoccupation of New World economists with urgent policy issues. In most of their meetings, monographs, and texts of the 1880's and 1890's they expressed an anxious impatience to get on with problems

15. Joseph Dorfman, "The Role of the German Historical School in American Economic Thought," *American Economic Review* 65 (Proceedings, 1955): 28; and also Jurgen Herbst, *The German Historical School in American Scholarship* (Ithaca, N. Y., 1965).

and not waste time on techniques. It had still to be demonstrated in the 1880's that marginal analysis could be useful in solving practical economic problems.

During the 1890's and the first decade of the twentieth century the true marginalist revolutionaries mounted the barricades in the New World and won the day. They exhibited certain distinct characteristics. First, they retained a clear consciousness of revolution and the importance of their struggles, typified on the one hand by the self-confidence of J. B. Clark, and on the other by the search for ancestors of Irving Fisher in connection with the publication in translation of Cournot's *Recherches*. There was high elan among the revolutionaries and a conviction that marginalism was the wave of the future. This view was expressed well by David I. Green, a minor figure, in 1894. He said:

> The older English and American economists, while recognizing that the Austrians have done careful and suggestive work in economic theory, do not seem to have been turned to any great extent from their former ways of thinking; but it is a significant fact that the young men whose ideas upon economic theory have been formed since the Austrian writings became accessible have quite generally adopted the leading conceptions and nomenclatures of the Austrian school.[16]

Publication of such a complete and obviously important work as J. B. Clark's *The Distribution of Wealth* (New York, 1899) gave a strong boost to this self-confidence.

A second characteristic of the third revolutionary stage was growing appreciation of the worldwide cast of revolutionary characters. All the members of the team, so to speak, became aware of the other players. In the new American professional journals of the 1890's, in addition to the works of English and domestic marginalists, the writings of Walras, Böhm-Bawerk, and Wieser were reviewed frequently and were published in translation. An indication that by the 1890's the marginal revolution was succeeding in America was the defensiveness of prominent non-marginalists. For example, Simon Nelson Patten considered it necessary to reply at length to criticisms

16. David I. Green, ''Wieser's Natural Value,'' *Annals of the American Academy of Political and Social Science* 5 (1894): 512.

from marginalists that he had used the term "utility" incorrectly to mean something like aggregate social welfare or "prosperity" instead of individual want satisfaction. He explained:

> The meaning I give to these terms is in harmony with the meaning attached to them by every economist who views political economy primarily as a theory of prosperity. If my usage differs from that of most of the writers of the present day it is because the theory of value has of recent years absorbed the attention of economists to a degree that causes them to neglect the theory of prosperity. Anyone desiring to revive the interest in the latter theory must use these terms with their earlier meanings, drawing some new distinctions needed to adapt the theory to our present knowledge of economic phenomena.[17]

An important characteristic of the successful "third-stage" revolutionaries in the New World is that they joined adherence to the marginal theory with continuing concern for a wide range of policy problems. Moreover, they soon found that their new body of tools did not necessarily either support or conflict with most policy proposals. E. R. A. Seligman, J. B. Clark, Frank Fetter, and others were all attracted to political economy by such reformist schemes as that of Henry George, and over their lifetimes they remained intensely involved with questions of tax reform, trade union regulations, relief of depressions, and antitrust legislation. Undoubtedly they were relieved that their adherence to marginalism did not predetermine their differing positions on these practical issues. J. B. Clark did make use of marginal productivity theory to refute socialist notions and to show the rationale for a distribution pattern which would hold with perfect markets. But he recognized also that markets were never perfect and that in real life the economist always faced great complexity.[18]

Unlike other bodies of economic doctrine, such as those of Smith or Marx, marginalism did not have a clear set of policy precepts attached to it. A marginalist could be a free trader or a protectionist, a monometallist or bimetallist. Except for the early controversy be-

17. Simon N. Patten, "Cost and Utility," *Annals* 3 (1892–93); 409–28.
18. See, for example, Benjamin J. Klebaner, "Trusts and Competition: A Note on John Bates Clark and John Maurice Clark," *Social Research* 29 (1962), 475–79.

tween European Marxists and marginalists, there were no crucial
incidents which committed marginalists for or against specific
policies. On the one side this relatively policy-neutral position may
have slowed down the spread of marginalism, but on the other hand
ultimately it gave the theory wider and stronger currency among pro-
fessionals who recognized that a marginalist training would sharpen
their wits and improve their skills while leaving them free to follow
the policy paths of their choice.

Some of the third-stage marginalists came to treat marginal theory
almost as religious doctrine divorced from day-to-day affairs; they
would say their marginal prayers, as it were, and then propose whichever policies were dictated by self-interest or by conscience. Irving
Fisher was a good example of the marginal purist and policy eclectic
who often left his mathematical studies to deal with the widest range
of unrelated contemporary issues, from conservation to the "com-
pensated dollar." One can also observe such later marginalists as
Herbert Davenport and Thomas Nixon Carver proposing creation of
interventionist economic institutions which would have horrified many
of the marginalist pioneers.

The last part of the third stage in the transfer of marginalism to
the New World was the widespread acceptance by the bulk of the
economics profession of marginal theory as the dominant paradigm.
Achievement of this position was facilitated by the publication of such
important texts as Marshall's *Principles* and the emigration of such
second-generation missionaries as Marshall's pupil A. W. Flux to
Canada, and Herbert Stanley Jevons, W. S. Jevons' son, to Australia
and India. Both Jevons and Flux wrote minor second-generation texts
aimed in part at the New World (*Essays on Economics*, Sydney,
1905; *Economic Principles*, London, 1904).

Into the twentieth century a desultory rearguard action against the
wholehearted adoption of marginalism was waged by the remaining
disciples of J. S. Mill (e.g., J. Laurence Laughlin or F. W. Taussig in
Wages and Capital, 1896), some of the products of the Scotch universities (e.g. John Davidson, the pupil of J. S. Nicholson, at the
University of New Brunswick), and a variety of persons sceptical of
all theory in the social sciences such as R. F. Irvine in Sydney and
Stephen Leacock at McGill. Ironically, one of the most prominent

snipers at the marginalists was another Canadian emigrant to the
United States, Silas MacVane at Harvard. But by now the former
revolutionaries had become the authorities in power. Mastery of
marginal techniques had become virtually a prerequisite for entry into
the economics profession. To some extent, one suspects, the complexities
of marginalism were welcomed by many economists as much for their
professional significance as for their capacity to explain economic
phenomena. It is the essence of a profession that the skills required
therein are not possessed by those without. Marginalism was the first
body of economic thought which provided the essential barrier of entry
to the profession.

II

It may be useful to reflect briefly upon additional instances of
the passage of economic doctrine from the Old World to the New
in order to observe if significant regularities and differences appear.
Only two other "revolutions" in economic thought seem at all comparable to the rise of marginalism, those associated with the writings
of Adam Smith and John Maynard Keynes. Elements of scholastic
and mercantilist doctrine had been brought to most parts of the New
World in the seventeenth and eighteenth centuries virtually with the
first settlers, and therefore these examples are not relevant. Sharp
changes in more specialized bodies of thought, like the ideas of the
banking-and-currency schools and the bimetallists, were too narrow
in focus to qualify as "revolutions." Some strands of thought, such
as the speculations of the Physiocrats or of J. A. Hobson, can best
be seen as progenitors of the later Smithian and Keynesian developments. Still others, such as the work of Malthus, Ricardo, and Harrod,
may be thought of as completing revolutions after they had already
succeeded. In recent years the transfer of bodies of economic thought,
such as complex theories of economic growth, have taken place from
the former New World to a newer New World, that of the "developing" countries; but this process is still too close in time and different
in context to provide a useful perspective for the marginalism case.

It seems fair to say that both the Smithian and Keynesian revolutions traveled somewhat better than did marginalism. Just as the
battle cry of the marginal revolution was the need to understand
marginal utility, that of the Smithian revolution was the need
to appreciate the operation of a free price economy and that of the

Table 1. *Elements of Difference Among Revolutions in Economics Relevant to Their Transferability*

ELEMENT	SMITHIAN REVOLUTION	MARGINAL REVOLUTION	KEYNESIAN REVOLUTION
Approximate time to revolutionary success	10 years	20 years	10 years
Technical content	low	high	medium
Links with economic policy	close	distant	close
Links with social philosophy	close	distant	close
Links with economics profession	distant	close	distant

Keynesian revolution the need to comprehend the macroeconomic determinants of employment and growth. But it took only about half as long for the last two cries to become clichés as for the first. One may take as the date of revolutionary success in each case the point when the new theoretical schema became widely understood and accepted as important for the discipline by a significant number of economists. For the sake of argument we might take as the time of triumph for Smithianism in the New World the publication of the *Federalist Papers*, 1787–88; for Keynesianism, 1944–47, when the various White Papers on employment and the postwar economies were published in Australia, Canada, and the United States. These transfer periods of about a decade each correspond to more than twenty years in the marginalism case, say from Jevons' *Theory* in 1871 to Irving Fisher's *Mathematical Investigations in the Theory of Value and Prices* in 1892.

A study of the similarities among these three major revolutions in economic thought may cast light upon those factors which determine the spread of intellectual innovations generally. Some of the most obvious similarities, which can only be mentioned here,[19] are as follows: (1) all three revolutions were international and multilingual in origin, thereby coming at the new countries from several directions; (2) the delay in the international transfer of the new ideas corresponds roughly to the length of the revolutionary episodes in the countries of origin, i.e., the revolutions succeeded in the New World at about the time they did in the old; (3) the missionary work of disciples and popularizations of seminal works both played vital parts in the transfer process; (4) the three-stage development sequence from

19. Among the large literature on the spread of Smithian and Keynesian doctrine see particularly Joseph Dorfman, *Economic Mind*, vols. 1 and 2; Robert S. Smith, ''The Wealth of Nations in Spain and Hispanic America, 1780–1830,'' *Journal of Political Economy* 65 (Feb. 1957): 104–25; Seymour E. Harris, ed., *The New Economics* (New York, 1952).

progenitors through assimilators to successful revolutionaries can be observed in all three cases.

But it is from the differences more than from the similarities in these three cases that understanding may come of the peculiarities in the marginalist experience. In Table 1 a number of the characteristics of the revolutions are listed which, a superficial examination suggests, varied significantly among the three. Mere guesses at the magnitude and direction of these differences are offered for consideration. More precise estimates, and even perhaps some quantification, might be provided to give this comparison greater meaning. The reasons for the variance ratings are as follows. First, with respect to technical content, Smithian doctrine could be understood by most educated laymen, in contrast to the relatively sophisticated formulation involved in marginal theory. Similarly, with a higher level of economic literacy by the 1930's, Keynesian theory did not have a dramatically novel technical content. In fact, Keynes used geometric and conceptual tools very similar to those of the marginalists. Second, it seems reasonable to speculate that the links these intellectual revolutions had with other bodies of thought are relevant to the transfer phenomenon. In this respect, a sharp distinction can be drawn between the Smithian and Keynesian flows on the one side, and the transfer of marginalism on the other. The first two were closely identified with policy precepts (free trade and public obligation to maintain full employment), while the other was not. Similarly, the first two were associated with a wider body of social thought (the notion of personal liberty on the one hand and of collective responsibility on the other) while it could reasonably be argued that marginalism was philosophically neutral as well as policy-neutral. In the case of the third link, that with developments in the economics profession, marginalism clearly had the closest relationship. This link was slight in the Smithian case because the economics "profession" at that time barely existed. Keynes on the other hand, while he undoubtedly helped to create a new subsect among economics practitioners, probably did not significantly reform the profession.

It would be unreasonable to suggest that such variations as these among the major revolutions in economics can explain entirely the unique characteristics of the one marginal case. But such comparisons may be fruitful avenues for future research.

The Adoption of the Marginal
Utility Theory

George J. Stigler

THE UTILITY theory was extensively developed as a theory of human behavior before the end of the Napoleonic Wars. This is a proposition supported in the first section of this paper, although it requires only modest support. The theory of utility was not deployed successfully in economics until after its introduction by Jevons, Menger, and Walras. This is a matter of common knowledge, although the time at which the theory was effectively adopted comes later than common knowledge would have it. The explanation for the retarded adoption and development of utility theory in economics constitutes the central task of this essay.

I. EARLY AND ACCESSIBLE UTILITY THEORIES

Of early statements of utility theory, incomparably the best-known to economists, intimately and not merely by hearsay, is that of Jeremy Bentham. Recall the soaring claims for the principle of utility which introduce *The Principles of Morals and Legislation*:

> Nature has placed mankind under the governance of two
> sovereign masters, *pain* and *pleasure*. It is for them alone to
> point out what we ought to do, as well as to determine what
> we shall do. On the one hand the standard of right and wrong,
> on the other the chain of causes and effects, are fastened to their
> throne. They govern us in all we do, in all we say, in all we
> think: every effort we can make to throw off our subjection,
> will serve but to demonstrate and confirm it.[1]

GEORGE J. STIGLER *is Charles R. Walgreen Distinguished Professor of American Institutions at the University of Chicago.*

1. J. Bentham, *An Introduction to the Principles of Morals and Legislation*, ed. J. H. Burns and H. L. A. Hart (London, 1970), p. 11.

Whatever the role of utility as a moral guide—and I believe it was
the intellectual tragedy of Bentham's life that he limited his analysis
of utility primarily to this role—it can hardly be disputed that the
principle of utility is an all-embracing theory of purposive conduct.
When a man acts with a view to anticipated consequences of the
act, the desired consequences (pleasures) and undesired consequences
(pains) surely govern his choice of action.

Already by Chapter 4 of the *Introduction* Bentham has listed
the dimensions of utility (intensity, duration, certainty, propinquity,
etc.) and asserted the universality of its domain:

> An article of property, an estate in land, for instance, is valu-
> able, on what account? On account of the pleasures of all kinds
> which it enables a man to produce, and what comes to the
> same thing the pains of all kinds which it enables him to avert.
> But the value of an article of property is universally under-
> stood to rise or fall according to the length or shortness of the
> time which a man has in it: the certainty or uncertainty of
> its coming into possession: and the nearness or remoteness of
> the time at which, if at all, it is to come into possession [ibid.,
> pp. 40–41].

Bentham did not perform *all* of the task of developing a utility
theory of economic behavior. He did not develop the marginal utility
theory of relative prices, and he did offer a variety of opinions which
we now believe to be at least obscure.[2] Yet he carried the analysis a
good way—well past the point where a Ricardo or a Mill could easily
have taken over the baton. The powerful chapter (14) on "The Proportion Between Punishments and Offences" is enough to support this
proposition. Consider a few of his Rules:

1. The value of the punishment must not be less in any case than
   what is sufficient to outweigh that of the profit of the offence.[3]

2. ". . . it is manifest, that there are occasions on which a given sum will be
worth infinitely more to a man than the same sum would at another time: where,
for example, in a case of extremity, a man stands in need of extraordinary medical
assistance" (*Introduction*, p. 59). The need for large medical expenditures may
not raise the marginal utility of a *given* number of dollars if the utility of
health is reckoned into the total wealth of the individual.

3. Ibid., p. 166. Profit is "not merely the pecuniary profit, but [also] the
pleasure" (p. 166 n). One striking passage, never published during Bentham's

3. When two offences come in competition, the punishment for the greater offence must be sufficient to induce a man to prefer the less.[4]

5. The punishment ought in no case to be more than what it is necessary to bring it into conformity with the rules here given.[5]

7. To enable the value of the punishment to outweigh that of the profit of the offence, it must be increased, in point of magnitude, in proportion as it falls short in point of certainty.[6]

The calculus of pleasure and pain extends throughout all human behavior: "all men calculate. I would not say, that even a madman does not calculate."[7]

Even fuller directions on the calculus of utility were given in the *Theory of Legislation*, synthesized from numerous manuscripts by Bentham's disciple, Dumont—a work well-known to the Benthamites.[8] The master seldom forgot the utility calculus for long, and our final quotation is from his *Rationale of Judicial Evidence*, a work which the young John Stuart Hill prepared with extreme labor and skill from a forest of manuscripts:

> ... the matter of wealth is of no value, but in proportion to its influence in respect of happiness. Multiply the sum of a man's property by 2, by 10, by 100, by 1000, there is not the smallest

---

life, was unusually explicit: "If I having a crown in my pocket, and not being athirst hesitate whether I should buy a bottle of claret with it for my own drinking, or lay it out in providing for a family I see about to perish for want of any assistance, so much the worse for me at the long run: but it is plain that, so long as I continue hesitating, the two pleasures of sensuality in the one case, of sympathy in the other, were exactly worth to me five shillings, to me they were exactly equal.

"I beg a truce here of our man of sentiment and feeling while from necessity, and it is only from necessity, I speak and prompt mankind to speak a mercenary language. The Thermometer is the instrument for measuring the heat of the weather; the Barometer the instrument for measuring the pressure of the Air. Those who are not satisfied with the accuracy of those instruments must find out others that shall be more accurate, or bid adieu to Natural Philosophy. Money is the instrument of measuring the quantity of pain or pleasure." See C. W. Everett, *The Education of Jeremy Bentham* (New York, 1931), pp. 35–36.

4. Bentham, *Introduction*, p. 168.

5. Ibid., p. 169.

6. Ibid., p. 170.

7. Ibid., p. 174.

8. Bentham, *The Theory of Legislation*, trans. Hildreth (London, 1864), esp. pt. 1, chaps. 6, 16.

reason for supposing that the sum of his happiness is increased in any such proportion, or in any one approaching to it: multiply his property by a thousand, it may still be a matter of doubt, whether, by that vast addition, you add as much to his happiness as you take away from it by dividing his property by 2, by taking from him but the half of it.[9]

A second and independent strand of utility theorizing can be disposed of more briefly: this is the calculus of moral expectation initiated by D. Bernoulli in dealing with the St. Petersburg paradox.[10] That paradox involved the proper price of a gamble in which a fair coin is flipped successively until a heads occurs, with payments to the player:

H	1 ducat
TH	2 ducats
TTH	4 ducats
. . .	. . .
T^nH	2^n ducats

The expected value of the gamble is infinite,[11] and to resolve this paradox Bernoulli postulates that the player seeks to maximize *moral* rather than mathematical expectation. He introduced the assumption that "the utility resulting from any small increase in wealth will be inversely proportionate to the quantity of goods previously possessed."[12] Using the law of utility,

$$du = \frac{bdw}{w}$$

where w is wealth, u is utility, and b is a constant, a finite value will be found for the gamble, and one dependent upon the individual's

9. J. Bentham, *Rationale of Judicial Evidence* (London, 1827), 5:656.

10. See D. Bernoulli, "Exposition of a New Theory on the Measurement of Risk," *Econometrica*, 1954; it first appeared in 1738. Also my *Essays in the History of Economics*, pp. 108 ff.

11. Since the probabilities of these outcomes are

$$\frac{1}{2}, \frac{1}{4}, \frac{1}{8}, \cdots \frac{1}{2^{n+1}}$$

and the expected gain for n infinite, is

$$(\tfrac{1}{2})1 + (\tfrac{1}{4})2 + (\tfrac{1}{8})4 + \cdots + \left(\frac{1}{2^{n+1}}\right)2^n + \cdots = \infty$$

12. Bernoulli, p. 25.

initial wealth.[13] The analysis is applied to the theory of insurance, and Bernoulli deduces among other things the value of risk diversification.

Bernoulli's essay provided stimulus to a number of the most distinguished probabilists to discuss moral expectation and diminishing marginal utility of income (and many more to discuss the paradox). Laplace devoted a chapter (10) of his great treatise, *Théorie analytique des probabilités*, to a restatement of Bernoulli's theory. Lesser names in this literature are Fourier,[14] Quételet,[15] and Cournot,[16] and of course most writers on probability touched on the St. Petersburg paradox. In addition, famous writers such as Buffon, the famous naturalist, devoted considerable attention to the subject.[17]

The availability of utility theory to economists differed immensely between these two literatures. The Benthamite version was directly addressed to social life and was enunciated with the very fullest possible generality; it was known, and known well, by at least three premier economists of the age—and probably to a degree by every educated Englishman. The Bernoulli version was less available to economists, since it came in a mathematical literature in several languages and over more than a century of writing, but in certain respects these

13. Integrating, one obtains $U = b \log(w/a)$. If the initial fortune of the player was W, his gain in utility if he wins 2^{n-1} ducats is

$$b \log \frac{W + 2^{n-1}}{a} - b \log \frac{W}{a} = b \log \frac{W + 2^{n-1}}{W}$$

and his expected gain of utility from playing the game is

$$\frac{b}{2} \log \frac{W + 1}{W} + \frac{b}{4} \log \frac{W + 2}{W} + \cdots$$

$$= b \log (W + 1)^{\frac{1}{2}} (W + 2)^{\frac{1}{4}} \cdots - b \log W$$

The sum D which would yield utility equal to that expected to be gained from the gamble is

$$D = (W + 1)^{\frac{1}{2}} (W + 2)^{\frac{1}{4}} \cdots - W$$

If $W = 10$, $D = 3$; if $W = 100$, $D = 4$; if $W = 1000$, $D = 6$.

14. See J. B. J. Fourier's remarkable essay, "Extrait d'un Mémoire sur la Théorie analytique des assurances," *Annales de Chémie et Physique*, 2d ser., 10 (1819): 177–89.

15. L. A. J. Quételet, *Letters addressed to H.R.H. The Grand Duke of Saxe Coburg and Gotha* (London, 1849), Letter VIII.

16. A. A. Cournot, *Exposition de la théorie des chances* (Paris, 1843), pp. 93, 106–9, 334.

17. G. L. Leclerc de Buffon, *Essai d'arithmétique morale*, in vol. 21 of his *Histoire naturelle* (Paris: Dufart, l'an VIII). Buffon was an independent and somewhat eccentric discoverer of moral expectation; see ibid., pp. 138–40 n.

attributes increased the probability of capturing the attention and interest of some economist—after all there were plenty of mathematically literate writers on economics before 1840, including Babbage, Whewell, possibly Malthus (a ninth wrangler), Thünen, Cournot, and Canard.

There is a separate reason for believing that utility theory was fully accessible to economics: it was closely approached, occasionally formulated, and then forgotten by its author and ignored by contemporaries. We may cite Longfield,[18] Lloyd,[19] Senior,[20] and Say:[21] a list long enough and illustrious enough to make indisputably evident the accessibility of utility theory to economists, and their want of interest in it.

II. THE HYPOTHESIS

The acceptance of a theory by a science is a social act, not an individual act. The genius of Babbage could not bring a computer into being in 1830; by 1940 the introduction of the computer required no major scientific advances, and in fact could not have been much delayed by any feasible social policy.[22] Similarly, we must not explain the general reappearance and acceptance of the marginal utility theory between 1870 and 1890 as the singular achievement of a Jevons, a Menger, or a Walras—indeed their multiplicity and near-simultaneity have often and properly been used to document the importance of the scientific environment.

I propose the following explanation for the fact that the utility theory was at hand for at least three-quarters of a century before it was accepted by the science. Economics became primarily an academic discipline in the last decades of the nineteenth century. Previously it was a science conducted by non-academicians whose main interest was

18. M. Longfield, *Lectures on Political Economy* (1834; reprint ed., London, 1931), pp. 27–28, 45–46, 111 ff.
19. "The Notion of Value," reprinted in *Economic History, Economic Journal Supplement*, May 1927.
20. *Political Economy* (New York, 1939), pp. 11–12.
21. See the letter to Ricardo in J. B. Say, *Mélanges et correspondance* (Paris, 1833), pp. 116–17, also pp. 287–89.
22. This position is strongly argued, and in fact moderately overstated, by R. K. Merton, "Singletons and Multiples in Scientific Discovery: A Chapter in the Sociology of Science," *Transactions of the American Philosophical Society* 105, no. 5 (1961). See also my "Does Economics Have a Useful Past?" *History of Political Economy* 1 (1969): 225–27.

in the policy implications of the science; thereafter it was conducted by professors who accepted the ruling values and incentives of scholarly activity.

The academic economist shares the general tastes of academicians, and they differ in important respects from those of the journalists, politicians, bureaucrats, and men of affairs who constituted the vast majority of economists in the earlier period. In the pre-academic period, the dominant purpose was to understand and to influence public policy, and fact-gathering and theorizing were both directed to the implementation of the primary purpose. Even Ricardo's highly abstract discussion of the measure of value was important to his main dynamical proposition that economic progress would lead to a rise in rents, and to a rise in wages "which would invariably lower profits."

Few academic economists separated themselves entirely from discussions of contemporary problems, but the sovereign importance of policy questions diminished as the science became more exclusively a university profession. A dominant value of the scholarly world is a certain disengagement from the contemporary scene and a search for knowledge more fundamental and durable than that required for practical and immediate purposes. Positively viewed, the academic mind places a special premium upon *generality*. The scholar is not a handmaiden of either local commerce or this year's congress.

A lesser, related scholarly value is the emphasis upon the paraphernalia of scholarship. The form of work takes on a value independent of its content: a scholar should be literate, and his work should be pursued with non-vulgar instruments. Ancient learning is often a constituent of this paraphernalia, but so too is the command over powerful mathematical methods. Words like rigor and elegance portray this element of academic taste, whereas the world of affairs prefers words such as *effective* and *persuasive*.

These values of disengagement from the journalistic crisis of the day or decade, vast generality of major results, and cultivation of scholarly techniques were reinforced by the major triumphs of the physical and biological sciences in the nineteenth century. These sciences sought and in great measure achieved deep unity of their central theoretical structures (Newtonian and Darwinian, respectively), and it became the hallmark of successful scientific work that it explained wide reaches of phenomena. Physics and astronomy already suggested that in a truly advanced science the main results lent themselves to a mathematical formalization which allowed extensive and beautiful derivations and applications.

Utility theory would have been a feeble ally to Ricardo or Mill. None of the great areas of classical economic literature would have gained much from utility theory even when it had reached the stage of development to which it was carried by Pareto and Fisher. Utility theory would have had little to say about corn laws and free trade (except that both countries gain!), about central banking and Peel's Act, about colonization and overpopulation, about Poor Laws or Factory Acts, even about Say's law or taxation. Indeed, after utility theory began to appear in the 1870's, it took no important part in any policy-oriented controversy up to World War I.

What utility theory contributed was precisely the values we attribute to the academic world and in particular to the academic sciences. The classical school had advanced one theory of value for producible goods and resorted to other theories (rent) or vague phrases ("passions of the buyer") for non-producible goods. Now the utility theory allowed a unified explanation of the value of shoes, wheat, and Shakespearean folios. The classical school had no central logic or behavior: the entrepreneur was a profit-maximizer while the consumer and laborer were opaque bundles of sociological behavior traits. Now the utility theory allowed a unified explanation of behavior: everyone was a utility-maximizer, and all economic problems became simply problems of tastes and obstacles (so, Pareto). The method of the classical school had been literary and numerical. Now the utility theory obviously permitted and even invited the use of mathematics.

There is a second stage of adoption of the utility theory: the period in which it was assimilated by the rank and file of competent economists. This period came after the theorists had developed the utility theory up to the point at which it had an operable role in substantive economic research. I also comment briefly on this process of professional adoption in the next section.

III. The Adoption of the Theory

When was the utility theory "adopted"? It is easy to give at least an approximate date for any given economist: the theory was adopted

Table 1. *First Dates of Recognition of the Marginal Utility Theory by Economists*

NAME	DATE	PLACE
Jevons	1862	British Association for Advancement of Science
Menger	1871	*Grundsätze der Volkswirtschaftslehre*
Marshall	1872	Review of Jevons
Cairnes	1874	*Leading Principles*
Walras	1874	*Eléments d'économie*
J. B. Clark	1881	Article in *New Englander*
Edgeworth	1881	*Mathematical Psychics*
Sidgwick	1883	*Principles of Political Economy*
Walker	1883	*Principles*
Wicksteed	1884	Review of *Das Kapital* in *To-Day*
Wieser	1884	*Über den Ursprung des Wertes*
Böhm-Bawerk	1886	*Theorie des Güterwerts*
Cannan	1888	*Elementary Political Economy*
Auspitz and Lieben	1889	*Theorie des Preises*
Pantaleoni	1889	*Principii*
Fisher	1892	*Mathematical Investigations*
Pareto	1892	Articles in *Giornale degli Economisti*
Taussig	1893	Proceedings, A. E. A.
Wicksell	1893	*Über Wert, Kapital und Rente*
Barone	1894	Articles in *Giornale degli Economisti*
Cassel	1899	Article in *Zeitschrift für die gesamte Staatswissenschaft*

at least by 1884 by Philip Wicksteed and not later than 1892 by Irving Fisher.[23] Since we are concerned with a science, and not simply with individual scientists, however, we require a method of characterizing adoption of a theory by the science.

Let us initially state as the simple law of utility: the marginal utility of every commodity diminishes for every man, and this phenomenon underlies his demand curve for each commodity. We can now go to the literature and classify economists in each year as to whether they did or did not "know" (understand) this proposition. We can grade each economist just as we now do in the classroom, classifying him (let us propose) under *Knows Law* and *Does Not Know Law* (and perhaps under *Knows Law* create two classes: *Accepts Law* and *Rejects Law*). Since forgetting and changing of minds are presumably uncommon, a single date will usually characterize each man: that on which he first showed knowledge of the law. We provide such a census of the leading theorists, including the main writers on utility, in the period 1860–1900 in Table 1. The dates are based upon

23. Wicksteed, review of *Das Kapital*, reprinted in *Common Sense of Political Economy* (London, 1934), 2:705; Fisher, *Mathematical Investigations in the Theory of Value and Prices* (1892).

Table 2. *Topics in the Marginal Utility Theory Literature*

1. The explicit relationship between utility and demand functions.
2. The implications of diminishing marginal utility for the shape of the demand curve.
3. Constancy of the marginal utility of income.
4. Definitions of complementarity in utility terms.
5. Measurability of utility with additive utility functions.
6. Measurability of utility with non-additive utility functions.
7. Indifference curve techniques.
8. The Edgeworth box.
9. Integrability problem.
10. The Slutsky equation: separation of income and substitution effects.

publications; often an earlier date could be assigned for knowledge on the basis of letters, recollections, etc.

The median date of first recognition of the utility theory by the economists listed in Table 1 is 1884, but several of the men had not begun to write on economics until later.[24] Professor Richard S. Howey provides a list of numerous minor writers on utility before 1890[25] in his treatise, *The Rise of the Marginal Utility School, 1870–1889.*

A later set of dates would be encountered if we raised the level of sophistication required to be classified as professional knowledge of utility theory. Some possible elements of a more complex standard of knowledge are given in Table 2. To require knowledge of even one of these elements of utility theory would remove perhaps three-quarters of the economists from Table 1, in any year. But the criterion of our simple law of utility will suffice, I believe, to support the following propositions:

1. Almost every economist who dealt seriously and professionally with utility theory in this period had an academic base. The

24. The later beginners were Pareto, Barone, Cassel, Wicksell, Cannan, and Fisher.
25. One interesting name is G. B. Shaw, who used marginal utility theory in a review of *Das Kapital* in the *National Reformer* in 1887. His ancient foe, H. M. Hyndman, has offered an explanation of Shaw's failure to scale the heights of logical analysis: "what a pity it is that Shaw should have stunted the natural growth of his mind and rocked his intellect to fiddle-strings by his confoundedly inappropriate diet. . . . Take Shaw now and feed him for a season on fine flesh foods artfully combined and carefully cooked, turn a highly skilled French chef on to him in every department of his glorious art, prescribe for him stout, blackjack, or, better still, the highest class of Burgundy of the Romanée Conti variety, born in a good year, and Shaw would be raised forthwith to the nth power of intellectual achievement." *Further Reminiscences* (London, 1912), pp. 233–34.

Table 3. *Number of Leading Economists and Academics*

PERIOD	TOTAL	ACADEMIC
1825–1850	14	0
1850–1875	10	3
1875–1900	7	2
1900–1915	8	5

only important exceptions are Auspitz and Lieben, and Barone, and (to a degree) Wicksteed.

2. The still substantial number of non-academic economists in this period, with the exceptions just noted, ignored the theory. This list would include names such as Giffen, Bonar, Farrer, Higgs, Ackworth, the Webbs, Palgrave, Hobson, Bagehot, Macleod, and Goschen.[26] It is not coincidence that the important writers in economics outside academic posts are names which one associates primarily with "applied" and policy-oriented problems.

3. By the time the theory in even this elementary form was generally known to theorists, the science was rapidly moving toward an academic character. If we date leading English economists by their mean year of publication, we find the academic participation to be rising as shown in Table 3.[27] A not dissimilar pattern is found in the United States, and perhaps a somewhat earlier dominance of academic economists was reached in France (see Note at the end of this article).

The remarkable fact that Germany, the leading scientific nation of the world in the late Victorian period, had not a single important utility theorist (although Launhardt deserves honorable mention) is of some relevance. German economics had an established, dominant academic base before almost any other European nation—why was utility theory so neglected?

The reception of utility theory in Germany was hardly helped by Menger's intemperate attacks upon the leading German econo-

26. Some violent attacks on utility theory can be found in the works of several of these men.

27. See my *Studies in the History of Economics* (Chicago, 1965), p. 38. After 1915 it is difficult to find important English economists outside academia except for Hawtrey and Stamp.

mist,[28] but personalities were at most a minor cause of German aloofness from utility theory. German economics was indeed scholarly; its emphasis upon erudition and its meticulous, highly specialized historical researches assuredly were not called for in order to use economics in the real world. German economics, however, had a profoundly antitheoretical position (which I do not attempt to explain); the disciplines of history and jurisprudence, not those of physics and biology, were the model for scientific work in the social sciences. The *Methodenstreit* was literally triggered by Schmoller's review of a book by Menger.[29] The juxtaposition of the leaders of the Austrian and the German schools was symbolic: the utility theory was the first formal, abstract, and (except in Menger's case) mathematically expressed theory of modern economics, and it emphasized the trend toward the physical science model to a degree that the workhorse theory of the classical school had not begun to do. A German

28. The attack on Schmoller in Menger's *Die Irrthümer des Historismus* (Vienna, 1884) may be quoted: "You have warned me, with friendly concern, that a dispute with Schmoller has not only a scientific side but also a very different side. There is not another scholar in Germany, or perhaps anywhere, who is so irresponsible in the choice of means when arguing with an opponent. I may be interpreted in every possible and impossible meaning of my words, and I myself have just received shocking proof that Schmoller is master equally of personality and vulgarity—incidentally, the only literary mastery which can be credited to him.

"You are right, my friend, when you look upon a scientific discussion with Schmoller as more than a scientific occasion: he is all too well known for his remarkable penchant for misinterpreting the meanings of others and equally well known as the unseemly participant in the area of scientific disputes (ibid., p. 6) . . . .

"Schmoller's historical and statistical labors are in any event very shaky performances; in fact our praise of the author could be much more enthusiastic if they came from a secretary of a chamber of commerce, the editor of a trade journal, or the historical society of some provincial city of Prussia. Historical and statistical works from such sources will be used by the theorist with a measure of caution appropriate to the guarantees of their reliability and the competence of their author. It is certainly an unusual phenomenon that a professor of political economy working in fields whose technique he does not fully command nevertheless demands that work of this quality be almost the only kind of work that is done. It would border on the laughable if Schmoller held himself as a serious historian for the sake of such works.

"Truly, the example of Schmoller is not so dazzling, that any political economist should be led to abandon his own field of scientific research to become a dilettante in the area of historical scholarship" (ibid., p. 41).

29. Gustav Schmoller, "Zur Methodologie der Staats- und Sozialwissenschaften," *Jahrbuch für Gesetzgebung, Verwaltung, und Volkswirtschaft* 7 (1883): 239–58.

Table 4. *Discussions of Utility Theory in the Journal of Political Economy and the Quarterly Journal of Economics*

	1893	1903	1913	1923
1. Number of articles devoted primarily to utility	2	2	1	4
2. Fraction of all articles	2/35	2/36	1/66	4/62
3. Number of other articles with non-trivial discussion of utility	2	1	0	1
4. Articles with trivial mention of utility	2	1	0	0
5. Pages devoted to utility discussion	54	68	32	93
6. Percent of all pages	6.7%	7.1%	2.5%	6.4%

historical economist could admire Smith and Mill and vent any antiformalism tastes upon Ricardo. With the advent of utility theory, the challenge of formal theory to the historical tradition became explicit. The English historical school was equally firm in its hostility to utility theory.[30] The sharp conflict of scientific and historical methods was consistent with the acceptance by both parties of the academic values of disengagement from immediate applications, the emphasis upon scholarly techniques, the appeal of intellectual work per se. The conflict, in short, was one of the strategy of economic research.

The Use of Utility Theory in Routine Analysis

It is one thing for the theoretical innovators in a science to occupy themselves with a problem; it is quite another for the new theory to become a part of the working equipment of the competent practitioners of the science.

Utility theory was not even a fashionable topic among economic theorists in the first two generations after it was introduced into economics. Some measures of the attention devoted to utility theory in American economic journals are presented in Table 4. Two characteristics stand out clearly: the interest in utility did not reach a high level, and there is no apparent tendency for it to increase over the thirty years covered by the table.

A fortiori, utility was not a part of the working equipment of economists during this period. An economist writing on taxes or trade

30. J. K. Ingram believed that Jevons' researches on utility "will in fact never be anything more than academic playthings." *History of Political Economy* (New York, 1888), p. 234; see also T. E. Cliffe Leslie, "Jevons' 'Theory of Political Economy,' " in *Essays in Political Economy*, 2d ed. (London, 1888), pp. 66–72.

or labor or the like did not introduce utility functions into his analysis and use them as a method of developing his subject. This absence of utility theory from theoretical work devoted to other subjects persisted for another two decades: not a single article in the *American Economic Review* of 1940 used utility theory in any fashion. It is only in the last two decades that this characteristic has emerged. A similar count of the articles in the *American Economic Review* for 1970 reveals that no fewer than fifteen of the articles introduce and utilize utility functions in the course of the analysis of other subjects. The effective acceptance of utility theory by economic theorists came almost a century after the marginal utility revolution. Science revolves slowly.

IV. Conclusion

These bits of evidence, I hope, create some support for the proposed explanation of the timing of the adoption of the marginal utility theory by the ruling theorists of economics. The explanation of the adoption in terms of the rise of new values as the discipline became increasingly academic has the additional merit that there does not appear to be any serious rival explanation.

However one views the persuasiveness of the present argument, the explanation of the adoption of theories by sciences is an important and neglected subject of scientific study. Once we accept the views that there are ruling theories in a science, and that these theories are replaced by new theories which are usually independently discovered by numerous persons, we are committed to the treatment of the change in scientific theories as a general scientific problem. We are not necessarily committed to Kuhn's particular sequence of scientific change, but we cannot any longer simply tacitly assume that genius leads its own mysterious and unpredictable life, nor that casual references to contemporary intellectual or social phenomena constitute a respectable explanation for particular changes.

The history of economics has become a nearly moribund subject in the United States, and has not failed to decline elsewhere. It is therefore a cause for rejoicing that the extraordinarily complex and subtle forces which dominate a science's evolution present a task of theoretical explanation comparable in intellectual demands to that presented by actual economic life.

Table 5. *Prominent American Economists, 1850–1915*

MEAN DATE OF PUBLICATION	NUMBER OF ECONOMISTS	
	TOTAL	ACADEMIC
1850–1875	4	3
1875–1900	14	7
1900–1915	23	21
1915 and after	9	9

NAMES

Adams, C. F.	George, H.	Seager, H.
Adams, H. C.	Green, D. I.	Seligman, E. R. A.
Anderson, B. M.	Hadley, A. T.	Smith, J. A.
Atwater, L. H.	Hoxie, R. F.	Sumner, W. G.
Bellamy, E.	Johannsen, N.	Taussig, F. W.
Bowen, F.	Johnson, A. S.	Taylor, F. M.
Carey, H.	Kinley, D.	Tuttle, C. A.
Carver, T. N.	Kleene, G. A.	Veblen, T.
Clark, J. B.	Laughlin, J. L.	Walker, A.
Commons, J. R.	MacFarlane, C. W.	Walker, C. S.
Cooley, C. H.	MacVane, S. M.	Walker, F. A.
Davenport, H. J.	Mitchell, W. C.	Wells, D.
Del Mar, A.	Moore, H. L.	Will, T. E.
Dunbar, C. F.	Moulton, H. G.	Wood, S.
Ely, R.	Newcomb, S.	Wright, C. D.
Fetter, F. A.	Patten, S. N.	Young, A. A.
Fisher, I.	Perry, A. L.	

NOTE: THE ACADEMIC STATUS OF ECONOMICS IN THE
UNITED STATES AND FRANCE

Preliminary studies have been made of the degree to which economics had become academic in the United States and France.[31]

A list of American economists was taken from Joseph Dorfman, *The Economic Mind in American Civilization*, vol. 3 (New York, 1949), and a corresponding list of French economists was taken from the well-known French textbook by C. Gide and C. Rist, *A History of Economic Doctrines* (New York, n.d.). The French list is more narrowly confined to theoretical economic literature and is therefore probably biased in the direction of overrepresentation of academic economists. In each case the mean date of publication of each economist was calculated from the usual encyclopedias, and the economists were classified as to occupancy or non-occupancy of an academic position. The results are given in Tables 5 and 6.

The American pattern is roughly similar to that of England, with academic economists becoming overwhelmingly dominant by the be-

31. In addition to my inevitable debt to Claire Friedland, I wish to express my obligations to T. Beatzoglou and Peter Kahn.

Table 6. *Prominent French Economists, 1800–1925*

MEAN DATE OF PUBLICATION	NUMBER OF ECONOMISTS	
	TOTAL	ACADEMIC
1800–1825	4	2
1825–1850	7	3
1850–1875	8	5
1875–1900	2	2
1900–1925	5	3

NAMES

Aftalion, A.	Cournot, A.	Proudhon, P. J.
Aupetit, A.	Dunoyer, C.	Rossi, P.
Bastiat, F.	Dupont-White, C.	Saint-Simon, C.-H.
Blanc, L.	Dupuit, J.	Say, J.-B.
Blanqui, J. A.	Fourier, C.	Simiand, F.
Cabet, E.	Garnier, J.	Sismondi, S. de
Chevalier, M.	Landry, A.	Walras, A.
Colson, C.-L.	Le Play, F.	Walras, L.
Courcelle-Seneuil, J.	Leroy-Beaulieu, P.	

ginning of the twentieth century. Few economists were interested in utility before 1900, and indeed the prevalence of German training was such as to instill a measure of historicism and antitheory in American economics.[32]

The French list seems short as well as biased: the number of prominent economists should be almost independent of the state of the science in a country! For what it is worth, the sample suggests an earlier and stronger academic base in France than in the English-speaking world.

32. J. Herbst, *The German Historical School in American Scholarship* (Ithaca, N. Y., 1965); also J. B. Parrish, "The Rise of Economics as an Academic Discipline: The Formative Years to 1900," *Southern Economic Journal*, July 1967.

Marginalism: The Harvest

G. L. S. Shackle

1. *The Nature of Marginalism*

Economic theory is about the sources of individual conduct and the consequences of its interaction. It is the intimate fusing together of the two questions, concerning the mode of choice of conduct and the outcome of the combination of many men's choices, that constitutes economics as a distinct body of ideas and a discipline on its own. Its identity and separateness are especially confirmed by its possesion of an incisive and, once its presuppositions are accepted, all-conquering principle. The method of the economic analyst is to assume that men pursue their interests by applying reason to their circumstances. A man will do what reason dictates: that is the key to all conduct in the business sphere, in the view of the economic theoretician. Therefore the theoretician has only to apply his own reasoning powers to a general, universally applicable description of men's basic predicament in order to know not only the essential character of a correct policy for the individual in each of his various business capacities but also what, in fact, the individual will do. The law of gravitation is hardly simpler in essence, and economics can aspire, so it might seem, to rival celestial mechanics in its sweep and certainty. It is small wonder that marginalism, the necessary reflection of reason confronted with diversity of need and scarcity of means, should have seized and held the imagination of the economists of the competitive world for half a century.

There were further considerations. Social experiment is possible, if at all, only to governments, and then only to governments willing to interfere with people's lives. But in a climate of austere liberal individualism, such a government attitude is a contradiction of its essential beliefs. A method of study which can eschew experiment

G. L. S. SHACKLE *was formerly Brunner Professor of Econmics at the University of Liverpool.*

was a solution of an otherwise insuperable difficulty. Economic theory, it seemed, could become a deductive science with ready-made, and exceedingly few, necessary and sufficient axioms. The temptation to follow this inviting road, once the nature of that road had been grasped, was irresistible. As has so often happened in the history of science, inspirations came to individuals here and there in time and space, without any notice being taken until some peculiar illumination of the intellectual and the social scene caused these scattered veins of gold to show up all at once and unify themselves in a striking pattern. This is the event we are here to discuss.

Even Robinson Crusoe, despite his unnatural situation, would have economic problems to solve. How often is his name invoked for this very reason. Yet these problems become more interesting when, with the arrival of Man Friday, they become interactive. Edgeworth invented the indifference curve and the contract curve to give an account of that central economic phenomenon, the bargaining process, but Crusoe could not bargain while he remained in solitary state. The chief difference between the Crusoe situation and the Crusoe-Friday situation is that it might, just conceivably, be possible for Crusoe, while alone, to have sufficient knowledge of his relevant circumstances to be able to act rationally, that is to say, to discern and adopt that course of conduct which was demonstrably the most advantageous for him. But with the advent of a second mind, *another* chooser, that knowledge could be attained, if at all, only by means of the most special arrangements and the most unlikely accidents. It requires only the presence of *other minds* than that of the particular chooser whom we are studying, and his awareness or acknowledgment of *other moments* than his present moment, to destroy the basis of *demonstrably optimal choice*. Rationality, as the method and basic procedure not only of the economic chooser under the microscope but also of the economic analyst with his eye to the instrument, thus makes two imperious demands in any non-Crusoe situation: first, for a *market*, and secondly, for a *timeless system*. It was the eventual recognition, in the post-Victorian era, that timelessness is an illusion of a peculiarly, extraordinarily stable and tranquil age, the kind of age which has scarcely occurred in history save under the Antonines or Queen Victoria's navy, and that as a general and universal assumption of

economic analysis it totally removes us from reality, which led in
the interwar period to the decline in the importance of marginalism.
It would of course be grossly misleading to suggest that the harvest
of marginalism is over. Logic, like Nature, can be expelled with a
pitchfork, but it ever returns. But logic, the pure logic of choice,
is seen since 1936 as only a constraint and not a complete and all-
sufficient guide. It provides some prohibitions, but it does not tell us
positively what to do. Marginalism, however, solved a crucial difficulty
which technics had failed to solve.

By technics I mean that view of the field of economic phenomena
which assumed their essence to belong to the visible, tangible scene of
things. The difference, expressed with some oversimplification, between the earlier economics and that of the Jevonsian or Mengerian
era, or to be more just, that of the Gossenian era, was the difference
between an economics of *things* and an economics of *thoughts*. The
effects of the division of labor is a theorem in the subject of industrial arts, a very general theorem, but one concerned with industrial efficiency, with *techne*, with the organization of manipulative
processes, with manufacture not with ingenio-facture (you will perhaps
forgive a little verbal ebullience on this exciting occasion); it is a
theorem which could have served as the ideal foundation of a new
discipline of industrial process organization, the heart and soul of
the management education of what was then the future; it could have
opened this path had the observer of the pinmakers been, let us say,
James Watt the engineer instead of Adam Smith the moral philosopher.
The notion of a *commodity*, as that word is used in the theory
of the perfectly competitive determination of price and output, is a
concept whose operational basis is an operation of the chemist or the
physicist or the housewife in her kitchen, making *physical* tests to discover whether two specimens belong to one and the same commodity.
The basic theory of value is an account of the exchange ratios of
things whose identity and nature is established *prior to* the discussion
of their value. These commodities are *objects*, valued by economic
subjects. But since the recognition of imperfect competition, that
is to say, since the early 1930's or, again to be more just, since 1838,
the notion of object and subject have become inseparably interfused.
Whether two specimens do or do not belong under the same heading,

are or are not representative of the same commodity, is a question which can only be answered by the *buyers*. Two specimens are one commodity if I and all other potential buyers are indifferent between them and unwilling to distinguish them; otherwise they are two commodities. Technics, in this respect, has survived as part of the mainstream of economics. It is scarcely recognized even nowadays that the competitive determination of price and output, in the old *simpliste* formulation of stable intersecting curves of supply and demand, mutually independent, refers to a technically and physically defined commodity, not to a *thought-commodity*. When economics was technics, value rested on technical considerations. The cost-of-production theory of value was a direct appeal to technics, for it regarded the physical character of the valued objects as dominating and almost exclusively relevant. If they were buried deep in the rocks, necessarily they were valuable, since so much labor was required to get them out. It was not thought necessary to add that they were valuable if *in fact* they were got out, since then someone would have actually given much labor to acquire them and must have thought the effort worthwhile. In the cost-of-production theory of value, value is *ex post* (as indeed it is in the revealed preference theory of value: economics has a remarkable cyclicality). We have to ask, therefore, Is an *ex post* account of value all that we require? May it not be argued that since the conduct-chooser whom we are studying needs to be able to discern value in a thing *before* he makes efforts to possess himself of it, value ought to be such as the analyst also can discern in advance? There is an answer to this question, which might make us content with an *ex post* conception of value if we were living in a period of stable tranquility and technological stagnation. For then a man's *ex ante* picture of a proper named calendar interval would be much like his *ex post* view of that interval. The unchanging society with an unchanging economy does not require the *ex ante/ex post* bifocal view. But this answer involves a sacrifice of generalness. Even Marshall would have been dissatisfied with it, for though he left many ideas unformulated, unseparated, and unnamed, he did refer habitually to what men expect.

But there is a more incisive and readily appreciated argument against our being satisfied with a physical, *ex post*, and cost-of-production basis of value. For if the relative values of two things, or the respective quantities of them which are deemed to have equal value, are made to depend on cost of production, *which* such cost are we to take? The cost per unit may vary greatly with the number of units produced per unit of time. What will be the *relevant* output? Will it depend upon price? But we are making price depend upon output. We have two unknowns but only one equation—the technological equation which makes the cost, and thus the price, of one thing in terms of another to depend on the relation of their respective daily quantities produced. It is this *indeterminacy* that is removed by marginalism. Marginalism provides the needed second equation, so that price and quantity depend upon a schedule of cost and a schedule of desire; or the needed third equation, so that quantity supplied, quantity demanded, and price, depend on the function which binds quantity supplied to price, the function which binds quantity demanded to price, and the stipulated equality of these two quantities. The length of the elastic string of output depends upon the tension, value; but there will be no tension unless there is a pull, or an anchorage at *both* ends of the string. Cost of production is only one anchorage.

We have suggested that economic theory itself consists of the unified answer to two questions, concerning the mode of choice of conduct and the consequences of the interaction of the courses of conduct that men choose, when the mode of choice itself is an endeavor to take account and advantage of those consequences. Marginalism also has a similarly dual character and is a fusing of two conceptions. For marginalism is (if I may be allowed to invent yet another word) simply maximalism or minimalism, when those are conceived in the formal mathematical sense. It is an application of the familiar technique offered us by the differential calculus, whereby those numerical values of an argument-variable are sought to which there correspond extreme values of a function depending on that argument. It is the technique which consists in setting the derivative equal to zero and solving the resulting equation. Now setting the derivative equal to zero will not give us an equation in which the argument appears, unless the function in question is non-linear. What happy circumstance is it that ensures the nonlinearity of the function connecting the total satisfaction derived from the daily quantity consumed of a good with that daily quantity itself? It is the circumstance of diminishing marginal rate of substitution, or (let us pay some tribute to historical modes of expression) diminishing marginal utility, a fact of human nature. Marginalism makes an extraordinarily felicitous use of a characteristic of the human psyche, or should we say, of the human predicament or the Scheme of Things Entire, to justify the appeal to a formal mathematical technique of the utmost generalness of application and total freedom from any essential connection with any particular subject matter.

2. *The Presuppositions of Marginalism*

We have ascribed to the economic analyst a particular view of human affairs and a method of procedure which follows from that view. Men pursue their interests by applying reason to their circumstances. Thus if the analyst can specify their circumstances, he can predict their action. Between these two propositions there is an unstated premiss of vital effect upon the resulting body of theory. We have to assume that reason dictates at each moment to each individual interest (each person or firm) only one course of action. This implies, on one hand, a certain character of the circumstances and a certain character of human interests, and to this we shall return. But it requires also that "applying reason" shall be interpreted in all strictness. For if our proposition meant merely a loose reflection by each man on the impressions casually gathered from his environment, and an impulsive response guided by some rough notions of logical implication, there would be no telling at all what action would result. In especial, there would be no telling what aspects and details of his real circumstances he might take into account or might, through indolence or ignorance, neglect. On the contrary, if the ascription to him of reasoned conduct is to mean determinate conduct, that reason must be applied in a strict manner to a *sufficiently known set of relevant circumstances*. It is the necessary *knowledge* of circumstances which economic theory may be thought to have overlooked and failed to provide for in its assumptions. Let us therefore reformulate the first of our two propositions. Men act *rationally*. And let us define rational conduct as that conduct which the individual can *demonstrate* (at

least to himself) to be the most advantageous for him. If conduct
is to be rational in this sense, the individual's knowledge of his circumstances must be relevantly complete, and known by him to be
complete. What are those circumstances, and what is required in order
that we may fairly suppose him to know them?

He will evidently need some technological understanding of the
world, but we shall not consider the question of the advance of
knowledge of technique. We shall suppose him to have some self-
consistent picture of the physical structure of things and of how things
work. If this picture is primitive by some standards, no matter, for
we are going to show that the question of its improvement does not
arise. He must also have a full knowledge of the effect upon his
feelings of every attainable set of supplies of the various goods which
he is aware of. The exact dependence of his comfort and efficiency
upon a variety of specific sets of daily or weekly quantities of the
various existing goods must be a matter of certainty and not of conjecture. For the freedom and the need to make conjectures would
destroy determinacy. Who is to know what guess I may evolve from
a stream of assorted impressions and suggestions?

Beyond all this, however, there is a requirement of a different
order. If an individual's choice of his own conduct is to be demonstrably the best for him, he needs to know what choices are being
made by others. For the character of their actions must inevitably
affect the outcome of his own. This requirement is the foundation of
much that economics has to say. For of course when we speak of "the
individual" we mean the *general* individual, any and every individual. What is true of one, what is conceded to one, must be true
and conceded in respect of every other. *All individuals simultaneously*
must, if they are each to act rationally, have a knowledge, at the
moment when each makes his choice, of what each other individual is
choosing. Each must be free to choose, but each must know what the
others' choices will be. In this paradox, in its mode of escape from it,
we see economic analysis at its best. General equilibrium, which solves
the problem by supposing the *pre-reconciliation of choices*, is a remarkable idea both in its powers and in its limitations. Its power
to solve the paradox of rational choice is intellectually beautiful and
must give it a grip upon our thoughts. But this power is condi-

tional upon the choices we are studying being *simultaneous*. If we are to claim that the world of men's actions is rational, that world or system of actions must embrace *every* action: there must be nothing left outside. If all such actions are simultaneous, it follows that the world we study must be deemed a timeless or momentary world. Rationality and time are alien to each other. This is the severe limitation imposed upon the analyst by his chosen method, that method to which marginalism must be taken to belong if it is to have its full meaning and effect.

Marginalism belongs essentially, and finds its role only, in the conception of general equilibrium. Marginalism is an aspect of a world of rationality, and a world of rationality must of its nature be all of a piece. A rational world cannot be a curate's egg, rational in parts. One cannot be an efficient railway traveler on a railway system which works chaotically. If there is no knowing what trains will run, there is no knowing how best to plan one's journey. Marginalism is logic, and logic to be applicable must be in possession of its sufficient data, and those data, to be sufficient, must cover the entire system which is being examined.

The notion of partial equilibrium plays a great role in Anglo-Saxon economics, but its special character and purpose ought to be kept constantly in view. It is essentially a means of insight, we might almost say a didactic method, depending upon assumptions which clearly exclude it from realism even of the most restricted kind. For it depends upon *ceteris paribus*, and that dependence forbids the conclusions of partial equilibrium to be built up, or as the statisticians say, blown up, into a description of the system as a whole. When the attempt is made to put all the partial equilibria together to compose a picture of the system as a whole, it is plain that each is thereby compelled to give up its *ceteris paribus* assumption: when all the partial systems, the small bits of the economy, are adjusting themselves to each other, *cetera* are no longer *paria*. If the general adjustment is successfully completed, the result is a general equilibrium. And a general equilibrium requires pervasive perfect relevant knowledge.

The choice which confronted the economic theoretician, at the beginning of the seventies of last century, was between adherence to

rationality, strictly defined, as the essential principle of his model of
the world and of his procedure in analyzing it, on the one hand; and
on the other, the abandonment of any aspiration to see the economic
aspect of human affairs as a self-contained, unified, and simple whole,
every feature of which would reflect one and the same natural law.
The marginal principle, uniting logical generalness (the classic method
of the differential calculus in locating an extreme value of a function) with an insight into a universal feature of the response of human
nature to its desires and scarcities in mutual confrontation, swung
him decisively in favor of unity, simplicity, and perfect intelligibility.
We do not suggest that this crux was recognized. Alfred Marshall none
theless devoted his life to finding an evasion of it, by recourse to
partial equilibrium and to deliberate imprecision of argument. He did
this in full awareness of an ultimately self-contradictory task. An
economist cast in Marshall's mold would have to be protean, changing
his assumptions, posture and approach as each fresh kind of problem
arrived, yet prepared to draw some distillation of insight from all
of the mutually exclusive sets of assumptions; taking them together,
by some extralogical or nonlogical process, despite their contradictions.

3. *Marginalism and Measure*

The task begun by Quesnay, of exhibiting economic society as a
system, an organism, and a unity, was essentially completed by the
marginalists. Quesnay's invention (perhaps suggested by the physiology which he knew as a physician) was that of the *system of
internecessary*, or *intertributary*, *activities*, a skein of activities each
supporting, and supported by, the system as a whole. The living
animal exemplifies and doubtless originated the idea. The organs and
their functions compose something which can operate only in virtue
of the combined presence and operation of these components, and
each component could have no continuing life except as part of the
living creature as a whole. Quesnay's analogy showed the Farmers, the
Proprietors, and the Artisans as necessary, each to all and all to
each. Moreover, their activities had to be conducted each on a scale
appropriate to that of the others. There was a *technological constraint*
on the sizes of the flows of goods going from one sector to another.
The artisans, for example, had to receive enough raw materials, di-

rectly or indirectly, from the Farmers to be able to manufacture the wares which they supplied in exchange for materials and sustenance combined. However, the technological constraint did not amount to determination of the flows. Had the Proprietors had a stronger taste for manufactures, relatively to their taste for food, it might (when we consider the matter in the light of our own insights) have been possible for the Artisans to exact from them a larger food supply. The total *value* of the flows supplied by any sector could still have been shown as equal to the total value of the flows received by it, even if the physical quantities involved had been changed. Something more was needed, beyond the bare principle of technological internecessity, to account completely for the precise character of a Tableau Economique. That something was the tastes of the participants. The notion of subjective marginalism made it possible to transform the Tableau into a General Equilibrium.

The self-containedness and self-sufficiency of the Tableau are, of course, necessary to the idea of the General Equilibrium. The General Equilibrium is an equilibrium of exchanges, and the exchanges form a closed system without loose ends or quantities not brought into a final balance. That self-containedness is equally necessary to the macroeconomic conception of society. The heart of the Keynesian theory, in its arithmetical aspects, is the necessity for output as a whole to be absorbed either in consumption or in investment. Both of these conceptions thus involve an accountancy, a procedure involving addition. Things which can be added together are, by the necessities of that procedure, either themselves scalar quantities, one-dimensional entities each representable by *one number*, or else are explicit arrays of such. Now the intersectoral flows of the Tableau or of the Leontief system or of the Keynesian macroeconomic system are composed of an ineffable diversity of real goods. How can they be so represented as to be *additive*? The answer may be said to be what makes economics possible, the notion of value. Value, however, is not something which resides in objects themselves, in the sense that mass or volume does. Value springs from a relation between the character of an object and the desires or needs of a human individual. Value is *subjective*. How then can value serve as a *public* measure, something recognized by all members of society as a universal standard? How can the value of a given object, or of a given quantity of some commodity, be one and the same for individuals of widely different temperaments, natures, and backgrounds? The public validity of value is achieved by the market. Those who exchange goods on a market adjust the daily or weekly (*et cetera*) quantities they offer or demand to such levels that, *at the margin*, their preferences, their rates of substitution, coincide with market prices, and these latter are, of course, the reflection of the mass of individual preferences taken as a whole. It is the notion of balance at the margin which makes possible the *scalar* measurement of collections of goods of wide-ranging diversity. Marginalism provides measure.

This measure is of course a very different thing from the length or mass which are attributes of an object in itself. Valuation is an act of some one mind. Many circumstances and considerations, unrelated to the object in question except via that mind, can influence and affect the evaluation. In particular, the daily or weekly quantity in which some good is already due to be received by the valuing individual will affect the price he is willing to pay for one extra daily or weekly unit. By altering his intake of this good, he can vary the number of weekly units of some other good, or of purchasing power in general, which he would regard as exact compensation for the loss of one marginal unit of the good in question. Thus he has under his control his own marginal rate of substitution of one good for another. But he will get the most possible anticipated satisfaction out of a given expenditure devoted to these particular goods taken together if he so adjusts his purchased quantities that his marginal rate of substitution is equal to the ratio in which the goods exchange for each other on the market. When *every* member of the society has thus adjusted his shopping list, there will be effective *unanimity* concerning the relative values of the two goods, and this unanimity will attach itself to the market prices, which are themselves a consequence of the mass of individual marginal valuations all taken together. The values of the two goods in terms of each other are thus public and generally accepted facts. For the moment, they represent for each private person as much an objective fact as the barometer reading. They will be seized upon by accountants and by statisticians and used as building blocks of a vast edifice of company accounts or of national accounts;

they will enter into the reckoning of GNP and of growth rates and of the balance of payments. The marginal principle will have conjured scalar objectivity and publicly accepted measure out of subjective diversity.

The central enigma, the most elusive and the most important theoretical problem for Adam Smith and his successors in the classical tradition, was that of the distribution of the total product. The length at which they discussed it was in inverse ratio to their success in solving it. It was not solved, in any incisive and complete fashion, until the marginalists in the second wave of their assault brought the new weapon to bear on the factor market as they had on the product market twenty years earlier. If it were asked who was the originator of mathematical economics, the masterly professional style and sweep of Cournot would give him the award. But another name deserves mention as the inventor of ideas peculiarly vital to economists. A conscript to the ranks of economic theoreticians, all unconscious of his plight, was Euler, Euler of the theorem. (Of course he has other claims: Euler's differential equation is the general basis of the turnpike theorem.) With Euler's somewhat posthumous assistance, the marginalists solved the income-distribution problem, within their own terms of reference, by means of the notions of diminishing marginal product, constant returns to scale, and perfect competition. The first two of these give us a production-surface generated by a straight ray pivoted at the origin of three mutually orthogonal axes, which at first coincides with one of the two "horizontal" axes and then swings up and over to coincide with the other. This is the linear homogeneous production function. The third notion, perfect competition, renders this linearity expressible in value terms as well as in physical terms. The demonstration of the exact exhaustion of the product under these conditions was the work of Wicksteed, Wicksell, and John Bates Clark. But let us instead consider the elegant simplicity of Irving Fisher's visual three-dimensional geometry.

Its essential element is a rigid rectangular plate, of which one corner is placed at the origin of the coordinate system while the diagonally opposite corner touches some point on the surface determined by making adjacent edges of the plate lie vertically above the two horizontal axes. We thus have the plate making contact with the surface along a straight line through the origin and the point which represents the actual combination of factor quantities and output quantity that we are going to study. It also makes contact with the two vertical walls of the coordinate system, which, if we call the vertical axis z, will be the xz-plane at the yz-plane. Now let a spider start walking from the production point, say (x_i, y_i, z_i) along one edge of the plate till it reaches the yz-plane. We may suppose without appreciable loss of generalness that this first leg of its walk is downhill. On reaching the yz-plane it turns through a right angle and marches down the next edge of the plate, along its contact line with the yz-plane, until it comes to the origin. It has now "exhausted the total product," z_i. But in doing so, it has paid the factor bill for factor x at the rate of that factor's marginal product, for that marginal product is represented by the slope of the first edge which the spider traced, namely, the edge parallel, in the horizontal plane, to the x-axis, while the quantity employed of factor x is represented by the horizontal component of the spider's walk along this first edge. Now the spider has also paid the factor bill for factor y, in walking down the second edge, by an argument precisely similar to that concerning factor x. It has precisely paid each of the two factor bills, and in doing so it has precisely exhausted the total product. It has out-Eulered Euler.

In the adding-up problem and its solution, marginalism is exhibited, I think, as indispensable to economic theory. For the abstract, idealized construction which we call the theory of value, the adding-up problem was a crucial test. All hung on it. To be able to show that Quesnay's self-sustaining, closed economy could be rendered determinate by a principle which met the overriding condition of balance and self-containedness was the conclusive triumph. And this truth, if accepted, illustrates another. Economic theory cannot be a logically unified, omnicompetent, and perfectly general system able to answer all questions and reconcile all insights. For the general rational equilibrium has to be timeless. Rational conduct must be fully informed conduct, the necessary data include the choices being made by others, the possession by each individual interest of a knowledge of the choices being made by all other individuals can be achieved only by a systematic pre-reconciliation, and this must encompass *all* choices with which our universe of discourse concerns itself. Thus these choices must be made simultaneously, the making of one involving and presupposing the making of all the others. Yet what has a time-less construction to say to the real Scheme of Things, the human predicament of consciousness, which consists in *perpetual finding out*? What has a world where knowledge is already complete, and everything is known, to do with a world where choice is about the future, but knowledge is only about the past? The whole business of choice, decision, policy making, deliberative conduct, is necessitated by our being at all moments headed into a void, a space empty of observed fact. There is an utter contradiction between the pre-suppositions of the general rational equilibrium and the actual sit-uation of human beings. Yet the general equilibrium indispensably illuminates our concerns. This is what I mean in claiming that the economist's great mosaic of theory must contain pictures somewhat mutually incongruous. We cannot expect to survey the whole without adjusting our mental posture from time to time.

Great themes are to be found in our discipline which make no use at all of the marginal principle. These themes, it therefore appears, are not concerned with economizing, with the search of men for the best use of their resources. In his classic article, "A Suggestion for Simplifying the Theory of Money," Sir John Hicks noted that the traditional quantity theory has no place for marginal analysis.[1] Indeed, the quantity theory in the form $MV = PT$ makes no mention of choice, preference, or utility, but is purely mechanical. In its Cambridge form, $M = kY$, it does refer to the desire of people to keep a money stock equal to some proportion of their income. But even here the notion of marginal balance seems to be absent. In the *General Theory*, Keynes says that "we can suppose that the schedule of liquidity-preference relating the quantity of money to the rate of interest is given by a smooth curve which shows the rate of interest falling as the quantity of money is increased." A smooth curve can, of course, be differentiated, and thus the notion of margin is plainly implicit in Keynes's statement. Even he, however, does not appear to use marginal terms explicitly. That final terminological clamp-

1. *Economica*, n.s., vol. 2, no. 5.

ing together of the theory of money and the theory of value was the work of Sir John Hicks in his remarkable article. There is one puzzle in that article. Although the *Treatise on Money* had long since presented the speculative motive for desiring a money stock (it is implicit in the discussion of the "two views" and the bull-bear position in the gilt-edged market), Sir John does not give it the prominence it seems quantitatively to deserve. Nonetheless, what Sir John Hicks did in his article was in effect to unify the two[2] valid Keynesian motives for holding assets in liquid form: the transactions motive and the speculative motive. Hicks shows that when money is held in preference to the income-earning assets it could buy, this is because of the expense and danger of investing it in such assets. By his explicit marginalization of the theory of money, Sir John Hicks gave the final touch of formal beauty to the work of Wicksell and Keynes (to leave aside Ricardo) in bringing together the theory of relative prices and the theory of absolute (i.e., money) prices in a single whole. Even here, there remains a difficulty and a doubt.

What is money doing in a theory of rational conduct which can, in the nature of things, in the Scheme of Things Entire, be set only in a timeless system? For money is that which is valued only because it can be exchanged for something else. And what would be the use, in a timeless world, of exchanging something which is enjoyable in virtue of its own properties for something which has no *inherent* desirability? What would be the use of a mere exchange counter in a world where there was not going to be any time to exchange it? Money is that asset which enables a man to *put off* deciding what to buy. It frees him from the barter necessity of making up his mind, at the moment of selling a real object, what other object to accept in exchange. In a world whence putting-off is excluded by assumption, there is no place for money. Pre-reconciliation must be in terms of objects wanted for their own sake. Money opens the Pandora's box of expectation and uncertainty, the limitless field of imagination is brought into view, and determinacy must evaporate.

Let me try to deal with a contention which may at this stage of my argument be justifiably raised. Even if the materials to which

---

2. The precautionary motive could be satisfied by holding nonliquid assets, were it not for the danger of their depreciating in money terms in the meantime. But such a fear of capital loss is simply the speculative motive.

marginal analysis is applied, it may be said, are mere figments and conjectures, does this invalidate or stultify the use of logic? Guesswork may be all we have to go on, but if so, will it not be logical to apply logic to our derivation of conduct and policy from our guesses? I think there are here two questions. First, are fine adjustments worth while, when the whole foundations upon which they are calculated are liable to unheralded and extensive shifts and upheavals? Speculation and marginalism are an uneasy team to drive. Secondly, is not marginalism intended to afford certainty and exactness, an unquestionable guide to the precise character of the most advantageous conduct? It is surely out of place in a world of restless conjecture, invention, and deliberately sought transformations of technology and taste. In the fluid unstable world which has so greatly accelerated from the manageable Victorian pace of change, marginalism must have lost some of its commanding influence and relevance.

And yet, we cannot make sense of things, even from the most pragmatic viewpoint and for the most practical purposes, without a frame of coherence, a glimpse of what *would* constitute an orderly, rational, unified economic organization of affairs. In finding my way from one place to another, I cannot follow the great-circle course, because there are streets, hills, rivers, and geographical "accidents" of every sort. But a conception of the terrestrial planet as a spheroid is not therefore dispensable.

Retrospect and Prospect

A. W. Coats

I

I<small>F</small> Mark Blaug's original provocative title, "There Never Was a Marginal Revolution," was justified, the Bellagio conference assembled under false pretenses to commemorate a non-event.[1] This was a disquieting prospect, since it was already apparent that no person of sound mind would willingly quit the Villa Serbelloni betimes! Fortunately no such drastic action proved necessary, for despite general agreement that the term "revolution" was too specific and too dramatic to describe the advent of marginalism in economics, especially if interpreted in a Kuhnian sense, most of the participants considered that Jevons', Menger's, and Walras's contributions constituted a genuine landmark or breakthrough in the development of economic theory. Even so, it proved surprisingly difficult to reach a consensus as to the common characteristics of their contributions. Close study of their works tended to focus attention on the differences rather than the similarities between them, and at first Erich Streissler doubted whether Menger could properly be termed a marginalist, arguing that there were such striking differences between the Jevonian, Austrian, and Walrasian streams of thought that it was misleading to regard them as component parts of a single whole. This issue recurred several times, but eventually there was unanimous agreement that all three authors had rejected cost-of-production theories of value and had acknowledged the significance of consumer's equilibrium at the point where the marginal utilities of all commodities purchased are proportional to their price. Hence if there was, in fact, a "multiple discovery"—a question considered in Section II below—then this was its central core.

1. Readers will note that the revised title is in a more defensive, interrogative form. However, as the main thrust of Blaug's argument is unchanged, it would be a mistake to interpret the revision as evidence that academic controversy merely destroys certainty and substitutes sophisticated doubt!

Beyond this, most participants also acknowledged other common characteristics of the three cofounders of modern marginalism—their emphasis on demand ("subjective") as against supply influence on price; the tendency to turn away from macro theory to micro theory; the narrowing of the scope of economics, by concentrating on analysis per se rather than its applications to practical problems; the impulse given to efforts to coordinate the theories of value and distribution; and the enhanced precision of language and techniques, especially (apart from the Austrians) by the use of mathematics.

Admittedly these conclusions are by no means startlingly novel; and there was no concerted effort to assess the importance of the various elements. Nevertheless, given the notorious difficulties of obtaining any consensus of opinion among a group of economists, the conclusions are worth recording. And while there was no disposition to apply either Kuhn's paradigm concept or his theory of scientific revolutions to the new economic theories of the 1870's, the Kuhnian framework helped to sharpen the focus of our discussion by pinpointing relevant questions. For example, how far did the marginal revolution constitute a break with the past? How far were any or all of the key concepts already present in the classical literature? Was there an intellectual "crisis" resulting from the acknowledged deficiencies of the cost-of-production approach to value? Did the new theories eliminate inherited theoretical or empirical anomalies, or did they merely entail a shift of attention to new, hitherto unrecognized problems? The list could, of course, be greatly extended; and at Bellagio issues of this kind were most carefully considered with reference to Jevons and the British tradition. The role of utilitarianism, stressed by Robert Black and George Stigler, is especially relevant here, while Neil de Marchi's essay represents a serious attempt to delineate the intellectual background to Jevons' *Theory* and to specify the precise reasons why his predecessors failed to actualized the possibilities inherent in earlier versions of marginalism. This example suggested the need for more detailed parallel studies of German and French economic writings which would reveal the precise intellectual qualities and the limitations of Menger's and Walras's predecessors.[2]

2. Of course, much preliminary work on these lines has already been undertaken. See, for example, the articles by Jaffé and Hutchison, above; and Emil Kauder, *A History of Marginal Utility Theory* (Princeton, 1965).

II

Although Kuhn's ideas did not figure prominently in the conference discussions, Robert Merton's concept of multiple discoveries was referred to in several sessions. It was agreed that Blaug should give the matter extended treatment in the revised version of his paper, as it was one facet of the general problem of explanation in the history of economics, a problem that underlay all our deliberations. Here I shall take the opportunity to comment on his views.

As Blaug rightly emphasizes, multiple discoveries are of limited interest if regarded merely as recurrent but isolated and accidental phenomena, and he considers that they become interesting only if seen as component parts of an explanatory model based on "the idea that the development of a science is to some extent predictable."[3] However, later in his essay, when discussing the diffusion as opposed to the genesis and emergence of marginal utility economics, he concedes a less rigorous criterion, contending that the historian is not called upon to predict, "retrodict," or even to explain, but merely to "make past events intelligible." The distinction between "predictable" and "intelligible" is significant, since Blaug is well aware of the protracted controversy about the nature of explanation in science and history which has continued among philosophers of science and historians intermittently since the 1940's. In my view, Blaug imposes too rigorous a standard in Section III of his essay, where he denies that Merton's concept of multiple discoveries is applicable to the so-called marginal revolution of the 1870's.

It is, of course, obvious that mid-nineteenth-century economics was very different from the highly institutionalized, densely populated kind of scientific community envisaged by Merton, in which repeated rediscoveries are so commonplace as to be hardly worthy of notice. But Merton did not hesitate to apply his concept of multiples to situations other than "mature science," as Blaug implies.[4] Admittedly

3. Blaug, "Was There a Marginal Revolution?," above. Throughout Section II of this Postscript, references to this source will be cited in the text.

4. Blaug, Section II. Merton in his essay, "Singletons and Multiples in Scientific Discovery," *Proceedings of the American Philosophical Society*, 105, no. 5 (1961), selected most of his examples of multiples from the nineteenth and twentieth centuries. But he added that the concept of multiples, which was in fact confirmed by its own history, had been "in the air" for three centuries. Ibid., p. 477.

in the decade or so before 1870 the number of "scientific" economists
was limited, the prevailing level of communications was imperfect,
and there were significant differences in the intellectual climate and
ruling economic ideas in the respective socioeconomic environments in
which Jevons, Menger, and Walras developed their ideas. Yet it is
surely unnecessary to require, as Blaug does, as a precondition of a
marginalist multiple that there should be "one economic science in
the 1860's . . . a heritage shared between economists all over the
world, studying the same treatises, reading the same journals, employing a common set of tools in the analysis of a similar range of
problems." Nor is it necessary to insist that "marginal utility economics was, in some sense, inevitable," "a perfectly predictable phenomenon," or that "economic science as such was inexorably moving
towards the discovery of marginal utility somewhere around the
middle of the century." The historian is concerned with probabilities,
not with certainties, with "empirical and contingent states of affairs,"
not with "unalterable logical necessities."[5] Hence, while it may be
impossible to account for the precise timing and location of the
discoveries or to explain why it was Jevons, Menger, and Walras rather
than some other individuals who made the decisive breakthrough,
there seems no reason to abandon the hypothesis that their contributions represented a natural and unsurprising (though by no means
inevitable)[6] product of the evolution of economic analysis "propelled
forward by the desire to refine, to improve, to perfect, a desire which
economists share with all other scientists."[7] Indeed, in the absence

5. Cf. Charles Frankel, "Explanation and Interpretation in History," in
Theories of History, ed. Patrick Gardiner (Glencoe, Ill., 1959), p. 416.
6. It has been well said that history is analogous to the development of a
play in which each step is explicable even though it was not fully predictable,
since "given the data we have up to a certain point, there are a number of
possible turns of fortune, none of which would seem to us inexplicable. . . . Explanation is retrospective, prediction prospective. . . . Hence, freedom of choice,
which is between future alternatives, is not compatible with the existence of
causes for every event." Michael Scriven, "Truisms as the Grounds for Historical
Explanation," in Gardiner, p. 470.
7. Mark Blaug, *Economic Theory in Retrospect*, 2d ed. (Homewood, Ill.,
1968), p. xi. Having on previous occasions criticized Blaug's "absolutist" approach from a moderate relativist standpoint, the writer derives some relish from
this apparent reversal of our respective allegiances. However, our difference is
doubtless a matter of degree rather than kind. In his revised Bellagio paper Blaug
does not deny that there was a breakthrough in the 1870's, though he rejects
the term "paradigm," preferring to say that after 1875 economists developed
"a new view of their research agenda."

of such an explanation the approximate coincidence in timing of the marginal revolution remains a mystery, a most unsatisfactory state of affairs.[8]

The principal grounds for this contention can be stated briefly. All three codiscoverers were concerned with essentially the same basic problems and, in certain crucial respects, arrived at the same solutions.[9] Their discoveries were not accidental in the sense that the innovators knew not what they were doing; on the contrary, the innovations were the direct outcome of deliberate and self-conscious attempts by serious scientific thinkers to dispose of unsolved problems in value and price theory which had long been recognized as obstacles to the analysis and comprehension of market phenomena. These problems were not peripheral, but central to economic science, and all three codiscoverers were aware of the scientific importance of their findings, although, being merely human, they could not foresee the long-run response of subsequent generations of economists. There were, of course, significant differences in the ways in which they presented and propagated their findings, differences largely attributable to personality traits. Yet it is significant that within a comparatively short period both Jevons and Walras grasped and vigorously proclaimed the importance of their findings, thereby behaving exactly like many other scientific discoverers; while Menger, though a less energetic self-publicist and less of a rebel against tradition, became the effective leader of perhaps the most coherent and tightly knit doctrinal school in the history of economics.

Blaug quite properly warns against the dangers of undue reliance on hindsight, "rational reconstruction" of the past, and *post hoc ergo propter hoc* reasoning. But given the historian's acknowledged inability to predict or "retrodict," how else can he proceed?[10] In the present instance hindsight is inescapable, for the scientific importance

8. "All explanations are attempts to explain away impediments of some kind. They are efforts to deprive puzzles, mysteries and blockages of their force, and hence, existence." Robert Brown, *Explanations in Social Science* (London, 1963), p. 41.

9. Cf. above, Section II.

10. In response to this question Blaug proposes counterfactual history. I would certainly welcome efforts to apply the multiple-discovery hypothesis to some of the unsuccessful claimants in the history of economics, such as the Marxists, underconsumptionists, or monetary cranks. Even so, no one familiar with the work of the so-called new economic historians is likely to overrate the prospects of successful counterfactual analysis in the history of economic ideas.

of any discovery or group of discoveries is seldom recognized immediately; it must await the collective judgment of the relevant scientific community. This judgment is neither eternally fixed nor irrevocable, nor should it be supposed that the process of assimilating new discoveries is predictable. Both these considerations help to explain "the ironic fate which history visited on the founders." Moreover, the delayed acceptance of marginal utility analysis does not prove that it was an anomaly, a sharp and wholly unaccountable breach with the past; it merely confirms our existing knowledge that the scientific community was small and unorganized, its members unresponsive to this particular innovation, and its communications inadequate. It is perfectly true, as Blaug insists, that the concept of a "marginal revolution" is the product of a belated historical *reinterpretation*; but the same cannot be said of the *fact* of multiple discovery. This was quickly and correctly perceived by Jevons and Walras, who not only soon knew of each other's work and acknowledged its importance but also quickly discovered several earlier anticipations, which they regarded as further evidence of the significance of their own discoveries. Menger, too, after some delay, recognized elements in common between his own work and theirs. Alfred Marshall not only acknowledged the significance of Jevons' ideas but also regarded multiples as familiar and recurrent phenomena in the history of economics;[11] while in the United States, J. B. Clark subsequently acknowledged the parallels between his own independent discovery and the new ideas of the 1870's. As we are concerned with probabilities rather than certainties, these facts constitute supporting evidence for the view that the Jevons-Menger-Walras discoveries were not merely random occurrences; and this view is reinforced by our knowledge of the six anticipations mentioned by Blaug, which serve to further diminish our sense of surprise at the approximate coincidence in timing of their publications.

As far as we know, the marginalist multiple occurred only in

11. Cf. Marshall to L. L. Price, quoted by Coats, above, in the essay "The Economic and Social Context of the Marginal Revolution," n. 10. In Merton's "Singletons" essay, p. 475, he quotes Macaulay as saying that "the doctrine of rent, now universally received by political economists, was propounded, at almost the same moment, by two writers unconnected with each other. Preceding speculators had long been blundering round about it; and it could not possibly have been missed much longer by the most heedless inquirer." Was this another "to some extent predictable" development in economics?

western Europe and the United States. It is therefore unreasonable to demand that it should be the product of "one economic science in the 1860's . . . a heritage shared between economists all over the world, studying the same treatises, reading the same journals, and employing a common set of tools in the analysis of a similar range of problems." On the whole the Bellagio participants tended to emphasize the differences rather than the similarities between the pre-1870 British, French, and German streams of economic thought. Nevertheless, given our limited knowledge of the dissemination of economic ideas in western Europe during that period, I submit that it is still too early to justify an outright dismissal of the possibility that Jevons, Menger, and Walras drew in some degree on a "shared heritage" of ideas. For they were, after all, reacting in their different ways against cost-of-production theories; and there were certainly some elementary economic ideas held in common in several European countries. Admittedly most conference members felt that the shared heritage consisted mainly of crude ideologies and simplistic policy recommendations. However, before casting a final judgment it may be advisable to reexamine the filiation of scientific ideas rather than the more obvious popular currents, and this may be another topic for future research.

III

Apart from the issue of multiple discoveries, the problem of explanation in intellectual history also underlay the repeated references to environmental influences on the formulation and diffusion of economic ideas which occurred throughout our discussions. Far more attention was paid to the circumstances directly impinging on intellectuals—the climate of opinion, the character and availability of teaching and research opportunities, and the channels of communication among scientists—than to more general socioeconomic conditions—the stage of economic development, the level of prosperity, or the social structure. It will therefore be convenient to dispose of the latter category first, before considering questions of professionalization and academicization. Environmental influences on individual economists will be considered in Section IV below in connection with the role of biography in the history of economics.

Although our Bellagio group contained no committed environmentalists, several participants were unwilling to endorse the writer's emphasis on conditions endogenous (or internal) to the growth of economic ideas.[12] Streissler, for instance, argued that Menger's interest in commercial crises and the marketability of commodities might be due to his experience of depression; that his stress on monopoly might reflect the inadequacy of transport conditions in Austria; and that the late nineteenth and early twentieth century growth of large-scale enterprise might explain the subsequent application of marginalism to problems of pricing policy. However, the last of these suggestions met with some scepticism from George Stigler and Donald Winch. Several participants tried to explain the marginalists' preoccupation with choice and allocation problems in environmentalist terms, and Ronald Meek displayed considerable enthusiasm for the hypothesis that Jevons' obsession with the scarcity of natural resources might be due to his contrasting experiences in England and Australia, where he was struck by the abundance of resources in a frontier society. Tamotsu Matsuura's suggestion that the reception of marginalism in Japan was influenced by the current concern with the imbalance between supply and demand provoked some controversy as others questioned whether this represented a problem of scarcity or of surplus. Moreover it was difficult to grasp the connection between these environmental conditions and the ideological motives to which Matsuura attached so much importance in explaining the development of Japanese economic thought. Finally, Blaug criticized Craufurd Goodwin's hypothesis that marginal utility theory was a luxury good produced (or consumed?) only in countries at a certain stage of economic development, an observation that provoked several comments on the relationship between GNP and the level of intellectual development in a given society. From Piero Barucci's account of the Italian case it appeared that the comparatively rapid assimilation of marginalism was mainly attributable to the compatibility between Italian and western European culture, rather than to the social or economic conditions in that country.

Throughout our discussions general socioeconomic conditions were usually considered only *en passant*, as possible sources of enlightenment on particular matters, not as component parts of a compre-

12. Cf. Coats, above, ''Economic and Social Context,'' Appendix. The following paragraph merely provides a sample of the issues raised.

hensive explanatory model. By contrast, environmental factors directly affecting intellectuals were examined much more fully, especially in relation to universities and the professionalization of economics. Several conference papers had suggested that the marginal revolution marked the beginning of modern professional economics, or that the diffusion of marginalist ideas was directly influenced by changing academic conditions, and in the course of our discussions efforts were made to distinguish between professionalism as such and academic or intellectual values and standards. Needless to say, there was no consensus of opinion on the choice of terms, and no disposition to accept Stigler's clear and simple definition of a professional as a paid specialist, as contrasted with a gentleman amateur. Most of the elements in customary definitions of a professional received some attention, such as source of income, type of occupation, nature of subject matter, level of expertise, and degree of self-consciousness (professional identity). But it was recognized that the nature of a profession probably differed from one society to another and changed over time, and as research on these aspects of the sociology of economics is still in its infancy, though growing rapidly, it is hardly surprising that no heroic attempts were made to provide a historical synthesis of the various elements.

In considering the impact of academic conditions on the diffusion of marginalism, Streissler was by far the most enthusiastic and committed environmentalist. His account of the origins and growth of Menger's Vienna "circle of patronage" may have aroused feelings of envy among some of the Anglo-American participants, and he agreed to expand his treatment of these matters in the revised version of his paper. It was generally accepted that the establishment of university chairs was neither a necessary nor a sufficient condition of the development of scientific economics, and this not merely because of the difference between quantity and quality. There were, for example, several chairs in Italy in the eighteenth and nineteenth centuries, but, like the cameralists in Germany, the incumbents would nowadays rarely be regarded as *bona fide* economists. This raised difficult semantic issues in defining the field; while Stigler stressed analytic ability as the principal criterion of scientific achievement in economics, others claimed that professionalism in applied economics should also be considered. The early Italian and German professors had been more concerned with practice than with theory, but in late-nineteenth-century Continental universities the fact that professors were state servants did not prevent them from undertaking serious scholarship of a highly theoretical character. In these circumstances, as in the Anglo-Saxon tradition, there was no necessary connection between the subject matter taught in universities and the careers followed by students; and the suggestion that Austrian ministers of finance were often economists who had failed to make the grade, whereas British chancellors of the exchequer were often successful classicists, provoked intriguing speculations.

It was clear that both strong personalities and institutional conditions could directly affect the growth of economic science—for example, by perpetuating certain conventional subdivisions of the discipline. Instances of this included the tripartite compartmentalization in Germany into economic theory, economic policy, and public finance; the position of economics in Continental law schools, where it was well supported, but inhibited; and the difficulty of establishing economics in British and American universities because the curriculum was dominated by traditional subjects. Most remarkable of all, however, was the extraordinary dichotomy between marginalist and Marxist economics in Japan. Matsuura's account of this situation both fascinated and baffled most of the conference members, and the mind boggled at the prospect of students writing two doctrinally inconsistent species of answers in examinations shared by professors of conflicting ideological persuasions.

The relationship between intellectual, academic, and professional values and standards was most thoroughly examined with reference to Stigler's paper. Blaug interpreted Stigler's argument as presupposing a direct causal sequence from professionalization to abstraction from policy questions, and thence to theoretical rigor and the predilection for marginal utility; but Stigler replied that although the logic of theoretical science had made academic economists receptive to marginalism, the adoption of marginal utility as such was neither an inevitable nor a necessary step. He considered that intellectualism —the quest for profound understanding of phenomena—was distinct from and antecedent to professionalism. While displaying genuine or pretended allegiance to intellectual values, the professional academic would also be motivated by other considerations, such as the desire to gain influence and authority, to occupy the most prestigious chair, or to become president of his professional association. Even so, academics also acquired, as a matter of training, habit, and self-esteem, a set of values that transcended those of the community at large. Winch, however, argued that Stigler had drawn too sharp a distinction between theory and policy and between intellectual and academic values. Despite their keen interest in policy questions, the classical economists had also upheld intellectual values and had formed a kind of quasi-professional self-conscious group or social circle, outside the universities.

Obviously the discussions of these matters, and the related questions of the diffusion of economic ideas considered in Section V below, were suggestive rather than definitive. A study of the growth of the economics profession must take account of a complex bundle of variables entering into the concept of a profession, any one of which is dependent on particular historical and environmental conditions. It must involve close examination of university conditions, including, as Black suggested, conditions of entry into academic appointments and the relationships between the academic establishment and intellectual deviants and outsiders. The extent to which academic institutions are subject to external pressures varies enormously from place to place and time to time, as students of the history of academic freedom know only too well; and the professionalization of academic science emphasizes the importance of professional self-consciousness, professional identity, and group relationships, all of which have important sociopsychological dimensions. The research possibilities for historians of economics are so obvious that they need not be enumerated here.

IV

The most explicit clash of opinions at Bellagio arose in connection with the role of biographical research in the history of economics. Discussion of this issue was focused on the conflicting views of William Jaffé and George Stigler, which had been mentioned in several conference papers, and most participants were already familiar with the general argument of Jaffé's 1965 paper, "Biography and Economic

Analysis.''[13] However the debate transcended the particular case of Walras and embraced more fundamental aspects of the problem of historical explanation. For example, what is the historian of economics seeking to explain? What kinds of data and methods of analysis are appropriate? And when can he feel confidence that a given explanation is sufficient for his purpose?

In this controversy Stigler played his accustomed role of principal iconoclast, claiming that the historian who merely collected biographical facts was setting himself too easy a task and arguing that too much knowledge of an individual's biography might well cloud the historian's judgment of his intellectual performance (as, for example, in the case of Wicksell). Others readily acknowledged the difficulty in deciding which facts to collect and when to stop accumulating data, but proposed no simple method of determining which facts were relevant. Thus there was general support for Jaffé's conviction that the details of Walras's toilet training and sexual proclivities seemed, a priori, to have little or no bearing on the genesis, development, or eventual significance of his general equilibrium theory. But it was less easy to say why this was so or to feel confident that these matters were totally irrelevant to Walras's professional career and effectiveness as an economist. Biographical information obviously has illustrative value and may serve as literary embellishment; but it is exceedingly difficult to draw the line between inconsequential descriptive and significant explanatory data.[14] At many points in our discussions the

13. *Western Economic Journal* 3 (Summer 1965): 223-32.

14. This may be an appropriate point to note that in recent philosophical discussions the interdependence of description and explanation has been stressed. As Karl Popper has noted, historical explanations frequently turn on ''the logic of the situation''; and as causal explanations are context-dependent and there is said to be a continuum linking causal and non-causal statements, it is hardly surprising if mere historians of economics fail to agree. Cf. William H. Dray, ed., *Philosophical Analysis and History* (New York, 1966), especially the essays by A. Donagan, ''The Popper-Hempel Theory Reconsidered,'' pp. 127-59; and Michael Scriven, ''Causes, Connections and Conditions in History,'' pp. 238-64. Also Gordon Leff, *History and Social Theory* (London, 1969), chap. 4; and Fred D. Newman, *Explanation by Description* (Paris, 1968), passim. On the variety of explanations in natural science and history, cf. Ernest Nagel, ''Some Issues in the Logic of Historical Analysis'': ''The explanatory premises in history, as in the natural sciences, include a number of implicitly assumed laws, as well as many explicitly (though usually incompletely) formulated statements of initial conditions. They may be statements of regularities well attested in some social science, or they may be uncodified assumptions taken from common experience; they may be universal statements of invariable concomitance,

dearth of relevant biographical data was a noticeable impediment to understanding. For some purposes it was necessary to know precisely how and whence an economist derived his ideas—whether from formal instruction, casual reading, or word of mouth—and this was as important in studying the diffusion of ideas as in studying their origin and development. At other times it was desirable to know why a given individual decried or rejected the currently accepted ideas or problems in his field, while elevating others to a central place in his work. Biographical information might also help to explain an economist's mode of presentation, not merely in a general sense (e.g., Jevons' eagerness as contrasted with Marshall's caution), but also in particular matters. The much-debated subject of marginalism and mathematics was relevant here. What minimal knowledge of mathematics, if any, was essential to an understanding of marginal utility or equilibrium analysis? How much mathematics did each of the cofounders know, and how far did they utilize their knowledge either in solving analytical problems or in publishing their findings? Several participants felt there was a need for more detailed and systematic information on the state of mathematical knowledge, especially calculus, in the mid and later nineteenth century. This aspect of the educational environment was relevant both to the individual case histories of the cofounders and their precursors and to the rate of acceptance of marginalism as a technical tool. It was recognized that an economist who possessed a thorough grasp of the relevant mathematics might dismiss it as misleading or inappropriate to the study of human affairs, whereas another, far less competent mathematically, might make very effective use of his limited equipment. Studies of individual biographies alone could determine how far these differences existed and were relevant in practice; and much the same was true of the sociology of economics, for example, in the processes of academicization and professionalization. Personalities and motivations were obviously important in the careers of key figures, those with leadership qualities or influence in developing and implementing institutional controls over the training, appointment, promotion, and publications of their students and colleagues.

---

or they may be statistical in form; they may assert a uniformity of temporal sequence; or they may assert some relation of co-existent dependence.'' In Gardiner, p. 377.

Having already declared an interest in these matters, I may now be in danger of overstating their importance in the Bellagio proceedings.[15] However, there is no doubt that the most significant point of disagreement during the entire conference arose from the question whether biographical information was more than just a source of convenient *ad hoc* explanations in the history of ideas. Was it true, as Jaffé had argued, that we must seek in any argument or theory ''the distinctive individuality of its author . . . [since] a great original discovery or . . . innovation, be it in economics or in any realm of scientific or artistic endeavor, is . . . the product of the imagination of some one individual whose identity marks the achievement indelibly in a thousand and one subtle ways.''[16] It should be noted that Jaffé might not now wish to stand by every word of this statement; indeed, he seemed surprised that it became the focus of controversy. But his remarks constitute an unusually clear and explicit formulation of a general issue of importance to intellectual historians. At Bellagio there was a clear division of opinion between those who (like Stigler and Blaug) called for a more explicitly analytical treatment of biographical data and those who (like Jaffé and Black) resisted the temptation to impose order and consistency on a man's life, since so many variables, including chance, play a part in determining his activities and achievements. The dangers of undue reliance on intuitive methods were recognized by all the participants, since efforts to explain a man's intellectual development in terms of this personal history could lead to bias and selectivity in the use of evidence, to the search for simple correlations between ideas and biography while subconsciously discarding evidence that failed to fit the model. This is not, of course, a problem peculiar to biographical studies; but the sceptics evidently considered that it was especially liable to occur in work of this kind. It was generally agreed that the historian of ideas must constantly ask himself whether additional knowledge of a man's life really adds anything to his knowledge of the subject's intellectual development; and while it might be impossible to discover all the relevant evidence, the grounds of explanation could be extended beyond the individual case by examining the careers of other thinkers in comparable fields, times, or places.

15. Coats, above, ''Economic and Social Context.''
16. Jaffé, p. 227.

In this connection Winch enquired whether it was thought necessary, in seeking counterexamples, to explain the individual case in terms of some general hypothetico-deductive "covering law"; but Stigler denied that this was so. In order to avoid the error of adopting a generalized explanation of an individual case it was sufficient to employ testable working hypotheses which were more general than the particular circumstance to be explained. At this point the subject was dropped, for the conference members displayed no inclination to press the issue beyond this limited, strictly pragmatic level. No attempt was made to inquire precisely what kinds of hypothesis might be appropriate to any given investigation, or to ask how such hypotheses should be tested or what would be the criteria of a satisfactory test. As a group, the conference members were reluctant to plunge too deeply into such logical and philosophical problems.[17] As Blaug remarked, while conceding that biographical information "shed light" on the development of economic ideas, he could not be sure precisely what was meant by such a statement.

No doubt some readers will regard this discussion as disappointingly inconclusive. Yet as far as I am aware, the methodological problems of biographical analysis in the history of economics were faced more clearly on this occasion than ever before. It would be optimistic to expect unanimity on a matter of this kind, where the individual historian's judgment (and perhaps his professional commitment too) may be deeply involved. Some scholars regard the

---

17. Cf. Nagel, in Gardiner, p. 385: ". . . we do not possess at present a generally accepted, explicitly formulated, and fully comprehensive schema for weighing the evidence for any arbitrarily given hypotheses, so that the logical worth of alternative conclusions relative to the evidence available for each can be compared. Judgments must be formed even on matters of supreme practical importance on the basis of only vaguely understood considerations; and in the absence of a logical canon for estimating the degree in which the evidence supports a conclusion, when judgments are in conflict each appears to be the outcome of an essentially arbitrary procedure. This circumstance affects the standing of the historian's conclusions in the same manner as the findings of other students. Fortunately, though the range of possible disagreement concerning the force of evidence for a given statement is theoretically limitless, there is a substantial agreement among men experienced in relevant matters on the relative probabilities to be assigned to many hypotheses. Such agreement indicates that, despite the absence of an explicitly formulated logic, many unformulated habits of thought embody factually warranted principles of inference. Accordingly, although there are often legitimate grounds for doubt concerning the validity of specific causal imputations in history, there appears to be no compelling reason for converting such doubt into wholesale scepticism."

investigation of an outstanding individual's life and thought as in-trinsically interesting irrespective of whether it serves to "shed light" on wider currents of thought and action. Even so, it appears that the consensus of opinion at Bellagio reflects the recent scholarly trend in the history of economics away from case studies of individual careers and key ideas towards broader sociological and comparative themes, such as the growth of scientific knowledge and the process of pro-fessionalization. Here, too, I may simply be expressing conclusions in conformity with my preconceived ideas.[18] However, the question of the diffusion of economic ideas, which is treated in the next section, represents another case in point.

V

During the past decade or so there has been a proliferation of research on the communication and assimilation of scientific ideas, much of it concerned with current conditions and future prospects, rather than past history. Quite recently, however, several historians of economics have taken an interest in these matters, and the con-ference organizers deliberately sought to encourage studies of the diffusion of marginalist ideas through time and space. The treatment of this theme in the conference papers was necessarily provisional and selective, even experimental. Nevertheless a number of significant general issues were raised in the course of our deliberations; and there can be no denying the potential riches of research possibilities in this field.

There is, of course, a close relationship between the diffusion of economic ideas and earlier themes in this postscript, such as the in-fluence of environmental factors and professionalization. Nevertheless it is convenient to consider the diffusion process separately, since it is a subject of formidable elusiveness and complexity. At the outset there are intractable definitional problems concerning the variety of eco-nomic ideas, changing channels of communication over time, and measures of the acceptance of ideas. For example, it is necessary to distinguish between scientific and popular ideas, between theoretical propositions or systems and policy recommendations; and beyond this it is essential not to confuse the mere citation of an idea (e.g.,

18. Cf. Coats, "Research Priorities in the History of Economics," *History of Political Economy* 1 (Spring 1969): 9–18.

in textbooks, whether for reasons of academic one-upmanship, or serious pedagogical purposes) with the process of substantial analytical adoption—a matter that figured prominently in Stigler's paper. It is obvious that new ideas may be mentioned and even embraced enthusiastically by persons who neither utilize nor even understand them (as, for example, in the case of Italian marginalism before 1890), and in such circumstances their scientific importance is negligible, zero, or conceivably even negative. Likewise, measures of acceptance are obviously dependent on the prior question: acceptance by whom? Is it sufficient merely to count heads; and if so, which heads? In a purely statistical sense some weighting of individual receptors is obviously needed, but this is no easy task.

Despite Stigler's effort to raise the scientific tone of the proceedings by drawing graphs to illustrate the rate of acceptance of marginal utility economics, little progress was made towards devising agreed measures of the acceptance of economic ideas. Indeed, Terence Hutchison considered that Stigler's paper significantly understated the importance of marginalism in the 1920's and 1930's; the writer expressed serious doubts about Stigler's method of identifying "prominent" American economists; and several participants questioned certain features of Goodwin's heroic typology of revolutions in economic thought. Nevertheless, in terms of the questions posed, this penultimate session proved to be one of the most stimulating of the entire conference. For example, why are certain ideas taken up and others neglected? What kinds of intellectual challenges inspire significant new ideas and what determines the length of time (i.e., "attention span") that elapses before the new impulse dies away? How far should the historian focus his attention on the scientific opinion leaders, rather than the followers? Is it possible to detect changes in the rate and quality of the acceptance of ideas as the advance of professional standards raises the "impermissible level of ignorance" in the field? How far do these standards vary between different segments of a given academic discipline, and why?

Other significant issues were mentioned in comments on media of communication, modes of presentation, and the timing of new ideas. For instance, while the presentation of new ideas in advanced scientific treatises, monographs, or learned journals necessarily restricts the potential audience, this is the relevant readership when we are considering the adoption and utilization of scientific ideas. Institutionalized communication of theoretical or scientific ideas, e.g., with the establishment of university chairs and scholarly publications, may either facilitate or inhibit the diffusion process; indeed, it may boost some signals while drowning or distorting others.

In determining the reception of ideas much will depend not only on the chosen mode of presentation (e.g., mathematical or verbal, abstract or policy-oriented) but also on the timing (e.g., the extent to which the relevant audience is preoccupied with other issues) and the existing state of scientific knowledge. If an idea is too far in advance of its time it may be ignored or dismissed, and the same may occur if it appears either irrelevant or threatening to the custodians of the ruling orthodoxy. This is why major scientific advances are so often made and initially welcomed by members of the younger generation. If the idea has practical as well as merely theoretical implications it may be embraced or rejected for non-scientific (e.g., ideological) reasons, a matter that was discussed with reference to both Meek's and Matsuura's papers. As already mentioned in Section III above, the assimilation of a new idea in economics may depend less on the prevailing level of economic activity than on the climate of opinion, and the examples of Italy and Japan were sufficient to provide a warning that the process of assimilation may depend as much on the general intellectual culture as on the state of knowledge in the discipline immediately affected. Matters are further complicated once it is recognized that a given new idea may not only be difficult to identify and trace through time and space but may also undergo significant modifications and reinterpretations during the process of diffusion. In this as in other respects, the diffusion process will differ between countries with no prior theoretical tradition (or a prevailingly antitheoretical climate of opinion) and those with an established, but hostile tradition. And there was some discussion of the possibility of comparing the international spread of economic ideas with that of technical ideas—e.g., as in engineering.

VI

Two further aspects of the marginal revolution merit consideration—the role of ideology, and changes in the scope and method of economics.

During our proceedings there were frequent references to the mixture of positive and normative elements in marginalist economics, especially in connection with Walras's treatment of pure competition, and the role of doctrinaire liberalism in the origins and development of the Austrian School. However, at the closing session it was generally agreed that we had devoted too little attention to these matters, despite the inducements provided by the Meek and Matsuura papers. No conference member believed that apologetics had been a primary motive in the early formulations of marginal theories; otherwise this aspect would have been far more prominent. But some evidently believed that ideological considerations were involved in more subtle ways, for example, when marginal concepts were applied to practical problems or used as the basis for policy recommendations. Of course, the difficulty here is that given sufficient ingenuity, a theoretical apparatus which is in principle ideologically neutral can be employed to defend almost any policy position. In considering individual motives there was no disposition to emphasize our differences of opinion, for it was generally recognized that posthumous psychoanalysis is rarely a fruitful activity. In Walras's case, for instance, there was a crucial distinction between the ideological background of his work[19] and his qualified use of the concept of pure competition as an "analytic convenience," a device for simplifying theoretical problems. Whereas Walras was preoccupied with relatively simple problems which he endeavored to solve completely, Menger's predilection for more open-ended questions reflected his complex vision of the economic process. Both were highly critical of dogmatic liberalism; but Streissler considered that Menger's social position as a professor in Vienna meant that he had to defend the existing order. Even so, apologetic features were less readily detectable in Menger's work than in the writings of Wieser.

19. "Underlying all of Walras' work, including his analytical contributions, there is an ideological substratum which is intensely personal. . . . It is a matter of no little importance to understand the provenance and the nature of this ideology, if for no other reasons, because it gave direction to Walras' inquiries and provided the hypothesis from which he derived the grandiose analytical vision which he bequeathed to posterity." William Jaffé, Preface to *Correspondence of Léon Walras and Related Papers* (Amsterdam, 1965), 1:ix.

When it came to the diffusion, as against the genesis, of marginalist ideas, most participants acknowledged the influence of ideological factors. In Italy, for example, it appeared that the leading marginalists were antisocialist; yet Barucci showed that marginalism initially penetrated Italy in "a very neutral way," and it was difficult to explain precisely why these ideas were so readily applied to public-finance problems. By contrast, in Japan marginalism was consciously adopted as an anti-Marxist weapon. But why had Marxism generally proved to be more readily exportable than marginalism? Did the ideological features of Marxism make it more acceptable? And if so, how far did ideological elements influence the international diffusion of other economic theories?

The narrowing of scope and the shift of emphasis from macro- to microeconomics during and after the marginal revolution was considered in general terms by Donald Winch and Vincent Tarascio and also, from a more limited standpoint, by Joseph Spengler. Various *ad hoc* environmentalist hypotheses were advanced to account for this shift, for, as Stigler observed, it was not inherent in the logic of marginalism. Perhaps utility theory served as a "trade union" device which helped to segregate the "professional" economists from the amateurs; or would the narrowing of scope have occurred even in the absence of marginalism? In general it appeared that the environmentalist interpretations failed even to account for the decline of interest in long-term economic growth, and the tendency to push macroeconomic questions into the field of applied economics. Some historians have attributed the narrowing of scope to a failure of nerve on the economists' part, a retreat to safer, more academic questions. But at Bellagio there was no general disposition to accept this explanation. On the contrary, attention was focused on the intellectual significance of the new ideas. Several participants attached considerable weight to the presumed defeat of the wages-fund doctrine in Britain, an event which, as Hutchison remarked, preceded an "anarchic interregnum" in distribution theory until the 1890's. It was agreed that the economists lacked neither opportunities nor inducements to develop theories to explain the size and trend of the distributive shares, for this was currently the subject of much public controversy. It was equally surprising that only a few heterodox economists made any efforts to develop macro theories of consumption, which nowadays appear as a logical extension of marginal utility. Admittedly the Austrians had raised fundamental objections to the process of aggregation, objections which had well-known ideological implications for some later exponents of that tradition. But it was difficult to find a convincing explanation of the origins of these ideas, or even to account for the deep-seated Austrian tradition of dissociating empirical work from theory. Was this due to basic philosophical ideas, or was it merely the result of a fortuitous institutional compartmentalization of the discipline? Meek's emphasis on the marginalists' extension of the concept of rationality to the household provoked much discussion, some participants expressing surprise that this fruitful new idea was so inadequately utilized, while others argued that the concept of rationality was incorporated in much earlier writing. The latter group argued that the important shift was not towards rationality per se—an elusive idea that can be defined in a variety of ways—but towards maximizing behavior, and several conference members thought that this concept should be more carefully defined and traced historically.

Taken as a whole, our treatment of the changing scope of economics was too circumscribed, partly owing to the general desire to steer clear of the issues raised in the *Methodenstreit*. Admittedly, if we had embarked on those troubled waters we might have been blown away from some of the issues more central to the marginal revolution. Moreover the *Methodenstreit* was a postrevolutionary development, and while possibly influential in the diffusion process was not relevant to the origins and formulation of marginalism. Nevertheless, methodological matters should have been more explicitly considered, for the conflict between the so-called inductive and deductive methods was an integral part of the contemporary climate of opinion which directly influenced the development of professionalism in the social sciences.

VII

As every academic conference organizer knows, not even the best-laid plans can ensure success; and the longer the proceedings, the greater the risk of unfulfilled expectations. In the present instance we encountered our misfortunes early, as two of our invited participants did not materalize. But from the time of our arrival at the Villa

Serbelloni the success of the venture was never in doubt, and if this lengthy but incomplete postscript does not communicate a sense of the vigor, stimulus, and fruitfulness of our discussions, it will not be doing justice to the case. At the outset there was, admittedly, a possibility that the main issues would be thrashed out in the early stages; but as it transpired, the interest was remarkably sustained, partly because the conference format was admirably suited to this complex, many-sided topic. Beyond this, it must be reported that the discussions were consistently relevant, good-humored, and infused with a sincere desire to understand and to reconcile conflicting viewpoints. And bearing in mind the idyllic setting, it may still be premature to dismiss the environmentalist explanation in intellectual history.[20]

20. The preceding account is based on notes compiled assiduously during the meetings at Bellagio (except when the scribe became too *engagé*) and supplemented by several nostalgic but attentive sessions with a tape recorder amid the lengthening shadows of an English winter. It is designed not to summarize but to supplement the essays printed in this volume (some of which represent revisions of the original conference papers) both by indicating the main issues considered in the formal meetings and by conveying an impression of the variety of viewpoints (and the occasional explicit clashes of opinion) expressed. In addition, I have drawn attention to some matters on which our exchanges proved inconclusive either because of a lack of relevant data or, more seriously, because of the absence of agreed criteria of relevance. Finally, I have attempted to pinpoint several potentially fruitful topics for future research even though—as one participant insisted—in this context an ounce of example is worth more than a wagonload of precepts.

Index